Accounting & Accountability

Accounting & Accountability

Changes and challenges in corporate social and environmental reporting

Rob Gray
Dave Owen
Carol Adams

FINANCIAL TIMES
Prentice Hall

An imprint of **Pearson Education**

Harlow, England · London · New York · Reading, Massachusetts · San Francisco
Toronto · Don Mills, Ontario · Sydney · Tokyo · Singapore · Hong Kong · Seoul
Taipei · Cape Town · Madrid · Mexico City · Amsterdam · Munich · Paris · Milan

Pearson Education Limited
Edinburgh Gate
Harlow
Essex CM20 2JE
England

and Associated Companies throughout the world

Visit us on the World Wide Web at:
http://www.pearsoneduc.com

First published 1996 by
Prentice Hall Europe

Typeset in Garamond 10½/12 pt
by MHL Typesetting Ltd, Coventry

Printed and bound in Great Britain by Antony Rowe Ltd, Chippenham and Eastbourne
Bookcraft (Bath) Ltd, Midsomer Norton, Somerset

Library of Congress Cataloging-in-Publication Data

Accounting and accountability/edited by Rob Gray, Dave Owen, and
  Carol Adams.
     p. cm.
  Includes bibliographical references (p.).
  ISBN 0-13-175860-8 (pbk. : alk. paper)
  1. Social accounting.   2. Industries—Social aspects—Accounting.
  3. Industries—Environmental aspects—Accounting.
  4. Social responsibility of business—Accounting.   I. Gray, Rob.
  II. Owen, Dave.   III. Adams, Carol
  HD60.A28 1996
  658.4′08—dc20   95-42790
                                            CIP

British Library Cataloguing in Publication Data

A catalogue record for this book is available from the British
Library

ISBN: 0-13-175860-8

---

10 9 8 7
06 05 04

Contents

Preface

Accounting and Accountability is a complete revision of *Corporate Social Reporting* (Gray, Owen and Maunders, 1987). *Corporate Social Reporting* attempted to provide a reasonably coherent overview of corporate social reporting (CSR). It codified the various manifestations of CSR, linked it to conventional accounting theory and attempted to show that there *was* a subject here which both deserved the attention of accountants *and* could be productively taught to aspiring accountants. It had a degree of success. Not only did it attract widespread attention — a significant proportion of which was critical of its view of the world (see below) — but it appeared to achieve its principal objectives in that (a) it encouraged more (usually younger academics) to begin to work in the area, and (b) the rest of the accounting community stopped complaining that CSR was ephemeral and nothing to do with accountants. That text finished on a bleak and pessimistic note. The 1980s were a time of increasing social injustice, a time of increasing emphasis on the worst forms of self-interest and a period when conventional accounting .and its calculative rationality was increasingly being used to justify morally bankrupt activities in the name of vacuous economic efficiency. The hegemony of the time — especially in the United Kingdom and Australasia — had successfully redefined issues such as income distribution, quality of employment, accountability, transparency, quality of life and broader notions such as 'justice', 'equality' and 'compassion' as heretical blasphemies to be despised as the bleating of effete ineffectuals. They were issues which, like the last-ditch attempts to prevent the desecration of public sector infrastructure, had to be swept away in the pursuit of the brave new world of the 'new right'. Never had CSR been more necessary. Never had it been less likely to succeed.

Much has changed — at least superficially — since then. By the late 1980s there was widespread acceptance that the natural environment *was* an issue of concern to us all; an issue which, for 20 years, had been impossible to raise on business and accounting agendas was brought back to centre stage. This concern for the natural environment, together with increasing disgust at the worst of the social consequences of the 1980s, suddenly re-opened the whole social justice, environmental concern and accountability debates. In a drastic turn-around, the heretics and sinners who had been preaching for a more socially and environmentally sensitive accounting and accountability found themselves as the new saints. Even the accounting profession began to recognise that there were important issues here. The fickleness of business, political and accounting agendas should never be underestimated.

This complete change in the social climate coupled with the exciting developments in (what has become known as) 'critical accounting theory' had the effect of making our earlier attempts in *Corporate Social Reporting* increasingly dated. This present text is our attempt to re-write that book with the benefit of nearly 10 years of further experience and a much more intellectually vibrant (though considerably more hard-pressed) academic accounting community.

Accounting and Accountability still has its primary focus as the role that corporate social and environmental reporting has played, and could continue to play, in meeting the demands for greater corporate social responsibility and accountability. However, it has been changed in a number of ways. The theoretical component has been significantly improved. In the present text we adopt a systems perspective to explore the failings of accounting and liberal economic democracy and undertake a critical examination of alternative theories of the organisation–society relationship and their implications for the development of corporate social and environmental accounting and accountability. We thus retain the central role of *accountability* in our discussion and analysis. The link between theory and practice is developed further through an examination of the various theories of corporate social and environmental accounting and an exploration of the historical emergence and patterns of social and environmental disclosure. The reviews of practice are updated and extended with especial reference to developments on the international and environmental agendas. Since further advances in social and environmental responsibility and accountability are influenced by the adequacy (or otherwise) of management information systems together with developments in the social investment and social audit movements, these areas are given particular attention in their own chapters.

The present text has benefited enormously from some severe, but cogent, critical comment (which we acknowledge below). As a consequence we have tried to be more positive — even, perhaps, aggressive. The text is founded on the basic principles that (a) modern society has an increasingly fatal sickness and that (b) conventional accounting, in reflecting that sick society, is fundamentally mis-specified. CSR is one of the ways in which that sickness may be exposed (if not changed). CSR is also a practicable alternative to conventional accounting practice. If you find these objectives either unacceptable or puzzling then the text will at least clarify why we think this and, perhaps, persuade you to a view closer to ours. Even if it does not, the material and the way in which the text is written should be accessible to all, of whatever political persuasion, whether accounting or non-accounting undergraduates, whether practitioners or researchers. Education — especially in the United Kingdom — is under violent attack and academics are under intolerable pressure. That is no reason to lie down and die. As long as we continue to teach the very thinking which is destroying academe we can only expect the situation to get worse. Enjoy the (remaining fragments of) intellectual freedom of student and researcher and pursue matters of greater importance and of more admirable potential than indoctrination of amoral accounting techniques. We hope this text will open up and offer you new possibilities.

Acknowledgements

There are far too many people we should acknowledge for us to be able to note them all individually. If you have read *Corporate Social Reporting* and/or are reading this, we thank you. First we wish to acknowledge our families and friends who make this book both necessary and worthwhile. We dedicate it to them and to all who believe 'love' is preferable to 'accuracy', 'compassion' preferable to 'efficiency' and 'justice' preferable to 'success'. Secondly we must acknowledge Keith Maunders, who was our co author on *Corporate Social Reporting* and who has been a major stimulus (in more ways than one) to our thinking and development. Thanks, Keith. Our close colleagues and friends sustain us in many ways. Our especial thanks to Roger Adams, Jan Bebbington, James Guthrie, George Harte, Linda Lewis, Reg Mathews, Lee Parker and Clare Roberts who have all been — and remain — crucial actors in the social accounting project and with whom we have worked and from whom we have learned. In a wider sense, we really should acknowledge most of the active academic community but, in the interests of practicability, we particularly acknowledge Paul Ekins, John Elkington, Ruth Hines, Richard Laughlin, Glen Lehman, Charles Medawar, David Power, Michael Power, all our colleagues in CSEAR (see below), Yvonne Laing of the University of Glasgow Wards Trust Library and Michael Gaull for their specific and professional assistance on parts of the project and, last but by no means least, our students of the last 10 years.

The final acknowledgement is perhaps, intellectually, the most important. Roger Halford, Christine Cooper and, most especially, Tony Tinker and Tony Puxty have all written papers highly critical of the CSR project. The stimulation, provocation and intellectual benefit (if emotional pain) that we have gained from this is immeasurable. Tony Tinker, in particular, has been a source of inspiration, friendship and downright conscience prodding for some years that has immeasurably (to our eyes at least) improved our work. Tony, thanks. Tony Puxty has been for many years the litmus test of the social accounting project — always there in the wings ready to pounce on sloppy scholarship and dishonest thinking. This he did to great effect on a number of occasions. The *fear* of him doing so had an even bigger impact on our work over the years! We will miss him terribly.

The Centre for Social and Environmental Accounting Research (CSEAR)

The Centre for Social and Environmental Accounting Research (CSEAR) is the recipient of all royalties earned by this text. The Centre was established as an international networking and research grouping for all those involved with teaching, researching and practising social and environmental accounting. CSEAR maintains a small library, organises summer schools, welcomes visitors and produces a twice-yearly newsletter for its members, who come from more than 20 countries worldwide. The Centre is an idea based on collegiality and cooperation with the objectives of supporting those involved in social and environmental accounting and helping to develop the teaching, research and practice of the subject. It is based at the University of Dundee in Scotland, from where further information can be obtained.

Rob Gray
Dave Owen
Carol Adams

chapter 1

Social accounting and systems thinking
The failures of accounting and liberal economic democracy

1.1 Introduction

How can we dance when our earth is turning?
How do we sleep while our beds are burning?

The time has come to say 'fair's fair',
To pay the rent, to pay our share.
The time has come, a fact's a fact.
It belongs to them, let's give it back
(Midnight Oil, 1987 on Aboriginal land rights)

'It's nothing to do with me!'

A major characteristic of twentieth century life is the constant barrage of seemingly unconnected images about the world in which we live. These images might seem to convey both 'good news' and 'bad news' about the conditions of human existence in roughly equal proportions. However, it is highly probable that the 'good news' and the 'bad news' are closely related – that, to a degree at least, they are two sides of the same coin. Catastrophic oil spills, destruction of habitat, famine and abject poverty, involuntary unemployment, destruction of the ozone layer, industrial conflict, stock market collapse, major fraud and insider trading, stress-related illness, violence, acid rain and exploitation are all major negative shocks to individuals, communities, nations and whole species of life. Rather than being isolated and unrelated phenomena they are, to a large extent, closely connected. They are the increasingly high price that the world pays for its 'good news'. The medical breakthroughs and the level of health care, the rising standards of living and the increased life expectancy of a proportion of mankind, rising gross national product (GNP) and profit levels, technological advances, increased travel opportunities and the rising quality of privilege experienced by many in the West are not unrelated or costless successes. Each economic or social 'advance' is won by the exceptionally successful business and economic systems in the West — but at a price. Economists refer to this 'price' as *externalities* — the consequences of economic activity which are not reflected in the costs borne by the individual or organisation enjoying the benefits of the activity.

1

While it might be convenient to consider the unforeseen spin-offs from successful economic activity as 'external' there are a number of essential problems with doing so:[1]

Timing All 'externalities' will, eventually, become 'internal'. The externality may take a long time before it is reflected in the organisation's activities or, perhaps, it may take an apparently unrelated form. However, eventually polluted land and air, an abused workforce or an exploited nation will create a situation in which organisational costs begin to reflect these things — to a degree at least. Accountants, adhering to the concepts of 'matching', 'accrual' and 'prudence', might wish to attempt to account for these issues as they arise.

Ethics By treating 'negative' environmental and social effects as external to a decision the decision maker is making a moral judgement that social exploitation, poverty and environmental degradation that are direct results of accounting practice are 'nothing to do with me'. This is not ethically defensible.

Practically (and more fundamentally), there is something both bizarre and offensive about constructs as ubiquitous as western economics and western business dominating the lives of all living things *but* assessing success in a manner which *excludes* most of the factors by which the quality of life might normally and reasonably be judged. Profit, although perhaps desirable, does not deserve unqualified praise if it is won at the cost of irreparable environmental degradation. Economic efficiency, although probably admirable, might attract less admiration when it involves the destruction of lives and communities. Increased consumer spending might be source of congratulation to industry and politicians but such congratulations may be muted when much of the world is starving.

Now, of course, the connections between the good and the bad news are neither as simple nor as direct as this implies. However, it *is* apparent that the world's economic, social, political and environmental systems are very closely interrelated. Events do not occur in a vacuum but have a whole array of consequences for other individuals, organisations and systems.[2] Accounting is implicated in this. The scorekeepers — accountants — measure, reify, encourage and reward behaviour that seeks profit, growth, economic efficiency, the maximisation of cash flow, etc. (Armstrong, 1991; Burchell *et al.*, 1980; Hines, 1988; Morgan, 1988). However, when conventional economic organisational activity — as measured by accounting and conceived and reified through its practice and study — is producing a growing list of social, ethical, environmental and political problems, then not everything in the garden is rosy.

Thus there is some sort of 'problem' — we will attempt some definition of this below. Accounting is somehow implicated in that 'problem'. Social accounting and corporate social reporting (CSR hereafter) are, at a minimum, an attempt to provide additional accounts which will capture some of these 'externalities' and, by doing so, to encourage behaviour which will ameliorate the consequences of western economic life.

This chapter is principally concerned with providing the beginnings of the theoretical basis for Chapters 2, 3 and 4 which, themselves, set the scene for the rest of the book. In the following section we briefly introduce and define CSR. Section 3 introduces a 'systems thinking perspective' which will be used to provide a framework within which we can analyse and criticise, in the rest of this chapter, taken-for-granted assumptions in conventional economics and accounting.

1.2 What is social accounting and reporting?

Gray *et al.* (1987) defined corporate social reporting as:

> . . . the process of communicating the social and environmental effects of organisations' economic actions to particular interest groups within society and to society at large. As such, it involves extending the accountability of organisations (particularly companies), beyond the traditional role of providing a financial account to the owners of capital, in particular, shareholders. Such an extension is predicated upon the assumption that companies do have wider responsibilities than simply to make money for their shareholders. (p.ix).

This definition[3] will need refining as we go along, both with respect to what we mean by these terms as well as to incorporate accounting and reporting within the organisation, that is, to the 'internal participants'. However, the definition will serve as a starting point.

CSR can take a potentially infinite range of forms. It can be designed to fulfil any one or more of a wide range of objectives. It can cover a myriad different subjects. CSR can be constructed around almost any type of information or with almost any sort of focus. It is not a systematic, regulated or well-established activity and so what is covered in the following chapters is limited (in description) only by practice and (in prescription) only by our imaginations. We will review many of the principal examples *from* practice and the better known suggestions *for* practice in the following chapters. However, in order to orientate the reader at this stage, Figure 1.1 provides three examples of CSR.

Some idea of the relationship between conventional accounting and CSR and of the extent and potential limits of CSR may be useful to begin with. At its most basic there are four necessary (although not sufficient) defining characteristics which enable the derivation of conventional western accounting practice (see Laughlin and Gray, 1988). These (four characteristics) are: that the world which the accountant recognises be restricted to:

1. the financial description;
2. specified (priced) economic events;
3. defined organisations or accounting entities;
4. provide information for specified users of that information.

This profoundly narrow image of all possible interactions between the 'world' and the organisation is created by the conventional accounting system. Conventional accounting thus stands as a political and social process that creates it own social reality (Cooper and Sherer, 1984; Gambling, 1977a, b; Hines, 1988, 1989, 1991a). In broad terms the social accounting literature has sought to challenge the propriety of the four characteristics of conventional accounting.[4] More specifically, social accounting is about some combination of:

a accounting for different things (i.e. other than accounting strictly for economic events);
b accounting in different media (i.e other than accounting in strictly financial terms);

Figure 1.1a *Extract from Tom's of Maine 1993 Annual Report (pp. 12, 13)*

Living Our Mission in the Community

As part of our efforts to integrate the pursuit of goodness into traditional business practice, we have made a commitment to donate at least 10% of our pre-tax profits each year to nonprofit groups serving the Common Good of our community, the environment and one another. Typical grants are small, from several hundred to two thousand dollars, and go to organizations whose projects overlap our grant categories. Special emphasis is given to ethically motivated and environmentally sustainable economic development projects, as well as projects which benefit Native Americans and other indigenous peoples.

We also encourage our employees to spend 5% of their paid work-time volunteering in the community for the organization or cause of their choice. And we continue to make significant in-kind contributions to many groups serving the needy. This commitment did not wane, despite a challenging year in the marketplace, and once again we found that we always receive more than we give.

Preserving the Rainforest and Its Native Cultures

We recognize that the health of our tropical forests is vital to maintaining the delicate balance of our life-giving ecosystem. We also believe that it is important to respect the indigenous cultures of our planet, and to listen, so that we learn from their knowledge and traditions. That is why in 1992 Tom's committed $100,000, paid over a three year period, to support the work of the *Rainforest Alliance*, a nonprofit organization committed to preserving the world's endangered tropical forests. Through their *Periwinkle Project*, *Rainforest Alliance* seeks out critically under-funded and under-"networked" projects for collaboration. The *Project* has three primary goals: to increase local appreciation of the tropical forests; to provide affordable health care for the region's indigenous peoples; and to prepare communities to enter into business relationships that allow them to make a living while at the same time protect forest resources. The funding provided by Tom's of Maine will benefit three projects in particular:

> Rubber tappers are being trained to collect samples of the many medicinal plants found in the Brazilian rain forest. This will allow scientists to create a much-needed database for future research into their medicinal uses.

> The "green pharmacy program" studies traditional medicines for use in modern health care. Plants which are found to be effective are then transferred to public gardens, for use by local doctors in the communities which surround the rain forest.

> Finally, the communities which surround a rain forest preserve south of Sao Paulo, Brazil, are supported in their efforts to develop ecologically sustainable sources of income from the harvesting of medicinal plants.

Figure 1.1a *continued*

The *Periwinkle Project* is already producing tangible benefits to the local economy and to the health care of poor Brazilians, as well as aiding conservation. Charles Zerner, director of the *Periwinkle Project*, says "Tom's support continues to make possible a wide variety of important work linking community health, medicines, and livelihood, with conservation of rain forests."

Smaller Grants Have a Big Impact

Our typical grant, unlike that given to the *Rainforest Alliance*, is to smaller organizations based in Maine which are pursuing innovative projects. For example, our grant of $1,500 to the *Maine Conservation School* helped fund their second annual summer camp for the children of migrant workers, as a similar grant did the year before. This small amount of money, when combined with grants from other organizations, allowed forty children a break from the bleak life of migrant labor. This outdoor conservation school provides the stimulating environment, including more individualized attention, that many of these children need to overcome their difficult circumstances and excel academically.

Supporting Harvard's New Center for Values in Public Life

Just as we are guided by values in our own workplace, we in turn support efforts to bring values into other arenas of business and public life. *Harvard Divinity School's Center for Values in Public Life*, funded in part by a grant from Tom's of Maine, integrates ethics and business in an educational program for matriculated and continuing education students. What makes this program most unusual is the introduction of spiritual analysis into a variety of disciplines. Our pledge of multi-year funding helped launch the project, which focuses on four overlapping areas of concern: public values and the environment; the ethics of international affairs; business, values and the economy; and domestic policy. Ultimately, the *Center* seeks clarity and common ground in our basic values, creating a starting point from which to creatively solve issues, regardless of industry.

Volunteering in Our Community Strengthens Us All

One of the programs at Tom's of Maine which provides the greatest return for everyone involved is our volunteer program, which encourages every employee to spend 5% of their paid work-time volunteering for the nonprofit community organization of their choice. We have often been asked if it doesn't cost us quite a bit of money to lose our employees for such a great period of time. The answer can be found in the renewed spirit and sense of pride that our volunteers bring back with them to work. Again, it is a matter of integration, of finding a middle way between competing values.

Occasionally a volunteer opportunity comes along which galvanizes the entire company into action. *Very Special Arts Maine (VSA)*, a long-time beneficiary of the Tom's of Maine grant program, approached us in the summer of 1992 about sponsoring an *Arts for All Festival* in

13

Figure 1.1b *Extract from Inveresk plc 1993 Annual Report*

Environmental

Report

Fig. 6

Caldwells Carrongrove Westfield
TOTAL SUSPENDED SOLIDS
(kg/nett tonne)
Note: TSS Consent does not apply to St Cuthberts

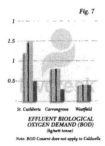

Fig. 7

St. Cuthberts Carrongrove Westfield
EFFLUENT BIOLOGICAL
OXYGEN DEMAND (BOD)
(kg/nett tonne)
Note: BOD Consent does not apply to Caldwells

91 92 93

MANAGEMENT SYSTEMS

Following adoption of an Environmental Policy in 1991, full external environmental audits were conducted on all sites in 1992 by PIRA International. Action plans for each site were developed and are regularly updated. A further limited audit was carried out in 1993 by the National Environment Unit of KPMG Peat Marwick.

All sites set up Environment Steering Committees in 1993. Training Seminars have been run for all managers and supervisors covering legal and operational aspects, and are now being extended to cover all employees. A Company Environment Handbook is in preparation and will be published during 1994.

To extend awareness of such matters, two editions of a newsletter "Environment Matters" have been published and widely circulated to employees, suppliers and customers. The Company features in a video "The Green Challenge" to be published by TV Choice in 1994.

INVESTMENT IN EFFLUENT TREATMENT *(Fig.6&7)*

Westfield Mill

A full secondary effluent treatment system was completed in 1990 at a cost of £0.8m. A revised consent from the Forth River Purification Board (FRPB) on ammoniacal nitrogen will be effective during 1994 and steps are in-hand to meet this consent level.

Carrongrove Mill

A full secondary effluent treatment system was completed in 1991 at a cost of £1.1m.

Caldwells Mill

Further investment of £670,000 in effluent treatment plant and improved operating procedures has reduced the effluent load by 80% since 1990. Consent conditions were met throughout 1993.

The FRPB has indicated its desire to improve the condition of Inverkeithing Bay which is almost landlocked and is also affected by other industrial discharges. A joint Working Party has been set-up to assess how to achieve this objective.

St. Cuthberts Mill

This site has a history of failure to comply with its discharge consent for ammoniacal nitrogen despite a series of improvements both to the effluent plant and to operating procedures. The Board in 1993 approved a further project in the sum of £680,000 to improve storage and remove the nitrogen from the final effluent. Initial pilot trials were not successful and it was necessary to change suppliers. Despite overall reduced nitrogen discharge levels the mill was prosecuted by the NRA for failure to meet consent and given a nominal fine. It is expected that the new plant will be commissioned during the second quarter of 1994 and construction is up to schedule. Performance guarantees have been obtained from the equipment supplier.

PERFORMANCE

Raw Materials

With the exception of very small tonnages of special pulps, all pulps used in 1993 were Elemental Chlorine Free (ECF) or Totally Chlorine Free (TCF) and meet the most stringent specifications.

All pulps are sourced from suppliers who pursue forest replenishment programmes and

Figure 1.1b *continued*

and this is backed by site visits from key managers. For example our major supplier, Georgia-Pacific Corporation, has won US Government recognition for its forest management policies.

Environmental assessment of major suppliers has started, with over 30% completed to date. This will be extended to cover all suppliers during 1994.

ENERGY *(Fig. 8, 9 & 10)*

Energy per saleable tonne improved at all mills except Carrongrove, where increased energy usage on new equipment was not offset by increased levels of output.

Environmental

Report

_____

Continued

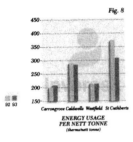

Fig. 8

ENERGY USAGE
PER NETT TONNE
(therms/nett tonne)

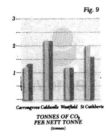

Fig. 9

TONNES OF CO₂
PER NETT TONNE
(tonnes)

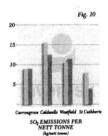

Fig. 10

SO₂ EMISSIONS PER
NETT TONNE
(kg/nett tonne)

SOLID WASTE & LAND *(Fig. 11)*

Projects are active to use process crumble and coating waste as a soil conditioner to improve agricultural land. This is expected to increase in 1994. A longer term project to compost waste is being assisted by Carrongrove. Boiler clinker and fly ash is increasingly used for building blocks.

As indicated in the flotation Prospectus, a ground survey was commissioned in 1993 at all four sites in the UK where paper making has been conducted for between 100 and 200 years.

The results for the four sites, with two minor exceptions, showed no significant evidence of land or groundwater contamination.

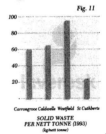

Fig. 11

SOLID WASTE
PER NETT TONNE (1993)
(kg/nett tonne)

SUMMARY

This report attempts to cover some key indicators for a multi-site and complex process industry.

Considerable progress has been made both to understand impact on the environment and to reduce it by investment and procedures.

Comments are welcome and should be sent to:

S.G. Kay, Managing Director,
Inveresk PLC,
3 Pitreavie Court,
South Pitreavie Business Park,
Dunfermline,
Fife KY11 5PU.

17.

Figure 1.1c *Extract from IBM (UK) Annual Review 1992 (pp. 35, 40, 41)*

People - not pounds

Community organisations approaching IBM for a cash donation are often disappointed these days. But the disappointment can be short-lived, because the company's creative approach to community investment often generates multiple benefits that financial donations alone could never achieve.

Sarah Portway is IBM's Public Affairs Manager. She says the economic reality is that nowadays there is less money to give. But she also says there is a growing realisation that companies like IBM have even more valuable assets to share – their business facilities and above all the skills, enthusiasm and time of their employees.

"We call it the 'people rather than pounds' approach," says Sarah. "Typically organisations ask us for a cheque when they might actually be better off asking for the time and expertise of some of our people. My role is to ensure that the contribution we make yields the maximum benefit, not only for the organisation concerned, but also for IBM."

Being able to justify IBM's continuing tradition of involvement with the community in business terms is an increasingly important aspect of Sarah's role in today's cost-conscious environment. Called 'community investment' it is precisely that – a long-term investment in the well-being of the society in which the company conducts its business.

"Wealthy high streets have their roots in healthy back streets. We believe that to secure the long-term success of our business we must play our part in meeting today's social challenges. The community at large expects it, our customers expect it, our employees expect it and the business demands it," says Sarah.

To avoid spreading resources too thinly, Sarah's team has taken its lead from IBM's mainstream business which is increasingly segmenting the marketplace into smaller, more highly-focused areas where expertise can be

IBM UK launches the IBM Consulting Group. With its headquarters in White Plains, New York, the group is a global network of local practices with more than 1500 consultants in 30 countries. There are 200 consultants based in the UK, able to undertake management and industrial consultancy assignments.

November

Hursley is the first laboratory to win a corporate Market Driven Quality (MDQ) bronze award. A team of assessors from Raleigh (USA) and La Gaude (France) scrutinises its performance in the seven MDQ categories: leadership; information and analysis; strategic quality planning; human resource development and management; quality and operational results; management of process quality; and customer focus and satisfaction.

IBM UK wins a top accolade in a national competition which recognises volunteer work in the community. The company is highly commended in the corporate category of the UK Award for Employee Volunteering, finishing second out of the 53 entries to the overall winners Allied Dunbar. IBM's Glasgow location is also highly commended in the company subsidiary category. The award comes from Business in the Community, in association with the award sponsor, Whitbread plc.

December

Customer satisfaction with IBM UK reaches a record high as Wave 2 of the Customer Satisfaction Survey records a rise from 71 to 75. Customers say that there is a new willingness in IBM to listen, to find solutions to problems and to be more flexible. Ten businesses achieve a 'very satisfied' rating of 75 or more.

Acknowledging that the company still has some way to go before reaching its goal of 'delighted customers', Nick Temple comments: "This vote of confidence in our company blueprint, and our new behaviour, should inspire everyone".

A new quality award scheme for the software industry is launched by the president of the Board of Trade, Michael Heseltine. Sponsored by IBM UK's Software Business, the 1993 TickIT awards are specifically designed to help raise standards across the industry and to encourage software developers to gain TickIT certification. TickIT gives the software industry a yardstick with which to measure the standards of its developers.

IBM and the Walt Disney Company join forces to produce one of the most endearing packages ever to be offered in the PC marketplace. The Disney Software Collection consists of nine educational and entertainment titles written to appeal to children between the ages of three and fifteen.

35

Figure 1.1c *continued*

Employee Statistics

Number of employees: 14,514 (15,665)

Customer facing employees (%)

| 1988 | 1989 | 1990 | 1991 | 1992 |

Non-services & administration

Sales & services

Age of employees*

1991	1992	
36	25	Over 60
1425	1319	51–60
5501	5369	41–50
5100	4968	31–40
3590	2829	21–30
13	4	Under 21

*The average age of employees was 39 years 9 months (39 years 2 months)

Wages, salaries & benefits

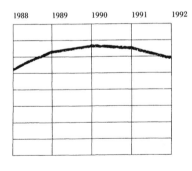

| 1988 | 1989 | 1990 | 1991 | 1992 |

Length of service*

1991	1992	
942	1032	Over 26 yrs
3135	2807	21–25 yrs
2173	2005	16–20
2728	2681	11–15
4082	3882	6–10
2605	2107	Up to 5 yrs

*The average length of service was 14 years and 6 months (13 years and 2 months)

40

Figure 1.1c *continued*

Women employees

1991		1992		
142	7.4%	141	7.7%	Managers
2063	18.9%	1851	18.4%	Professionals
792	27.6%	661	25.2%	Administration & technical
2997	19.1%	2653	18.3%	In all jobs

Labour turnover rate

The 1992 rate was 7.2% of which 1.8% was attributable to normal attrition.

Speak Up!

The Speak Up! programme gives employees the opportunity to request clarification on any matter related to IBM's business.
Correspondence is forwarded to the appropriate senior manager for reply, the writer's name being known only to the Speak Up! co-ordinator.
During 1992, 529 (981) letters were received in the Speak Up! programme. Of these 80 (127) required some further management action. Top subjects were:

1991	1992	
75	43	Company cars
0	43	Office systems
57	32	Company policies
47	28	Communications/miscellaneous
65	22	Office/administration procedures
60	16	Benefits
156	15	Pay/compensation/allowances
46	9	Promotions/transfers

Open door
In 1992 there were 34 (37) cases. They concerned:

1991	1992	
0	3	Appeals
1	4	Advancement/Promotion
3	1	Appraisal & counselling
0	1	Behaviour of others
1	1	Discrimination
1	7	Employee/Manager relations
3	7	Policies and practices
2	5	Pay and compensation
4	2	Reassignments
0	1	Suggestion plan
1	2	Other
		Outcome
5	5	Upheld
5	4	Partially upheld
27	20	Not upheld
0	2	Withdrawn
0	3	Pending

41

c accounting to different individuals or groups (i.e. not necessarily only accounting to the providers of finance); and

d accounting for different purposes (i.e. not necessarily accounting only to enable the making of decisions whose success would be judged in financial or even only cash flow terms).

Thus we might consider traditional financial accounting as a significantly and artificially constrained set of all accountings. That is, traditional accounting is one particular form of the broader, richer 'social accounting' or social accounting is what you get when the artificial restrictions of conventional accounting are removed. However, while we might wish to encompass all possible 'accountings' (which would include everything from descriptions of one's time at university to novels, from journalism to advertising, from prayer to excuses) this will be somewhat impracticable. As a result, CSR tends to restrict itself:

First to *formal* (as opposed to *informal*) accounts.

Secondly to formal accounts that are prepared *by* organisations either for themselves or which are (less commonly) disclosed to others.

Thirdly the social accounting literature tends to assume that the reports are prepared *about* certain areas of activities — typically those which affect:

- the natural environment;
- employees;

and wider 'ethical' issues which typically concentrate upon:

- consumers and products;
- local and international communities.

As we shall see, especially when considering the 'social audits', this can be a very narrow range of concerns. Other issues, such as ethical stances, and action on race and gender issues, are clearly also important elements of an organisation's social activity. An indication of the potential range of issues that CSR might need to address is given in Figure 1.2, taken from the *Ethical Consumer* criteria for evaluation of products and companies. Throughout the book we will tend to concentrate on the four principal areas we have identified above. However, the reader is reminded that this is an artificial limitation of the issues. Some of the effects of this limitation will be re-examined as the book develops.

Fourthly Social accounting tends to assume that in addition to reporting to shareholders and other owners and finance providers, organisations should report to their 'stakeholders' — the other internal and external participants in the organisation. These are normally assumed to be:

- members of local communities;
- employees and trade unions;

Figure 1.2 The Ethical Consumer *criteria for evaluation of products and companies*

- Animal testing;
- Armaments;
- Environment;
- Irresponsible marketing;
- Land rights;
- Nuclear power;
- Oppressive regimes;
- South Africa;
- Trade union relations;
- Wages and conditions.

Figure 1.3 *The basic elements of the conventional corporate social accounting model*
- a formal account;
- prepared and communicated by an 'organisation';
- about social and environmental aspects of the organisation's activities;
- and communicated to the internal and external 'participants' of the organisation.

- consumers;
- society at large.

This is also a limiting and potentially dangerous assumption which we will examine below.

These, then, are the basic elements of the social accounting/CSR framework — the basic (but often implicit) assumptions that the CSR literature adopts. They are summarised in Figure 1.3. These basic characteristics are, however, *underspecified* in that they do not tell us (for example) why an organisation might self-report, or why it might (or should) report on particular aspects and to particular groups of individuals. Clearly international companies do not (for example) communicate to everybody the detail of their environmental impacts, their impacts on communities in lesser-developed countries or their attempts to persuade governments not to pass legislation that might restrict their commercial activities. So why do organisations report at all and, more importantly, why do they *not* report and why *should* they report?

These are questions which raise ethical, social and political — as well as economic — issues. In fact all of accounting, and as a result all of CSR, implicitly begs a whole range of fundamental questions about the structure of and power in society, the role of economic as opposed to social and political considerations, the proper ethical response to issues and so on. Sadly, these matters are rarely made explicit in accounting and finance education and training and so, as a result, we as accountants tend to be ill-equipped to consider these issues. Therefore, the bulk of the rest of this chapter will introduce some of these issues — albeit in a simple manner — in order that we might be able to consider the implications of our accounting and social accounting activities in an informed way.

To do this we will begin by providing a 'systems perspective'. The principal advantage of this is that it provides an explicit contrast to the 'reductionism' which more typically characterises thought in economics, accounting and finance. However, the systems perspective provides a wide range of additional insights into the world in which we live and, especially, is something of a *sine qua non* for the serious environmental thought which we will consider later in the book.

1.3 Systems thinking and general systems theory

The genesis of systems thinking is normally attributed to the pioneering work of Ludwig von Bertalanffy (see, for example, von Bertalanffy, 1956) which derived from his concern over the way in which the natural sciences were developing. Von Bertalanffy's conception of what he called General Systems Theory (GST hereafter) was an attempt to break down the barriers between knowledge systems and to reverse — or at least slow down — the tendency in scientific thought towards reductionist reasoning. The essence of the concern was that:

- the attempt to study a part without understanding the whole from which the part comes (reductionism) was bound to lead to misunderstandings. The part can only be understoood in its context;

- understanding tends to be directed by and limited to one's own discipline. Natural phenomena are complex and cannot be successfully studied by artifically bounded modes of thought; in Ackoff's famous dictum:

... we must stop acting as though nature was organised in the same way as university departments are. (Ackoff, 1960)

This led to an expansion of systems thinking and it was soon recognised that the conception of systems was not restricted to natural science. In fact, most phenomena with which the human species interacts could be usefully considered in a systems way. GST could provide a framework for thought throughout the natural and the social sciences *and* capture the interactions between the two.[5]

Kast and Rozenweig (1974) define a system as:

An organised unitary whole, composed of two or more components or subsystems and delineated by identifiable boundaries from its environmental suprasystem . . . (p.101).

That is, a system is a conception of a part of the world that recognises explicitly that the part is (a) one element of a larger whole with which it interacts (influences and is itself influenced by); and (b) also contains other parts which are intrinsic to it. Ultimately, therefore, nothing can be understood without a complete understanding of everything else. Although possibly desirable, this is clearly impossible. However, we are counselled by GST to be aware that each attempt to focus on a manageable chunk of experience — one system or subsystem — *must* risk misunderstanding through loss of the interactions between the system and other systems.

With such a wide definition it is apparent that *everything* can be seen as a system. Systems thinking has been applied successfully to social science (and, in particular, to organisations and their internal and external interactions), to systems of thought and, especially relevant, to the interaction between human and other systems of natural ecology. Systems thinking has also had an obvious influence on thinking about accounting systems, control systems and management information systems, for example. Unfortunately, attempts have also been made to apply systems thinking in a specifically 'scientistic' and functionalist manner to the articulation and solution of specific problems. This has highlighted an essential tension in the use of GST. That is, GST is especially helpful as a way of thinking — as a mental framework with which to stand back from issues and see them in their broader context. It is not particularly good at helping to solve specific, closely defined problems. If one seeks specific and precise solutions one is in real danger of 'reducing' the problem artificially to produce that solution. In such circumstances, one is using a *constrained* systems thinking — which always runs the risk of missing the point of GST by excluding from the problem the complex and irreducible elements of the system under consideration.[6]

Accounting is too often considered in a severely constrained systems perspective, but accounting is not a system which operates in isolation. Nor is it simply part of some system which we might decribe as 'economic'. Accounting also interacts with systems which we might call 'social', 'political' and 'ethical' as well as being directly related to interactions within and between organisational systems and between those organisational systems and individuals, groups, communities, societies, nations and the non-human elements of the planetary natural environment.[7] Conventional accounting too often ignores these interactions and so it falls to social accounting to attempt to account for some of these missing elements from conventional accounting study and practice.

1.4 Using the GST framework

Imagine yourself sitting on the moon, comfortably equipped, and looking down on planet Earth with an all-seeing telescope.[8] We are familiar with the concept of the solar 'system'[9] of which the moon and Earth are a part. However, with the dominant exception of the sun (to which we return later), we are not especially concerned here with this 'level' of system.[10]

So we increase the level of resolution of our telescope to look at the Earth. Looking at planet Earth, we might observe climate, weather, oceans and physical features. These we might observe within the mental constructs of climatology, meteorology, oceanography, geology, geography, etc. These are clearly human-constructed categories and our understanding and familiarity with these categories is automatically influencing what we see and how we see it. This will become more obvious as we move into social systems but the general rule that 'observation is theory-laden' — that how we think affects what we see — is an important insight of GST (see also Tinker *et al.*, 1982). A second insight from GST is that there is a wholeness to the planetary systems that is lost as soon as we begin to break down categories of experience. We do this (isolating experience into categories — reductionism) in order to increase the depth of our knowledge but in doing so we immediately lose sense of the completeness (the holism) of the thing experienced; *and* in doing so we risk failure of understanding at the boundaries of our 'ologies' and 'ographies'. Thus, for example, attempts to explain a particular weather phenomenon without reference to the oceans, mountains, seasons and other physical characteristics are obviously doomed to failure.

Increasing the level of resolution of our telescope further will perhaps bring biological systems ('life' as we humanly understand it) to our attention. We might see vast numbers of species (categories) with one — humanity — seemingly the most ubiquitous and intrusive. Raising the level of resolution still further may bring to sight those systems which are clearly of human construction (i.e. things which do not exist if humans are not present); for example, nations, states, regions, organisations, households, groups, political parties. That is, we might choose to 'see' the human system as consisting of organisational subsystems. We might equally, however, choose to 'see' systems of activity that we might call 'economic systems' (typically distinguished in modern conventional economics by the presence of priced transactions), 'political systems' (in which power is exercised and imposed), 'social systems' (in which humans organise their activities and support systems), 'ethical' systems, 'metaphysical' systems, etc.

This might all seem self-evident but we rarely make it explicit in accounting. While we may wish to believe that accounting is no more than a (complex) set of (socially neutral) techniques and skills and that economics is a 'science' abstracted from ethics, values, human emotions, exploitation, quality of life and the state of the physical environment, such beliefs are untenable at best and destructive, dishonest and immoral at worst. If we think that economics and accounting have anything at all to do with human and non-human systems then it is the worst sort of reductionism to draw our systems boundaries around those parts we might choose to ignore. Societies, organisations, economics, accounting, ecology are all systems and they interact. Simply assuming that accounting is unrelated to societal or environmental desecration *does not make it so*!

However, simply to identify economic, social, political, etc. systems is not enough. We need to be able to say something about the *nature* of these systems. That is, there are different ways of conceiving of the systems we think of as 'economic' or 'social'; there are different ways of interpreting the *same* social or economic systems; and, there are different ways of conceiving of the interactions between these systems. This is far from trivial. If we wish to have any understanding of conventional accounting — the role it does, can and should play — and extend that to social accounting, we must have some conception of the world in which that activity can, does and should take place.

The most common way of articulating this conception in the western developed nations is by way of **liberal economic democracy**. This is not only the most common conception in the rhetoric of western (and especially North American, British and Australasian) politicians and business leaders but it is the root metaphor and an essential *but implicit* factor in the way in which conventional accounting is taught and conceived. By making those assumptions explicit we can identify many of the systems interactions, identify the limitations and myths of the conception and thereby identify the absolute failure of the intellectual foundations of conventional accounting. This failure of conventional accounting extends by default into CSR and may undermine any claims that CSR might aspire to (see Tinker *et al.*, 1991[11]).

1.5 Liberal economic democracy

It has been said that democracy is the worst form of government except for all those other forms that have been tried from time to time. (Sir Winston Churchill, House of Commons, 1947)

Sitting on the moon with our all-seeing telescope we have already organised many of the things we see by reference to categories of thought: to theories and theory-related conceptions. We observe human action and, for convenience and simplicity, divide human action into systems — groups of individuals being 'social', 'political' 'religious', 'economic', 'ethical', etc. Potentially there is an infinite number of ways in which human action might be categorised and analysed. Liberal economics and democracy is only one such way, but in the 100–200 years of its growth and maturity it has become by far the most influential and ubiquitous in the so-called developed world and, globally, in accounting thought.[12]

At its simplest, the liberal economic democratic conception envisages a world of equal individuals, free to act (liberal)[13] and to express choice through actions in markets (economic) and actions in the political arena (democratic). The State (the government and its organs and institutional structures) is presumed to be small, to act to maintain freedom and, most importantly, to be *neutral* with respect to serving particular group's interests.[14] The liberal economic democracy conception is both a *positive* conception (i.e. an attempted description of how the world *is* presumed to be), and a *normative* conception (i.e. a conception of how the world *should* be).[15] The essence is that the individual's freedom is paramount, that we all come to economic exchange equally able and free to express our personal economic choices. For those choices which cannot be expressed through economic exchange, we are presumed to be able to express them through either individual or group social action or through exercising equal power through the ballot box or other political action. As power (the ability to influence others) is assumed to be equally distributed no single individual or group can systematically dominate (or impose their preference upon) any other. However, occasionally it may be necessary for individuals to form, disband and re-form (probably temporary) groups as coalitions to make a political point — for example, political parties, pressure groups, representative groups, etc. Everyone is assumed to be free to join these groups or to form alternative groups. This 'refinement' of liberal economic democracy to allow for 'groups' as opposed to just 'individuals' is, at its simplest, what is known as *pluralism*.[16]

The claimed analytical power of the liberal economic democratic conception develops when each agent is presumed to be acting in their own self-interest. The sum total of all these individual social, political and, especially, economic actions of self-interested individuals does, it is claimed, produce maximum economic efficiency fettered by minimum social and political interference. The self-interested pursuit of economic efficiency seeks out the 'best' economic choices and ensures that finance, labour, know-how, physical capital and materials are put to the 'best' economic uses. As a result this generates maximum profits and economic growth (via maximum efficient output from scarce resources). Thus, it is concluded, an economy which is generating more (financial) wealth must also make society better off and thus make everyone within that society better off. Minor inequalities arise either through choice (e.g. leisure versus work) or can be eroded through political action (e.g. pressure groups of the disadvantaged).

The individual is thus free to be rich, free to starve, free to be politically active or inactive. In this world the institutional framework — and thus the law and government — represents the wishes of the (actively choosing) people (the demos) and is brought into existence because the majority acting freely, rationally and in their own self-interest wish them to be.

Finally, this pen-picture[17] of liberal economic democracy has avoided any explicit reference to emotive matters such as ethics and morals. This is because embedded, implicitly, in the assumed workings of liberal economic democracy is a version of the ethic of *utilitarianism*. This ethic states that every action should be judged by the consequences of that action and, in particular, by reference to the consequences to the agent — the change in his/her utility. In the liberal economy of recent history this utility is to be measured by cash flows, profit and gross national product (GNP) and thus, the consequences (and thus the 'rightness') of an action are captured in profit. A profitable action is a good action. (This matter of *ethics* we will return to later.)

This is a brief a statement of the 'pristine' liberal economic democratic position associated with the 'New Right'.[18]

1.6 Accounting as liberal economy

Throughout conventional accounting theory, teaching and practice there appears to be a widespread acceptance that (for example) the purpose of financial accounting is to inform the self-interested decision maker in order that they may maximise their personal wealth and (explicitly or implicitly) thereby ensure the efficiency of the capital markets (AAA, 1977; Beaver, 1981; Benston, 1982a, 1984; Dyckman *et al.*, 1975; McMonnies, 1988; Solomons, 1989). Why such a highly talented and privileged group as accountants should exert so much effort in order to ensure that the richest and apparently most powerful group in society become still richer and more powerful is rarely explored. When such matters *are* touched upon they are usually justified by reference to (a) serving the clients or (b) because the law requires it. Both retorts are fraught with contradiction.[19] The situation assumed within accounting *could* be justified by reference to the liberal economic democratic conception. Thus accounting is a major part of the information necessary for the (implicitly equally able and powerful) agents to act in their self-interest to maximise their personal returns and *thereby* maximise the economic efficiency that will ensure the maximum wellbeing of a society. More formally, economic actors seeking out economic gains in response to accounting information, moving capital through informationally efficient markets in order to make those markets allocatively efficient. Maximal allocative efficiency generates maximum economic growth (via profit) and thus maximum economic well-being. This ensures maximum social welfare. Such a goal would be a noble and worthy one for accountants and accounting practice. Such is the world assumed in, for example, Benston (1982a; and throughout the so-called Agency Theory literature and the so-called 'positive accounting theory' (see, for example, Armstrong, 1991; Arrington and Francis, 1989; Jensen and Meckling 1976; Roslender, 1992; Tinker and Puxty, 1995; Walker, 1989).

If all agents were equal and *if* markets were information efficient and *if* this led to allocative efficiency and *if* this led, in turn, to economic growth and *if* this ensured maximum social welfare and *if* maximum social welfare is the aim of the society *then* accounting is morally, economically and socially justifiable and may lay claim to an intellectual framework.

Of course, this is not the case.

None of these 'ifs' can be shown unequivocally to hold and most of them can be shown *not* to hold. This leaves pristine liberal economic democracy, accounting which is implicitly justified by reference to it and CSR (if based upon accounting thinking) with no moral, economic or logical theoretical foundation. If the pristine liberal economic democracy conception was reliable *and* desirable then we could assume that the casualties of economic activity — species extinction, exploitation, pollution, poverty, community destruction — were voluntary choices: the eggs which had to be broken in the making of the developed country omelette. Such is the implicit assumption in most accounting teaching, research and theory: accounting is amoral and its responsibility is to develop and enhance the workings of the economic system to the benefit of the wealthy. In such a world there is little need for such soft-hearted ideas like CSR except perhaps to legitimise the system, to perhaps paper over or explain away occasional excesses or as an occasional tool for use by corporate management (Den Uyl, 1984; Mulligan, 1986; Walton, 1983). This is the position taken by Benston (see, for example, 1982a, 1984) in his liberal economic analysis of CSR. It is *also* the conclusion reached by Puxty (1986, 1991) from a critical theoretic, anti-liberal point of view (see also Tinker *et al.*, 1991). In a pristine liberal economic democracy world CSR is largely irrelevant at best and damaging at worst, because it interferes with freedom and makes no contribution to liberalism. In a critical theoretic world, in a 'radical' conception[20] CSR is also largely irrelevant because it cannot achieve any change of substance as it is essentially part of liberalism and controlled by corporations (capital). Both views have some substance but we find neither view conclusively persuasive.[21] We will attempt to demonstrate this in Chapters 2 and 4 when we will briefly consider both the radical critique — Marxist, Critical Theory and including the persuasive deep green position — and the more 'pragmatic' issues that arise from a business-centred point of view.

In the meantime, what are the failings of the pristine liberal economic democratic model that make CSR desirable —or even essential? What we need to show is that while pristine liberal economic democracy may be the conceptual model that is widely assumed and adopted, the world in which we live cannot be shown to be consistent with that model. There are so many empirical failings that the pristine version of the model is no longer descriptive. What we may have, however, is a *version*, albeit a badly perverted and twisted version, of liberal economic democracy. (Do note that while we may be able to come to conclusions about aspects of the world in which we live, in which accounting operates and in which we wish to place CSR, it is probably the case that the *actual* form of power distribution, how economies and societies *actually* operate, etc., is virtually unknowable in any ultimate, 'factual' sense. Our assumptions about societies are just that — assumptions, faiths, in fact. We return to this in Chapters 2 and 4.) If we do in fact face some version of liberal economic democracy then we have to come to some conclusion on how 'bad' or 'good' this is. Will sticking-plaster solutions work? Do we need something more substantial in the way of encouraging social change? Or should we simply attempt to get rid of the system and replace it with something (hopefully) better?[22] What role does, can and should accounting (in some form or other, including social and environmental accounting) play in this? This will prove to be a major theme throughout the book.

1.7 The failings of liberal economic democracy

The pristine liberal economic democratic model can be severely criticised on a number of important issues.

In the first place, all individuals are clearly not equal economically, equal politically, or free to act in abstraction from their background, experience and the system in which they operate (Marcuse, 1955; 1964). The differences in economic and political power and freedom between even the average professional household (to which most readers will be aspiring we suspect) and the homeless, the destitute, the mentally ill, the victimised and the abandoned, etc., in (for example) Australia, New Zealand, the United States, Canada, Germany and Holland are clearly enormous. Suggestions that an individual chooses to be born to a homeless, unemployed parent in a major city (with whatever 'social disadvantages' one may care to acknowledge) or else to a stable, wealthy and privileged middle-class household in 'pleasant' suburban surroundings is an essential tenet of liberal economic democracy and clearly it is nonsense.[23] If that professional household in a developed country is then compared with an Ethiopian peasant family caught in a famine, some idea of the full extent of the inequities start to become apparent.

Secondly,[24] individuals cannot act independently of their framework and it is *not* individuals that exercise the real power but institutions — States, governments, corporations, etc. That is, there is 'power asymmetry' between the actors — Gray, Owen, Adams and General Motors are four actors in the liberal economic democratic world acting with equal power, wealth and freedom? Hardly! But more far-reaching than this is *how* that power is used by corporations and States. The Marxian critique, simply stated, suggests that:

- power is held by 'capital' and exercised on its behalf;
- conflict is the natural state in capitalism and, in particular, conflict between capital and labour;
- the state is 'captured' by capital and operates on its behalf to protect, reinforce and support capital's expansion and to maintain the suppression of labour;
- the emergence of a middle-class does not necessarily change anything in that it (and especially professionals such as accountants) acts on behalf of capital, is privileged by it (as long as it serves capital) and is beholden to it.

One does not need to be a 'Marxist' or any other kind of 'ist' — nor does one have to accept the whole panoply of Marxism[25] to be persuaded that Karl Marx was, at a minimum, one of the brightest and wisest minds commenting on human conditions in recent centuries. One does not need to accept 'capital' and 'labour' as discrete and identifiable groups in a constant state of conflict to recognise that companies and their owners hold vast power (unelected) throughout the globe and exercise that power in pursuit of organisational goals (however defined). One does not need to believe that the State works entirely on behalf of capital to be well aware of the very many examples of governments acting — willingly and under pressure — to protect companies and their shareholders.[26] Furthermore, one does not need to be convinced of the ubiquity of the bourgeoisie to recognise that many professionals act to support and strengthen 'capital'

— after all, what else is financial accounting? When was the last time any country's Companies Acts established the information rights of the poor, the starving, the unemployed, the homeless, environmentalists, employees, communities, etc., above the rights of the financial community?[27]

Thirdly, the model of liberal economic democracy has many internal contradictions. Some of the most important are:[28]

a   the links between individual self-interest ('greed' as it is manifested in conventional economic, finance and accounting literature) and social welfare cannot be demonstrated. It is vaguely possible that such a link exists — and, in very specific circumstances might actually do so — but it cannot be shown to hold for everyday western economies;

b   increases in income (whether measured by, for example, personal income, profit or GDP), while typically related to an increase in the consumption of certain things, does not measure quality of life, health, happiness or the 'consumption' of other things such as pleasurable activities, spiritual experience or the quality or quantity of the individual's relationship with community or nature;

c   the measure of society's wealth (GDP) has many anomolies in it such that, for example, an increase in road accidents and environmental degradation count as *increases* in wealth rather than decreases (see, for example, Anderson, 1991; Ekins, 1992b);

d   increases in financial wealth say nothing about the distribution of that wealth. Although total financial wealth as measured is increasing, the gap between rich and poor within and between nations is increasing and the increased wealth in the 'developed' nations has been achieved at the expense of the 'lesser developed' nations (see, for example, Daly and Cobb, 1990; Ekins, 1992a).

Fourthly, the model of pristine liberal economic democracy makes no allowance for environmental matters except in so far as they are represented in price. Nature is assumed to have no worth independent of its provision of economic facilities and environmental, ecological or nature-centred values can find no space within the conception. Just as social desecration is possible — and even encouraged — within liberal economic democracy, so ecological desecration is an inevitable consequence of a model of the world based upon the liberal economic democratic view (Gray, 1990a, Gray and Morrison, 1991). However, the Marxian analysis is also guilty of ignoring the environmental issues (Gray, 1992). Accounting (and CSR if derived from it) which is based upon either the liberal economic democratic vision or the Marxian vision is almost certain to encourage and reward ecological desecration (Gray, 1990a, 1992: Maunders and Burritt, 1991). We will reconsider this in Chapters 2 and 4.

Fifthly, ethical problems are also crucial and significant. In the first place, 'more' is not necessarily 'better' (see, for example, Gorz, 1989, Power, 1992). Gorz's widely repeated statement is very apposite:

Accountancy is familiar with the categories of 'more' and 'less' but doesn't know that of enough. (Gorz, 1989, p.112)

The pursuit and reward of 'more profit' is not amoral — it also tends to bring with it more environmental degradation, exploitation, inequality, etc. We are familiar in accounting with measuring the desirability of action by reference to cash flow and/or profit results. In this we follow most of conventional economics — that the desirability of an action be judged by its (financial) consequences. This is a *moral* position based upon a particular interpretation of utilitarianism (Mill, 1863/1962). Choice must always have some moral element — some suggestion that the action is better or worse, more or less desirable, is essentially more good or more bad. That conventional economics and conventional accounting have attempted to strip the explicitly moral from decisions should not blind us to the fact that decisions are still moral choices. Even the attempt to make financial and economic decision making non-moral is itself a moral choice (Cartwright, 1990; Gray, 1990b; Malachowski, 1990).[29] It is a form of intellectual dishonesty to claim, as do accounting, finance and economics, that moral issues are 'nothing to do with me' (see, for example, Gray *et al.*, 1994).

Within the pristine liberal economic democratic vision, self-interested utilitarianism *is* moral because its consequences — economic efficiency, growth, maximal social welfare — *are* assumed to be morally desirable. It is essential to know that the shareholder's hold–sell–buy decision or the determination of a DCF-based investment decision are *moral* acts. They are implicitly justified in terms of the assumed economic (and therefore the assumed social welfare) consequences of the actions and the criteria (self-interested utility maximising – i.e. greed) on which they are based.

However, 'consequentialism' (of which utilitarianism is one part) has a fatal flaw: not all consequences can be identified or known. Of course, accounting and economics avoid this by completely ignoring all non-financial (human, social, environmental) consequences and using statistical analysis to deal with the unknown elements of the *identified* consequences. (That is, the unidentified consequences are ignored.[30]) Furthermore, consequentialism is only one way to assess the rightness or wrongness of actions. It is also possible to assess an action by reference to the motives of the actor (motivism) or by reference to the intrinsic rightness or wrongness of the act itself (deontological).[31]

There can be no unequivocally correct way in which to judge an action and, one might suppose, a truly good action would satisfy all three criteria by reference to some 'higher' set of moral standards deduced from some conception of the actor's relationship with society, the natural environment and the metaphysical (e.g. a deity). More usually, however, the criteria will conflict. A common example of this is provided by questions about whether ends (consequences) justify means (motive and deontology). Under utilitarianism as practised by accounting and economics the answer must be 'yes'. Under other frames of reference (e.g. the pacifist deep green position — see for example Gray, 1992 and Chapter 2) they may not (see Figure 1.4).

No human action can be wholly amoral — attempts to remove the moral is a deliberate (if often unconscious) ethical choice. The world of accounting and finance within a world of conventional economics based as it is, in essence, on liberal economic democracy has recourse to moral justification in terms of (financial) consequences — the rise in (financial) utility generated. This is only one way of ethically justifying a moral

Figure 1.4 *An example of conflicts in ethical codes*

The decision to invest in a new plant and where to site it is a situation potentially fraught with ethical conflict.

Which consequences should be taken into account and if so how? This may lead to the sort of ethical conflict *within* a criteria that can occur with cost–benefit analysis. That is what costs (e.g. damage to life, communities, environment) and what benefits should be recognised and, if recognised, how should they be introduced to the decision? Should they be 'valued' and if so whose valuation? Are the consequences to the corporation taking precedence over those to the local community? Why? Is it ethical?

The siting of a plant may involve bribery, for example. Is that ethical? In consequential terms it may well be so but for many people, bribery is intrinsically wrong.

Why is the company (and why are you) considering this investment? What are the motives? Is making profit an ethical motive?

Is the plant an intrisically 'good' thing? By what criteria? While it may be consequentially desirable it may not be deontologically ethical. Thus, given a particular frame of reference we might find an energy efficient plant of elegant and non-intrusive technology located in a sympathetic way an intrinsically good act. What is the plant to produce? Is producing deodorants or computer toys for rich western children an intrinsically good thing to be doing?

And so on. (For more detail, see, for example, Mintz, 1990; Donaldson, 1988)

stance. Actions which may be judged moral by reference to consequentialism may be judged immoral by reference to motivist or deontological reasoning. We can now see that the consequential justification for actions taken in a liberal economic democratic conception is based upon an assumption of the mechanisms within liberal economic democracy producing social welfare consequences: a link which cannot be shown to exist.

Thus accounting and finance — and any system of social and environmental accounting based upon them — cannot demonstrate any moral justification. Certainly, accounting, finance and CSR within a liberal economic democratic vision cannot take the morality of choices for granted. So, recognition that certain of the assumptions of liberal economic democracy are incorrect plus the persuasive nature of a number of the Marxian critiques (see, for example, Tinker 1984a, b, c, 1985) and environmental critiques (Gray, 1990c, 1992; Maunders and Burritt, 1991) lead to a recognition that however desirable one might perhaps find the liberal economic democratic conception as a normative model, it has major flaws as a positive one. We do not live in a pristine liberal economic democratic world.

1.8 Social accounting and liberal economic democracy

Halford (1989), Puxty (1986, 1991) and Tinker *et al.* (1991) have argued correctly that most exploration and practice of social accounting is grounded in liberal economic democracy. As such, they say, social accounting is really no more than a sticking-plaster over the worse excesses of capitalism and that it is frequently employed to justify and legitimise the way things are and the way organisations behave. That is, it not only fails to achieve change of any substance it actually works to prevent it. The arguments of such authors are predicated upon the assumptions that the very system of power, economic activity, social organisation and so on is fundamentally wrong and must be removed before environmental protection, social justice, spiritual enlightenment, even mechanisms for the survival of the species and the planet have any chance of developing. With this last point we agree (Gray, 1992; Maunders & Burritt, 1991; Owen, 1990). Clearly social change, of a fairly fundamental nature, is required; but how to do this? and can CSR deliver?

At its simplest we may choose to work with 'the system' (whether described as liberal economic democracy or not) or against it. This might consist of:

- An intellectual route of exposing the failures of a system in the hope that it will either crack under the weight of its own inconsistencies or that a sufficient proportion of the demos will rise up and do something;

- A path involving more 'direct action' against the system — in the manner of some sort of terrorist activity as favoured by Earth First! and animal rights activists or, in a less violent way, take the approach of organisations such as Greenpeace;

- Working in, through and around the system in order to either gain some control over the system or else persuade the demos (and the system) of the inappropriate nature of its ways. Such would be the approach of the Green Parties, peace campaigners, Friends of the Earth, trade unions, most of the women's movements and most campaigning charities, for example;

- Working with the system in attempting to change its existing forms, institutions and organisations — for example, working with the established political parties or attempting to reform the existing corporate reporting regime, etc.

In its various guises CSR *could* play a role in each of these but in seeking some degree of social change there are a number of decisions to be made:

- does the system need change?
- if so how much?
- is it anything to do with me?
- should I do something?
- what is the route most appropriate to take to achieve change?

These are clearly ethical and beg a larger, more difficult ethical question: 'who is to choose what is right?'

Within this book we will be working predominantly within a heavily modified conception of liberal economic democracy — what is known as 'neo-pluralism and participative democracy' (Held, 1987; Macpherson, 1973, 1977, 1978, and see Chapter 2). This decision has been taken, despite the critique above, for the following reasons:

- **Pragmatic** To entirely abandon liberal economic democracy runs into some pragmatic problems. *First*, as we have already said, most CSR is fairly firmly embedded in liberal economic democracy. To apply a critique from some other system of reference is to run the risk of dismissing most, if not all, CSR practice to date. It is improbable that there is nothing to learn from existing experiments. To extract the lessons from the experiments a review which is more sympathetic to assumptions and principles of those experiments is needed. *Secondly*, experience tells us that students, academics, politicians and business people are more sympathetic to the liberal economic democracy than to either (for example) a deep green perspective or a detailed Marxian analysis. We believe it is more constructive to avoid the risk of alienating readers at this stage. *Thirdly* (and relatedly), by coming onto the intellectual ground of those we wish to persuade we avoid the charge of irrelevance. It is too easy to avoid debate if one's debating contestant chooses a set of premises which can themselves be dismissed — regardless of their quality and regardless of the arguments that flow from them. We wish to engage debate with accounting and finance academics, students and practitioners and achieve more by working with the conventional preconceptions; but do note, this is not to say that we are looking for an apologists' compromise. The development of CSR is both a *potentially* radical project seeking change in the structure of our society *and* a practicable project that deals with daily action through accounting. CSR is one of the very few areas of accounting and finance that can offer this.

- **Strategic** More can be achieved, in the short term at least,[32] by working with those who hold the power — business, economics and politics — and within their terms of reference to try to get them to achieve change. At the moment, 'the only game in town' is set by business, the professions and politics. One can choose to play or not to play. We choose to play.

- **Democratic** Choosing a framework other than some version of liberal economic democracy requires a difficult decision — on what grounds is one to choose? If one is not to 'let the people choose' then there needs to be a deity or else the chooser has to take to themselves some mantle of enlightenment. This can produce bigotry, chauvinism, intolerance, arrogance and religious fundamentalism. For example, the majority of individuals who are informed about environmental matters and who have no apparent axe to grind have been saying, for 20 years, that the planet will cease to support life within the foreseeable future. Until very recently they have been dismissed as cranks. However, their arguments are still resisted by big politics and big business and, as a result, are not widely accepted by western populations. Are they morally right to impose their views on the rest of society who may be lazy, uninformed, self-interested, etc.? On the grounds that everyone considers that benign dictatorship is an ideal form of government — as long as they are the dictator — we see no option but to subscribe to a form of democratic process. The demos must choose about what is done to their communities, environment and social structures — but choose in an informed and enlightened way. CSR at its best should be a democratic force (see Chapter 2 and Medawar, 1976).

- **Intellectual** In the interests of intellectual honesty we need to mention that we consider current forms of liberal economic democracy a travesty of justice to human and non-human life, and subscribe to some form of deep green socialism. However, we three disagree on the form of that and (i) believe each individual has a right to choice and (ii) that there is little point in confusing the reader at this stage with a plethora of conflicting analyses. It will be a sufficient achievement of this book if these alternatives are introduced (see, e.g., Chapters 2 and 3) and that the implicit assumptions of liberal economic democracy are clearly exposed.

We will examine, in Chapter 2, the components of our chosen (pragmatic) position and attempt to demonstrate that CSR has great radicalising potential through the way in which it might contribute to a more democratic world of greater accountability and transparency. CSR as a legitimation device — as a sticking plaster — strikes us as without merit. Only if CSR has this potential to enhance democracy can it be justified morally and professionally.

1.9 Social accounting and the accounting profession

On the face of it, we should not look to the accounting profession for leadership in the CSR field. This pessimism might be based on three factors:

- First, if the Marxian critique is correct — and there is enough evidence to give it some credence — then accounting must act on behalf of corporations and capital (see, for example, Lindblom, 1984, for a non-Marxian analysis that comes to a similar conclusion);

- Secondly, the accounting profession has had golden opportunities to introduce CSR (see, for example, AAA, 1973; AICPA, 1977; ASSC, 1975) but chose not to follow them through. Why might the 1990s be different?

- Thirdly, the accounting professions are not widely renowned for their innovation and originality. Why might the accounting profession choose to be innovative in this field (see, for example, Bebbington *et al.*, 1994)?

The basic debate as to whether or not social and environmental accounting was anything to do with accountants has had a long run (see, for example, Birnberg and Ghandi, 1976; Campfield, 1973; Churchill, 1973; Francis, 1973; Gray, 1990d; Gray *et al.*, 1987; Mathews, 1985; Parker, 1976; Perks and Gray, 1979). We believe that the case is made — accountants do have a responsibility to contribute to social and environmental accounting. (We rehearse the arguments for and against the adoption of CSR and the involvements of accountants in Chapter 3.) Why, though, might the professional accounting bodies be *expected* to take a lead?

Here again there are various reasons. For pragmatic reasons the profession may wish to be represented in an area potentially fruitful for future work. For practical reasons, any developments of social and environmental accounting will need the abilities and experience of accountants. However, the primary argument relates to the profession's purported responsibility to the 'public interest' (see, for example, Allen, 1991; Briloff, 1986; Hines, 1989; Robson and Cooper, 1990; Sikka, 1987; Willmott, 1986). The accounting profession enjoys considerable status and in part this is due to its particular position as a 'profession' (but see Booth and Cocks, 1990; Robson and Cooper, 1990; Sikka *et al.*, 1989). A profession, within a liberal economic democratic world at least, is supposed to have two essential and defining characteristics — a body of theory and knowledge which guides its practice and a commitment to the public interest (see, for example, Armstrong and Vincent, 1988; Gerboth, 1987, 1988; Greenwood, 1957; Millerson, 1964; Sikka, 1987; Zeff, 1987). If the pristine liberal economic democratic conception cannot be shown to hold then the 'public' whose 'interest' accounting serves is a very small (but rich and powerful) one. Outside a pristine liberal economic democracy, accounting must seek some expression of public interest that it attempts to serve (Bloom and Heymann, 1986). This, we believe, must take two forms:

- Taking responsibility for the negative consequences of current accounting practice. For example, recognition, ameleoration and eventual removal of many of the 'externalities' of current accounting practice (a reactive approach); and,

- Attempting to positively seek out and contribute to the public interest. For example, contribution to society — however we might define that (a proactive approach). In our case, a contribution to democratic development, to environmental protection and a reduction in exploitation, for example, should be easy to demonstrate as in the public interest. In Chapter 2 we will attempt to show that CSR should ideally contribute to this sort of development.

It might be naive to assume that the upsurge in the accounting profession's involvement in environmental accounting in the late 1980s and early 1990s (Adams, 1990; CICA, 1993a,b; FEE, 1993; Gray, 1990a; Huizing and Dekker, 1992; ICAEW, 1992; Kestigan, 1991; Owen 1992; Owen *et al.*, 1992) owed its existence to the public interest. However, there are signs that many of the lessons from the 1970s (see Chapter 4) were learnt and, as Owen (1992) notes, the failures of the profession to grasp the social opportunities in the 1970s was a tragedy that the profession had, in the early 1990s, an opportunity of redressing. The 1990s presented the accounting profession with a second opportunity to really contribute to the public interest. It may not get another.

1.10 Summary and conclusions

General Systems Theory and the systems perspective provide us with a way of conceiving of the human, non-human, physical, planetary, metaphysical, etc., systems in which we act. The first half of the chapter introduced this way of thinking which we then employed throughout the rest of the chapter. The human constructed categories of systems tend to provide our mental framework for thought and action. However, no particular framework can be thought of as immutably 'right' as all categories of systems are artificial and all frames of reference are conditional upon some set of underlying faith — whether about deities, the purpose of the human species or about the functioning of markets. Any delineation of systems, and in our particular case, the attempt to restrict accounting to the conventionally economic, is *bound* to be artificial. At a minimum there must be interactions between the systems — between the economic (and thus accounting) and the social, the political, the ethical, the environmental, etc. We cannot begin to understand one (the economic, the accounting) without understanding others (e.g. social, environmental, political). A coherent body of thought would attempt to capture this richness and this is what is claimed for liberal economic democracy.

However, the pristine liberal economic democratic conception, as we have seen, is fatally flawed in a number of important ways. Other frameworks (e.g. Marxian, deep green, various religious faiths) exist but are, themselves, human, flawed and conditional matters of faith. This is not to deny their value or their insights; rather, all we deny is their perfection. However, we do not believe that the absence of a 'perfect perception' permits inactivity in the face of problems, social ills, injustice and environmental desecration. We are of the view that an *explicit* intellectual framework is almost always preferable to an implicit one. With an explicit framework, the assumptions and implications of those assumptions are more clear and can be more easily debated. With an implicit framework, as we have seen, one will usually lapse back into an unproven, pristine form of liberal economic democracy without any recognition of the implications of so doing. As a result we have selected an explicit framework within a neo-pluralistic conception of participatory democracy. This is spelt out in Chapter 2.

Until there is a great deal more political will in governments, a far more informed and active demos, an explicit recognition of the failings of liberal economic democracy and/ or a reintroduction of human values and ethics into the corporate world, CSR and social accounting must be restricted to less than radical initiatives and so stand (potentially at least) guilty as charged by the Marxian analysis. However, the challenge of CSR is to make the loss of democracy and accountability explicit while demonstrating how accountability and democracy can be improved and developed. It is this that we see as the purpose and worth of CSR and to which we now turn.

Notes

1. For more detail see, for example, Daly (1980); Daly and Cobb (1990); Gray (1992); Maunders and Burritt (1991); Owen (1990).
2. This essential interrelatedness of events and things can be articulated through something known as 'systems thinking' and this we will examine in some depth below.

3. There is a plethora of terms used to describe social (and environmental) accounting and corporate social (and environmental) reporting. We will tend to stick with these two terms to refer to the construction, presentation and communication of an account of social and environmental phenomena. We will also use the terms 'social audit' and 'environmental audit' in specific ways later on. Other terms used to mean much the same thing include 'social responsibility accounting', 'corporate social disclosure', 'social accountability disclosure' and so on. The sense is usually obvious from the context and the variety of terms (with the possible exception of 'audit') rarely causes serious confusion. The terms 'social accounting' and 'environmental accounting' are also both employed in economics in reference to national income accounting (the calculation of GNP and GDP — see, for example, Anderson, 1991; Lutz *et al.*, 1990).

4. In general the 'defined organisation' or 'accounting entity' characteristic has been retained in social accounting as this remains the focus of some process of accounting. There are problems with retaining the entity definition (see, for example, Hines, 1988; Tinker, 1985) and, as we shall see, attempts have been made to soften, if not remove, the characteristic.

5. GST is not, strictly speaking a 'theory', more a way of thinking about things. Hopefully this will become obvious as we progress. GST is also not without its criticisms which we will touch upon below but see, for example, Bryer (1979), Hopper and Powell (1985).

6. For more detail about systems thinking in general see, for example, Ackoff (1960), von Bertalanffy (1956, 1971, 1972), Laughlin and Gray (1988), Carter *et al.* (1984), Checkland (1981), Emery (1969), Gray (1992), Kast and Rosenweig (1974).

7. See, for example, Gray (1990a), Laughlin and Gray (1988), Lowe (1972), Lowe and McInnes (1971).

8. You would be looking at the (fairly recently) familiar image of the Earth in space — 'Spaceship Earth' (see, for example, Boulding, 1966).

9. Although this is a 'conception', a 'category'. This issue of how we categorise things and the effects of so doing will be important in what follows.

10. However, before increasing the level of resolution of our telescope to focus on the Earth we should perhaps ask the reader to decrease the level of resolution of their mental telescope to expand their vision to the metaphysical level — to the (scientifically) unknowable system within which all systems — planetary, solar, galaxy, etc., may purportedly exist. That is, we must ask the reader to answer a personal question as to whether or not deity or deities exist (and if so which) as the creator, controller and/or framework for all systems. The answer to this will logically influence reactions and conclusions later on.

11. This is the essence of the Tinker *et al.* (1991) criticisms of Gray *et al.* (1987). A similar set of criticisms were launched by Halford (1989). We consider the criticisms to be very well founded.

12. Democracy has a history of more than 2500 years (see, for example, Held, 1987). Liberal economics and its relationship with democracy (hence 'liberal economic democracy') has a much more recent history and is usually dated from the work of Jeremy Bentham (1748–1832) and James Mill (1773–1836) which itself grew from the work of Hobbes, Locke and Rousseau and provided the foundation for the much richer work of John Suart Mill (1806–1873). By contrast, this intellectual tradition

also provided the basis for the very different interpretations of the world offered by Marx (1818–83) and Engels (1820–95). It is democracy that will be discussed (and painfully simplified) here.

13. The word 'liberal' tends to cause problems for those not versed in political thought. It refers to the freedom of action of the agent and, in the modern context, the economic agent. It bears little correspondence with modern manifestations of political parties with 'liberal' in their titles.

14. In large part this occurs 'naturally' in the conception because there are no systematic or systemic conflicts of interests between identifiable groups — itself because there are assumed to be no systematic or systemic groupings of 'classes'. That is, the model is 'atomistic' — a conception of a social world which consists entirely of individuals who may coalesce into groups (see below) but then fly apart again, constantly moving.

15. See, for example, Friedman (1962); Hayek (1960, 1982); Nozick (1974).

16. See, for example, Barach and Baratz (1962), Dahl (1970, 1972), Held (1987), Lukes (1974) and for a brief introduction see, for example, Abercrombie *et al.* (1984), Robertson (1986), Speake (1979).

17. A 'pen-picture' because one cannot summarise all of 150 years of modern liberal economic democracy in a few pages! For more detail see, for example, Held (1987) and Macpherson (1977).

18. Experience suggests that students — especially those who have only known the 1980s and 1990s in the 'developed' English-speaking world — have little appreciation of concepts like 'left' and 'right' wing in political terms. We have just outlined the right wing position — pristine liberal economic democracy (the extreme of the 'right' wing is assumed to be Fascist). Pristine liberal economic democracy does not exist (and probably cannot exist) anywhere in the world but is presumed to come closest in the United States and possibly in Hong Kong and Singapore. The other end of the left/right political spectrum is usually attributed to a form of Marxism and, in particular, socialism. The pure form of socialist utopia similarly does not exist in the world (its extreme counterpart is usually assumed to be the State Communism of the former USSR, Cuba and China). In the socialist (left wing) model the State plays a greater role in (putting it simply) protecting and supporting the less able and less privileged but the 'cost' of this is the reduced freedom of economic agents. Most countries exist somewhere along this spectrum with a very noticeable move towards the 'right' during the 1980s. A third dimension to the spectrum has been introduced by the deep greens, which is reviewed in Chapter 2.

19. To do something simply because one is paid to do so may be practical. It does not, however, have any ethical or theoretical justification; does not warrant the status of 'profession'; and, does not warrant its place as an educational experience (at the State's expense) within universities. Attitudes such as this would place accounting in the same category of action as mercenaries, prostitutes and SS camp commandants. To do something because the law says so again denies a personal decision and has no theoretical foundation, is an insufficient explanation (not everybody obeys the law) and ultimately fails to address the crucial question of *why* the law requires this bizarre state of affairs.

20. When we use the term 'radical' without any qualifying adjective we will be referring to thought stimulated by Marx and post-Marxist critical theory and most usually

associated with the radical left wing. Benston and his ilk are also radical — right wing radicals.

21. As evidenced by our continuing to write a textbook on the subject!
22. The possibilities with which one might replace liberal economic democracy are infinite and limited only by imagination. They include variants of socialism, feudalism, anarchy, monarchy, dictatorship, theocracy, etc. Democracy may be the best of a bad bunch that we have so far tried but it may not be enough to undo the appalling social and environmental conditions that exist in the world today. If we do not allow democracy — or at least a version which empowers the choice of the people — and we have no wholly accepted form of authority (e.g. a deity) then whose vision of utopia and justice should be allowed to dominate? These are fundamental questions which will be touched upon throughout the book but see also, for example, Adorno and Horkeimer, 1947/1972; Dobson (1990); Marcuse (1955, 1964); Weston (1986).
23. While it is clearly possible for some especially able, tenacious or lucky individuals to 'claw their way out' or substantially 'advance themselves' and it is probably the case that 'social mobility' has increased in certain parts of the world, this does alter the basic premise that privilege generally encourages privilege and deprivation tends to lead to further deprivation. To give a simple example to which most readers of this text can relate, the probability of someone with a 'professional' background being able to go to university and subsequently earn a 'professional' salary is very significantly higher than for someone from a 'manual' or 'unemployed' background. To believe that one attained university entrance simply because one was *intrinsically* more able or hard working — rather than because one had a background which encouraged opportunity — is the worst kind of arrogance. All peoples, even in the affluent West, are far from equal.
24. This is a very simple summary of the Marxian critique of liberal economic democracy.
25. 'Marxism' comes in myriad different forms and so to talk of just 'Marxism' is misleading. It is probably more accurate to refer to 'Marxian' meaning forms of thought influenced by Karl Marx's insights and arguments.
26. There are far too many documented examples of this to make it really contentious. One of the most obvious would be the constant lobbying by European and North American companies to persuade governments to forbear from legislation. In the 1990s such pressure was best illustrated in the attempts of companies to avoid environmental legislation. On the other side, the Companies Acts are among the most detailed legislation and are unique in being focused entirely upon the companies' right to operate and providing the only real means of power and control in the hands of a select group — the shareholders. No other group in society has such an enabling piece of powerful legislation.
27. See later chapters for evidence of such moves in this direction as *have* occurred. While not trivial, they are not radical either and certainly do not challenge the apparently immutable rights of the shareholder.
28. See, for example, for more detail Galbraith (1973, 1991), Hahn (1984a, b).
29. The attempt to strip the explicitly moral from economics was an essential element in leading to economic's undoubted analytical power. This is associated, primarily, with the work of Bentham and James Mill. It *does not*, however, make human action free of moral choice. The difficulties arising from this attempt are clear in John Stuart

Mill's refinement of Bentham and James Mill's work. Furthermore, the 'invisible hand' which amorally achieves this mythical rise in social welfare derives from Adam Smith's work which was known to Bentham and Mill. However, Smith's 'self-interest' is wholly predicated upon the assumption of a moral and spiritual individual acting in a reasonable, moral, caring and thoughtful way. His understanding of 'self-interest' was much different from that of Bentham and wholly different from that of modern conventional economics (see, for example, Coker, 1990; Jacobson, 1991; McKee, 1986; Raines and Jung, 1986; Reilly and Kyj, 1990).

30. Even within a simplistic accounting world this has problems, as research work on the post-audit (or lack of it) of investment decisions adequately shows (see, for example, Neale, 1989; Pike, 1984; Scapens and Sale, 1981).

31. The deontological approach bears a close relationship with Sartre's notion of 'integrity' of actions and actors.

32. The problem with this argument is that from a deep green perspective there *is only* a short term left for the species. This is a view to which we subscribe. However, business' ability to control the environmental agenda and to marginalise extremism (as they see it) has slowed down development. Pragmatism may be self-defeating but we tend to believe that by subjecting business and politics to arguments based upon their own preconceptions some of this — potentially fatal — resistance may be reduced, if not actually overcome.

chapter 2

Social accounting and accountability

2.1 Introduction

Chapter 1 examined a number of the assumptions that tend to be taken for granted in accounting and finance. We have recognised some of the major limitations of our implicitly assumed world of pristine liberal economic democracy; we have begun to see the sheer complexity of human systems; and we have explicitly recognised the essentially limited and artificial nature of our attempts to conceive of those human systems. Yet all observations are governed — to a greater or lesser extent — by the (implicit) theories we use. All action is, to some extent, influenced by implicit theory and any attempt to justify and evaluate new action (e.g. accounting policy making) is guided by theory — whether or not we are aware of this (see, for example, Tinker *et al.*, 1982). Thus, if we are to make any progress in examining, evaluating and prescribing CSR in anything other than an *ad hoc* or instinctive way[1] we need to establish some bones of a framework of explicit theory.

We will touch upon a wide range of theories throughout this book — the problem is choosing one which can act as a sort of 'anchor' for the discussion. Let us say, from the outset, that while some theories have greater or lesser claims to 'truthfulness', virtually all have *some* truth claims and *none* can claim complete truth. Any theory, mental framework or way of visualising the world is therefore temporary, conditional and debatable. Our objective is to analyse CSR usefully in a way which (a) does not entirely alienate accountants and accounting students and scholars (who are, on the whole a traditional and atheoretical lot), (b) leads us to a better understanding of the society in which we live and of the role that accounting plays in that society, and (c) allows for the possibility of serious social change in ways in which humanity orders its life.

We continue to believe that the **accountability framework** is the most useful one for analysing accounting information transmission in general, and CSR in particular (Gray *et al.*, 1986, 1987, 1988, 1991) but that framework (and its potential affiliation with liberal economic democracy) is subject to substantial criticism (see, for example, Puxty, 1986, 1991; Roberts and Scapens, 1985; Tinker *et al.*, 1991; we will return to this again below and in Chapter 3). What we now need to do is take the major themes from Chapter 1 and use them to provide a way of visualising the world that will permit us to see the role that accounting, accountability and CSR can play.

In this chapter we will provide a broad theoretical view of the world that argues that social and environmental accounting and disclosure are essential to the development of accountability. Accountability, we will argue, is the necessary link between a (neo-pluralist) view of how our world *is* currently ordered and a democratic view of how it *should be* ordered.

2.2 A neo-pluralist vision of the world

Chapter 1 introduced the idea of **neo-pluralism**. In this section we will attempt to explain the neo-pluralist conception of the world. The 'plural' in 'pluralism' refers to the idea that there are many sources of power and influence in a society. As we saw in Chapter 1, neo-classical economics (and thus a great deal of accounting and finance) implicitly assume that power is widely distributed between all individuals — that all individuals are equal. While we might wish this to be the case *in principle*, it is clearly not so *in fact*. 'Neo-pluralism' recognises this and assumes that while power is not located in a single individual or group (e.g. the State, capital, a ruling elite, etc.), nor is it evenly distributed (General Motors is clearly more powerful than you are and therefore has more influence in political, economic and social matters than do you).[2] While we can develop this idea a lot further, for our present purposes we can summarise the main elements in the visualisation presented in Figure 2.1 (for more detail see Held, 1987).

That is, again using the systems perspective introduced in Chapter 1, Figure 2.1 presents the 'economic domain' as being located within the 'societal, cultural and ethical domain'. The society, its culture and ethics determine, to a considerable degree, the structure and the acceptable modes of behaviour in the economic domain. Society is, itself, located within — and perhaps should be thought of as indistinguishable from — the natural environment. It is a very modern, western conceit to think of society and economics as distinct from each other and both as distinct from the natural environment in which they are located. Within these systems we have identified the organisations, the State and the plurality of individuals, groups and 'stakeholders' that are the dominant players in the economic domain. Traditionally, accounting attempts to restrict itself to a consideration of the relationships between companies and a very restricted set of stakeholders[3] (typically investors and other providers of finance) within a strictly economic domain — the State, society, ethics, culture and the natural environment are virtually ignored and effectively assumed away. In doing so accounting not only ignores the effect that these wider systems have on the accounting and business functions but, in effect, also ignores the influence that accounting and business, in turn, have on these wider systems. In thinking about CSR we shall try to maintain this more complex, and thus richer, model of the world in which we live.

In Chapter 1 we saw that social and environmental accounting in the widest sense concerns itself with (a) the effects that the flows of traditional accounting information have in this wider context, (b) the way such flows reflect and construct the relationships in society (Hines, 1988), (c) flows of information about the wider-than-economic activities of the companies, and (d) flows of information to a wider set of stakeholders.[4]

The flows of information that we know as accounting and CSR reflect and construct

Figure 2.1 *A simple neo-pluralist visualisation of society*

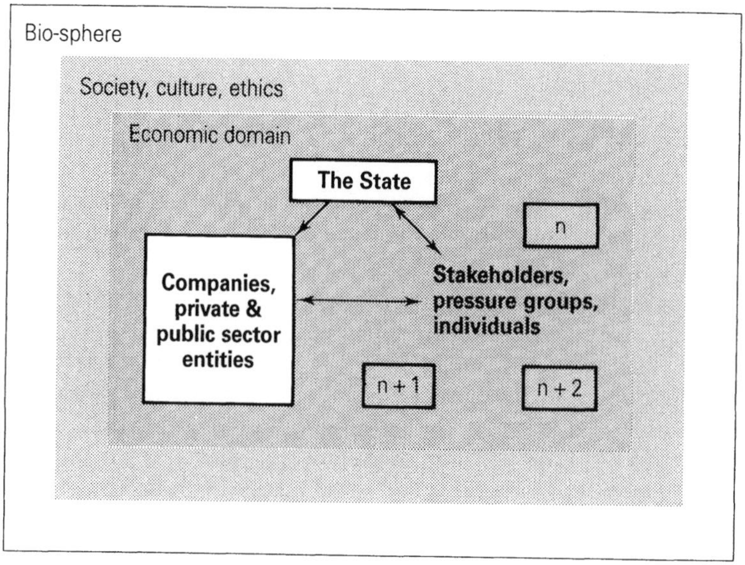

the society of which they are part. Different forms of accounting reflect different distributions of influence. That is, uneven distribution of information can, to a considerable degree, be taken as reflecting an uneven distribution of power. Accounting contributes to that essentially undemocratic situation. Similarly therefore, a change in information — including accounting and CSR — can be taken as reflecting a change in society and can even perhaps be used either to reinforce or change the distribution of influence in a society. Thus if some information on polluting discharges to water (for instance) is provided to society by companies there may have been a shift in the relative power of these two groups which brought this about and that switch in the levels of information asymmetry may reinforce that change. That is, the information is never neutral.

This leads us to one of the so very important assumptions missing from conventional accounting — what are its purposes in terms of society and change therein? In CSR we must make this explicit. Perks and Gray (1978) identified four objectives behind the development of CSR. These can be expanded somewhat (Gray *et al.*, 1988) and must also take account of the wider issues raised by the environmental accounting debate (see, for example, Gray, 1992; Gray and Laughlin, 1991; Maunders and Burritt, 1991). The potential role(s) of CSR in terms of societal change are summarised in Figure 2.2.

The essence of Figure 2.2 is this. To what extent are you content with the way society is currently ordered? If not entirely content do you want to see change? If so how much?

Figure 2.2 *Societal purposes behind social accounting (adapted from Gray et al., 1988, p. 7)*

ASSUMPTIONS ABOUT CHANGE IN SOCIETY	Assumptions about CSR's role in the society/ organisation relationship	Assumed and/or imputed purpose for CSR	Criteria to be adopted in selection of information to be reported	Form that CSR should take
RADICAL CHANGE (Left wing)	Controlled and innocuous legitimation of the corporation	To enhance corporate power	Not relevant	Perhaps the External Social Audits (see Chapter 9)
EVOLUTIONARY CHANGE	Element of the social contract, developing of democracy	Discharge accountability and increase transparency	Accountability and transparency. Possibly stewardship.	Compliance-with-standard. External social audits. Development of legally required disclosure
MARGINAL CHANGE	Demonstrates corporate benificence	Enhance corporate image	Convenience and cost to the corporation	Narrative disclosure reflecting well on the corportion. Legally required disclosure
NO CHANGE	None	Perhaps increase property rights of special interest groups (e.g. accountants)	User needs, total impact accounts, 'truth'	Social income statements and balance sheets.
RADICAL CHANGE (Right wing)	Interferes with liberty	Perhaps to deflect corporate criticism	Not relevant	Minimisation of legally required disclosure

The figure then provides current best thinking on the extent to which social and environmental accounting — *within the present structure of society* — might contribute to your preferences.[5,6]

As we have been at pains to point out, our view is that:

- **First** CSR can be used to illuminate the extent to which our society is distorted in its power distributions and the way traditional financial accounting not only supports this essentially undemocratic structure but does so in a way that dismisses the social, ethical and environmental from consideration.

- **Secondly** CSR presents new ways of accounting that not only attempt to overcome these limitations but do so in a way that makes more about organisational life **visible**[7] and, in so doing, makes organisations more transparent.[8]

- **Thirdly** CSR should seek to achieve this in pursuit of enhancing a society's democracy via the development and discharge of accountability (see also Medawar, 1976).

In the next section, we explore the connection between:

a Organisational reporting (e.g. Monsanto reporting data about its environmental interactions to society at large, British Petroleum reporting data about its social and educational provisions in Southern Africa or Rhone Poulenc describing its management of chemical wastes) and internal social and environmental accounting systems (e.g. IBM's internal monitoring of social investment, Van den Burgh/ Unilever's environmental management system or Volvo's employee and accident monitoring);

b the advancement of democracy through the mechanism of accountability.

2.3 Accounting and democracy

Democracy is a very broad term and, at its simplest:

> means little more than that, in some undefined sense, political power is ultimately in the hands of the whole adult population, and that no smaller group has the right to rule.
> (Robertson, 1986, p.80)

There are, very crudely, three forms of democracy. **Representative democracy** is the sort of democracy which most of us in the (so-called) developed western nations associate with the term. The 'will of the people' is operated through the election of representatives to speak and act on their behalf. It is usually operated through a party-political system which, while being politically expedient, vastly reduces the choices of the demos to the selection between two or three political parties every few years. Representative democracy is thus basically a fairly passive form of democracy and wide open to abuse. **State democracy** was conceived by Marx and developed by Lenin as an intermediate step towards a 'truer', socialist democracy. In this conception, the State first removed all the inequalities in the nation which prevent the essential democratic ingredient of equality of power being exercised. (This fairness is an essential element of socialism and, as we saw, one of the major flaws in liberal democratic economy.) The State then acted on behalf of the people, rising above individual exercise of power, with the assumption (in Marx's conception at least) that an equality of power would slowly be handed back to the people in a socialist utopia. Versions (albeit somewhat perverted versions) of such a model operated in, for example, the former USSR, Cuba and China and in these nations the major disadvantages — and the far from trivial advantages — could so clearly be observed.[9] Finally, there is something called **Participative (or participatory) democracy** which requires a much higher level of personal involvement of the demos in the political process through, normally, a major devolution of power to 'local level' politics. Such was the basis of the Athenian model and, very importantly, is the sort of democracy assumed in (liberal democratic) economics where 'active votes' are expressed through 'markets' by *informed* and active individuals. As we have seen, the modern economics version does not exist and Held (1987), for example, shows that the Athenian version was only a myth.[10] However, its attractions are considerable and have led Macpherson (see, for example, 1973, 1977, 1985) — one of the leading modern political commentators — to see it as the last untried possibility for democratic organisation of society.[11]

Each model of democracy has its share of strengths and weaknesses (see, for example, Held, 1987; Macpherson, 1977).[12] However, modern political thinking suggests that characteristics such as fairness and justice can be married with other desirable characteristics such as freedom and opportunity through a re-democratisation of society.[13] This can only be achieved through the return of power to the people. A necessary, but by no means sufficient,[14] requirement for this is that information flows are themselves more 'democratic'.

The importance of participatory information flows is emphasised by the considerable importance placed on them by environmentalists. Their argument is that planetary ecology is so complex that no one can possibly know how to solve it and no individual or group can possibly have the right to take decisions which affect the planet and the life expectancy (or non-expectancy of life) of large swathes of the world's population. Only through empowering the individual to make informed and caring choices might there be any chance of ameliorating the environmental crisis — or at least permitting the species to make itself extant in an informed way (Gray, 1992).

In a participative democracy there must be flows of information in which those controlling the resources provide accounts to society of their use of those resources. This is *accountability*, the development of which we see to be the major potential for CSR.

To recap: we have introduced a neo-pluralist visualisation of society which conceives of power and influence as widely spread — but not evenly. Neither political power (the power of 'votes') nor economic power (the power to 'vote with dollars in the market place') is distributed with equality, justice or fairness. The distribution of and access to information in general and accounting in particular also follows this asymmetry. Information reflects, reinforces and/or helps to create those inequalities. In a participatory democracy those inequalities would be less pronounced and certainly more visible — the demos would have rights to information and actions on their behalf would be more transparent. **Accountability** would be more developed and more widely discharged. So, what is accountability?

2.4 Social accounting and accountability

Accountability can be simply defined as:

> **The duty to provide an account (by no means necessarily a *financial* account) or reckoning of those actions for which one is held responsible.**

Thus accountability involves two responsibilities or duties: the responsibility to undertake certain actions (or forbear from taking actions) and the responsibility to provide an account of those actions. In the simplest case — that of the shareholders and a company — the directors of a company have a responsibility to manage the resources (financial and non-financial) entrusted to them by the shareholders *and* a responsibility to provide an account of this management. We can therefore see the annual report and the financial statements as a mechanism for discharging accountability (how well the statements succeed in discharging the accountability is another matter). The essential elements of this process arise from a **relationship** between the directors and the shareholders, a relationship **defined by society** (in this case through, *inter alia*, the Companies Acts) and which provides the shareholders with a **right to information**.

This specific case of the accountability model can be generalised to apply to all relationships and rights to information in Figure 2.3.[15] Figure 2.3 is an extremely simplified model but can be used to explore many complex situations.[16] This basic version of the model hypothesises a simple two-way relationship between an accountee (who we might call the 'principal' and in conventional financial accounting would be the shareholder) and accountor (who we might call the agent and in conventional financial accounting would be the director of a company). The terms of the flows between the parties and the actions and accountability required will be a function of the relationship (which might be thought of as a 'contract') between the parties (in conventional financial accounting this contract is set by the Companies Acts). This, in turn, will reflect the social context of that relationship (e.g. the importance that society places on the flow of capital to the company in return for the privileges of limited liability and rights to information[17]).

The model is a great deal more flexible than it might look. For example, the accountee and accountor may be individuals, organisations or groups. A particular pair of accountor and accountee might have several different relationships and thus be accountor in one and accountee in another — thus an employee may be accountable to the management of an organisation for his/her work performance while the management may be accountable to the employee for the extent to which the company is complying with health and safety at work legislation. The employee may also be a shareholder and thus able to hold the management to account while both employee and management, as members of the community, may wish to hold the company to account for its pollution record.

Figure 2.3 *A generalised accountability model*

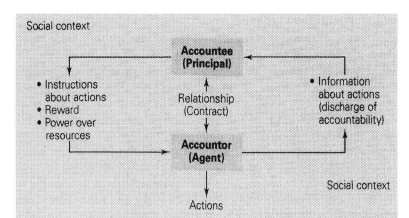

The essence of the model is the relationship between the parties and the role that society ascribes to it (we need not, of course, necessarily agree with society). It is this relationship that ascribes responsibility and permits right to information, and thereby determines the accountability. So the crucial issue is how the relationship — the 'contract' — is determined.

What we are envisaging here (referring again to Figure 2.1) is that a society may be thought of as sets of relationships — for example, between individuals, between organisations, between the State and the individual or organisation and between individuals and the rest of the natural environment and so on. In essence, a society can then be thought of as a series of individual 'social contracts' between members of society and society itself.[18] Those contracts can be thought of as both legal and non-legal — that is, moral or natural contracts; that is, some relationships and parts of some relationship are governed by law whereas other relationships — and some parts of all relationships — are governed by the ruling ethics, values and principles of society. These 'contracts' provide the basis for the rights of the parties in that relationship — including rights and responsibilities relating to information flows.

To see what this means for accountability, we therefore need to distinguish between **legal** and non-legal, or **moral** or **natural**, rights and responsibilities (Likierman, 1986; Likierman and Creasey, 1985). The most obvious rights and responsibilities are those established in law. However one feels about the justice of laws of a country or about the processes that generate the laws,[19] they are certainly the 'rules of the game' by which each of us — including organisations — are supposed to play.[20] The law lays down the **minimum** level of responsibilities and rights and thus the **minimum** level of legal accountability at any given time in any given country (Tinker *et al.*, 1991).

While law frequently identifies responsibility for actions it rarely specifies the responsibility to account for those actions — the accountability. So, for example, in the United Kingdom a company is legally reponsible (*inter alia*) to protect the health and safety of its workforce, to give equal opportunities to all members of the workforce and to give special attention to the employment of the disabled. Only in the case of employment of the disabled is that legal responsibility accompanied by a legal responsibility to disclose. Even then, the information the company is required to disclose — the discharged accountability — is trivial and certainly does not provide information to permit any assessment of whether the responsibility has been met. Therefore, we can note that the legal responsibility for action and the legal responsibility for accountability are not equal — the *legal* responsibility for action brings a *moral* responsibility to account which is only partially discharged by the *legal* responsibility to account. If we were content to leave accountability to only legal forces and voluntary initiatives, the demands of accountability would rarely be satisfied. This represents one of the major reasons why CSR, if it is to be a meaningful activity, *must* be mandatory. Evidence is quite clear that the encouragement of voluntary CSR has little lasting or substantive influence on reporting practices (see Adams *et al.*, 1995a; and Gray *et al.*, 1995a; for summaries of this evidence).

Indeed, the requirement to report to shareholders (financial accounting) is one of the very few instances of explicit accountability being established within the law itself[21] and thus, one of the very few examples of where there is *any* sort of congruence between an organisation's defined responsibility and its discharged accountability. The first role for CSR, therefore, is to fill this gap: to develop means for the moral responsibility for accountability required in law to be satisfied. The range of responsibilities upon the organisation are considerable. A **Compliance-with-Standard Report** (Gray *et al.*, 1986, 1987; and see Chapter 3) would provide much of the information necessary to assess the extent to which organisations had met their responsibilities; that is, it would discharge the organisation's accountability for legal responsibility.[22]

If legal rights have the advantage of being relatively easy to identify (if not to enforce), non-legal or moral and natural rights and responsibilities are far more difficult to establish in any unique way. Again, it is therefore useful to split these non-legal rights and responsibilities into **quasi-legal** and other, **philosophical** rights and responsibilities. The quasi-legal rights and responsibilities are those enshrined in codes of conduct (e.g. in the United Kingdom the Code of Conduct on Employment Practices in Southern Africa, in the United States the Sullivan Principles; the Montreal Protocol on CFCs; Agenda 21 from The Earth Summit in Rio de Janiero in 1992), statements from authoritative bodies to whom the organisations subscribe (the Confederation of British Industry, the International Chamber of Commerce, the United Nations, for example), plus other 'semi-binding agreements' — possibly from the organisations themselves — such as mission statements, published social and environmental policy statements, statements in speeches from chief executives or statements of objectives. In effect, a 'contract' is established by an authoritative body, by an organisation to which the 'accountable' organisation subscribes or by the 'accountable' organisation itself.

The 'philosophical' rights and responsibilities are the most tricky but probably the most important. These relate to rights and responsibilities that are not enshrined in statute or other forms of authority or agreement but which, nevertheless, may be thought to exist in principle. They may, themselves, be of two sorts: those that we might argue are **absolute** (that is unvarying with time and place), and those which are **relative** (changing with time and place). The establishment of 'philosophical' rights and responsibility can only really be achieved through debate, education and agreement. While it is possible to construct some fairly substantial arguments to the effect that (for example) every individual has an absolute duty to show respect to others and an absolute right to expect it, one would be hard pushed to show, *conclusively*, that this was always so. Hence one might personally believe in the absolute nature of a right or responsibility but recognise that it is only absolute for the society if the society agrees with you, hence most societal values end up being relative. To illustrate — we, the authors, have to varying degrees believed, for some 20 years or so, in the *absolute* duty to respect the natural environment of the planet. Such views only became widespread in the 'developed western democracies' from about the late 1980s. There is now *agreement* that respect for the natural environment is a responsibility (of, among others, business), but the view is a relative one because no one can show *conclusively* that respect for the natural environment is *absolutely* essential to a single criteria by which the species evaluates its actions. The *societal* (as opposed to individual) responsibility for the natural environment is therefore relative.

The nature of what is considered to be responsibility is constantly changing and developing; moral and natural rights in a society exist but are changing and developing over time (see Tinker *et al.*, 1991). Natural and moral rights and responsibilities will always be of this nature and thus the levels of accountability needed will be constantly changing. However, simply because it is difficult, if not impossible, to establish such rights, responsibilities and accountability with certainty (but see Cartwright, 1990; Malachowski, 1990) does not mean that these things do not exist or can be ignored. The case of responses to the natural environment eloquently demonstrates this.

If we can see society as a social system (and it is difficult to think of it as anything else — a system which includes the economic and interacts with, *inter alia*, the natural, ethical and metaphysical systems) which is determined by a whole complex of social relationships which bring with them constantly developing and changing rights, responsibilities and accountability and if we consider active democracy as the appropriate moral basis upon which to organise society, then we can identify a complex of information flows — actual and potential — which do define and can be developed to redefine the society in which we live. A major source of those information flows are the 'accounts' prepared and presented by organisations. Currently, such 'accounts' are predominantly financial and predominantly directed towards the most powerful groups in society and are therefore a source of anti-democracy (that is, they represent and reinforce the neo-pluralist view of an unbalanced distribution of power: power includes the ability to require accountability). CSR, through the accountability framework, can be used to develop the democratic functioning of information flows relating to responsibilities established in law, in quasi-law plus those we must constantly debate: the philosophical (natural/moral) responsibilities (for more detail see Birkett, 1988; Pallott, 1991; Williams, 1987). Indeed, as we shall see, External Social Audits (see

Chapter 9) can be viewed as part of this debate about moral and natural rights in that they are constantly challenging and extending the actual recognised responsibilities and actual discharged accountabilities (see, for example, Gray *et al.*, 1988, 1991).

2.5 Some limitations and extensions of accountability

Accountability does hold out the possibility for the development of accounting in a way which both contributes to and reflects the sort of democratic society in which individuals are better informed and more empowered, in which the inequalities of wealth are potentially exposed and the inequalities of power are somewhat reduced. The conventional approaches to accounting (and, most directly, decision-usefulness) are themselves based on a sort of democratic principle (pristine liberal democratic economy), but one which is a complete abstraction from the world as it exists and ignores many of the basic inconsistencies which are necessary for its derivation. Accountability is also based upon an ideal and an abstraction (participative democracy) *but* its assumptions can be made more transparent and — in principle — it does not depend upon any particular assumptions about the ways in which society is currently organised. That is, although we find the neo-pluralist conception of society usefully illustrative, it is not a prerequisite for the development of the accountability model. The accountability model can be used to analyse current practice under whatever assumptions one chooses to make about the organisation of society. In the proactive rather than analytical sense accountability is essentially a mechanism, the development of which contributes to the normative position of a more justly organised and better informed democracy.

Establishing how information in general and social and environmental accounting and accountability in particular will actually contribute to the desired social change is largely guesswork. However, two things are apparent. First, a prerequisite of an active (participative) democracy is information and, virtually by definition, social and environmental accounting and accountability are necessary, but not sufficient, conditions for greater democracy. Secondly, an increase in organisational transparency through more formal social and environmental accounting and accountability has (at least) three effects:

a The increased and *different* information will help to socially reconstruct the organisation (see, for example, Hines, 1988). More aspects of organisational life will be made visible[23] and the consequences of organisational activity and the actions of society with respect to the organisation will become more transparent;

b The increased and *different* information will tend to cause *information inductance* (Garrod, 1987; Prakash and Rappaport, 1977) whereby the type of information one is required to report tends to influence the behaviour of not just the recipient of the information (e.g. society) but the creator and transmitter of the information (e.g. company management);

c The transparency engendered by the accountability can have the effect of bringing the organisation and the results of the actions of the organisation into closer conjunction.[24] There is some evidence to suggest that 'closeness' between actors themselves — as well as between actors and the results of their actions — decreases conflicts of interest and increases the exercise of responsibility. That is, accountability is a result of responsibility and, in turn, increases responsibility.[25]

These effects must have influence on business, society and environment relationships and, we can only hope, will move them towards more democratic relationships. We also see this process as essentially emancipatory and evolutionary. That is, the process is driven by the rebalancing of power relationships through a changing of control over, and access to, information. This will produce change which, while starting from and grounded upon present practice, will be a constant and developing process. More information usually leads to different actions and demands for even more, rather than less, information. The demos becomes increasingly empowered to demand more democratic relationships.

However, for some commentators accountability still has major problems. These are principally to do with 'power'. For example, we have already seen that a case might be made for a particular set of rights and responsibilities — let us say, for illustration, the preservation of whales. Those making the case believe an accountability is due to them. Those from whom the accountability is owed do not. Who is right? Tricker (1983) and Stewart (1984) argue that unless the principal can enforce the accountability, then no accountability is due. This might be called 'positive accountability': what *should be*, is considered to be identical to *what is*. Tricker goes on to argue that if the agent voluntarily chooses to disclose some or all of the information that (an assumed) accountability might demand and the principal is unable to enforce that disclosure then we should think of this as '*ex gratia* disclosure'. That is, the agent, for reasons of his/her own (see section 2.6) in placing information in the public domain should not be thought of as acknowledging and discharging a (non-existent) accountability. This theme can be developed further. Many of the types of information with which CSR is concerned can be, indeed often are, made available to the State. That is, the State can (and occasionally does) enforce the accountability but the demos is unable to enforce the next step in the accountability chain onto either the agent or the State. In this we certainly learn something about the nature of the State, not least that it is not accountable to the demos and, perhaps more disturbing, it is perhaps not a democratic institution itself! (See, for example, Tinker, 1984a, b.)

Be that as it may, we insist that accountability can be due, even when it cannot be enforced. A moral or natural right to information flows from an established (legal or non-legal) responsibility and the fact that it is not discharged at least reaffirms our (reluctant) arguments about the lack of democracy in modern western industrialised society. Roberts and Scapens (1985) take this further. They argue, as we have done above, that accountability is essentially a reflection of a social process. However, they go further and, following Giddens (1976), deduce that this suggests that power rests with the principal who is able to impose his/her social values on the agent. The accountability relationship is thus potentially exploitive. The irony, in the present context, is that in

CSR we are generally concerned with principals (e.g. society, employees, etc.) unable to enforce their accountability onto the agents (e.g. the State or companies), and therefore with no chance to exercise exploitation even if they wished to.

This is where the flexibility of the accountability model comes into play. Remember that we said that the accountor and accountee (agent and principal) can change and swap places. Take the society–State–company relationship. Accountability relationships are far from simple. We might think that society elects the State which controls and enfranchises the company. Certainly one set of relationships runs that way, but the company can control the State (the simplest illustration is by threatening to move overseas and create unemployment and a reduction in tax revenue, etc.) and the State can also, to a fair degree, control society. The relationship can thus run the other way; so, each party can be both an agent and a principal to the other. When explicit, actual and perhaps economic power outstrips moral or natural rights (as seems to be increasingly the case in a less and less moral world) then only those relationships in which the principal can enforce accountability are positively observable; and 'yes', such relationships will impose one group's view on another — whether that is better or worse, good or bad will depend upon point of view and moral position.[26]

Similarly, there may be situations in which the principal is able to enforce accountability but chooses not to — through trust, ignorance, lack of concern, laziness, stupidity, for example. Does accountability also fail here? Stewart (1984) argues that it does but we are unconvinced. Certainly principals which fail to exercise their rights are also failing to exercise a *duty* of control (an important argument in the shareholder/ director relationship) but it seems that the *principle* of accountability still obtains. This is the argument of Hedlund and Hamm (1978) and Greer *et al.* (1978) in which a natural or moral right does not wither through lack of use. It may encourage a self-interested agent *not* to discharge accountability but it need not suggest that the agent *should* not discharge it. Indeed, Gray (1978) has argued that accountability can be discharged by the *existence* of a channel of accountability — a means whereby the information can be obtained — and that this is far more significant than the existence of the account itself.

Although charges can be brought against the accountability model (and these are only some of them), it is nevertheless a useful means for analysing information in a society which claims to be a democracy (It thus provides a particularly useful normative basis for a profession such as accountancy which claims to serve the public (democratic?) interest.) In other words, the model allows analysis, it has some positive (descriptive) power — as with, for example, the shareholder/director relationship, but is predominantly a normative model — a model of the world as it should be from a particular point of view. Such normative models are essential, not just for planning one's route (where do we want to get to?), but also for evaluating the steps along the way (do we wish to be here? how well are we progressing in our development towards our goal — whatever that is?).

However, social and environmental accounting theory is still in its infancy and, recognising that the 'normative' and the 'positive' work closely together (see, for example, Tinker *et al.*, 1982), it is worth spending a little time on the descriptive (positive) 'where are we?' questions as well as prescriptive (normative) 'where should we be?' questions.

2.6 Descriptive theories of CSR: what is social accounting when it is not accountability?

Throughout the book we will be reviewing developments in both the theory and the practice of CSR. As we shall see, there are many possible explanations of current CSR practice (and non-practice). In this CSR is very similar to conventional financial reporting where the range of competing theories, all of which have some descriptive power, has prevented any arrival at 'theory closure' (AAA, 1977; Davis *et al.*, 1982; Laughlin and Gray, 1988; Laughlin and Puxty, 1981). For example, Dierkes and Antal (1985) have argued that CSR is a response to the information needs of users. This theme is present in the studies of investor and share price response to social disclosures (see, for example, Ingram, 1978; Ullmann, 1985) but has been, at best, fairly inconclusive (Mathews, 1987; Owen *et al.*, 1987; Ullmann, 1985; and see also Cooper, 1988) and, as we shall see in the development of ethical investment (Chapter 8) frankly misleading.

Of more recent vintage and of more promising descriptive power are the theories which attempt to explain CSR practice within a more systems-orientated view of the organisation and society (and usually do so within an implict conception of society not incompatible with the neo-pluralist conception). These theories permit us to focus on the role of information and disclosure (accounting and CSR) in the relationship(s) between organisations, the State, individuals and groups. In the accounting literature, the most widely employed of these theories are: **Stakeholder Theory** (see, for example, Roberts, 1992; Ullmann, 1985); **Legitimacy Theory** (see, for example, Guthrie and Parker, 1989a; Lindblom, 1994; Patten, 1992) and **Political Economy Theory** (see, for example, Cooper and Sherer, 1984; Guthrie and Parker, 1990).[27]

Stakeholder theory

A 'stakeholder' is any human agency that can be influenced by, or can itself influence, the activities of the organisation in question. An organisation is likely, therefore, to have many stakeholders. These will include the groups we have already discussed — employees, communities, society, the State, customers — but will be extended beyond this to include, for example, suppliers, competitors, local government, stock markets, industry bodies, foreign governments, future generations, non-human life, etc. So, the first thing about stakeholder theory is that it is an explicitly systems-based view of the organisation and its environment which recognises the dynamic and complex nature of the interplay between them. This applies to both variants of stakeholder theory.

The first variant relates directly to the accountability model we have discussed for much of this chapter. That is, the organisation-stakeholder interplay can be seen as a socially grounded relationship which involves responsibility and accountability. Thus, the organisation owes accountability to all its stakeholders. The nature of that accountability is determined by the relationship(s) of that stakeholder with the organisation. Thus, to all intents and purposes, this is the normative accountability approach we have examined in depth. We can leave it for now as it has little descriptive or explanatory power in a CSR context. We will return to it in Chapter 3 and examine how it can be (and is) applied in practice.

The second variant of the stakeholder theory relates more closely to Tricker's (1983) concern over *empirical accountability*. That is, stakeholder theory may be employed in a strictly organisation-centred way. Here, the stakeholders are identified *by the organisation of concern* (not by society as they are in the accountability framework), by reference to the extent to which the organisation believes the interplay with each group needs to be managed in order to further the interests of the organisation. (The interests of the organisation need not be restricted to conventional profit-seeking assumptions — as we shall see in Chapters 3 and 7.) The more important the stakeholder to the organisation, the more effort will be exerted in managing that relationship. Information — whether financial accounting or CSR — is a major element that can be employed by the organisation to manage (or manipulate) the stakeholder in order to gain their support and approval, or to distract their opposition and disapproval.

Roberts (1992) argues that CSR has been a relatively successful medium for companies, in particular, to negotiate their stakeholder relationships. Certainly, it is quite possible to interpret a proportion of CSR as commensurate with an organisation operating in accordance with a stakeholder theory. Stakeholder theory encourages us to interpret examples of voluntarily disclosed CSR as indicative of which stakeholders matter most to an organisation and, thus, those which the organisation may be seeking to influence. Again, we will return the practical implications of this in Chapter 3.

Legitimacy theory

While stakeholder theory can be used to explain some CSR practice, legitimacy theory can be employed to explain a little more. Basically, it takes the second variant of stakeholder theory above and adds conflict and dissention to the picture. Legitimacy theory, at its simplest, argues that organisations can only continue to exist if the society in which they are based perceive the organisation to be operating to a value system which is commensurate with the society's own value system. Organisations may face many threats to their legitimacy. Lindblom (1994) argues that an organisation may employ four broad *legitimation strategies* when faced with different legitimation threats. Thus, in the face of failure of the organisation's performance (e.g. a serious accident, a major pollution leak or a financial scandal), the organisation may:

a   seek to 'educate' its stakeholders about the organisation's intentions to improve that performance;

b   seek to change the stakeholders' perceptions of the event (but without changing the organisation's actual performance);

c   distract (i.e. manipulate) attention away from the issue of concern (concentrate on some positive activity not necessarily related to the failure itself); or

d   seek to change external expectations about its performance (by, for example, explaining why a competitive, profit-seeking, wealth-creating company is not actually responsible for human-rights abuses to its employees in a repressive regime in which it operates).

Legitimacy theory, in this general form, offers important insights into CSR practice. Frequently, many major CSR initiatives can be traced back to one or more of Lindblom's suggested legitimation strategies. For example, the general tendency for CSR to emphasise the positive points of organisational behaviour, rather than the negative elements, may be explained as commensurate with a legitimation action on the part of the organisation.

However, legitimacy theory also has two variants. The first tends to be concerned with the legitimacy of individual organisations — for example, a company which is involved in a major oil spill, a charity caught up in a financial scandal. The second variant takes a wider perspective (a lower level of resolution) on the issue of concern. This wider perspective is, principally, informed by Marxian thinking and raises questions about the legitimacy of the *system* (e.g. capitalism) as a whole. Such a perspective might lead one to ask, for example, why shareholders have the dominant role in external information provision, or why companies are permitted to act in ways that most individuals would find unacceptable in their private lives.[28]

Under the first perspective, as we saw above, one can find many illustrations of where CSR is employed to close a 'legitimacy gap' (Lindblom, 1994). Under the second perspective, CSR is more subtly employed. CSR might be used by an organisation to (for example) either 'explain' about changing organisation–employee relationships which may appear, on the surface, to be an attempt to educate stakeholders but which is probably more usefully interpreted as an attempt to cover moves towards the emasculation of trade unions. Similarly, we can see trends in CSR which can be interpreted as attempts to maintain public perception of the importance of a company, an industry and a system in the 'creation' of 'wealth' and 'jobs'. Such uses of CSR can be interpreted as attempts to continue the legitimacy of the system rather than of individual organisations.

Political economy theory

This second variant of legitimacy theory brings us close to the idea of political economy. Political economy is certainly not a new concept[29] but its application in accounting is fairly recent (see, for example, Cooper and Sherer, 1984). In essence, all we talked about in Chapter 1 plus much of this chapter has been concerned with political economy. In essence, the 'political economy' is the social, political and economic framework within which human life takes place. By adopting a political economy theoretic perspective on CSR, one is lowering the level of resolution to widen the focus of analysis, as we did in Chapter 1. In doing so one is explicitly attempting to introduce wider, systemic factors into the interpretation and explanation of the CSR phenomenon.

There are also two variants on political economy theory. Political economy can be viewed as either 'classical' (most usually associated with Marx) or 'bourgeois' (most usually associated with John Stuart Mill and subsequent economists). The essential difference between the two lies in the level of resolution of analysis and, thus, the importance placed on structural conflict within society. A classical political economy places structural conflict, inequality and the role of the State at the heart of the analysis.

Bourgeois political economy, by contrast, tends to take these things as given and thus exclude them from the analysis. As a result, bourgeois political economists tend to be concerned with interactions between groups in an essentially pluralistic world (for example, the negotiation between a company and an environmental pressure group, or between a local authority and the State). While this produces useful analysis it does, according to classical political economists, entirely miss the more important point of how those relative differences in power, wealth, etc., were generated and maintained by the system in the first place.

Bourgeois political economy can be employed successfully to help explain much of CSR practice. It is especially useful in helping to explain the *absence of CSR* — why, for example, UK companies do *not* report much detail on their equal opportunites performance (see Adams *et al.*, 1995a). Classical political economy, however, has little to say about the detail of CSR practice, maintaining that CSR produced voluntarily can only be the crumbs of legitimation dropped from the table of capitalism (see Puxty, 1986, 1991) and therefore largely irrelevant other than as another mechanism by which capital protects its own interests. Where classical political economy *does* offer direct insights is with regard to *mandatory* disclosure rules. In these cases (usually) the State has chosen to impose some restriction on organisations. Classical political economists would interpret this as evidence of the State acting *as if* in the interests of disadvantaged groups — the disabled, minority races, for example — in order to maintain the legitimacy of the capitalist system as a whole (see, for example, Arnold, 1990). Similarly, classical political economy encourages us to interpret general trends in CSR in systemic political terms. Thus the growth of environmental disclosure by companies in the late 1980s and early 1990s can be seen as an attempt to act *as if* in response to environmental pressure groups while, actually, attempting to wrest the initiative and control of the environmental agenda away from these groups in order to permit capital to carry on doing what it does best — make money for capital (for more detail on these issues see Gray *et al.*, 1995a).

These theories certainly offer a variety of ways of looking at the CSR phenomenon but they are neither discrete nor wholly specified theories. Figure 2.4 may help to put them in (a tentative) context. For our purposes, we can perhaps see these as broadly similar theories in that each is concerned with, on the one hand, the power of the society (or groups within it) to pressurise organisations into disclosure (whether through legislation or the threat of legislation) while, on the other hand, the desire and ability of the organisation to use information (and particularly social and environmental accountability) to legitimate, to deflect criticism and to control the debate being held in the wider community. These theories do not deny that an organisation might disclose for ethical reasons, but they do lead us to see organisations as wishing to be left alone by public pressure, governments, environmentalists and others (and using information and disclosure to achieve this) while these groups, in turn, attempt to bring more control to bear upon the organisation — a control made possible by, and reflected in, published information like social and environmental disclosures.

These theoretical perspectives, informed by extensive empirical work, lead to a few tentative inferences. Thus, we might expect corporations to undertake social disclosure when they have a particularly bad, and widely publicised, accident (as has happened in the

Figure 2.4 *A tentative schema of political and systems-based theories of CSR*

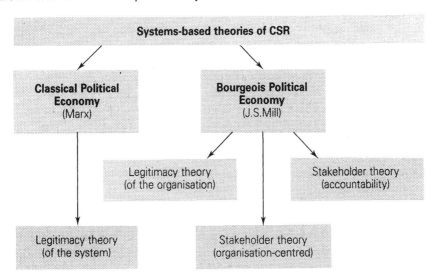

oil industry throughout the 1980s), when there is a major decline or increase in society's values and expectations (as with, for example, the importance placed on employee issues — see, for example, Burchell *et al.*, 1985 — or with environmental issues — see, for example, Gray, 1990a) or when a particular (stakeholder) group in society gains an increased influence (by whatever means) as happened with trade unions in the United Kingdom in the late 1960s and 1970s.

These broadly plausible expectations seem compatible with what happens in CSR practice and offer much scope for further work. They are not as yet fully fledged theories (in the CSR context) but provide useful frameworks within which to study the developing practice of CSR, but we should note that we are a very long way from any complete understanding of why organisations do (and do not) undertake social and environmental accounting and disclosure. At a simple level these theories are attempting to recognise that management is primarily concerned with the control of their organisations and will use social and environmental accounting and accountability to the extent that this aids them to achieve that control. The extent to which social and environmental matters are disturbances to which management need to respond (and thus for which social and environmental accounting may provide solutions) will be largely a function of pressure exerted by forces outside the dominant coalition of the organisation. To a degree, this — if accurate — is depressing in that it suggests that managements of organisations have no intrinsic desire to contribute to transparency and accountability. That is, something in modern organisations removes them from any civilising, morally proper desire to account for their effects on society and the natural environment.

Western industrial 'democracies' are clearly dominated by organisations and other forces which permit accountability to be treated as an unnecessary activity. It is difficult to feel any pleasure in such a conclusion (these issues are touched upon again in Chapter 3).

This leads to the realisation that in addition to our analysis of social and environmental accounting and accountability practice and our exploration of predominantly normative models of accountability we need to know a great deal more about the *absence* of social and environmental accounting and accountability (see, for example, Choudhury, 1988). That is, it becomes useful to our understanding of the society we live in, the society–organisation relationship and the role(s) that accounting plays in this if we study both the actual practice of CSR *as well as* the absence of CSR. The absences are examples, it would seem, of the successful exercise of power and influence by organisations (and perhaps states) to keep themselves unfettered by society. They are thus examples of failures of democracy — of the exercise of unequal power in society. Accounting, by inaction as much as action, is an important player in this. The corollary is that the examples of CSR can perhaps be seen as successful developments in accountability and democracy and instances in which society or groups in society have succeeded in taking power back to themselves. It may tell us much about the role of accounting in society when the accounting profession *has* backed such developments.

2.7 Summary and conclusions

Chapters 1 and 2 have provided the broad theoretical structure within which we will examine the development (and non-development) of social and environmental accounting and accountability. We have recognised that traditional accounting adopts (usually implicitly) a very right wing, pristine liberal, economic democracy view of the way society is, and should be, organised. We have identified some critical problems with this; but because of (a) our intention to study actual practice; (b) the lack of practical alternative solutions deriving from critical theory; (c) our appreciation of the relativist nature of moral judgement in society; and (d) our wish — as accountants — to be involved in the process of change, we have chosen to adapt, rather than wholly adopt, the sorts of more 'radical' positions with which we might, ourselves, feel more comfortable (see also Chapter 3). We are far from happy with many of the current manifestations of present society — whether it be starvation, poverty, exploitation or environmental desecration, for example — but are seeking *evolution* to a more just society, leaving the preaching and practice of *revolution* to others and to other forums.

As a result we have adopted a neo-pluralist vision of how society is currently organised. This is a plausible conception that many will find new but not entirely surprising. We have identified improved democracy as our aim (and few could argue with that we think) and, perhaps more surprisingly, seen traditional accounting as anti-democratic while we see social and environmental accounting and accountability as pre-eminently mechanisms for the furtherance of a fairer, more just, democracy. Our model of *accountability* is the link between these ideas. In our conception of society, we can identify a number of *legal* and *quasi-legal responsibilities*, only some of which are matched by discharged accountability. We can add to this *natural* or *moral* responsibilities which are matters for continual debate within the society. CSR, at its broadest, is to fill the gap between responsibility and accountability and to act as constant challenge to the extant positive state of responsibility and accountability — working, principally, upon a society's acceptance of moral and natural responsibilities and rights. Accountability will, therefore, be a constantly changing notion (see especially Tinker *et al.*, 1991).

For convenience, despite the necessary narrowing that this brings, our 'societies' are conceived of as comprising, in addition to the State and organisations, stakeholder groups representative of interests in community, employment, consumption and environment. If this is set within an explicitly ethical atmosphere, then most of the information rights that accountability must discharge can be identified within this framework.

No framework can be complete, no social theory can be all-embracing. To place the accountability perspective in context we have briefly reviewed some of the other significant ways in which CSR has been interpreted. These theories, summarised in Figure 2.4, implicitly highlight some of the major limitations of the accountability approach. At least, with our systems-based accountability model, we have now moved beyond the claustrophobic confines of conventional accounting and recognised that there are activities other than economic, morals other than self-interest. Accounting is anything but a 'neutral' and 'unbiased' technical activity. The study of social and environmental accounting and accountability, if nothing else, at least makes that both explicit and obvious.

Notes

1. An increasing element of post-modern thought and, in particular, the deep green and feminist thinking is the growing disenchantment with modern, western conventions of logic, problem formulation and reasoning. The model 'rational' man (and it usually is) denies the value of instinct, intuition and spirituality in guiding action. This is not necessarily wise (see, for example, Cooper, 1992; Gray, 1992; Hines, 1991a, b; Robertson, 1978b, 1984).
2. See also Neimark (1992) on this issue and General Motors in particular.
3. Stakeholders are re-examined in section 2.6 below.
4. The third and fourth of these are more typically what constitutes social and environmental accounting while the first and second are more typically part of the 'accounting and society' issues (see, for example, Burchell *et al.*, 1980, 1985; Perks, 1993). While we will be emphasising the third and fourth elements, they are not really separable from the first two.
5. We have already seen that conventional accounting and finance tends to assume that it falls into the 'no change' category, whereas the assumptions underlying conventional accounting and finance actually place it in the 'radical change–right wing' category.
6. We should also note that the 'no change' category may seem misleading. In essence this category captures those who are quite content with their world and have no

burning ambition to change it. If change does come along, this category will seek to ride with the tide. Hence, the professional accountant does not seem overly exercised by the moral imperatives for social change but is quite happy to try to develop new forms of accounting if it means more work. The irony is that such new forms of accounting may very well produce a form of social change to which the conventional accountant feels antipathy.

7. It is now widely recognised that the very act of accounting in any single way must have the effect of focusing attention on one attribute of a selected group of phenomena. Thus in accounting for goodwill, we make certain aspects of the concept of goodwill 'visible'. It therefore follows that whatever is excluded in our accounting is de-emphasised and, in effect, made 'invisible'. For more detail see Hines (1992) and Hopwood (1978, 1984, 1986).

8. 'Transparency' is a very simple idea — that one can see into or through something. Information is one way in which one can 'see into' organisations — by which they become more transparent. (Other ways include working for the organisation, site visits, genuine community involvement, etc.; see, for example, Gray, 1992.)

9. One should note therefore that the collapse of the Soviet Union has nothing at all to say about socialism as such. The Soviet Union was a monolithic dictatorship that was frozen on its path towards socialism by the attentions of a few serious psychopaths and a moribund and self-serving elite. The USSR was, nevertheless, a form of democracy, and perhaps no further from a democratic ideal in its own way than the United Kingdom, which is sometimes claimed to be the cradle of democracy.

10. 'Mythical' because the franchise (the right to vote) was only given to males of wealth and thus *disenfranchised* the very system which supported it — women, slaves and freemen without wealth.

11. It is doubtful whether this actually adds to the notion's appeal but participative democracy is a central plank in Green Party policy.

12. Nothing we say here is suggesting we know how to get to Utopia — or even what it might look like.

13. This *does not* suggest that necessarily everyone should have the same — differences are always inevitable — but that all people are created equal demands respect for all people. Otherwise, one is back to dictatorships or the present 'I've got the power and I don't see what is wrong with the present system' attitude.

14. Why information is probably insufficient in itself lies in the considerable imbalance in the current distribution of power and opportunity.

15. *Please note* that. this model bears only the slightest resemblance to the Principal–Agent or Agency Model so popular in accounting and finance research in the 1980s and 1990s (see, for example, Jensen and Meckling, 1976). The Agency model is a two-person model based upon Coase's Theorem and makes a whole raft of assumptions about the motivations and characters of the principal and agent — most notably that they are so-called 'rational' economic actors who are wholly selfish and wholly greedy. These are the sort of people you hope never to meet but when you do, you may find that it is in your short-term self-interest to smack them in the mouth (see, for example, Gambling, 1978; Tinker and Puxty, 1995). The present model makes none of these assumptions, predates 'Agency Theory' by several centuries and is subject to none of the fatal criticisms that make Agency Theory such an intellectual dead duck (see, for example, Armstrong, 1991; Arrington, 1990;

Arrington and Francis, 1989; Christenson, 1983; Noreen, 1988; Tinker and Okcabol, 1991).

16. For more detail on the derivation of the simple model, on the basic notion of accountability and on the involvement of accountants see, for example, Bird (1973); Bird and Morgan-Jones (1981); Gjedsal (1981); Gray *et al.* (1987, 1988, 1991); Ijiri (1983); Jackson (1982); Jones (1977); Munkman (1971).

17. Apparently (if puzzlingly) there would not appear to be any moral duties or responsibilities in return for this privilege.

18. This 'social contractarian' tradition is well established in political philosophy and while, like most models, is an oversimplification it captures a richer set of actual and potential social relationships than are present in, for example, the atomistic view of pristine liberal economic democracy. We should stress that we acknowledge a greater intellectual debt in this model to Rawls than we do to Coase.

19. See, for example, Dowling and Pfeffer (1975), Lindblom (1994), Stone (1975).

20. Nothing we say here should be taken to imply that we believe there is a moral imperative to obey the law. Indeed civil disobedience and direct action (e.g. demonstrations and the actions of Greenpeace and Earth First!) may be essential democratic mechanisms to the maintenance of accountability. This is a complex matter but space prevents us dwelling upon it here.

21. Although this is beginning to change with Freedom of Information in the United States, Canada, and the EU: see Chapters 5 and 6.

22. Given that accountability is an essential element in democracy and given that most countries of the world do not require organisations to be accountable for their legally established responsibilities, you can surely infer something about the nature of societies and organisations.

23. And while total visibility will probably increase, each increase in visibility, in focusing attention on some matters, decreases attention on others and, thus, inevitably makes other things 'invisible'. See, for example, Broadbent *et al.*, 1991; Hines, 1992; Hopwood, 1990.

24. This relates to a reduction in what is known in Marxian analysis as 'alienation' and to an increase in what is called in the work of John Rawls 'closeness' (see, for example, Rawls, 1972). For more detail in an accounting context see, for example, Lehman (in press).

25. Some evidence to this effect is quoted in Gray (1992). Indeed, a major element in 'deeper green' thinking is the recognition that being accountable, the giving of an account, is often a morally sound and spiritually uplifting thing to do. There are frequently times in normal human relationships when an 'agent' wants, even demands, to give an account of themselves. It is only habit, social convention and the conditioning effects of large organisations that make the idea of freely giving an account so bizarre.

26. For example, do you believe it is necessarily a good thing that companies can impose their views on society but not the other way around?

27. For a more detailed exploration of these theories in a CSR context see, for example, Adams *et al.* (1995a), Gray *et al.* (1995a), Guthrie and Parker (1989a, 1990).

28. One illustration of this in the United Kingdom arises from the Church of England which, as a Christian Church, is committed to the principle of 'thou shalt not kill' and yet did, for many years, have a substantial number of financial investments with

weapons manufacturers. Somehow, weapons manufacturing is a legitimate form of business — even to people who are sworn to uphold the sanctity of life.

29. In fact, it predates the separation of 'politics' and 'economics' that we currently take for granted in our schools and universities. Until relatively modern times — the late 19th century and increasingly through the 20th century — one would have studied political economy on the understanding that society, politics and economics were inseparable. Sounds like a good idea to us.

chapter 3

Corporate social reporting, social responsibility, accounting and accountants

3.1 Introduction

Chapters 1 and 2 provided an introduction to social accounting and considered some of the theoretical perspectives with which to begin to analyse the issues that arise when we consider CSR. Of necessity, this introduction and overview has been heavily theoretical. We have already noted in Chapter 1 that as accountants, our education and training place a very heavy emphasis on learning accounting skills and acquiring accounting knowledge. While this emphasis may be necessary in an accounting degree it does not equip us to analyse carefully the assumptions and theories which underlie conventional accounting thinking. As a result, it is necessary to re-examine conventional accounting before we can make any serious progress with social and environmental accounting. The only way to do this is to employ some theoretical 'spectacles' in order to give us a perspective on accounting (in both its conventional and broader sense) which will allow us to see the (social, economic and political) wood for (the technical and knowledge-based) trees. Without access to theory, we will find ourselves quite unable to offer any systematic analysis of what accounting actually is, can be or should be. Theory gives us a basis from which to evaluate both current accounting and other forms of accounting (e.g. social and environmental accounting). Only by careful evaluation will you be able to judge whether, for example, conventional accounting has serious or trivial limitations, whether social and environmental accounting is a waste of time or not, and whether the whole issue of the social and environmental effects of accounting are, indeed, anything to do with accountants.[1]

We have so far concentrated upon the 'right wing', liberal economic democracy arguments and counter-poised this with a little Marxian analysis. This gives us what is often called a *dialectic* between, for example, the views of Benston (1982a, b) and those of Tinker *et al.* (1991) or Puxty (1986, 1991). It lays out two ends of a spectrum (see Figure 2.2 in Chapter 2)[2] and shows the implicit assumptions that ensure that accounting stays towards the 'Benston end' (liberal democracy) of the spectrum. This spectrum of world views also demonstrates that the 'Tinker end' (Marxian) of the spectrum has important insights to offer us. We then showed in Chapter 2, using the accountability model, that there was an intervening position which could, perhaps, take the best from both extremes. However, the later stages of Chapter 2 also introduced other (related) theoretical points of view — legitimacy theory, political economy theory and stakeholder theory; thus demonstrating that how you see the world naturally leads to a different theoretical perspective and this, in turn, profoundly influences your conclusions about accounting in general and social and environmental accounting in particular.

This chapter will attempt to bring all these themes together in a more systematic (and simpler) way focusing on social accounting, accountants and conventional accounting theory. We will make more of a link between the practice of social accounting and your wider experience of studying accounting. To do this we will borrow a range of views on such matters as the role of business and its responsibilities, the role of accountants and the elements of accounting theory. This will lead us into the body of the book and its more detailed examination of social and environmental accounting theory and pratice.

This chapter is principally an attempt to synthesise and re-organise the material from the first two chapters in a more accessible manner. The chapter is organised as follows. The next section reviews the principle elements in the 'corporate social responsibility' debate. One's views on the relationship between organisations and society strongly colour how one thinks about CSR. Section 3.3 reviews the role(s) that CSR can play in this relationship in Section 3.5. Section 3.4 briefly examines the role that the State plays in the development of CSR before we go on to look at why organisations actually do produce CSR information. Section 3.6 examines different views on the role that accounting and the accounting profession should play in CSR, following which we provide a very brief review of current accounting theories and the extent to which they can help accountants make a bridge between 'conventional accounting' and social and environmental accounting. Section 3.8 reviews the chapter.

3.2 The social responsibility of organisations?

We have already seen (in Chapter 2) that one objective of CSR might be to discharge the social accountability of an organisation. Social accountability only arises *if* the organisation has a *social responsibility* — otherwise there is no social accountability to discharge. The accountability model we introduced made this explicit. However, what happens if we disagree about that social responsibility? Is there then a need for CSR? Indeed, is CSR the only way to discharge that responsibility?

One's views about the nature and extent of organisational social responsibility derive from one's views about how you believe the world to be and how you would like the world to be. There are widely different views on this. For illustration, we will run through a few general ways in which different groups in society might envisage the organisation–society relationship — how they might see the nature of social responsibility.[3]

1. The *pristine capitalists* are those who see liberal economic democracy (see Chapter 1) as a good approximation of how the world works and also as the way in which the world *should* work. Consider the following quotations:

In a free enterprise, private property system, a corporate executive is an employee of the owners of the business. He has a direct responsibility to his employers. That responsibility is to conduct the business in accordance with their desires, which generally will be to make as much money as possible while conforming to the basic rules of society, both those embodied in law, and those embodied in ethical custom. (Friedman,1970)

There is no reason to think that shareholders are willing to tolerate an amount of corporate non-profit activity which appreciably reduces either dividends of the market performance of the stock. (Hetherington, 1973)

If you subscribe to these views then, while there are still good educational reasons for examining the extent to which the current social, economic and political systems do, in fact, work in this way, any notion of social responsibility is dominated by the need to make money for shareholders, to grow, make profits and seek economic efficiency. It should be obvious from Chapters 1 and 2 that this view is implicit in most accounting and finance (both theory and practice) but is a view which we consider both wholly untenable and highly undesirable.[4]

2. Alternatively, you might subscribe to an *expedient* point of view. Such a view considers that long-term economic welfare and stability can only be achieved by the acceptance of certain (usually minimal) wider social responsibilities:

The important issues involve accommodation between different and often conflicting values. There are the values associated with the market economy — efficiency, freedom, innovation, decentralisation, incentive, individual achievement. And there are the values associated with political and social rights — equality of opportunity, the right of an individual to participate in important decisions affecting his or her life, the right to standards of health, education, personal privacy and personal dignity. What we are constantly faced with are the difficult choices and trade-offs needed to achieve balance among all these values. (Clarke, Exxon Corporation, 1981)

Business must learn to look upon its social responsibilities as inseparable from its economic function. If it fails to do so, it leaves a void that will quickly be filled by others — usually by the government. (Champion, Chase National Park, 1966)

Such a view might be thought of as 'enlightened self-interest' — the sort of concern that current economic systems generate unacceptable excesses and so some additional moral content must be added to the organisation–society relationship through, for example, a fairly minimal acceptance of some limited social legislation and a recognition of 'business ethics' (see also Donaldson, 1988; Gray, 1990b; Schmidheiny, 1992).

3. The *proponents of the social contract*, on the other hand, tend to consider that companies and other organisations exist at society's will and therefore are beholden (to some degree) to society's wishes:

> Any social institution — and business is no exception — operates in society via a social contract, expressed or implied, whereby its survival and growth are based on:
> 1) The delivery of some socially desirable ends to society in general and
> 2) The distribution of economic, social or political benefits to groups from which it derives its power.
> In a dynamic society, neither the sources of institutional power nor the need for its services are permanent. Therefore an institution must constantly meet the twin tests of legitimacy and relevance by demonstrating that society requires its services and that the groups benefitting from its rewards have society's approval. (Shocker and Sethi, 1973, p. 97)

> . . . every large corporation should be thought of as a social enterprise; that is as an entity whose existence and decisions can be justified in so far as they serve public or social purposes. (Dahl, 1972)

This group would accept the principle of accountability as we have outlined in the opening chapters of the book but might have very severe doubts about the extent of the responsibilities and, subsequently, the accountability that was implied by this contract (see also Gray *et al.*, 1988, 1991).

4. We could use the term *social ecologists* to describe those who are concerned for the human environment (in the widest sense, who see serious problems developing if nothing is done about organisation–environment interactions soon, and who consider that large organisations (in particular) have been influential in creating the social and environmental problems and so could be equally influential in helping to eradicate them:

> The principal defect of the industrial way of life with its ethos of expansion is that it is not sustainable. Its termination within the lifetime of someone born today is inevitable — unless it continues to be sustained for a while longer by an entrenched minority at the cost of imposing great suffering on the rest of mankind. We can be certain, however, that sooner or later it will end (only the precise time and circumstances are in doubt) and that it will do so in one of two ways: either against our will, in a succession of famines, epidemics, social crises and wars; or because we want it to — because we wish to create a society which will not impose hardship and cruelty upon our children — in a succession of thoughtful, humane and measured changes. (Goldsmith *et al.*, 1972, p. 15)

> The rapid succession of crises which are currently engulfing the entire globe is the clearest indication that humanity is at a turning point in its historical evolution. The way to make doomsday prophecies self-fulfilling is to ignore the obvious signs of perils that lie ahead. Our scientifically conducted analysis of long term world development based on all available data points out quite clearly that such a passive course leads to disaster. (Mesarovic and Pestel, 1975, as quoted in Robertson, 1978b, pp. 22–3)

Most of those exercised by the 'greening of business' and the environmental debates of the early and mid-1990s (in particular, see Chapter 4) would fall into this group. The implicit element here is that something has gone wrong with the economic system and, at a minimum, the economic processes that lead to resource use, pollution, waste creation and so on must be amended if the quality of human life is to be improved — or held constant (see also Gray, 1990a; Gray *et al.*, 1993; Owen, 1992).

5. The *socialists* — although this is a very general term covering a wide range of views — tend to believe that the present domination of social, economic and political life by capital is inimical. There thus needs to be a significant re-adjustment in the ownership and structure of society:

> We shrink back from the truth if we believe that the destructive forces of the modern world can be 'brought under control' simply by mobilising more resources — of wealth, education, and research — to fight pollution, to preserve wildlife, to discover new sources of energy, and to arrive at more effective agreements on peaceful co-existence. Needless to say, wealth, education research, and many other things are needed for any civilisation, but what is most needed today is a revision of the ends which these means are meant to serve. And this implies, above all else, the development of a life-style which accords to material things their proper, legitimate place, which is secondary and not primary. (Schumacher, 1973, p. 290)

> From the political point of view it is important to emphasize that the problems associated with advanced technology cannot be framed merely in terms of economic categories, concerning solely the ownership and control of the means of production, but challenge the political nature of our social and cultural institutions, that of the concept of the nature of man to which they have given rise, and the technological practices which have been based on them. Institutions that promote social hierarchies must be confronted with demands for the recognition of the equality and shared collective experience of all men. Not only must the division of society into oppressors and oppressed be broken down, but so too must the barriers that separate mental activity from manual labour, and abstract theory from concrete practice. Only through such changes can we create a situation that will enable us to reintegrate all aspects of social life and experience and to establish a situation in which man can be liberated to fulfil his full potential as a sensitive, creative and social being. (Dickson, 1974, p. 203)

You should be able to see here a strong sympathy with the views expressed by a number of influential accounting scholars (see, for example, Armstrong, 1991; Lehman, 1992; Neimark, 1992; Puxty, 1986, 1991). In general terms, if you hold these views you are likely to be very suspicious of accounting in general and social and environmental accounting in particular. We shall return to this below.

6. There is also an increasingly influential voice from feminism and, in particular, the *radical feminists*. The essence of the view expressed here is that our economic, social, political and business systems — and thus the language of business and accounting — are essentially 'masculine' constructs which emphasise, for example, aggression, traditional success, achievement, conflict, competition and so on. Our world thus

denies a proper voice for, for example, compassion, love, reflection, cooperation and other 'feminine' values:

> . . . most people and societies in the present planetary order are dominated by the un-
> balanced Masculine or Yang worldview. In order for a balancing, an emergence of the
> Universal Feminine or Yin is necessary, so that a genuine union or integration may
> occur between the two: an integration of thinking and reasoning with intuition and
> feeling; a balancing of active and productive doing with stillness and contemplation; a
> preparedness to receptively wait as well as aggressively confront; a blending of
> material concerns with spiritual realization; a dilution of the respect for analysis,
> discourse and argument with a love of silence; a contemplating of dualistic thought
> with intuitive holistic seeing; a softening of the attachment to logic with a receptivity
> to imagination and dreams; a turning of the coin, to see that the other side . . .
> (Hines, 1992, p. 337)

> Mas(k)culine gestures based on the notion of unified, self-present subjects of
> rationality are made here and there in accounting. But there is no recognition of the
> masculine fear of thinking the unthinkable, giving up power and control and struggling
> for difference. Calls are made for corporate social reporting, 'participative budgeting',
> accountability (in terms of masculine power or agency relationships). They are all in the
> end doomed to the masculine proliferation of the self-same (what is like me and hence
> is good/safe) — a feminine affective economy of gift, affirmation and love would be
> more disruptive. . . . At present, environmental accounting too, being founded on
> phallogocentric understandings, will be unable to bring about revolutionary change
> despite the high hopes and desires of some of its proponents. (Cooper, 1992, p. 28)

Such a view then suggests that there is an essential 'sickness' in much of what we take for granted. Even the way in which we think about apparently benign concepts such as 'social responsibility' (for example) completely misses the point that this is no way for wise and compassionate human beings to organise their world.

7. The *deep ecologists*, in many regards, hold views closer to the *radical feminists* than their more obvious bedfellows, the *social ecologists*. This is because the deep ecologists hold that human beings do not have any greater rights to existence than any other form of life. Such views inform animal rights activists and organisations such as Earth First!:

> . . . the world is an intrinsically dynamic, interconnected web of relations in which there
> are no absolutely discrete entities and no absolute dividing lines between the living and
> the nonliving, the animate and the inanimate, or the human and the non-human. This
> model of reality undermines anthropocentrism . . . which may be seen as a kind of
> ecological myopia or unenlightened self-interest that is blind to the ecological
> circularities between the self and the external world . . . (Eckersley, 1992, pp. 49, 52)

> This is not to claim that accounting information plays one of the primary roles in either
> creating or inhibiting the solution of ecological problems. Such primacy can, arguably,
> be attributed to cultural factors — nationalism/parochialism, anthropocentrism,

selfishness and ideologically induced attitudes towards the desirability of economic growth, efficiency and property rights. . . . [S]ome of the attributes of conventional accounting information and its uses act to exacerbate or reinforce the effects of these primary factors. (Maunders and Burritt, 1991, p. 10)

The essence of these views is that the very foundation — even the existence — of our economic (and social) system is an anathema. Put at its simplest, our economic system can, and does, contemplate trade-offs between, for example, the habitat of threatened species and economic imperatives. To a deep ecologist it is inconceivable that a trade-off could have any form of moral justification. Such a view therefore challenges virtually every aspect of taken-for-granted ways of human existence, especially in the western developed nations.

While we are contemplating this range of views it is an appropriate point at which to introduce the concept of **sustainability**. Sustainability (or, as it often called, *sustainable development*) is most commonly defined as a system of development which:

meets the needs of the present without compromising the ability of future generations to meet their own needs. (The Brundtland Report, United Nations (UNWCED), 1987)

The essential idea behind sustainability is that current modes of behaviour — especially in the developed world — are *un-sustainable* and therefore threaten current and future ways of life. Sustainability is important for at least two major reasons: *first*, it brings firmly onto the political and business agendas of the world that present ways of doing things do, indeed, have 'externalities'; and *secondly*, it is an almost universally accepted principle. This does mean that members representing virtually the whole spectrum of views given above can, to a degree at least, debate matters around a single concept with which they are all, in principle at least, in agreement (see, for example, Pezzey, 1989).

Sustainability, however, is something of a wolf in sheep's clothing. First, although it is generally used to refer only to planetary environmental issues, it is also an essentially social concept. That is, sustainability can be thought of as consisting of both *eco-justice* (social) and *eco-efficiency* (environmental) elements (Gladwin, 1993). That is, not only must we all be more careful with our use of scarce planetary resources but we must also have regard for the wealth distribution (intragenerational equity) as well as the wellbeing of future generations (intergenerational equity). This raises major questions about such matters as current distributions of wealth, current levels of consumption in the West and population growth and there are, unsurprisingly, widely differing attitudes to these things. Secondly, there is widespread dispute about how big is the current gap between our current patterns of consumption and production on the one hand and a sustainable way of life on the other. This disagreement naturally leads to very different views on how substantial a change is necessary to bring us round to sustainability.

Consequently, although sustainability has provided a new, demanding and potential holistic basis on which to discuss such matters as organisational responsibility and society it has also brought out into the open many differences of belief which will remain sources of continuing conflict. What is almost universally accepted is that businesses in the developed world are certainly not sustainable. It is quite apparent that they must become so — through government action and/or through their own actions. Such a change will have a major impact on organisational life and the way in which the changes come about will depend significantly on which of the above groups' opinions finally prevail (for more detail see, for example, Gray *et al.*, 1993, Chapter 14; Jacobs, 1991).

As a final point at this stage on sustainability it is worth highlighting that many of the *deep ecologists* have very serious reservations about sustainability. This is because they are concerned about the continued viability of the human species — not about all species. At one extreme a very plausible argument can be made that humanity has had its chance. It is now the chance of other species and life-forms to escape from domination of people and if this involves the extinction of humanity, this is a reasonable and natural consequence. Such views are increasingly widely held (Gray, 1992; Maunders and Burritt, 1991).

There are, of course, yet other points of view (we have not, for example, considered religious points of view here). The range we have identified is probably sufficient for our purposes as it highlights that the organisation–society relationship is far more complex (and is continually becoming more complex) than we are inclined to think of it. This complexity means that the roles we may envisage for accounting in general and social and environmental accounting in particular are far from simple.

3.3 What, then, is the role of CSR?

The role that one envisages for CSR depends, then, upon one's view of how the organisation–society relationship operates, and how one would like it to operate.

The *pristine capitalists* and the *expedients* are both predominantly conservative, pro-capital, pro-corporations and generally content with the basic structures of the existing system of economic activity. For people holding such views, CSR is *only* desirable to the extent that it is in the corporation's (and/or capital's) own interests and/or leads to a greater economic efficiency as currently defined by markets. The value or otherwise of CSR may, therefore, be judged as if from the point of view of the reporting corporation — as long as the organisation is pursuing traditional wealth creation, profit growth and, perhaps, maximisation of shareholder wealth (for more detail see, for example, Benston, 1982a, b). This does not suggest, however, that there may not be conflict between the management of an organisation and its shareholders over the way in which CSR is employed. A management's desire to, for instance, improve accountability or manipulate its stakeholders may be at variance with a shareholder's right to information and/or may cost money which a shareholder might consider was better spent on other, either social or financial, projects (see, for example, Mintzberg, 1983). At its simplest, CSR is likely to involve some opportunity cost over which all stakeholders may not be in agreement (we return to this in section 3.5).

For those whose views lean towards either a *social contract* or *social ecologist* point of view, CSR will probably be an extremely important factor in the development of accountability, democracy and transparency. For the 'social contract' view, some significant flow of information between, for example, companies and society is a *sine qua non* of democratic life. This is the view we took in Chapter 2 and which will dominate the rest of the book. We need say no more at this stage. For the 'social ecologists', however, the matter is perhaps more complicated because there is a fundamental concern that it is the very working of the system that has led to problems. CSR is therefore seen as having the potential to generate a wider accountability which will, in turn, lead to fundamental change in the system itself. While, from the social contract viewpoint, CSR is useful for its evolutionary potential, for the social ecologist there is more than a hint of revolution in the change that is intended. In this social ecologists overlap with the more radical groups.

The essential concern for the more radical groups, the *socialists, radical feminists* and *deep ecologists* is that the very way in which society is ordered, the distribution of wealth, the power of corporations, the language of economics and business and so on, are so fundamentally flawed that nothing less than radical structural change has any hope of emancipating human and non-human life. The social, economic and political systems are seen as being fundamentally inimical. The role of CSR is therefore seen as, at best, severely limited and, at worst, downright destructive. That is, CSR *may* be able to raise the visibility of different groups in society — constituencies such as the underdeveloped nations, the unemployed, women, ethnic minorities, the natural environment — and thus give them a voice. This voice *may* lead to fundamental change. To this extent CSR is desirable; but — and it is a major 'but' — the more radical groups would see that CSR can only express views which are, more or less, in harmony with the current way of doing things (the current 'hegemony', as it is called). Therefore, because CSR will be controlled by the reporting corporations and a State which has a vested interest in keeping things more or less as they are, CSR has little radical content. Furthermore, CSR may do more harm than good because it may give the *impression* of concern and change but, in fact, will do no more than allow the system to 'capture' the radical elements of, for example, socialism, environmentalism or femininism and thus emasculate them (see, for example, Cooper, 1992; Power, 1994).

Perhaps the best example of this relates to the radical ecology debate. A 'social ecologist' might argue, correctly (see, for example, Gray, 1990a; 1992; Gray *et al.*, 1993), that current business practice, economic thinking and accounting make environmental crisis virtually inevitable. The social ecologist may well believe that we need, therefore, to adjust our current business, economic and accounting practice to take account of environmental issues. One strategy would be to place an economic value on all aspects of nature so that 'nature' is 'fully integrated' in decision making (see, for example, Milne, 1991; Pearce *et al.*, 1989). By doing so one is using the very process (current economics and accounting) that caused the problem (environmental crisis) to try to solve the problem. This is known as the process of 'juridification' (see, for example, Power and Laughlin, 1992) and it is well established that one is unlikely to solve a problem by applying more of the thing which caused the problem (this case is well made in Hines, 1991b; and Maunders and Burritt, 1991).

We share these concerns to a considerable degree (see, for example, Gray, 1992; Owen, 1992). The forms of social and environmental accounting that we are recommending make less use of conventional economic thinking and conventional financial accounting than they attempt to devise *new* ways of accounting for social, environmental and political issues. Whether CSR *can* achieve more good than ill from these radical perspectives is still an open question and one which must be treated with great care (see, for example, Power, 1994).

Therefore, if you subscribe to a radical point of view, whether radical right, radical left, feminism or ecologist, you will probably have very limited use for CSR. If you are quietly content with the way the world currently works you will also have little use for social and environmental accounting. From a societal point of view, CSR is an essentially *evolutionary* mechanism designed to develop and enhance the current processes of accountability. It is thus a generally implicit political tool designed to enhance democracy. From almost any other point of view CSR is an explicitly political tool which should be used (or not used) in the furtherance of the political ends of seeking radical change by particular groups, whether they be radicals, companies, expedients or, even, accountants.

Look at the problem another way. If we think that the world is less than perfect and we decide we would like to try to do something to limit that imperfection, what should we do? Each group discussed above has some broad view on what the world should look like as well as a broad view of how the world now is. The central question is how do we get there from here? To answer such a question accurately we would need a complete understanding of how societal change comes about. This is not something we possess at the moment — nor, perhaps, are we ever likely to possess. As a result, any efforts to bring about social change will be partly based on faith as to likely outcomes as well as an element of trust in the deontological (intrinsic) rightness of the actions themselves. While we cannot say with any certainty whether CSR will produce change and, indeed, whether such change will be predominantly positive or negative, we can judge that social and environmental accounting seems to us intrinsically good actions which accord with a set of principles (accountability and democracy) and which seems likely to encourage movement towards a more democratic future. Seeking to change accounting seems an appropriate act for accountants. While accounting may not be the best place to start when seeking to change society it is clearly an important element for any significant change and, as accountants define and reify accounting, it seems reasonable to assume that accountants are an appropriate group to explore such a change.

It is this issue which we will now explore, looking first at the State's response to social and environmental accounting issues, then the response of companies before trying to establish what, if anything, accountants should do about the situation.

3.4 The State's role in CSR

The State lays down a minimum set of conditions for organisation behaviour in law. This law, for our purposes, comprises two elements: responsibility for action; and responsibility for *disclosure* about action (i.e. accountability). There is always a gap between these two and, generally speaking, law governing actions is more demanding than that governing disclosure about actions. This is generally true in the social and environmental sphere of organisational activity (as we shall see in Chapters 5 and 6) but, strangely enough, is not the case in the financial sphere. Here, the disclosure requirements — the financial reporting rules — generally exceed the requirements governing the financial actions themselves. More particularly, Companies Acts tend to be the most demanding requirement of disclosure placed on any organisation. From this we may infer one of three things. First, we might infer that an organisation is a predominantly economic and financial entity. While we *may* wish to see organisations as dominated by financial issues, it is certainly not the case that organisations are exclusively economic creatures. Secondly, we might infer that the information needs or wants of financial participants are considered by the State to be significantly more important than the non-financial information needs and wants of financial participants. There is little reason to suppose either that this is true or, more especially, that it *ought* to be true. Finally, we might conclude that the State places the information needs and wants of financial participants above those of other participants. Why should this be? The answer to this, once again, depends on your point of view. You may well choose to agree that the current level of regulation of both actions and disclosure is indeed at an 'ideal' level and reflects the wishes of society at any one time. If, however, by 'society' one means the wishes and needs of the whole populace you will find it difficult to sustain such an argument. The linkage between societal preferences and legal pronouncement is shaky and involves many lags (see, for example, Dowling and Pfeffer, 1975; Stone, 1975). If, on the other hand, by 'society' one means an imbalanced distribution of power, then one probably could argue that law reflects the more powerful elements in society's preferences. Indeed, a Marxian argument would be that the State is actually 'captured' by capital and will only normally act to protect the interests of capital. The evidence certainly seems to suggest that the State, in the developed countries at least, must be thought of as having objectives commensurate with the *pristine capitalists* or the *expedients*.

This is where the political economy theory arguments from Chapter 2 come into play. For example, environmental protection is clearly an increasingly essential element in any economic system and poverty, oppression, homelessness and unemployment are generally considered undesirable elements in a society. Why, then, does the State not introduce more legislation to govern these issues? As we saw in Chapter 1, we could answer this quite simply if we believed in the liberal economic democracy position. The alternative explanations — of which there are many because State legislature is a complex matter — include the idea that the State will only act if it has the backing of capital. Thus, it is possible to see regulations governing CSR — and other areas of disclosure — as arising either when the whole corporate economic system is struggling to maintain legitimacy (for example over protection of the environment or the employment of women and ethnic minorities) or when particular elements of the corporate system start abusing the system to the detriment of companies as a whole (for example over health and safety issues or pension fund management) (for more detail see, for example, Adams *et al.*, 1995a; Gray *et al.*, 1995a).

We shall see some of these interpretations in action when we look at the development of CSR in subsequent chapters. However, it does suggest that attempts to influence government thinking on matters of social and environmental disclosure will be largely doomed to failure if such disclosure is not in the interests of organisations in general and companies and capital in particular. That is, we find it difficult to maintain an argument that the State is a fundamental force for democracy and accountability. If it were, at a minimum we might see a great deal more in the way of disclosure requirements covering extant areas of law. We now turn to look, briefly, at why organisations *do* introduce disclosure.

3.5 How should companies respond?

Companies — and other organisations — generally comply with disclosure requirements. Such compliance is, again generally speaking, at a minimum level. That is, all things being equal, a company will disclose just sufficient information to meet the legal requirements. This should come as no surprise. Companies have many pressures on them and it is generally difficult to see why extensive disclosure might be something that a company pursued or was especially happy to encourage. However, companies in particular do undertake voluntary disclosure in terms of both disclosure in excess of the minimum on regulated issues and in areas where no disclosure is currently required. Companies' reasons for doing this are varied and complex (we will see in Chapter 4, Figure 4.1, a list of the range of these motivations behind corporate disclosure); but what can we reasonably *expect* a company — or other organisation — to undertake voluntarily?

It is easy enough to see that any organisation will undertake disclosure if it sees that by so doing it will enhance its corporate goals. We normally assume that such goals are dominated by economic criteria — especially profit — and thus that the desirability of CSR will be judged by reference to how it affects that goal. Thus, we will normally assume that companies, in particular (as well as the State) also fall into the *pristine capitalists* or *expedients* groups with respect to the objectives for CSR.

To this extent, the theories of social disclosure which we outlined in Chapter 2 are particularly helpful. That is, political economy and legitimacy theories suggest that we may interpret most corporate social disclosure as concerned with maintaining the legitimacy of the company and/or the capitalist system. Similarly, we may wish to see the organisation as managing its strategic environment through the use of 'stakeholder analysis'.

As we saw in Chapter 2, we might think of a 'stakeholder perspective' as comprising a company-centred view of the world (stakeholder analysis) and a society-centred view of the world (accountability). From the company's point of view, one is interested in assessing the *empirical* (Tricker, 1983) accountability that stakeholders can enforce on the company and which is thus in the company's interests to acknowledge and manage. To do this, the company needs, first, to assess its 'substantive environment'. This is shown, for a mythical company, in Figures 3.1 to 3.3. Figure 3.1 shows the *primary level* of a company's interactions with its substantive environment. These are the organisations with which the company interacts — at least in part — financially and

Figure 3.1 *Primary level influences of organisational activity*

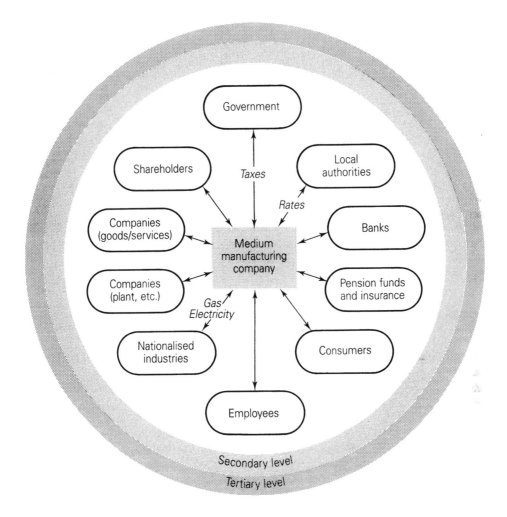

which are thus recognised in the financial accounting system of the organisation. However, as we have already seen, current accounting practice does not capture all of even these primary level interactions. From society's point of view these groups and organisations have rights to information (accountability) which is not fully discharged by current accounting practice or other sources of information. From the company's point of view these are organisations which, to a greater or lesser extent, have a direct influence on the continued existence and success of the company. They are thus

Figure 3.2 *Secondary level influences of organisational activity*

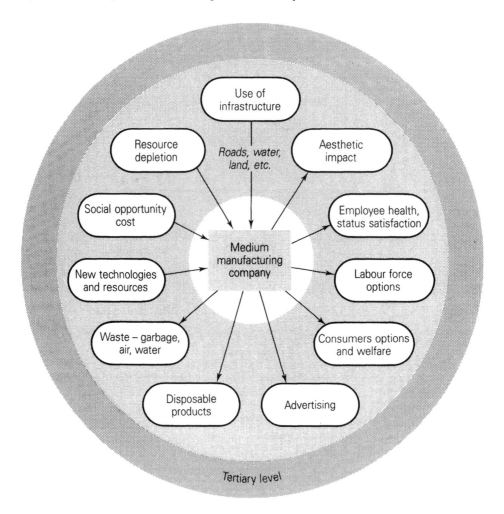

stakeholders which it is in the company's interest to manage and with whom to maintain goodwill — or legitimacy.

The company's interactions are, however, a great deal more complex than this. Figure 3.2 illustrates some of the *secondary* level interactions. These secondary level interactions reflect, to a greater extent, the societal interactions of the company. The company, assuming that it pursues a narrow profit-orientated goal, will wish to manage these more ephemeral 'stakeholders' to the extent that groups in society (e.g. pressure groups,

Figure 3.3 *Tertiary level influences of organisational activity*

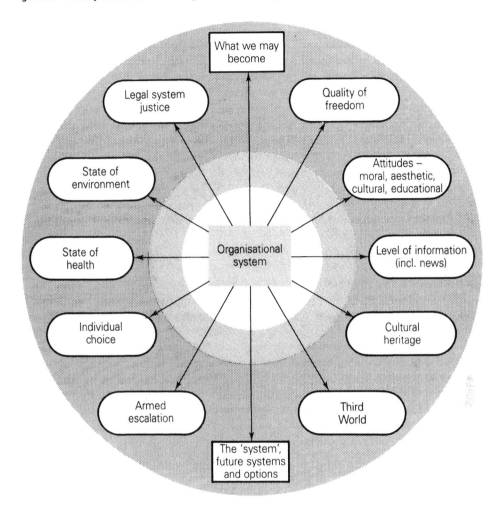

customers, employees) are actively concerned by them and/or that the company believes that its image is enhanced by being seen to be benign in these areas of activity. The upsurge in environmental concern is a typical example of this. As the 1990s progressed it became increasingly important to companies to be seen to be managing the 'environmental stakeholder' because this was both 'good business sense' and because the companies' legitimacy as a responsible environmental citizen was under threat. From society's point of view, these secondary level interactions tend to be the areas in which accountability is more hotly contested. It is here that we see increasing legal and moral pressure on companies as society's rights to information in these areas are developed.

Finally, we can identify a *tertiary level* of interactions. At this stage the interactions between the individual organisation and society are less important than the interactions of the organisational economic system as a whole. This is illustrated in Figure 3.3, which captures the theoretical underpinnings of organisational existence. The influences on and by the organisational system are far more subtle and elusive. Generally speaking it is only when we make our theoretical assumptions about the world explicit — as we have done in the preceding chapters — that we make any kind of useful statement about these interactions. Interestingly, the emergence of *sustainability* (as a theoretical perspective on the world) has raised the awareness of these tertiary level interactions and made them explicit. For the first time within recent decades, the concept of the organisational system as a powerful influence at this tertiary level is being more widely discussed and recognised. From society's point of view this raises questions about a broader sort of accountability that organisations owe to society — through, for example, reporting on sustainability (see, for example, Bebbington and Gray, 1993; Gray, 1994b). From the companies' point of view explicit acknowledgement of such a wide range of potential responsibilities and influences raises difficult questions about the limits to their legitimacy (see, for example, Bebbington and Gray, 1995a, b).

How a company selects its stakeholders (and thus chooses to manage them through CSR) is a strategic choice by the company, but for a number of companies and for many non-company organisations it is *not* simply a matter of identifying which groups influence one's profitability and working to influence those. There are an increasing number of *values-based* companies to whom there is a goal beyond profitability.[5] Such companies are often taken to include The Body Shop, Traidcraft, Shared Earth, New Consumer, Shared Interest, The Centre for Alternative Technology in the United Kingdom, Ben and Jerry's in the United States, Earth Sanctuaries in Australia and, if we broaden our definition of values just a little, very many household company names in many countries (see, for example, Centre for Social Change/New Consumer, 1993). For non-company organisations there is frequently an even greater commitment to accountability and genuine response to stakeholder views — as opposed to 'managing' one's stakeholders.

The point is not to simply assume a pernicious and rapacious selfishness on the part of the company or organisation when it is considering its social disclosure policy. It may be a complex matter (we return to this in more detail throughout the book and in Chapter 9 in particular).

3.6 What is the role of the accountant?

Whatever one decides about the desirability or otherwise of CSR, there is no incontrovertible necessity that the accountant should become involved. It may be that a substantial case can be made to support the argument that accountants should have nothing or little to do with CSR and social and environmental accounting.

If we think of accountants as the sum of the skills and knowledge that they acquire through professional examinations then there is no reason to anticipate that we have the requisite orientation for reporting across a wider range of issues to a wider range of stakeholders. Similarly, if accountants perceive themselves as rule-followers (whether legal rules or those issued by the accountancy profession) then the absence of appropriate guidance on social and environmental accounting would exclude the accountant from the development of these areas. Furthermore, research suggests that accountants, as a whole, are not an innovative breed partly as result of their education and training (see, for example, Bebbington *et al.*, 1994; French *et al.*, 1992) and partly as a result of the nature of the role of the accountant itself. Recent work suggests, in fact, that accountants are actually unable to take new initiatives without formal guidance (see, for example, Bebbington *et al.*, 1994). There are also more pragmatic reasons that may encourage the accountant to stay away from CSR. For example, busy accountants certainly need no extra tasks with which to fill an already hectic working life. Similarly, as most accountants are employed by organisations (either directly or indirectly), their freedom for innovation is limited to the roles expected of them within those organisations. Additionally, as accountants may believe that they enjoy a reputation for impartiality and reliability, involvement in a new area such as CSR may damage that reputation (see, for example, Gray and Perks, 1982). Finally, the 'critical theorists' have identified (as we discussed above) that accounting and accountants are frequently responsible for many of the more socially, culturally and environmentally damaging practices of — and in — organisations. There are many, therefore, who would not adjudge accountants the most attractive group with whom to entrust a new, important and demanding function.

All these points have merit and some evidence to support them: so much so that any argument we might assemble to argue for the desirability of the accountants' involvement must, of necessity, be tempered by the above limitations.

The case in favour of accountants' involvement in CSR is only partly founded on *positive* arguments — on the way that accountants currently behave and on the way that they are currently educated and trained. Such arguments supporting CSR as a suitable area of accountants' activity tend to be more *normative* in nature. The positive arguments are briefly reviewed first.

CSR, in whatever form it takes, involves the design and management of information systems, the collation and verification of data and the reporting of information to those outside the organisation. These are skills which accountants do — or should — possess. For social and environmental accounting systems, the accountant *qua* accountant need not necessarily be an expert on environmental or employment matters any more that s/he need be an expert on engineering or construction issues for conventional accounting systems. Indeed, there are aspects of accounting training which are especially apposite in CSR. Accountants may well take the accounting, reporting and disclosure and auditing issues for granted in conventional accounting, but this ability to clarify the different stages of an 'accounting' process has proved especially useful in the design of social and environmental accounting systems: so much so that experiments have been undertaken to replicate a conventional accounting system as a *social bookkeeping and accounting* system (see Chapter 7 and Dey *et al.*, 1995, for more detail). Finally, using a 'skills-based' argument, while we would not wish social and environmental accounting to be dominated by financial information it is inevitable that some CSR will involve financial numbers and the actions underlying the disclosure (e.g. development of better health and safety procedures, measures to reduce pollution) will have financial consequences — especially at the investment appraisal level. This seems like an important area for accountants' involvement (for more detail see, for example, Gray and Mallon, 1994; Gray *et al.*, 1993).

A more pragmatic — although less admirable — reason for the involvement of accountants relates to the expansion of 'professional' expertise. Not only might accountants think 'if we do not do it, who will?' but there are business opportunities for accountants in exactly the same way as many large firms of accountants found significant business opportunities in the environmental accounting and auditing developments of the 1990s (see, for example, Perks and Gray, 1979, 1980).

The most persuasive arguments for the involvement of accountants, in our view, relate to issues we have already considered. First, accounting purports to be a profession with a committment to the *public interest*. The development of accountability is clearly, to our eyes, a central element of accounting *and* in the public interest. It is, thus, an inevitable task of the accountant. Secondly, we have identified CSR as attempting to fill an increasing hole left by the increasingly worrying failures of conventional accounting systems. If there are major failures in the accounting systems, it seems to us that accountants must take a major responsibility in trying to overcome those failures.

In essence, our view is that if accounting is not about *accountability*, what is it about? Conventional accounting cannot wholly discharge accountability. CSR, it seems to us, is an essential element in any attempt to explore and develop current levels of organisational accountability. In this sense we find the case self-evident (as we indicated in Chapter 1, section 1.9). We do not, however, consider that accountants are likely to find CSR easy nor will the current educational experience of accountants help them to fulfil the demands that CSR will impose. This is less a problem with accounting than what currently passes for accounting education (see, for example, Gray *et al.*, 1994; Lewis *et al.*, 1992; Owen *et al.*, 1994).

To finalise this review of the role of accountants — and, perhaps, to emphasise the need for additional developments in the education of the accounting profession — we need to introduce a very brief review of those theories which we so frequently take for granted in accounting.

3.7 A brief review of accounting theory

If only for completeness, it seems appropriate to spend just a few moments examining what we more conventionally think of as 'accounting theories'. That is, we have attempted, throughout this and the preceding chapters, to link CSR with conventional accounting. We have carefully examined the underpinnings of conventional accounting but then reviewed a range of theories (e.g. accountability and legitimacy theory) which are rarely placed at the centre of accounting teaching and debate. To what extent are the more frequently referenced accounting theories useful in attempting to understand social and environmental accounting in general and the role of accountants therein in particular?

There have been a number of influential attempts to codify conventional accounting theories. These complex and scholarly analyses (see, for example, AAA, 1977; Davis *et al.*, 1982; Laughlin and Puxty, 1981; and see, for example, Belkaoui, 1986; Gray *et al.*, 1987, Chapter 4, for more detail) identify a range of accounting theories by reference to, for example, the way in which the theory has been developed (e.g. 'normative deductive' or 'positive inductive')[6] or the objective of the accounting process which lies behind a particular attempt to theorise. This work is too extensive to review thoroughly in this context but we can usefully identify a number of key themes. Although this will, of necessity, be cursory, it should serve for our purposes.

If we can be forgiven a high degree of simplicity, conventional accounting theories might be thought of falling into four broad (although overlapping) groups: *classical inductive theories*; *income theories*, *decision usefulness theories*; and *information economics/agency theories*. All these theories work within the four characteristics which define conventional accounting[7] and each behave as if CSR was nothing to do with accounting. This suggests that if the theories are a good basis for accounting we may be able to dismiss CSR. They also suggest that conventional accounting training — in so far as it depends on these theories — will have little to offer for our understanding of CSR. We will briefly look at each of these in turn.

The *classical inductive theories* were, principally, attempts to codify current accounting practice and draw out the principles, themes and conventions on which current practice was based. Our identification of the four characteristics which delineate conventional accounting are 'inductive' in this sense (see Note 6). One of the most important insights to emerge from the classical inductive approach has been the identification of the characteristics of accounting such as accrual, prudence, representational accuracy, periodicity and so on.[8] Without in any way wishing to dismiss this approach, it does not help us a great deal. First, you need a definition of 'accounting' before you can begin to codify it. 'Accounting' therefore becomes what you define it to be. This is essentially reactionary and does not allow for *any* change in what constitutes accounting. More importantly, the 'accounting' you are codifying cannot be justified as being the 'right accounting'. Accounting is a man-made artefact. It has no independent existence and therefore its existence cannot be taken as a given in the way we accept the existence of stars, worms and atoms; so while we may wish to codify what we might like to think of as 'accounting' there is no basis for saying that this *is* or this *should be* what accounting is. Thus, although the classical inductive school excludes CSR it is unable to offer any justification for doing so.[9] This is not persuasive!

The *income theories* are an attempt to measure some sort of objective 'truth' about an organisation. Their principle aim is to identify the 'real profit' of an organisation. Much of value has emerged from these attempts — not least the identification of how difficult (if not impossible) it is to measure a single income figure. First of all, there is the issue of 'whose income' one is seeking to measure. Is it the income of the organisation (the entity concept) or that of the owners (the proprietorship concept)? Further, why are we not trying to measure, for example, the employees' income (see, for example, Bougen,

1984; Glautier and Underdown, 1976) or that of communities? Secondly, there has to be a major question as to whether such a thing as a 'true income' can exist. After all, profit is a function of a measurement system designed to measure profit. This is disturbingly circular reasoning. Finally, the central theme in income measurement is the elegance of Hicks' calculations of economic income (Hicks, 1946). We already know that the 'economic' restricts itself to that for which there is a price. It therefore, by definition, excludes anything for which there is no price — employee health, community well-being, environmental quality.

Income theories, even without their philosophical problems, implicitly exclude the very things that CSR is concerned with. As we have seen, this can only be justified in a pristine liberal economic world — which does not exist. So the justification for excluding CSR is, as with the classical inductive theories, pretty vacuous.

However, the income theories *do* offer lines of development for CSR. First, there is an emerging line of evidence which suggests that the 'economic income' (however defined) of the wealthy nations — and the shareholders therein in particular — has been gained at the expense of the less developed world and/or at the expense of the poor in any nation. Thus, the 'income' which is, for example, attributable to developed-country shareholders overstates their 'earnings' to the degree that, for example, the TNCs (transnational corporations) have managed to exploit their relative power. This profit does not reflect some 'true' and 'objective' measure of earnings but is more a reflection of power and exploitation (for more detail see, for example, Bailey *et al.*, 1994a, b; Ekins, 1992a, b; Jacobs, 1991). Taking this one step further it is quite a simple matter to demonstrate that company 'income' contains a significant element of capital distribution — in this case 'environmental capital'. An essential tenet of accounting is that income must allow for the maintenance of capital. Current organisational behaviour clearly does not maintain environmental capital and so overstates earnings (see, for example, Gray, 1991a; Gray *et al.*, 1993). If diminution of environmental capital is factored into the income figure it seems likely that no company in the western world has actually made any kind of a profit for many years (see, for example, Gray, 1992; 1994b; Gray *et al.*, 1993; Bebbington and Gray, 1993).

While conventional income theory may (unconsciously?) exclude CSR, it is relatively simple to show that a 'full and proper' examination of income and profit must take account of those matters to which CSR gives attention. The corollary is that the reasoning behind income theory offers intellectual mechanisms for thinking about some of the issues which will exercise us in our attempts to understand and articulate social and environmental accounting.

If there is one set of theories that have dominated accounting thought in recent decades it must the *decision usefulness theories*. While these theories have enormous power in a management accounting (internal to the organisation) context and have encouraged much important research (on the use of accounting numbers, the impact on share price behaviour and so on) it is difficult to understand how *decision usefulness* has maintained its prominent position. First of all, *decision usefulness* has little 'positive' value. Decision usefulness purports to describe the central characteristics of accounting in general and financial statements in particular. To describe accounting as useful for decisions is no more illuminating than describing a screwdriver as being useful for digging a hole — it is better than nothing (and therefore 'useful') but hardly what one might ideally like for such a task. The research literature is fairly clear that current financial statements do not represent the information that investors most desire (see, for example, Gray, 1994a; Lee, 1978; Puxty and Laughlin, 1983). Secondly, and far more importantly, there is no obvious justification for the *normative* position of decision usefulness. Why should accounting be useful? Especially, if it is to be useful, why should it be only useful to investors? Once again, we can only justify such an assumption in a pristine liberal economic world (see Gray, 1994a).

Whatever one concludes here (and we would have the most serious reservations about deriving accounting from a decision usefulness point of view) it is certainly possible — should one wish — to recognise that CSR can be useful to all sorts of groups. Remember that decision usefulness also fails to distinguish between information *needs* and information *wants* (see, for example, Sterling, 1972). Many non-financial participants *want* CSR as it provides insight into the processes that affect their lives. Our contention is that the financial participants *need* CSR so that the owners of the business are constantly reminded of the social and environmental costs that their wellbeing and wealth has imposed on others (see, for example, Cooper, 1988; Owen *et al.*, 1987).

Thus, despite the ubiquity of decision usefulness in accounting, and despite the fact that decision usefulness has prompted valuable insights and ways of thinking about accounting it is, at base, an empty *raison d'être* for either accounting or CSR. It has neither descriptive power nor any normative justification. Examination of CSR tends to illuminate this lack in conventional accounting theorising (Cooper, 1988; Owen *et al.*, 1987) and goes some way to explaining why CSR has, on the whole, been little influenced by decision usefulness thinking (see, for example, Dierkes and Antal, 1985).

Finally, we can turn to the *information economics/agency theories* of accounting. The essence of these theories is that the world is *explicitly* limited to the economic and accounting information is considered exclusively as a 'good' which preparers (company management) and users (typically investors) fight over, bargain for and buy and sell to each other. All parties are assumed to be rational economic men (*sic*) and to be acting in their own financial short-term self-interest, (i.e. to be selfish, gambling and greedy). In this, we are once again back into a liberal economic world. There is little doubt that these theories have provided *some* useful insights in the way in which they model the world. There is equally little doubt that some company management and many gambling investors may appear to act in line with these theories. It is also the case that some authors have found the form of analysis employed in these theories useful in examining CSR (see, for example, Ness and Mirza, 1991; and see also Mak, 1991); but apart from the limitations which must arise from a prisitine liberal economic perspective on the world and the profound philosophical limitations of the approach (see, for example, Armstrong, 1991; Arrington, 1990; Christenson, 1983; Tinker and Okcabol, 1991) the approach cannot offer any justification for *why* we might accept this description of the world as a desirable one. As we noted in Chapter 2, it is a morally bankrupt view of the world in general and accounting in particular. Its (usual) exclusion of CSR is therefore actually attractive as an argument *for* CSR!

This very brief review of possible links between CSR and conventional accounting theories has shown (we believe) that, in general, it is the very weaknesses of the way in which accounting practice is constructed and its lack of a theoretical underpinning and justification which actually supports the development of CSR. That is, conventional accounting theory does not do much for conventional accounting — primarily because (a) conventional accounting practice is so piecemeal and thus defies systematic codification; and (b) the theories offer no realistic moral or descriptive basis from which to build a normative theory about accounting.[10] Thus accounting — as currently practised — cannot be justified as in the public interest. To bring it closer to the public interest probably requires the addition of CSR. Alternatively you may choose, after this review, to agree with (particularly) the Marxian scholars who suggest that accounting simply reflects the power distribution in the *status quo* and theories are, thus, no more than 'excuses' to justify and bolster that distribution.[11] This may, indeed, be the case. If it is, then accounting is a sham and not worthy of our support (although it is still worthy of our attention). We choose to believe that accounting can be in the public interest but that only by placing the theoretical model of accountability at its centre and the resultant development of social and environmental accounting can this be achieved.

We hope that this and the preceding two chapters have provided some useful insights into 'accounting' in a general sense and into CSR in particular. Although we have tried to offer the cases against a need for CSR, we can no longer sustain such a point of view. Accounting has much to recommend it but it is a fatally flawed activity and has few reliable claims to be a profession. It also has little in the way of theoretical and moral justification. These can be provided by accountability and the development of CSR.

The chapters in the rest of the book will trace and explain social and environmental accounting practice within the broad theoretical framework we have introduced here. However, experience suggests to us that we must, before we go much further, give some indication of what we think CSR should look like. It is far too easy to criticise if one has nothing to put in its place. This we try to do in the last section.

3.8 A way forward?

We will return to prescription for social and environmental accounting — including CSR — in Chapter 10. We have already seen a number of examples of CSR and, in the following chapters, we will present a very wide range of experiments which offer examples of what a (possibly) 'ideal' CSR might look like. For the time being, however, it may be appropriate to give some indication of the sort of minimum proposals which we believe the accounting profession must take on board. These can be broadly itemised as follows.

a Some means must be found to reverse the ethical and intellectual atrophy that accounting education and training appears to encourage. The evidence is increasingly alarming. Accountants seem incapable of, for example, taking new initiatives, considering issues at an abstract and theoretical level and/or examining the moral impact of their activities (for reviews of this evidence see, for example, Gray *et al.*, 1994; Lewis *et al.*, 1992; Owen *et al.*, 1994). This is wholly unacceptable in any educated profession, but does go some way towards explaining why, for example, the 'Conceptual Framework' projects have been such abject and expensive failures. Some of the fault for this state of affairs lies with educators who must help accounting students to develop more independent and critical minds — the *raison d'être* of education after all; but much blame also lies with the profession as a whole in the emphasis it continues to place on training and skills acquisition. This is clearly an essential issue (see, for example, AECC, 1990) and one which, we believe, must be addressed as a prerequisite to accountants being in a position to develop a significant role within CSR.

b Secondly, we believe that the accountancy profession must raise the issue of accountability as the founding basis of current accounting practice and commit to it as a central principle. We are bewildered by the continued confused emphasis on — and incorrect application of — the (largely vacuous) 'decision-usefulness' basis of accounting (*sic*). The profession must serve its public interest duties through a commitment to accountability.

c Thirdly, we believe that continued experimentation with all aspects of social and environmental accounting and CSR is especially helpful. It opens up new possibilities and permits 'ivory tower' ideas to be tried out in practice. We will see many such examples throughout this book. Historically, various professional accountancy bodies (see, for example, ICAEW, 1992; ACCA, 1990 (see Gray 1990a); AICPA, 1977; ASSC, 1975; CICA, 1993a, b) have lent their support to these experiments. Much more could be done.

d Finally, we believe that the *minimum* form of CSR must be the **Compliance-with-Standard Report (CWS)**. The reasoning behind the CWS approach has been explained in earlier chapters (see also Gray *et al.*, 1986, 1988, 1991) and in its emphasis on disclosing the extent to which organisation has complied with existing responsibilities, it is clearly an approach which places accountability at its centre. As an indication of what such a report might look like, we include an extract in Figure 3.4.

In the examples which follow in later chapters, especially examples relating to environmental disclosure (but see also the work on social audits in Chapter 9), it will be apparent that organisations do not find the *principle* of an — at least minimal — practice of the CWS beyond them. These are, however, partial attempts whose critique we will return to in Chapter 10.

The CWS is certainly not without its difficulties. Some of these are practical in that (i) companies may not know to what extent they comply with the law!; (ii) large TNCs (transnational corporations) not only have to comply with a very wide range of standards but have to do so across many sites in many countries — this may produce a practical data overload problem;[12] and (iii) many organisations will probably be fairly reluctant to release this information to the public domain — although that is what accountability is all about!

Figure 3.4 *An extract from a Compliance-with-Standard report summary*

Area of standard	Previous year: level	Previous year: standard	Current year: level	Current year: standard	Source of standard	Explanation of standard and performance
Natural environment						
Water discharges: 1. to ground: Discharge 1 etc. ... 2. to mains: Discharge 1 etc. ...						
Disposal of wastes: 1. Controlled substances Substance 1. etc. ... 2. Landfill volumes 3. Incineration volumes						
Discharges to air: Substance 1. etc. ...						
Employees						
Accidents Type 1: no. etc. ... Days lost:						
Health and Safety infringements						
Staff turnover: Resignations Redundancies etc. ...						
Overseas communities						
Fair Trade:						
Employment Code						

However, CWS also has its own theoretical problems. These are the problems of CSR itself which we have briefly reviewed above, plus a set of its own particular difficulties. The more important of these include its essentially conservative nature (in that it follows the law) and its essentially reactionary nature (in that law tends to be more influenced by companies and capital than by communities, employees and the natural environment). For these reasons we were careful to specify the CWS as a *minimum* basis for the development of CSR. It will, thus, provide us (and you) with a minimal benchmark against which to start the process of assessing and evaluation the examples of CSR we review throughout the book.

Notes

1. Put more simply, if there is nothing wrong with conventional accounting then we probably do not need social and environmental accounting. The corollary is that if there *is* something less than perfect in conventional accounting, then we need to do something about it. Social and environmental accounting is one, major, potential solution to the information-flow problems that have arisen in the organisation–society relationship. Theory is the basis on which we judge these things.
2. We will show below that the spectrum may be more usefully thought of as comprising three or more dimensions (e.g. left wing, right wing, deep green and feminist), rather than just the two of Benston and Tinker.
3. For more detail on these issues see, for example, Bailey *et al.*, 1994a, b; Kempner *et al.*, 1976; Lehman, 1992; Mathews, 1993; Perks, 1993; Tinker, 1985.
4. For more detail see, for example, Benston, 1982a, b; Gray, 1994a; Owen, 1992.
5. This cannot imply that maintaining cash-flow or even maintaining some degree of profit is not important in these companies. It is the relative emphasis that is given to the various organisational goals that is important. In some cases, it might even be that a company would prefer to go out of business rather than compromise some set of values. While this might seem outrageous in a wholly economic world, it is nowhere near as crazy as some of the things we take for granted in the name of accounting and economic orthodoxy.
6. Recall that 'normative' refers to 'should' statements — how things ought to be (e.g. accounting policy is normative as it states what accounting should do about an issue). 'Positive' statements purport to be descriptive statements about the world as it is (note that Tinker *et al.* (1982) demonstrate successfully that all positive descriptions have a normative basis so the distinction should be treated with care). 'Inductive' refers to the intellectual process of reasoning from specific instances to the general situation — for example, from specific instances of accounting practice to a general rule about accounting practice in general (e.g. all debits are on the left, all balance sheets balance). 'Deductive' reasoning goes in the other direction and links the general statement to the specific instance — for example, the Companies Acts require a profit and loss account, therefore company X will have a profit and loss account, or financial statements are intended to be useful to investors therefore investor Y will find financial statements useful.
7. These were the characteristics of: *accounting entity, economic events, financial description*

and *assumptions of usefulness*, which we introduced in Chapter 1.

8. Although there must be doubts as to (a) the consistency with which these characteristics are applied in conventional accounting and therefore the extent to which they can really be deemed to be essential characteristics of the practice of accounting; and (b) whether 'representational accuracy' is any kind of possibility (see, for example, Laughlin and Puxty, 1981).

9. There is an implicit justification in this literature based on the 'it exists therefore it must be right' sort of reasoning. This is seriously fallacious. War exists, disease exists, fascism exists, abuse and rape exist, etc. These are not 'good things'. Existence is therefore not a sufficient condition for the value of something.

10. It is quite striking how very few accounting theorisations even mention the Companies Acts when, in most countries, this is the foundation for the acts of accounting and one of its primary justifications. Any such starting point would need to consider such matters as 'stewardship' (a close relation of accountability) and to examine the extent to which a profession might like to see company law as the sole expression of what is in the public interest. None of the theories we (and others) have reviewed in conventional accounting give more than the briefest lip-service to these essential and elementary questions. No wonder that accounting is a bit odd.

11. An argument also voiced, surprisingly, by some arch right wing scholars. See, for example, Tinker and Puxty (1995), Watts and Zimmerman (1979).

12. Notably, many experimental companies producing environmental reports managed to overcome these problems. See, for further detail, Gray *et al.* (1993), Gray *et al.* (1995d), Owen (1992), Owen and Gray (1994).

chapter 4

The development of social and environmental accounting and reporting

4.1 Introduction

Social and environmental accounting and reporting are not simply recent phenomena which have sprung up as a result of increased concern over environmental issues in the late 1980s. 'Modern' CSR can be thought of as one manifestation of the concerns over corporate social responsibility and the organisation–society interactions that have grown during the decades since World War II. While both corporate social responsibility and CSR have histories stretching back well before WWII[1] it is convenient for our purposes to concentrate upon developments in the second half of the 20th century.

In this chapter we shall be attempting to provide a brief history and overview of the developments in CSR in recent years. However, if we are looking for a neat and tidy history which systematically chronicles the developments of the organisation–society relationship, the emergence and development of CSR and the accounting profession's response, we will be disappointed. Corporate social responsibility has rather advanced in fits and starts, ebbing and flowing through the decades, and CSR has the look of an *ad hoc* spasmodic response to it. CSR is *not* a precisely definable or systematic activity — nor is it likely to become so in the absence of detailed regulation. The attempts to derive theoretical explanations for CSR which we have examined in Chapters 2 and 3 illustrate that the ways in which social and environmental accounting have advanced are, at least, complex matters driven by a changing array of influences and motivations.

Therefore, in this chapter we will try to provide as coherent as possible an overview of what we understand to be some of the important milestones in (i) the modern development of the organisation–society relationship (as they relate to CSR), (ii) the accounting profession's response to this and (iii) the development of CSR practice during the last few decades. In the interests of clarity what follows may seem more simple than, in fact, was the case. Further, as a result of our own experience and other experience published (typically) in the English language what follows will, probably, also provide a more British, Anglo-American and, latterly, European emphasis than would justify a truly worldwide perspective on CSR. Such biases are probably inevitable but should be borne in mind nevertheless (but see Chapters 5 and 6 for a more international emphasis).

Before attempting this sort of 'psuedo-history' of CSR it is necessary to explain in rather more detail what might be meant by the concept of social and environmental accounting and reporting. This we do in the next section.

4.2 Characteristics of social and environmental accounting

Chapter 1, section 1.2 provided an initial definition of, and introduction to, social and environmental accounting and reporting. We now need to flesh that out somewhat. You will recall that CSR was, in essence, defined as all possible forms of accounting — or what 'accounting' would look like if it were not necessarily limited to a very particular set of four characteristics.[2] Furthermore, CSR is only partially regulated and such regulations as exist vary considerably from country to country (see, for example, Guthrie and Parker, 1990). As a result, CSR is a virtually limitless area of potential activity.[3] Some idea of the potential range is given in Figure 4.1. A few words about Figure 4.1 are appropriate:

Subject As we mentioned in Chapter 1, CSR tends to focus on the areas of employees, 'ethical issues' (emphasising community and consumers) and the natural environment. However, as Figure 4.1 illustrates it need not do so and we can find examples of accounting and reporting on other matters such as ethics, standards and characteristics of organisational investment.

Audience While some examples of CSR are closely defined for a specific target audience (for example employee reports, information for collective bargaining, local environmental information, information for use in schools or internal documents for management use), it may often be difficult to establish for whom a report is intended. Certainly, as much of the regulated disclosure appears in Annual Reports it must, therefore, be assumed to be intended primarily for shareholders. This suggests that, although the *general* or social accountability of companies may still be relatively under-developed, social disclosure to shareholders *has* shown a steady increase over time. This has, however, tended to emphasise non-financial, or at least non-traditional, areas of disclosure (see, for example, Gray *et al.*, 1995a).

Content When one speaks of conventional accounting and reporting one can typically expect to find, at a minimum, some sort of income statement and balance sheet: not so with social and environmental accounting. Examples of what passes for CSR might vary from brief assertive statements from the Chairperson or Directors through to the far rarer attempts at full social or environmental accounts. We will meet examples from the full spectrum throughout the book and a number of illustrations are provided later in this chapter. For reference and illustration at this stage, Figure 4.2 is another set of examples of CSR (see also Figure 1.1 in Chapter 1).

Motivation As we saw in Chapter 3, it would be both interesting and useful to know why an organisation chooses to produce a social and environmental account and report. Motives are notoriously tricky to infer with any fairness or accuracy and to simply assume 'self-interest' is both trite and, potentially, deeply offensive to the individuals in the reporting organisation (see also Chapter 2). Figure 4.1 therefore lists many of the motives that have been stated or suggested in the literature as potentially leading to CSR. Some may dominate, but experience suggests that any individual example of CSR will

Figure 4.1 *Some aspects of corporate social reporting*

Subject	Audience	Content	Motivation	Reliability
• Shareholders	• Shareholders	• Narrative	• Ethics	• Estimated and
• Investments	• Financial	assertion	• Individual	partial data
• Employees	markets and	factual	commitment	• Internal audit
• Consumers	intermediaries	intentions	• Accountability	and information
• Community	• Employees	• Quantitative	• Legal	systems
• Environment	• Management	actual	• Code of	• Externally
• Total impact	• Trade unions	targets	practice	prepared
• General	• Potential	comparative	• Anticipate	• Externally
policy	employees	• Financial	regulation	commented
• Ethics and	• Communities	expenditure	• Forestall	upon
standards	• Pressure	commitment	regulation	• External audit
• National and	groups	requirement	• Marketing	
local	• Media	valuation	• Public image	
governments	• National	impact	• Defence	
• Dealings	governments	liability	• Distract	
with other	• Local		attention	
countries	governments		• Influence	
	• Regulatory		perceptions	
	bodies		• Response to	
	• Competitors		pressure	
	• Peers		• Get ahead	
	• Industry		of/stay with	
	groups		competitors	
	• Consumers		• Experimentation	
	• Suppliers		• Previously	
	• Society in		given	
	general		commitment	
			• Ethical	
			investors	
			• To overcome	
			fears of	
			secrecy	
			• To maintain	
			position of	
			power	
			• Legitimation	

Figure 4.2a Extract from Noranda Minerals Inc. 1993 Environmental Report

Water

THE MINING INDUSTRY USES LARGE AMOUNTS OF WATER IN MINING
AND MILLING PROCESSES, WHICH MUST BE TREATED BEFORE BEING
RELEASED BACK INTO THE ENVIRONMENT. THIS TREATED WATER,
PARTICULARLY FROM OLDER OPERATIONS, MAY CONTAIN SOME
CONCENTRATIONS OF METALS. OVER TIME, THESE METALS CAN BUILD
UP IN SEDIMENTS OF LAKES, RIVERS, AND OCEANS DOWNSTREAM FROM
A MINING FACILITY. AT CERTAIN CONCENTRATIONS, AQUATIC LIFE
MAY BE AFFECTED.

❖ One operation had a compliance level ranging between 90% and 94% also an improvement from 1992, when five operations had compliance levels between 87% and 94%. This operation, Brunswick's zinc mine near Bathurst, New Brunswick, started up its new $22 million water treatment system in October 1993. It has since achieved full compliance with the water discharge requirements.

WATER DISCHARGES

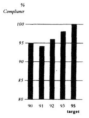

A new water treatment plant at Brunswick's zinc mine and improvements at the lead smelter in New Brunswick contributed dramatically to our improved compliance level of 98%

COMPLIANCE

Water discharges are regulated by federal, provincial and municipal governments in Canada and by federal and state agencies in the U.S. Water discharge permits may require measurements for lead, copper, zinc, arsenic, nickel, pH (an indicator of water acidity) and total suspended solids (particles of fine-grained materials that remain suspended in flowing water). In 1993, samples of our water discharges were also collected and analyzed by government officials on 34 occasions as a check on our own results. No significant differences between government measurements and our own have been found.

NORANDA ACTION

At our facilities, 29 water discharge locations operate under 33 separate permits. Several of our sites have more than one permitted discharge location.
❖ Twenty-five water discharge locations were at 100% compliance in 1993 compared to 10 in 1992.

❖ Seven others had compliance levels averaging between 95% and 100%, an improvement from 14 last year. All of these operations have corrective action plans in place.

METALS DISCHARGED IN WATER

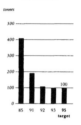

Metal discharges have decreased by 74% since 1985. In 1993, 105 tonnes of metals were discharged from Noranda Minerals' operations, five tonnes fewer than in 1992. Operating plants which were shut down due to weak market conditions and scheduled maintenance decreased the total metal discharged by less than one percent

SPILLS

Although the mining industry has measures in place to prevent spills, incidents do occur. Spills can result from transportation accidents, flooding conditions, operating errors, equipment malfunctions, and failures in pipelines that transport tailings and water to holding ponds. Metals discharged as a result of spills accounted for approximately 3% of the 105 tonnes.

Figure 4.2a *continued*

COMPLIANCE

Noranda Minerals' operations are subject to federal, provincial and municipal regulations in Canada and state agencies in the U.S. All spills have been reported in compliance with applicable laws and regulations. Sixteen spills resulting in discharges leaving our property occurred at Noranda Minerals' operations in 1993.

NORANDA ACTION

❖ Six spills occurred at CEZinc in Valleyfield, Quebec.

Three spills contained untreated run-off water after an unusually heavy snowfall and a rapid spring thaw exceeded the plant's ability to store and treat water. A pipeline has been cleaned to increase flow capacity into the water treatment system. As well, clean cooling water from the steam-generating plant will be removed from water requiring treatment. These steps will increase the ability to handle large flows.

Approximately 200 kilograms of dissolved zinc leaked from a broken pipeline. It was repaired and a drainage channel was blocked to divert future leaks into the water treatment system.

A solution used to clean a waste-heat boiler was discharged into the environment. A procedure for directing the cleaning solution into the water treatment plant has been developed.

An estimated 1.7 cubic meters of jarosite residue containing iron, zinc and copper were discharged from a broken pipeline. All material was reclaimed. After a similar event in 1991 when 600 cubic meters were released, the pipeline was equipped with flow monitoring equipment. This system allowed the pipeline to be shut down very quickly when the 1993 event occurred.

❖ Heavy rainfall, extremely cold weather, and leakage through a discharge structure resulted in five spills at our Heath Steele mine in New Brunswick.

High water flows from melting snow and heavy rainfall caused an overflow of three collection structures at the same time. A blocked culvert and a pump failure contributed to this event. The culvert has been removed and the pump replaced.

In the fourth spill, ice build-up in a creek diverted water into an adjacent collection pond during very cold weather. The overflow containing some untreated water re-entered the creek.

In the last case, tailings flowed across ice and a small amount of solids leaked through an inactive discharge structure in the tailings pond. An internal dam is being constructed within the tailings area to improve solids retention.

❖ Three releases occurred at our Geco zinc-copper mine at Manitouwadge, Ontario.

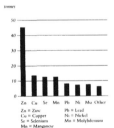

METALS DISCHARGED IN
WATER BY METAL TYPES

tonnes

| Zn | Cu | Se | Mn | Pb | Ni | Mo | Other |

Zn = Zinc   Pb = Lead
Cu = Copper   Ni = Nickel
Se = Selenium   Mo = Molybdenum
Mn = Manganese

One hundred and five tonnes of metals were discharged at 29 locations. The "Other" category includes six tonnes of aluminum, arsenic, antimony, cobalt, chromium, mercury and silver. The total amount of mercury was 0.07 tonnes.

A large quantity of water is used in mining, milling, smelting and refining processes. Our environmental efforts in this regard are two-fold: first, to reduce consumption of fresh water; second, to effectively treat water used in various processes. These efforts may serve to reduce the quantity of metals discharged into the environment and the effect on aquatic systems. For example, in 1993 Hemlo Gold's Golden Giant Mine near Marathon Ontario, conducted a review of its fresh water use. The review identified where fresh water was being used and how much was actually required. The follow-up action plan has resulted in a 40% decrease in the amount of fresh water required from a nearby creek. Recycled water has increased to 87% of total consumption, up from 72% in 1992. The operation's goal is to further reduce fresh water use by an additional 20% in 1994.

Approximately 3,000 cubic metres of fresh water and untreated water were discharged into Fox Creek when a check valve failed. The valve has been replaced with a more reliable manual unit.

Failure of a plastic pipeline and a pump in the mill caused two small spills into Fox Creek totalling less than one cubic metre. Replacement units have been installed and a concrete curb has also been constructed to provide a second level of containment in this part of the mill.

❖ Two additional spills involved less than one cubic metre of material. One involved a product shipped from our CCR copper refinery in Montreal-East and the second was a discharge from a tank at our closed Brenda mine in British Columbia. Action plans were implemented in both cases.

Figure 4.2b *Extract from 3M (UK) Group 1989 Annual Report*

COMPANY INFORMATION

COMMUNITY RELATIONS ~ 3M believes that community support in the areas where we are located is an essential and important corporate responsibility. In the United Kingdom, 3M is a member of the "Per Cent Club", whose members commit to contribute a certain percentage of profit to good works in the community. Under this banner, we donate to a large variety of organisations committed to relieve, reduce or eliminate suffering. In particular, in common with our associates throughout Europe, we have given substantial support to "Europe against Cancer", an initiative designed to increase awareness of the causes of cancer. We also support educational causes in and around our seventeen U.K. sites. Our work to improve links between education and industry is extensive, including sponsorship of "Young Engineers" regional events, and "Young Investigators", a nationwide programme designed to interest young people in the world of science. During 1988, 3M played a significant part in persuading British industry to raise funds to contribute towards the cost of sending British athletes to compete in the 1988 Winter and Summer Olympic Games, as well as donating to the fund in its own name. In 1989, 3M's worldwide chairman and chief executive officer, Allen Jacobson, announced our sponsorship of the 1992 Olympic Games, adding that "3M is sponsoring the Olympic Games because they represent in athletics what the company strives for in business - competitive excellence".

EMPLOYEES ~ Without a dedicated and talented work force, 3M could never have enjoyed sixty years of growth and success in the United Kingdom. We believe that our ability to respect the dignity and worth of individuals, to provide equal opportunity for all, our promotion of entrepreneurship and insistence upon freedom in the work place to pursue innovative ideas have contributed in no small way to our success as employers. 3M people who perform exceptionally well enter our "Bond of Excellence" programme, as a recognition of their contribution. 3M's company goals link employees and shareholders in a mutually beneficial common enterprise - and we are confident that our ability to recruit and retain the best people will continue during the coming decade.

British Sports Association for the Disabled southern region final sponsored by 3M

Micropore" surgical tape launched

63

Reflective products group formed

58

Adhesive tapes first manufactured at Gorseinon

57

Figure 4.2b *continued*

ENVIRONMENT ~ Preventing or reducing environmental pollution has been called "the greatest imperative facing industry today", and in this, as in many areas, 3M has been a pioneer with its "pollution prevention pays" (3P) programme. Long convinced that a sound waste reduction programme makes economic sense, we

adopted the "3P" programme in 1975. Four different "3P" concepts encourage technical innovation to prevent pollution at source.

1. *Reformulation of products or processes so that they pollute the environment less, or not at all. For example, our manufacturing facilities use solvent-less coating solutions where possible.*

2. *Manufacturing processes are adapted to reduce or control by-product formation.*

3. *Equipment may be modified to perform more efficiently, or to make better use of available resources, such as steam from another process.*

4. *By-products are recycled and then either sold, or used in other 3M products or processes.*

Since its introduction in 1975, "3P" has become a way of life for our employees in the United Kingdom, and they are constantly encouraged to look for pollution prevention solutions.

COMMITMENT TO CUSTOMER SERVICE ~ 1989 has been a year characterised by great achievements in quality. At the same time, there have been cost reductions for our distribution, engineering and manufacturing groups and we have seen considerable service enhancements at all of our major plants throughout the United Kingdom. Changes in the way that we manufacture and distribute products from our plants and distribution centre have allowed us to offer customers a faster, more efficient and reliable service. In addition, reorganisation of our manufacturing operations into business-focussed units should ensure greater responsiveness to customer needs. This commitment to excellence is not simply a group mission, but a personal objective for distribution, engineering and manufacturing employees, who have been awarded with over 300 Bonds of Excellence for their contribution over the past three years.

QUALITY ~ 3M's achievement in winning a British Quality Award is a great source of pride for all our employees, who have successfully integrated "total quality management" practices into every area of their everyday work since the process was introduced formally to the U.K. in 1984. Some typical results of this quality emphasis within 3M in the United Kingdom have been a 3M global process engineering award, and a 3M quality award for personal achievement made to our distribution, engineering and manufacturing groups during 1989. Within 3M in the United Kingdom, over 600 teams are currently working on projects that aim not only to prevent defects in the company's products, but also to meet customer expectations through improvements in all areas of operation. During the past two years, 3M in the United

Kingdom has won more awards than any other operating unit in the worldwide 3M quality programme. In the U.K. we are at the forefront of total quality management implementation in achieving BS5750/ISO9002 accreditation for all of our major manufacturing sites.

Minnesota Mining and Manufacturing Ltd formed

51

New factory opened at Tredegar

50

"Scotch" magnetic tape is launched in the UK

45

Figure 4.2c *Extract from Ben & Jerry's 1993 Annual Report (pp. 14, 15)*

The 1993 SOCIAL ASSESSMENT

Employees

☑ As a socially progressive employer, Ben&Jerry's has worked hard at creating an outstanding work environment and a generous compensation package. In most of the areas where its plants are situated, it is the preferred and most sought after employer by residents seeking work. People who work at Ben&Jerry's are loathe to leave, and turnover is quite low.

☑ During the past year, there were no significant changes in the compensation arrangements at Ben&Jerry's. As befitting a low inflation and low growth year, starting wages remained at $8/hour, high by Vermont standards. Employment remained nearly constant during the year, increasing from 476 in 1992 to 500 at the end of the year in 1993. All full-time and regular part-time employees receive health and dental coverage on the 1st of the month following their initial date of employment. Dependent coverage for children, spouses, or gay or lesbian partners, is available for $2.10 per week, or $4.93 for a family. Coverage includes life insurance up to twice the employee's annual salary, and additional coverage up to five times annual wages can be obtained at low rates. Ben&Jerry's instituted paid family leave in 1992 and actively lobbied for state and federal legislation supporting leave. Mothers receive short-term disability insurance granting them full pay for six weeks, and 60% pay for up to six months. Fathers can also obtain two weeks of paternity leave at full pay, and the primary caregiver in the case of an adoption receives 4 weeks leave at full pay. Employees also have the option of contributing up to $5000 per year pretax to a Flexible Spending Account which will pay for non-covered medical expenses such as eye, orthodontic or dependent care. The Company continues to provide its Employee Assistance Plan (EAP) which provides free and confidential counseling to employees needing help with substance abuse, marital or family problems, or other personal issues.

☑ Compensation at Ben&Jerry's is remarkably balanced between top and bottom. Although the company had to expand its top ratio from five to seven-to-one in 1990 in order to attract and retain skilled and trained management, the overall ratio from top to bottom is still very equitable when compared with any other company in America of comparable size. For example, the average pay per worker including benefits for the top decile in the company is $79,734 whereas the lowest decile receives an average compensation of $20,372, a ratio of only four-to-one. Monies paid to employees from the profit sharing program totaled $671,675 in 1993, as compared to $636,447 in 1992.

☑ Last year's social assessment recommended that the Company extend its concept of linked prosperity by creating some form of an employee stock ownership program. At that time, employees, excluding founders and top management, owned only .04% of the company's stock. Plans are underway to grant stock options to employees at all levels of the Company in 1994.

☑ Employee life at Ben&Jerry's is as varied as the flavors. Befitting a company of 500 employees, there is a wide variety of tasks and jobs, ranging from the sedentary and

14

probably have been the result of more than one motivation and usually the motivation of more than one individual.

Reliability As with any information, it is necessary to know to what extent one may trust it to (for instance) present a complete, fair, balanced or reliable picture of the issues and/or organisation in question — in so far as this is possible at all (see, for example, Hines, 1988; Morgan, 1988). Of course, a report prepared by an organisation and un-audited does not mean it is a pack of lies, any more that a report prepared by an external party can be assumed to be a full and balanced picture. However, the source and reliability of the preparer of the information should be taken into account when reading the social and environmental reports — especially by accountants who place such an importance on the statutory audit of companies' financial statements!

We mentioned earlier the question of the motivation of a reporting company. This is important because much, if not most, social and environmental accounting is voluntarily produced (for more detail see Chapters 5 and 6). Figure 4.3 gives some indication of what

Figure 4.2c *continued*

cerebral to jobs of considerable physical strain and exertion. Furthermore, the company has several sites, from the central administrative core to three manufacturing plants and a distribution center. It is fair to say that each plant or building has created a different Ben& Jerry's culture, and that as time goes on, they are becoming more distinct as opposed to being more amalgamated. If you inquire about the quality of work life at the Company, most people will reply by asking "Where?" In keeping with this, the report will try to reflect the conditions for employees at each facility.

The Waterbury Plant
◾ The Waterbury plant was opened in June 1985, built during a period of rapid company growth. Its capacity had been planned to serve the company for years ahead; although it was the biggest plant the Company could afford to build, by the time it opened it was too small. Like many first plants, once it was built, some planning and engineering flaws were readily apparent. From the outset, employees had to work hard and adaptively because no one had foreseen how successful Ben&Jerry's was going to be in the marketplace. Production facilities were somewhat cramped, six-day shifts were often required, and workplace injuries were a constant concern. The demands on employees were ameliorated by the fact that the plant was the center of attention because it contained the administrative offices. Company meetings were truly the whole Company. Ben and Jerry worked there. Reporters, TV cameras, tourists, and admirers also showed up there. Although the stress and strains of being a rapidly growing company affected everyone, there was in those first years the compensation of working together as one community. When the Company moved the administrative headquarters down the road in 1991, the loss of togetherness allowed some resentments to surface or grow. Today, many problems that go back a number of years still appear to be festering at Waterbury and are affecting morale. Compounding the problems of the plant has been a series of plant managers who may have been less than exemplary in their leadership and delegation skills.

◾ The morale has been partially improved by some recent personnel changes. Yet, it is clear that some people at Waterbury do not feel a "part" of the Company. Others feel that they have not been getting as good treatment as people at newer plants. It was difficult for me to accurately measure the nature of the concerns or how widespread they were because there was no climate survey undertaken in 1993 (the next will be Fall 1994). In many cases, employees at Waterbury are reticent to talk about their problems because they feel people don't want to hear it. In other instances, they no longer want to talk because they feel that is all there has been - talk - and they want to see action. Nonetheless, it is clear that people at Waterbury, including production workers with considerable seniority, care deeply about the Company. Waterbury continues to be the breeding ground of some of the Company's top managers who are running other plants and programs in the Company. And despite some morale problems, there is an elan or culture that is both proud and highly content.

15

this means in a United Kingdom context. Figure 4.3 identifies those areas governed by a statutory — or other form of — authority to disclose social and environmental information. With the exception of some of the employee and pension data, the disclosure which results from these regulations is relatively trivial — but at least it is regular and systematic. By contrast, the voluntary areas of disclosure (and the list in Figure 4.3 could be a great deal longer) vary from organisation to organisation, from year to year, from country to country, from the utterly trivial to the path-breaking and informative.[4]

Finally, in this section, it is necessary to dwell briefly on the distinction between 'internal' and 'external' accounting and reporting. Indeed, we should note distinctions between internal and external *preparation* and internal and external *consumption* of the accounts and the reports. These sources and destinations tend to result in different forms of CSR. Figure 4.4 seeks to illustrate this.

Organisations will frequently prepare information for their own internal use, provide

Figure 4.3 *Typical areas covered by CSR in UK company Annual Reports (adapted from Gray (1991b, p. 3)*

Voluntary	Required/mandatory
• Environmental protection	• Charitable donations
• Energy saving	• Employment data
• Consumer protection	• Pension fund adequacy
• Product safety	• Consultation with employees
• Community involvement	• Employee share ownership schemes
• Value-added statement	• Employment in South Africa
• Health and safety	• Employment of the disabled
• Racial and sexual equality	• Contingent liabilities and provisions for
• Redundancies	health and safety or environmental
• Employee training	remediation
• Mission statement/statement of social responsibility	

information for use by regulatory authorities[5] or contract with external consultants to provide information for them.[6] Only rarely does such information reach the public domain and so little is known about it outside the organisation, but its principal purpose will be to help guide management decisions within the organisation (for more detail see Chapter 7). As a result, the emphasis in CSR tends to be on published material for external consumption — although this may be only the tip of a social and environmental accounting iceberg. Organisations have the full range of possible approaches to CSR from which to choose if they decide to proceed with a published social and environmental account (Figure 4.4 illustrates some of these possibilities). Increasingly, various independent bodies have developed the ability to produce and publish information about other organisations. So a multinational company, for example, which is reluctant to produce data on, for example, its environmental performance may find that the public, its employees, shareholders and others are increasingly well informed about that company's performance as a result of the ferreting activities of bodies such as the CEP (Council on Economic Priorities) in the United States, New Consumer in the United Kingdom, Friends of the Earth and Greenpeace (for more detail see Chapter 9). This provides yet another pressure upon organisations to undertake the disclosure of their social and environmental performance themselves before 'less sympathetic' organisations do it for them![7]

The foregoing, then, provides some idea of the range of possibilities that can fall within the ambit of CSR. We could perhaps now turn to look at how it appears to have developed in recent years. However, particularly given the orientation we adopted in Chapters 2 and 3, it is inappropriate — and less illuminating — to consider CSR as

Figure 4.4 *Different approaches to social accounting (adapted from Gray (1991b, p. 3)*

| Report for the consumption of ... | Report compiled by ... | |
	Internal participants	External participants

Internal participants	• Social accounts
	• Programme evaluation
	• Attitudes audit
	• Indicator
	• Compliance audit
	• Environmental audit and
	  accounting
		• Quango Reports, e.g.
		  Health and Safety
		  HMIP
		  EPA
		  Water pollution
		  regulators
		• Environmental consultants
		• Waste and energy audits

External participants	• Social accounts
	• Social reports
	  narrative
	  quantitative
	  qualitative
	  financial
	• Compliance audit
	• Mission statements
	• Environmental performance
	  report
		• Social Audit Ltd
		• Counter Information
		  Services
		• New Consumer
		• Consumers Association
		• Friends of the Earth
		• Greenpeace
		• Journalists
		• Ethical investment/EIRIS
		• Social audits

occurring in a social, political and economic vacuum. Therefore, in the next section we attempt to provide a brief introduction to some of the social, political and economic context within which modern CSR has occurred.

4.3 The changing context of CSR

The recent history of CSR is usually assumed to have started in the early 1970s. As far as we can tell, the origins of this CSR lie in the 'social responsibility of business' debates of the preceding decade or so (see Chapter 3 for more detail).

It is, however, useful to point out that there are, in effect, two strands to any debates about issues as complex as social responsibility. The first strand comprises the debates held by what are normally considered the 'extremists' — the reformers, radical theorists and environmentalists, for example, whether coming from 'extreme' socialist, right wing or deep green points of view (see Chapter 3). The second strand comprises the debates held in the powerful, apparently orthodox, 'middle-ground' of a society — businesses, government, business schools and the large sweep of public concern. The former strand of debate will usually pre-date the latter by many years — even by decades and centuries. So, for example, 'popular' concern over the social responsibility of business arose nearly a century after the seminal work of Marx and Engels, and the popular awareness of environmental issues post-dates initial awareness and concern by nearly 30 years (see, for example, Gray, 1990a; Owen, 1992). That business, governments, business schools and the popular consciousness (for example) are resistant to new areas of concern and enter the debates belatedly and reluctantly should not be forgotten in what follows. This is because we will be largely emphasising the 'conventional' (e.g. business and governments) progress of social and environmental debates in the following chapters.[8]

Modern thinking about business and its (actual or potential) social responsibility is normally dated from Bowen (1953), who was one of the first 'non-radical' commentators on business[9] to identify a separate — and largely new and unrecognised — potential for responsibility in business and its managers. By the 1960s such concerns were very much live issues — especially in the United States — and were widely debated in business, government and business school circles. By the mid-1960s Peter Drucker, a well-respected establishment figure in the field of management, was able to report that young, white, middle-America was increasingly disappointed with the level of social responsibility exercised by American corporations (Drucker, 1965). Although these concerns were far from radical (it was some years before the middle classes of the 'developed' nations began to wake up to the structural inequities, environmental degradation, exploitation of labour and irresponsibility of dealings with 'developing nations' and repressive regimes arising from 'normal' business practice) it represented a major shift in thinking where it mattered — in the business and government. No longer could middle-class society and business assume that the corporations of market capitalism were unequivocally benign institutions. By the late 1960s the social responsibility of business debate was in full swing in North America and similar debates were an increasing feature of continental Europe[10] — although it took some years to really reach the United Kingdom and Australasia.[11]

Meanwhile, other developments were afoot. Probably the most important (for the planet and society if not for business and accounting) was the emerging environmental movement which laid the groundwork for the environmental revival in the late 1980s. At the same time, and of more political importance, the power of labour was rising and rights for labour and labour unions were of increasing concern. At this time we see the first discussions of whether employees might be considered to have rights similar to those of shareholders. More prosaically, accounting itself was coming out of the shadows and was increasingly recognised as not only an economically important activity but one of great political significance. It was in the late 1960s that the whole area of accounting standards and regulation became a matter of debate. As a result, by the 1960s the identification of political problems in the regulation of business was, for the first time, likely to see accounting as both part of the problem and a potential source for solving the problem. One manifestation of this was the increase in disclosure required in the United Kingdom's 1967 Companies Act which, for example, introduced the requirement that companies disclose their charitable and political donations.

It was against this backdrop that the emergence of CSR in the early 1970s should be set. Some of these issues, and their development, are shown in Figure 4.5. From Figure 4.5 we can identify a number of major trends relevant to CSR in the last two decades or so.

Social responsibility

General social responsibility was a major theme throughout the early 1970s. The debate was significantly enlivened by Milton Friedman's stating of the pristine liberal economic democracy argument (see Chapters 1 and 3 where the pristine capitalists' point of view is stated). (We should emphasise that Friedman's view was considered an 'extreme' view in the 1970s and not the apparently 'reasonable' view that was so widely held in the 1980s. For counter views see, for example, Dahl, 1972; Dickson, 1974; Goldsmith *et al.*, 1972; Mulligan, 1986; Robertson, 1978b; Schumacher, 1973; Shocker and Sethi, 1973). In the United Kingdom the social responsibility debate arrived rather later than in the United States, but was apparently accepted across a broad front (CBI, 1973) and even came close to entering UK company law (Cmnd 5391, 1973; Cmnd 6888, 1977). However, with the onset of the purported worldwide recession of the late 1970s (Gambling, 1984), the broad notion of social responsibility quietly slipped off the political and business agenda — and only really showed any signs of returning by the mid-1990s by way of the Trojan Horse of 'environmental' issues which brought social responsibility debate back within the citadel walls of corporations. As a general rule, in so far as 'social responsibility' is discussed at all in the United Kingdom, the United States and Australasia, it is generally discussed either in the context of specific constituencies (see below) or in the much narrower concerns of 'business ethics' and issues such as insider trading. The atmosphere in continental Europe, however, has been notably different. For many of the, particularly northern European and Scandinavian countries, social responsibility never left the agenda. A striking feature of EU and Scandinavian discussion of social responsibility is its much greater acceptance of social issues that countries which have fallen under North American dominance find hard to accept within their ideology (for more detail see Chapters 5 and 6). We must, once again, emphasise the difficulties of making general statements about worldwide social responsibility issues.[12]

Community and customer

In the United States, 'social responsibility' translated most directly to a responsibility for the community in which the organisation operated. This reflected the North American culture and, as we shall see below (see also Chapter 5) much early American CSR had a strong 'community' emphasis. However, this broad concern with community did not bed very deeply into other cultures until the 1980s when, with the massive lurch to the political right that occurred (with the Thatcher and Reagan eras, for example, in the United Kingdom and United States — somewhat later in New Zealand and Australia and continental Europe) the more aware — and perhaps socially concerned — members of corporate management realised that the community support which was no longer to

Figure 4.5 Background to CSR

	SOCIAL RESPONSIBILITY ETHICS AND MORAL VALUES	COMMUNITY (LDCs) AND CONSUMERS	EMPLOYEES AND TRADE UNIONS	NATURAL ENVIRONMENT	RESPONSE OF ACCOUNTING PROFESSION AND PRACTICE
1950s	H.R. Bowen (1953: USA)		Treaty of Rome (1957: EC)		
1960s	P. Drucker (1965: USA)	Charity Donations (1967: UK)		Silent Spring (1962: USA)	Concern with financial reporting
1970s	Milton Friedman (1970: USA) CBI Report (1973: UK) White Paper (1973: UK) Green Paper (1977: UK)		Emp. Protect. Act (1974: UK) Sudreau Report (1977: France)	Stockholm Conf. (1972: UN) E.F. Schumacher (1973: UK) Energy Crisis (1976: The West)	Linowes (1972: USA) AAA Reports c. 1973: USA) ASSC Report (1975: UK) Empl. Reports (1970s: EEC/USA) AICPA Report (1977: USA) Study Gp Report (1977: Germany) Ernst & Ernst (1978: USA) Value Added St. (1979: UK)

Figure 4.5 continued

1980s

Insider Dealing (1985: USA/UK)	TNCs (1982: UN)	Employment Act (1982: UK)	CERCLA (1980: USA)	Energy, CIMA (1982: UK)
Business Ethics (c. 1988: USA)	Bus-in-Comm (1980s: UK)	Vredeling (1983: EEC)	Bhopal Disaster (1984: India)	UEC Report (1983: Europe)
		Employee consultation and Disabled employment (1985: UK)	Brundtland Report (1987: UN)	Accounting for wastes and liabilities (1980s: USA)
			M. Thatcher (1988: UK)	
			Exxon Valdez (1989: USA)	

1990s

	Treaty on the European Union (1992: EU)	Treaty on the European Union (1992: EU)	Res. Man. Act (1991: NZ)	CICA Handbook (1990: Canada)
		European Works Council Directive (1995: EU)	UNCTC (UN: 1992)	ACCA Report (1990: UK)
			Earth Summit (1992: UNCED)	ICAEW Report (1992: UK)
			5th Action Plan (1993: EC)	CMA Report (1992: Canada)
				FEE Report (1993: EU)

be provided by the State institutions should be provided by a paternalistic corporation culture concerned to maintain its legitimacy.[13] 'Community' thus became very much the apparent theme of social responsibility in the 1980s.[14] On the other hand, concern for customers has remained a steady subtext since the 1960s — at least in so far as it relates to the campaigning consumer organisations which have remained lively throughout the period. However, the concern for the well-being of the consumer — as distinct from protection and maintenance of a walking, consuming purse — has never been an especially strong element of social responsibility practice, particularly outside the United States.[15]

Employees and trade unions

Probably *the* major area of 'social responsibility' debate and action has been in the area of employees and trade unions. Indeed, the 1970s saw significant changes in labour law, in the empowerment of employees and trade unions, in the rights of employees to information and so on. (This was especially true in the United Kingdom, but see Chapter 5 and 6 for developments elsewhere.) Or, rather, it looked as though these things happened. Certainly, for much of the 1970s there appeared to be the real possibility of a major shift in employer–employee relations — a real development of one sort of socialism. However, the 1980s showed just how insignificant the changes had been. The 1980s saw massive unemployment, the repealing of much labour law and pulling of the teeth of much of the rest. The power of the unions was broken and the major manufacturing industries — traditionally the locus of union and employee power — were broken up and moved to developing countries where labour legislation was so much less 'constraining' on the business. The alacrity with which so much of corporate United Kingdom, United States, Australasia, etc., abandoned the higher-wage economies of the West for the low (exploitive) economies of the developing nations was proof enough of how seriously the social responsibility with respect to employees had been taken by business. There were, however, *some* potentially positive developments of note during the 1980s. The attempts to rewrite employer–employee relations as a partnership with employees becoming, increasingly, shareholders in the businesses in which they worked (employee share ownership schemes: ESOPs) and legislation requiring more employment of the disabled, the increasing emphasis on race and sex equality and the legislative requirement to inform and consult with employees, could all be taken as positive steps forward if one wished to do so. Again, one should note that major differences occurred between countries. While, for example, the United Kingdom, United States, New Zealand and Australia appeared to be working hard to remove employee rights from the political agenda, many of the countries of the European Union continued to develop more mature employee policies. The development of the *bilan social* in France and, in the early 1990s, the EU's Social Charter illustrate a very different approach to employees from that adopted in the Anglo-American countries (for more detail see Chapters 5, 6 and 7).

Natural environment

Concerns over the natural environment have been voiced for more than 30 years — it is not just a phenomenon of the late 1980s and 1990s. This concern did surface in the social responsibility debates of the early 1970s — albeit briefly — in North America and parts of continental Europe (most notably Germany, the Netherlands and Scandinavia). However, the concern appeared to be largely restricted to issues of pollution and not to the broader matters of the business–environment relationship (see also Chapter 3 and Gray *et al.*, 1993; Owen, 1992; for more detail). The mid-1970s saw the emergence of the 'energy crisis' which arose from a combination of the Middle Eastern conflicts and a recognition of the West's vunerable dependence upon essentially limited fossil fuels — oil and coal. This did generate concern about energy and energy-efficiency for a while but again, by the early 1980s the concern had passed back to a peripheral issue of concern only to 'extremists'. That failure to address what has proved to be a major, substantive concern for the human race once again illustrates the fickle nature of business 'social responsibility' and counsels great care in accepting 'business' as a responsible group capable of sensibly determining the agenda of society. In the United States and many parts of Northern Europe the environmental concern was never entirely removed from the political agenda. In 1980, the United States issued the Comprehensive Environmental Response Compensation and Liability Act (CERCLA) — also known as 'Superfund' — to deal with the devastating issue of contaminated land.[16] By the mid-1980s European countries — most notably Germany and the Netherlands — had major programmes in place to remediate and limit the effects of economic expansion on the fragile natural ecology upon which we all depend. However, it was not until the late 1980s, enhanced by a growing series of major environmental disasters, that worldwide concern among business, governments and the general public reached sufficient levels to place environmental issues at the core of political and business thinking.

Every country is very different in the way it perceives, discusses and responds to issues. While we can perhaps see some very broad worldwide cycles, the only major theme that holds for all countries throughout this period is the fragility of business responsibility over and above growth, profit and economic power. Unlegislated, 'social responsibility' is left in the hands of business who, voluntarily, will respond at the margins to probably only one issue at a time. This is starkly illustrated by the trends in the United Kingdom: the early 1970s focused on social responsibility; by the mid-late 1970s this had shifted to employees and unions; the 1980s saw explicit pursuit of economic goals with a thin veneer of community concern and a redefinition of employee rights as the major theme; while in the 1990s attention shifted to environmental concern. We can assert, from considerable personal experience, that if you wanted to talk about the environment in business circles in the 1970s and 1980s you would be considered a lunatic. In the 1990s everybody wants to talk about the environment but, in the United Kingdom notably, if you also would like to talk about employees and trade unions, you will again find yourself classed as a lunatic. Social responsibility, as defined by business, follows fashions. As far as business is generally concerned Friedman's views (quoted above) are about the only views upon which one can rely (see also Adams *et al.*, 1995a; Gray *et al.*, 1995a; Tinker *et al.*, 1991).

4.4 The response of the accounting profession

Fashion, it seems, not only dictates what areas of social responsibility a company will concern itself with, but is brutally apparent in the attitude of the accountancy professions. Figure 4.5 also illustrates some of the milestones of the accounting professions' responses to the developing social responsibility agenda. One will look without success for any consistency of purpose in this.

The accounting profession in the United States responded with alacrity to the social responsibility of the early 1970s. David Linowes, himself an influential practising accountant in the United States, was one of the first to see the potential link between social responsibility and accounting (Linowes, 1972). More particularly, Linowes argued that a 'good' company — a company which embraced the highest standards of social responsibility — should not be penalised in its financial statements. Linowes argued that social responsibility will, at least in the short term, cost a company money. This will in turn reduce profit and, as a result, the 'responsible' company will appear to be less successful. He went on to propose an additional accounting statement that could be published in the Annual Report which would show how well the organisation had performed in the social domain. His proposal is summarised in Figure 4.6.

Linowes' proposal was especially important for a number of reasons. First, this was a practising and respected accountant making the proposal — not an academic or 'other impractical extremist'. Secondly, it was the first concrete suggestion as to how a 'social account' might be prepared. Thirdly, it explicitly attempted to link the 'social' and the 'economic' in one statement. As we shall see, this last point remains one of the more difficult challenges for social accounting. However, the proposed statement was not without considerable problems — not least of which were that (a) it was highly subjective; (b) it used different valuation and cost bases in different parts of the statement and then added and subtracted the resultant oranges, apples and pears; and (c) Linowes was unclear as to whether he was taking the corporation's view looking out to society, or the society's view looking into the corporation.[17] Linowes' work was, and remains two decades later, seminal and an important starting point for any discussion about the practicalities of social accounting (for more detail see, for example, Burton, 1972; Estes, 1976; Jensen, 1976; and, especially, Gray *et al.*, 1987).

There was a considerable initial response from the accounting profession. Throughout the early 1970s the American Accounting Association issued a series of thoughtful reports on many aspects of the social responsibility debate (including environmental matters) as they applied to accounting. These reports remain as fresh and as illuminating today (see, for example, AAA, 1973; 1975b).[18] There were many discussions about — and commissioned reports on — the accounting issues surrounding reporting to (employee reporting) and about (employment reporting) employees as well as investigation into the issues concerning the reporting of accounting information to trade unions for the purposes of collective bargaining (see, for example, Foley and Maunders, 1977; Maunders, 1984; and Chapter 7). In the United Kingdom the (then) Accounting Standards Steering Committee published the widely quoted *Corporate Report* (ASSC, 1975) which attempted to establish a programme to develop accounting

Figure 4.6 *Socioeconomic operating statement. Source: Linowes (1972), reproduced with permission*

X Corporation
Socio-economic operating statement for the year ending December 31 19x1

I Relations with people
A. Improvements
    1. Training program for handicapped workers $10,000
    2. Contribution to educational institution   4,000
    3. Extra turnover costs because of minority hiring program   5,000
    4. Cost of nursery school for children of employees voluntarily set up   11,000

    Total improvements $30,000

B. *Less* Detriments
    1. Postponed installing new safety devices on cutting machines
    (cost of the devices) $14,000

C. Net improvements in people actions for the year $16,000

II Relations with environment
A. Improvements
    1. Cost of reclaiming and landscaping old dump on company property $70,000
    2. Cost of installing pollution control devices on Plant A smokestacks   4,000
    3. Cost of detoxifying waste from finishing process this year   9,000

A. Total improvements $83,000

B. *Less* Detriments
    1. Cost that would have been incurred to relandscape strip-mining
    site used this year $80,000
    2. Estimated costs to have installed purification process to
    neutralize poisonous liquid being dumped into stream   100,000

     $180,000

C. Net deficit in environment actions for the year $97,000

III Relations with product
A. Improvements
    1. Salary of vice-president while serving on government Product
    Safety Commission $25,000
    2. Cost of substituting leadfree paint for previously used poisonous
    lead paint   9,000

    Total improvements $34,000

B. *Less* Detriments
    1. Safety device recommended by Safety Council but not added to
    product $22,000

C. Net improvements in product actions for the year $12,000

Total socio-economic deficit for the year $69,000

Add Net cumulative socio-economic improvements as of January 1, 19x1 $249,000

Grand total net socio-economic actions to December 31, 19x1 $180,000

Figure 4.7 The Corporate Report (ASSC, 1975)

The Corporate Report was based upon the basic idea that all organisations owe a duty to 'public accountability'. External reporting should, it was argued, satisfy the information needs of those 'who have reasonable rights to information concerning the reporting entity'.

These were identified as:
● the equity-investor group;
● the loan creditor group;
● the employee group;
● the analyst-adviser group;
● the business contact group;
● local and national government;
● the public including consumers, community, environmental protection groups, etc.

In addition to developments in the financial statements, The Corporate Report recommended that entities publish additionally:
● a value-added statement;
● an employment report;
● a statement of money exchanges with government;
● a statement of transactions in foreign currency;
● a statement of future prospects;
● a statement of corporate objectives.

Further, the report emphasised the potential desirability of CSR and identified the need for further investigation into practical ways of providing a social account.

to become more responsive to the wider social responsibility issues. Figure 4.7 summarises some of the main points from the *Corporate Report*.[19] Other reports in other countries followed (see, especially, AICPA, 1977) and they still represent an excellent bank of thinking and ideas on the whole spectrum of social accounting and account-ability. *However*, with very few exceptions, notably at the periphery of employee and employ-ment reporting, these excursions by the accounting professions had little long-term effect on practice and virtually no effect on accounting regulation.

As we noted above there appears to be a response akin to fashion in the profession's reaction to 'new' issues. That few, if any, of the developments that attracted so much attention at the time have passed into the core of the account-ing curriculum is depressing and, we would suggest, indicative that accounting still has no coherent way of thinking about its mission (no 'conceptual framework': Macve, 1981; and see also Hines, 1991a). As a result it reacts to issues and, when those issues pass from the political agenda, the accounting profession abandons them.

Such a view is supported in Figure 4.5 by the environmental issues. Neither the early 1970s reports from the AAA nor the path-breaking work on energy accounting (see, for example, CIMA, 1982) were re-activated when accounting for the environment became such a live issue in the late 1980s. A principal challenge faced by those supporting environmental accounting is to ensure that 'environment' is not hustled offstage in the way all previous social accounting initiatives have been. Further, it is worth remarking that this ebbing and flowing of various aspects of CSR is as good an indication as one could ask for that *voluntary* solutions to accounting problems, however desirable they may be in principle, simply do not work in practice. Only when a 'new' accounting problem is established in an accounting standard or the Companies Acts does it become part of the core knowledge of the profession. This is very depressing and hardly a cause for congratulation to a group such as accountants, with such high aspirations to be a profession (see, particularly, Bebbington *et al.*, 1994; Gray *et al.*, 1994; Owen *et al.*, 1994; Sterling, 1973; Zeff, 1987, 1989).

4.5 The development of CSR practice

As may be inferred from the foregoing, CSR practice has not evolved in any systematic manner. However, we can identify a series of 'milestones' in the development of CSR practice. These can be used to illustrate the different themes we have been speaking of. These themes and the examples (and 'milestones') we can use to illustrate them, are shown in Figure 4.8.

Before going into the detail of Figure 4.8 a few words of explanation seem appropriate. First, the figure identifies both individual examples of CSR (those in lower case) and general trends in reporting (those in upper case). Illustrations of some of these are presented below but it is hoped that the combination helps to illustrate the themes we have been discussing in this chapter. Secondly, the theme of 'employees and trade unions' in Figure 4.8 contains a range of approaches including human resource accounting as well as reporting *to* and *for* employees. These are touched upon in Chapters 5 and 6 and examined in a little more detail in Chapter 7. Thirdly, a number of the examples cited in Figure 4.8 relate to externally prepared reports (see also Figure 4.4). These (which include the Council on Economic Priorities, the consumer movements, Social Audit Ltd, Counter Information Services, local authority and plant closure audits) are what we shall refer to generally as 'Social Audits' and are dealt with in more detail in Chapter 9. Fourthly, the relatively new phenomenon of 'ethical or social investment' which was such an important part of the trends in the late 1980s is dealt with in detail in Chapter 8. Finally the more recent trends, and notably the recent emergence of environmental reporting and accounting, will be given some detailed examination in Chapters 5 and 6. In this section of this chapter we will just concentrate on those examples from the past that remain important milestones; that help illustrate the trends we have pulled out earlier in the chapter; and which fall, generally, into the category (in Figure 4.4) of internally prepared for external consumption. We will do this, again, under the four broad headings of social responsibility; community and consumers; employees; and natural environment.

Social responsibility reporting

Social responsibility reporting or — as Mathews (1984) calls it — 'total impact reporting' is concerned with trying to present a comprehensive picture of the full extent of the organisation's interactions with its external environment. Although this is, it would seem, an impossible (although laudable) aim, there have been useful, substantial attempts in this direction. Indeed, two of the very first examples of internally generated social

Figure 4.8 *Milestones in practice and experimentation in CSR*

	SOCIAL RESPONSIBILITY AND TOTAL IMPACT	COMMUNITY AND CONSUMER	EMPLOYEES AND TRADE UNIONS	NATURAL ENVIRONMENT
1960s	Council on Economic Priorities (USA)	Ralph Nader (USA)		
		Consumer Assoc. (UK)	R.G. Barry Corp (1968: USA)	
1970s	Social Audit Ltd (1971: UK)			
	Counter Info' Services (c. 1972: UK)			
	Linowes (1972: USA)		SOCIALBERICHT (Germany)	
	Clark C. Abt (1972: USA)			
	Eastern Gas (1972: USA)	BankAmerica (1974: USA)	EMPLOYEE REPORTS (UK, Germany)	Philips Screw (1973: USA)
	Deutsche-Shell (1975: Germany)	1st Nat. Bank Minneapolis (1974: USA)	The Lucas Plan (1975: UK)	
	Atlantic Richfield (1974–1977: USA)		EMPLOYMENT REPORTS (UK)	EXPERIMENTS IN ENERGY ACCOUNTING (Germany, UK)

Figure 4.8 continued

VALUE ADDED STATEMENTS (UK)

BILAN SOCIAL (France)

CERCLA DISCLOSURE (USA)

PLANT CLOSURE AUDITS (UK)

Ciba-Geigy (1989: Switzl)

SOUTH AFRICAN EMPLOYMENT (MNCs)

1980s

Cement Corp India (1981: India)

PUBLIC SECTOR REPORTING (UK)

SOCIALBILANZ (Germany)

ETHICAL INVESTMENT FUNDS (USA/UK)

LOCAL AUTHORITY SOCIAL AUDITS (UK)

Noranda (1990: Canada)

Norsk Hydro (1990: UK/Norway)

BSO/Origin (1990: Netherlands)

Danish Steel Works (1991: Denmark)

ÖKOBILANZ (Germany/Austria)

1990s

Changing Corporate Values (1991: UK)

SbN Bank (1992: Denmark)

Traidcraft (1992: UK)

Ethical Consumer (1990: UK)

New Consumer (1990: UK)

reporting were of this sort. Both from the United States, the 1972 reports from Clark C. Abt and Associates and from Eastern Gas and Fuel Associates represent very different approaches to the same basic problem.

Clark C. Abt was a consultancy firm which initiated and developed a set of 'social accounts' that were intended to show the total impact of the company in financial terms. The accounts were intended, in part, as a public relations device but were published (and refined) by Abt throughout the 1970s. Although accompanied by very detailed and thoughtful notes on how items such as pollution or employee remuneration were treated, the accounts demonstrated (rather more clearly than was intended) that it is very difficult (if not impossible) to capture all social and environmental interactions in financial terms *on the same valuation basis*. Even more acutely than Linowes (see Figure 4.6) the accounts end up comparing, adding and subtracting figures calculated on fundamentally different bases. What, if anything, the resultant bottom-line purports to represent is therefore anybody's guess.[20] However, the method was applied in one other case of which we are aware. The Cement Corporation of India produced Abt-based social accounts for 1981. These are reproduced in Figure 4.9.

The two major importances of the Abt attempts were that (a) the company encouraged and undertook experimentation in the area of social accounting — such experimentation is far too rare and urgently needed if advances are to be achieved; and (b) the Abt accounts, like the Linowes, do attempt to link the economic and the social/environmental activities of the company. An essential tenet of CSR is that a large part of what CSR seeks to represent is that economic activity and the pursuit of profit is not a costless activity to the host society. The Abt accounts move us, albeit oddly, in this direction. Finally, as we shall see in Chapter 6, attempts of this sort are still being made. Chapter 6 will introduce and explore the environmental accounts of BSO/Origin, a Dutch company, that bear a notable resemblance to the Abt accounts (for more detail see also Gray and Symon, 1992).

A complete contrast is offered by the Eastern Gas and Fuel Associates 1972 Report. In general terms this is much closer to what normally passes for social and environmental reporting, in that it is descriptive with the intermittent use of quantitative data (see Figure 4.10). The Eastern Gas Report is clearly addressed to shareholders and suggests that it covers those matters thought to be of greatest concern to the shareholders. In this we see that management still have something approaching total control over the social reporting process and, as a result, we cannot expect such reports to be either unbiased (even if that were possible) or complete. In fact, the Eastern Gas report has one quite glaring omission in that, given the business it is in, the company's greatest impact is likely to be in the area of air and land pollution — about which the report is silent.

Two further illustrations will serve to complete the early picture of attempts at social responsibility accounting. Figure 4.11 shows an extract from the Deutsche Shell 1975 Report. The Deutsche Shell Report is a combination of a set of social accounts (derived, so it would appear, from the Linowes model), plus a series of more general statements. An attempt at comprehensive reporting is provided by an orientation to assessing the extent to which the company contributes to social welfare. Thus the Deutsche Shell model relies on costs (and not valuations like the Abt model) and relates the whole to

Figure 4.9 *Extract from Cement Corporation of India Ltd 1981 Social Account*

			(Rs. in Lakhs)
Social Accounts	**I Social benefits & cost to staff**	**1980–81**	**1979–80**
Social Income	A. Social benefits to staff		
Statement	1. Medical and hospital amenities	**32.14**	20.35
	2. Educational facilities	**4.10**	2.39
	3. Canteen facilities	**5.71**	3.46
	4. Recreation, entertainment & cultural activities	**3.07**	1.77
	5. Housing and township facilities	**112.54**	84.33
	6. Water supply, concessional electricity and transport	**18.15**	13.59
	7. Training & career development	**4.93**	3.85
	8. Other benefits to employees	**192.01**	149.97
	Total benefits to staff	**372.65**	279.71
	B. Social cost to staff		
	1. Lay off & involuntary terminations	**0.86**	—
	2. Extra hours put in by executives voluntarily	**9.26**	7.75
	Total cost to staff	**10.12**	7.75
	Net social income to staff (A–B)	**362.53**	271.96
	II. Social benefits & cost to community		
	A. Social benefits to community		
	1. Local taxes paid to Panchyat/ Municipality	**0.21**	0.08
	2. Environmental improvements	**6.97**	7.01
	3. Generation of job potential	**550.69**	448.67
	4. Generation of business	**95.63**	75.90
	Total social benefits to community	**653.50**	531.66
	B. Social cost to community Increase in cost of living in the vicinity on account of cement plants	**155.00**	127.40
	Net social income to community (A–B)	**459.50**	404.26

Figure 4.9 *continued*

III. Social benefits & costs to general public

A. Total benefits to general public		
1. Taxes, duties, etc. paid to State Governments	**735.55**	496.80
2. Taxes, duties, etc. paid to Central Government	**1499.61**	1284.77
Total benefits to general public	**2235.16**	1781.57
B. Costs to general public		
1. State services consumed: electricity charges paid	**519.72**	325.20
2. Central services consumed: telephones, telegrams, postage & bank charges	**14.37**	11.96
Total cost to general public	**534.09**	337.16
Net social benefit to general public (A−B)	**1701.07**	1444.41
NET SOCIAL INCOME TO STAFF, COMMUNITY AND GENERAL PUBLIC (I + II + III)	**2562.10**	2120.63

Social Balance Sheet

LIABILITIES			ASSETS		
	(Rs. in Lakhs)			(Rs. in Lakhs)	
	As at 31.3.81	**As at 31.3.80**		**As at 31.3.81**	**As at 31.3.80**
I. Organisation Equity	**720.48**	546.54	**1. Social Capital: Investment**		
II. Social Equity			1. Township land	**15.74**	15.73
Contribution by staff	**3584.15**	2869.11	2. Buildings (i) Township (residential & welfare buildings)	**581.51**	444.23
			(ii) Canteen buildings	**9.36**	5.49

Figure 4.9 *continued*

Social Balance Sheet				
LIABILITIES		ASSETS		
		3. Township water supply and sewage	**47.16**	24.56
		4. Township — roads	**29.13**	23.51
		5. Township — electrification	**17.33**	15.07
		II. Other social assets		
		1. Hospital equipments	**1.38**	0.59
		2. Hospital vehicle/ ambulance	**4.66**	4.00
		3. School equipments	**0.76**	0.71
		4. Club equipments	**0.80**	0.74
		5. Play ground/park	**0.32**	0.20
		6. School buses	**12.33**	11.71
		III. Human assets:	**3584.15**	2869.11
4304.63	3415.65		**4304.63**	3415.65

corporate social objectives via the establishment of and reporting against internally generated standards (for more detail see Schreuder, 1979; Van den Bergh, 1976). Such an approach has attracted a great deal of attention (see, for example, Dierkes, 1979; Jaggi, 1980).

The final illustration in this section comes from another American company, Atlantic Richfield (see Figure 4.12). The Atlantic Richfield Company 1977 Report consisted of more than 60 pages, principally of narrative but with a selective disclosure of quantitative information. Before publication of the report the company prepared a summary and asked Milton Markowitz, a well-known critical journalist of the period, to provide a 'critique' of the report. This critique appears alongside the summary in Figure 4.12 and acts as a sort of audit of the report.

The Atlantic Richfield summary illustrates two useful points at this stage. First, the extent of the criticism that the 'auditor' is able to bring acts as a stark reminder of just how partial and biased a self-reported, un-audited social or environmental report is likely to be. As most CSR is of this sort, it is not surprising that Estes (1976) refers to most CSR as 'blatantly self-serving' and 'incomplete, defensive and sprinkled with propoganda' (p. 55). We do well to remember this. Secondly, Atlantic Richfield also illustrate a somewhat

Figure 4.10 *Extract from Eastern Gas and Fuel Associates 1972 Annual Report*

Toward Social Accounting

TO OUR SHAREHOLDERS:

There has been much talk in recent years of corporate social responsibility and of the need to develop some sort of social accounting to gauge how well a given firm is performing – not just as an economic unit but as a citizen. Indeed, some have suggested that these measures of corporate performance beyond net profit should be subjected to an independent social audit.

This insert for the 1972 Annual Report of Eastern Gas and Fuel Associates has been designed as an experimental exploration of two aspects of social accounting for "self-auditing" purposes:

(1) What are some internal topics on which management can presently assemble and organize reasonably accurate and coherent data?

(2) Which issues of social accountability are of external interest and to what extent are shareholders in particular interested, if at all?

To explore the first of these aspects we have gathered statistical information that covers four topics from among the many that are currently of concern to those studying corporate social responsibility:

● Industrial safety
● Minority employment
● Charitable giving
● Pensions

To explore the second aspect we have included, at the end of this insert, a short questionnaire which, if you will mail it back, will serve as a useful measure of shareholder concern with corporate social responsibility and the reporting of it. No generally accepted standards or methods of presentation have been developed for shareholder reporting on such topics nor is there clear evidence as to shareholder interest.

The topics for this first report were not chosen because they are necessarily the most important ones. or the ones that might make us look good, but because they are the most readily measurable, because our goals with respect to them are comparatively simple and clear, and because they lie in areas where management can rather directly influence results. In addition, managerial decisions on these topics can have a significant impact on earnings per share.

In the process of making this first consolidation of social data from our various operations, we found that our records were less complete and less certain than we had believed. We also found that even inadequate disclosure begins to exert a useful pressure on management to comply with new public expectations as to the conduct of large corporations. It may also be some of the best evidence that management is sincerely concerned and making an effort to meet proper expectations.

Four major recurring principles for the quantification of social responsibility have been suggested:

The first is that our priorities have been changing with some rapidity. Many of our political, economic and commercial measures of progress have become obsolescent. We need a new kind of social accounting that goes beyond GNP for the nation and goes beyond net profit for the firm.

Second, while we think of our current economic and accounting measures of GNP and net profit as very precise when you really get into the nitty gritty of how they are put together, their certainty is delusive.

Third, many proposed imprecise measures of social accounting can be sufficiently accurate to be instructive. They are not hopelessly less accurate than GNP or net profit, and so they can be quite useful, even though they lack precision, for many purposes for which we cannot use GNP and net profit.

And finally, while our efforts to calibrate our concerns by social accounting will reflect this new sense of priorities, without personal observation in the field and a weighing of the figures that we create with moral concerns, social accounting itself becomes only a new numbers game.

As we proceed with these early attempts to develop some form of internal social accounting, we should acquire additional useful insights into this new art.

Eli Goldston, *President*

1 INDUSTRIAL SAFETY

Recent legislation has demonstrated that a major current public concern, especially in the heavy industries in which Eastern is involved, is the health and safety of employees.

Our industrial accident record in recent years has not been very good. One standard measurement is the accident frequency rate (number of accidents versus hours worked), and our rate has almost doubled in the last three years, going up most dramatically in gas operations. It is clear that our safety performance has been slipping. In addition it seems that our record is poorer than that of a number of firms with whom we have compared specific records. Just where we stand in our various industries is difficult to gauge because meaningful comparative figures are not available.

ACCIDENT FREQUENCY RATE
(Lost time accidents per million employee hours)

	1970	1971	1972
Coal & Coke	43	61	78
Gas	14	26	30
Marine	34	41	43
EGFA Avg.	36	50	64

Another measure of safety performance is the severity rate, which takes into account time lost as a result of accidents. Here Eastern's record has been steadier, and apparently more in line with other firms for our industries. But much room for improvement remains.

ACCIDENT SEVERITY RATE
(Employee days lost per million employee hours)*

	1970	1971	1972
Coal & Coke	2,948	3,427	4,209
Gas	222	191	303
Marine	1,707	2,015	1,423
EGFA Avg.	2,225	2,516	3,033

*Excluding days charged for fatalities.

Figure 4.10 *continued*

Frequency and severity rates, either for a single firm or for an industry, are rather elusive statistics. They may appear worse simply from improved reporting, or may appear better if excessive pressure to improve the record results in variable reporting practices. Comparisons are complicated by numerous variables. Our river towboat crews, for instance, live aboard the boats and so are at their workplace even when not actually working. A greater awareness by both employees and management of the importance of safety may increase the number of reported accidents. Improved benefits could encourage accident reporting. Comparisons are also difficult because of different bases of reporting. We are trying for 1973 to improve both our performance and our ability to supply managers with comparable industry statistics.

Job related fatalities, of course, are the most salient and tragic accidents. We require full reports to top management on all serious injuries and fatalities along with proposals to prevent recurrence. At Eastern we are constantly trying to develop more effective ways to impress on all our people the need to guard against the ever present hazards in their particular line of work. Here is our recent record of fatalities:

FATALITIES

	1970	1971	1972
Coal & Coke	8	3	4
Gas	0	0	0
Marine	1	1	2
EGFA Total	9	4	6

Critics of industry often assume that management has more ability to reduce accident frequency and severity and to eliminate fatalities than may be the case. We do not accept at all the rationalization that "accidents just happen" and we would be the last to suggest that a victim alone is at fault. But it is obvious that we need to be better persuaders and to improve training, motivation and enforcement when it is considered that in at least five of the six 1972 fatalities, the victim was an experienced employee who was clearly violating a standard safety work rule of the company at the time of his death. The need for and difficulty of broad safety indoctrination is evidenced by the fact that 11 employees were fatally injured in 1972 in accidents off the job.

The economics of safety reinforces our social/humanitarian concerns. Compensation of employees injured on the job cost Eastern at least $3,600,000 last year, or about 20¢ in earnings per share.

We are continuing to increase our commitment of men and money to ongoing safety programs in all operations. One of our headquarters officers has been assigned to regular field checks of safety practices and the compilation and analysis of accident statistics. Eastern Associated Coal Corp. has further strengthened its existing safety program by engaging the highly respected safety department of a firm in another industry to help us improve our safety performance in coal operations. In Boston Gas Company, a safety campaign has commenced that focuses not only on safe work habits but also on continuing "defensive" use of equipment and procedures to avoid dangerous situations.

2   MINORITY EMPLOYMENT

An important thrust of Eastern's social concerns effort is to respond positively to the apparently clear national desire to bring an end to discrimination in employment and promotion because of race, religion or other difference from that elusive notion of "the majority."

It is difficult to generalize fairly and judiciously about Eastern's minority employment statistics. Numerically, minority employment in the company has increased in recent years, but has not quite maintained its percentage proportion. This has been particularly noticeable in coal operations, but in this instance, the increased employment has come in areas where there has been a smaller minority proportion in the local population. And it may be that the improving employment prospects for minority members either with our competitors or in fields previously closed to them have reduced the relative attractiveness of jobs with us. Boston Gas has had an excellent record of integrating its work force, but the addition of new territory with a different population mix has appeared to slow the trend.

MINORITY EMPLOYMENT

	1970	1971	1972
Coal & Coke			
Total	5,703	6,050	6,448
Minority	526	544	517
% Minority	9.2%	9.0%	8.0%
Gas			
Total	1,466	1,500	1,611
Minority	66	96	115
% Minority	4.5%	6.4%	7.1%
Marine			
Total Employees	1,077	1,332	1,358
Minority	64	84	79
% Minority	5.9%	6.3%	5.8%
EGFA*			
Total Employees	8,349	8,995	9,526
Minority	659	727	716
% Minority	7.9%	8.3%	7.5%
* Includes Boston Office			

Measuring progress in integration is further complicated by the fact that companies were forbidden to record the race of employees until quite recently. Many of our operations are so geographically scattered that it is difficult to determine in many cases if our percentages of minority employment are in line with the minority population in reasonably relevant areas, although this does seem to be true.

MINORITY EMPLOYMENT LEVELS

	1971	1972	1972 Total in Category	1972 % of Total
Officers & Managers	15	12	1,229	1%
Professional & Technical	19	34	648	4.9%
Clerical	58	56	895	6.1%
Skilled	364	398	5,091	7.8%
Unskilled	271	216	1,663	1.3%

Passing over complicated matters of definition, the figures seem to indicate that Eastern has done a reasonable job but still has some distance to go in reaching a fair proportion of minorities in the work force and in levels of employment. Our effort in recruitment and advancement is to give due recognition to merit and performance while still showing concern for the need to achieve appropriate representation of minorities. There are local instances in our operations which will require continuing attention and prodding if this is to be accomplished.

Figure 4.11 *Extract from Deutsche Shell 1975 Report*

THE GOALS OF SHELL'S CORPORATE POLICY

Every company in a free market must achieve a reasonable return on the capital that has been invested, to a large degree, at high risk. On the other hand, we are aware of our responsibility in a social market economy and, besides its purely economic activities, we see the company as a part of society, as the employer of those working for us, as a part of the whole. As long ago as 1974 we laid down in our principles of management the following five goals. Each carries the same weight, but they do not always operate in the same direction.

– Supplying the consumer on conditions determined by the market;
– Developing new applications of techniques and products;
– Achieving a reasonable return on investment;
– Taking into account our employees' interests;
– Paying regard to the general public welfare.

This overall objective explains why we have extended the Annual Report, which was in the main a report intended for the shareholders, to include a complete account of the degree to which all five of these corporate goals have been achieved.

Table of Contents
1. Introduction.
2. The framework of Shell's policy; general developments in the energy market;
   2.1 The policy of the OPEC countries.
   2.2 The impact on the German mineral oil market.
   2.3 The Federal government's energy program.
   2.4 Obligation to maintain minimum stock levels.
   2.5 Structural and business activity problems of the
   mineral oil industry.
   2.6 Special levies on domestic oil and natural gas
   production.
   2.7 Long-term aspects.
3. The goals of Shell's corporate policy.
4. The performance of Deutsche Shell A.G.;
   4.1 Supplying the consumer on conditions determined by the market.
4.2 Development of new application techniques and
    products.
4.3 Achieving a reasonable return on investment.
4.4 Taking account of or employees' interests.
4.5 Paying regard to the general public welfare.
5. Explanations pertaining to the German Shareholders' Act;
   5.1 Explanations of the balance sheet.
   5.2 Explanations of the profit and loss account.
6. Tables;
   6.1 Social accounts.
   6.2 Relations with investors.
   6.3 Account of performance.
   6.4 Balance sheet.
   6.5 Profit and loss statement.

Social accounts

RELATIONS TO PERSONNEL	Report page	P & L position	Cost (000 DM) 1975	1974
I Wages	24	16	60,725	58,894
Salaries		16	133,249	131,341
Total I			193,974	190,235
II Benefits accruing directly to employees (excl. wages and salaries)				
1 General				
(a) Christmas bonus (13th month)		16	16,055	15,764
(b) Holiday pay		17	5,750	4,590
(c) State sponsored saving scheme (employer contribution)		16	3,099	3,262
(d) other (incl. rebate on Shell products)	1 and 26		1,821	1,753
2 For special reasons				
(a) Suggestion scheme	28	16	90	64
(b) Long service bonus		16	300	395
(c) Birth grant		18	32	32
(d) Marriage grant		18	173	131
(e) Work safety competition	26/28	16	646	712
(f) Rent subsidies		16	398	424
Total II			28,364	27,127
III Benefits accruing indirectly to employees				
(a) Employer contribution – pension insurance				
(b) Employer contribution – health insurance		14,16,17	20,857	13,852
(c) Employer contribution – unemployment insurance				
(d) Employer's liability insurance		17	1,670	1,643
(e) Work undertaken for company health scheme (salaries, rent etc.)		various	622	612
Total III			23,149	16,107
IV Benefits accruing directly to personnel as a group				
1 (a) Company medical service	28		806	799
(b) Accident prevention	26–28		2,000	2,000
(c) Holiday homes		various	130	112
(d) Subsidies to sports associations	25		514	493
			3,450	3,404
2 Education and training				
(a) Training centre			523	546
(b) Language courses	25	various	64	46
(c) Other training			1,401	1,372
(d) Trainees and apprentices			1,136	1,289
			3,124	3,253

	Report page	P & L position	1975	1974
3. Other				
(a) Works clothes		26	624	538
(b) Cost of canteen		26	4,023	4,400
			4,647	4,938
Total IV			11,221	11,595
V Benefits to pensioners and dependants				
(a) Pension payments			27,030	22,772
(b) Transfer to pension reserves	24	18	77,329	74,107
(c) Insolvency insurance			669	74,017
Total V			105,028	96,789
VI Works councils		various	1,579	1,559
Relations with Personnel Total I – VI			363,315	343,412
Less double counting (especially personnel costs)			(6,507)	(7,012)
			356,808	336,400
ATTENTION TO PUBLIC CONCERNS				
I Relations to the consumer				
(a) Research and development	18/19	various	35,717	32,578
(b) Cost to secure supplies	11		NA	NA
Total I			35,717	32,578
II Relations to environment				
(a) Air purification				
(b) Noise control				
(c) Preservation of the countryside	33/34	various	62,000	NA
(d) Waste-water control				
Total II			62,000	NA
III Relations to the public				
(a) Youth work	30/31	various	722	590
(b) Donations and charitable contributions	32	26	390	363
(c) Publications etc.	28/29	various	1,791	2,697
(d) Taxation and rates (incl. capital gains tax)	35	24 a,b,c	138,870	209,782
(e) Subscriptions to associations, institutes etc		26	5,225	4,705
(f) Other contributions		26	3,721	2,786
Total III			150,719	220,923
Total I – III			248,436	253,501
Less double counting			(10,747)	(11,109)
			237,689	242,392

Figure 4.12 *Extract from Atlantic Richfield Company's 1977 Social Report*

ASSETS

Minority Affairs

Atlantic Richfield has worked hard to provide job opportunities for minorities. Minority group members account for 13 percent of the total work force, a ratio that ranks Atlantic Richfield at the top of the petroleum industry.

Jobs formerly restricted to men – such as refinery work – have been opened up to women.

The number of minorities and women in professional, managerial and sales positions has nearly doubled since 1970.

To aid minority economic development, Atlantic Richfield maintains deposits of over $1 million in minority-owned financial institutions across the country.

Atlantic Richfield reported purchases of $3.2 million from minority suppliers in 1974. This was double its 1973 purchases.

Contributions

Its $5.5 million of charitable contributions in 1974 supported a large number of educational, health and cultural organizations in the United States.

Atlantic Richfield matches, dollar for dollar, employee contributions to educational institutions.

One unusual grant in 1974 was $10,000 to the Council on Economic Priorities, an organization that monitors corporate social responsibility.

Community organizations backed by Atlantic Richfield Foundation grants include the Boy Scouts, YMCA, Junior Achievement, Urban Coalition, American Red Cross, Salvation Army and Urban League.

Shareholder Information

The firm's Form 10K financial report, which contains more detailed information than the annual report and which all corporations must file with the Securities and Exchange Commission, was offered free of charge to all shareholders in 1972 and 1973.

Environment and Conservation

Atlantic Richfield was the first company in the petroleum industry to announce that it would make a lead-free gasoline.

In the interests of what it called "America's natural beauty," the Company in 1972 cancelled its entire out-door advertising – 1,000 billboards in 36 states.

Its Cherry Point refinery in the state of Washington has been recognized as a model nonpolluter.

It has emphasized energy conservation in its own operations.

Consumerism

It was one of the first companies in the petroleum industry to post the octane levels of its gasolines at the pump.

Social Management

The Company's public affairs program in Alaska is outstanding, far surpassing any comparable effort by Atlantic Richfield in the lower 48 states both in the range and depth of activities. The Company has made its presence felt in Alaska as a concerned corporate citizen.

LIABILITIES

Most minorities and women who work for Atlantic Richfield hold low-level jobs. There is not a single black or female officer.

More than 70 major U.S. companies have elected blacks to their boards of directors. Many have also named women directors. The petroleum industry has resisted this trend – and so has Atlantic Richfield. Its board is all-white, all-male, all-Christian.

The Company has not been aggressive or innovative in its support of minority enterprise. Standard Oil of Indiana, for example, requires its purchasing agents to set goals and goes out of its way to help fledgling companies. Result: Indiana Standard spends four or five times what Atlantic Richfield spends in purchases from minority suppliers.

To encourage charitable contributions, the Internal revenue Service allows corporations a deduction of up to 5% on pretax profits. At least two companies – Dayton Hudson and Cummins Engine – takes this full deduction. Other companies – Aetna Life & Casualty, for example – have sharply increased their giving. Atlantic Richfield gives away 1.3% of pretax profits.

The pattern of Atlantic Richfield's giving is in the traditional mold, with most money going to old-line, established institutions. Of the $850,000 committed to education in 1973, for example, more than a quarter went to one school, the Massachusetts Institute of Technology.

Black colleges receive only minimal support.

The Company's annual report has been niggardly in providing meaningful details of pollution control programs or specific information about social responsibility activities. The tendency has been to substitute rhetoric for hard data. Shell Oil Company has consistently released far more information.

Atlantic Richfield was slow to comprehend the environmental problems connected with the Alaskan pipeline and for too long resisted protection measures later incorporated into the project.

The Company, while paying its respects to the conservation ethic in solving our energy problems, persists in the view that more development and more growth can solve our energy problems.

At many U.S. companies the concept of social responsibility has been institutionalized at least to the extent that new positions and/or committees have been created, some of them with high standing in the table of organization. Atlantic Richfield has floundered through a series of organizational reshuffles, with the social responsibility functions still scattered, relegated to lower levels of the Company and concerned largely with peripheral areas outside the mainstream activities.

CONCLUSION

As the youngest of the petroleum giants, the Company carries less baggage from the past. As a company still in transition, it is more conscious that its future lies ahead. And that is perhaps what is most hopeful; it is a company not yet fully formed. When oil from Alaska begins to flow and Atlantic Richfield becomes even bigger than it is today, it will have a splendid opportunity to demonstrate that social concerns can be built into the day-to-day operations of a petroleum company. More than most giant companies, it has its future in its hands. It need not relive or repeat the mistakes of the past.

depressing characteristic related to the motivation for social and environmental disclosure. Atlantic Richfield, according to Patterson (1976), had been responsible for a major environmental catastrophe involving the leakage to groundwater of nuclear waste material. The production of this social report — with no mention of that catastrophe — appears to lend support to the hypothesis that social and environmental disclosure will often be used to distract attention from other, more major issues. Sadly (but perhaps unsurprisingly), if one digs deeply enough one can usually find some social or environmental crisis in the company which produces the report and which, one may infer, provided the motivation for its production. It is this sort of evidence which leads to the use of legitimacy theory and political economy theory in an attempt to explain CSR (as we saw in Chapters 2 and 3). While there may be many instances of disclosure for reasons of accountability and social responsibility, there are also many examples where the disclosure would appear to have been driven by concerns to, for example, maintain the legitimacy of an organisation, a sector, or capital itself.

Community and consumers reporting

Apart from the activities of the consumer movements (see Chapter 9) organisations have generally given less attention to detailed experimental approaches to reporting about their consumers' well-being (see also Chapter 6). One major exception to this was the development in the UK public sector (which in the early 1980s still included many public utilities) of external accountability reports. Except for the (then) nationalised industries (which, incidentally, produced many of the United Kingdom's leading examples of social and environmental disclosure) these public sector reports tended to ignore all social and environmental issues *with the exception of* the quality and quantity of service delivered. Figure 4.13 gives two examples by way of illustration. These reports contrast starkly with some of the early attempt at 'community accounting' in the United States. The two most celebrated examples of this approach are The First National Bank of Minneapolis (whose social indicator approach to social accounting is extensively reported in Jensen, 1976) and the BankAmerica 1974, an extract of which is shown in Figure 4.14.

In keeping with our suggestion that CSR follows the fashions of 'social responsibility' we are aware of few detailed, published reports of more recent vintage which continue or develop the initiatives of these organisations (some of these examples, for example from Traidcraft plc and SbN Bank, are covered in Chapter 9).

Employee-related reporting

Until the 1990s a greater number of examples of CSR relate to employees than to any other area of concern — although with the exception of reporting about 'minorities' in the United States, it is a predominantly United Kingdom and European phenomenon (see, for example, Lessem, 1977; Preston *et al.*,1978; Schreuder, 1979). There are many reasons for this (see, for example, Maunders, 1984) and, in the United Kingdom at least, one major reason is that both reporting to employees ('employee reporting') and

Figure 4.13a *Public sector reporting: extract from Tayside Regional Council 1993–94 Annual Report and Statement of Accounts*

PUBLICATION OF INFORMATION
(STANDARDS OF PERFORMANCE)

EDUCATION:

Pre-School	1	(a) Quantified statement of local authority objective in provision:	
		Target % of Primary 1 pupils with experience of pre-school education	90%
		(b) Target % of Primary 1 pupils with experience of Education Department pre-schooling	59%
		(c) % of pupils enrolled in Primary 1 with experience of Education Department pre-schooling	53.0%
	2	Expenditure per place	£1,805.13
Primary School	3	Service cost per pupil for	
		(a) teaching staff	£1,208.76
		(b) support staff (school-based)	£92.27
		(c) educational support services (central)	£38.30
		(d) administrative support (central)	£55.49
	4	Expenditure per pupil on individual teaching materials and equipment	
		(a) total budget allocated (£/pupil)	£36.49
		(b) actual expenditure per pupil (£/pupil)	£35.84

		5 % of classes in which the number of pupils fall within the following bands:	(1) Non-Composite Classes	(2) Composite Classes	
		(a) less than 15	0.3%	5.9%	}
		(b) 16-20	5.7%	6.3%	}
		(c) 21-25	16.7%	17.8%	} 100%
		(d) 26-30	28.7%	0.3%	}
		(e) 31 or more	18.3%	—	}

	6	Occupancy: % of schools where ratio of pupils to places is	
		(a) 40% or less	8.0%
		(b) 41-60%	23.0%
		(c) 61-80%	29.4%
		(d) 81% or more	39.6%
Secondary School	7	Service cost per pupil for	
		(a) teaching staff	£2,121.88
		(b) support staff (school-based)	£155.19
		(c) educational support services (central)	£134.43
		(d) administrative support (central)	£96.91
	8	Expenditure per pupil on individual teaching materials and equipment	
		(a) total budget allocated (£/pupil)	£59.40
		(b) actual expenditure per pupil (£/pupil)	£62.57
	9	Occupancy: % of schools where ratio of pupils to places is	
		(a) 40% or less	6.2%
		(b) 41-60%	18.8%
		(c) 61-80%	21.9%
		(d) 81% or more	53.1%
General	10	Assessment of special educational needs: average time taken to complete assessment	32.2 wks
	11	Repairs and maintenance costs per m² floor area	£10.97

Tr
Tayside

Tayside Regional Council
Annual Report and Accounts 1993/94

93

Figure 4.13b Public sector reporting: extract from University of Dundee 1992–93 Annual Report

GRADUATE CAREERS

You're the Tops....

UNIVERSITY of Dundee graduates were again among the most adept in the UK at avoiding unemployment, against a national background of fewer opportunities even for well-qualified job seekers.

In 1992, figures compiled from the Universities Statistical Record show that Dundee graduates were more successful than those of any other Scottish university in going on to full-time employment or further study. Just 11.6% of Dundee's 1992 graduates were unemployed or still seeking employment at 31 December 1992, against a Scottish average of 16.6% and a UK average of 17.2%. Dundee graduates' performance put the University fifth in the equivalent UK league table.

The graph on this page shows information collected by the Careers Service on new graduates from courses in the Faculties of Arts & Social Sciences, Law and Science & Engineering.

UK Employment
(excluding short-term employment)

		%
A1	Industry, Commerce, & Public Utilities	20.2
A2	Government, Local Government, NHS etc	3.3
A3	Universities, Colleges, Schools	1.1
A4	Other	2.3
A	Total	26.9

Full-time Study, Research & Training

B1	Full-time academic study/research	15.8
B2	Teacher-training	4.5
B3	Vocational and other training courses	22.6
B	Total	42.9

Other Destinations

C1	Employment overseas (UK graduates)	0.6
	Short-term UK employment	4.5
	Not available for employment	5.5
	Overseas graduates returning overseas	2.0
C2	Seeking employment	7.6
C3	Destinations unknown or not confirmed	10.0
	Total	100.0

University Of Dundee

24

Figure 4.14 *Extract from BankAmerica Corporation Annual Report 1974*

Urban Affairs

Urban Affairs assigned new officers, called regional urban development officers, to major metropolitan areas in seven of the bank's eleven California regions. These officers, all specialists in minority business lending, work closely with community offices and minority businesses to encourage and expand minority customer relations.

Two new programs were developed in Los Angeles to provide better career information for junior and senior high school students. One program includes a slide presentation on banking careers and trips to Bank of America facilities. The other acquaints students with a variety of career alternatives and provides visits to various industries.

Affirmative Action

Significant strides were made in the continuing efforts to identify, develop and upgrade minority and women employees as the chart below illustrates. Through intensive recruitment, training and development efforts, further Affirmative Action progress was made in 1974.

Overall, minorities represent the same proportion in Bank of America's staff as in the State of California.

The Equal Opportunity Section in Personnel Administration monitors all employment activities to insure equal opportunity for all persons.

The following chart shows the gains Bank of America has made since 1971 in its continuing commitment for equal opportunity in hiring and advancement for women and minorities:

	March 1971	March 1972	March 1973	March 1974	Dec. 31 1974
Women					
Total Bank Staff	72.4%	72.9%	73.4%	73.8%	74.3%
Officers	23.1%	25.3%	29.9%	32.4%	34.0%
Minorities					
Total Bank Staff	20.8%	22.5%	23.7%	25.3%	26.6%*
Officers	6.6%	7.4%	9.0%	10.4%	11.6%

* Minorities constitute 26.5% of California's population, according to the 1970 Census.

Investments

Bank of America's Trust Department in 1974 gained the services of an analyst whose full-time duty is to advise on the social responsibility of businesses as their conduct affects investment decisions. The corporate responsibility analyst was appointed by BA Investment Management Corporation, wholly-owned subsidiary of BankAmerica Corporation, which serves as investment advisor to the Trust Department.

Contributions and Grants

Bank of America made charitable contributions of $2.7 million to Bank of America Foundation and to other deserving organizations. These funds were distributed in the following approximate proportions: Health, 48 percent; Education, 31 percent; Community Involvement, 18 percent; other, 3 percent.

Public Broadcasting Service: Bank of America made two gifts to PBS television stations. It gave $57,000 to KQED, Inc., and the Pacific Film Archive of the University of California at Berkeley, to partially fund the showing of a series of 13 Japanese film masterpieces on the 240-station network.

The bank also made a $104,000 grant to seven California PBS stations for three series of programs: "Evening at Symphony," "Romagnoli's Table," and "Animated Film Festival."

Poppy Park: Bank of America Foundation supported a statewide effort by school children to preserve the best-known stand of the state flower, the California poppy. The pupils raised $18,000 and the foundation matched that amount to save a 1,000-acre area in Lancaster, California. The children have named the wildflower preserve "Poppy Park." It will be officially established as a state park in 1976.

Multicultural Resources: The Foundation also gave $30,000 to support a library of 5,000 books and other publications for and about various ethnic cultures. The library, a one-of-its-kind collection called "Multicultural Resources," is also receiving administrative and staff assistance from San Francisco State University and the San Francisco School District.

Paper Recycling

The corporation continued its program of using recycled paper and recycling waste paper wherever practical. More than 2,650 tons of used paper – principally old records, used corrugated cartons, and obsolete forms – were turned over to secondary fiber companies in 1974.

On the other side of the cycle, many bank forms and almost all bank envelopes use stock containing at least 75 percent recycled paper. All general bank letterhead stationery is 100 percent recycled paper.

However, scarcity and cost of recycled paper for production of the 1974 Annual Report forced the corporation to forego its use this year.

reporting about employees ('employment reporting') have some standing in law. Figure 4.15 provides illustrations of both of these from a United Kingdom and a Spanish company.

It was the decade of the 1970s that saw *employee* reporting appear to enter the established reporting practices of many organisations. The employee reports were in no sense standardised and so covered a very wide range of styles and subjects. Some were used by the management as a means of communication, others as an attempt to head off industrial action, yet others were part of the industrial and collective bargaining that was such a major economic feature of the UK 1970s. The reports might contain abbreviated financial statements, a review of the organisation's progress during the year, any changes in policies and, perhaps, data on staff turnover, health and safety issues and so on (for more detail see, for example, Maunders, 1984). These latter, statistical issues were more normally associated with the dedicated *employment* reports. These, however, never achieved the same popularity as reporting to employees themselves. As can be expected with voluntary reporting, the 1980s saw a reduction in the emphasis given to the non-statutory elements of both employee reporting and employment reporting. Except in so far as reporting to and about employees was covered by law, it largely went the way of all voluntary disclosure initiatives and, for most companies, became a matter of reduced interest (see Gray *et al.*, 1987; Chapter 3; Gray *et al.*, 1995a; Maunders, 1981; 1982a, b).

This waxing and waning in voluntary reporting is illustrated graphically in the United Kingdom by another, purportedly employee-related, development of the 1970s — the value-added statement. The value-added statement is, in effect, no more than a restatement of the profit and loss account which shows employees, governments and providers of finance and recipients of 'value added' rather than as costs-to-the-business. On the positive side, it is a statement which asks 'whose profit is it anyway?' and ranks the employee on a par with the providers of finance. On the negative side, it has been used to persuade employees that they already take more than their fair share out of the business (see, for example, Bougen, 1983, 1984). An example of a value-added statement is shown in Figure 4.16.

The value-added statement has been strictly a European phenomenon (Meek and Gray, 1988) and strictly a voluntary development. It rose in popularity in the 1970s and by the early 1980s, in the United Kingdom, something in the region of 30 per cent of the larger companies produced such a report (see, for example, Bougen, 1983). In one sense this might be considered something of a triumph for voluntary disclosure except that this still leaves something over 80 per cent of all UK companies *not* producing value-added statements and, as Burchell *et al.* (1985) argue successfully, the climate of business (and, specifically, the political environment) changed drastically through the 1980s: and with it went the value-added statement. In the United Kingdom, it remains very much a minority sport among a very few companies. Once again the context-based attempts to explain CSR (through, for example, legitimacy theory or political economy theory) have some important supporting evidence.

Before leaving this section, however, there are two other employee-related areas of reporting that deserve mentioning. The first relates to reporting about employment in southern Africa. Arising from the concern over apartheid and related social conditions in southern Africa there was a considerable popular movement for information about about companies' involvement in southern Africa.[21] This manifested itself, eventually, in a code of practice for multinational corporations (MNCs) proposed by the United Nations (and implemented in the United Kingdom by Cmnd 7233 in 1978) which, *inter alia*, called for the voluntary disclosure of employment information in southern Africa. Once again, the voluntary approach had some limited success but response by companies was patchy and frequently partial in content (for more detail see, for example, Patten, 1990).

The second of these final elements in employee-related reporting is that of *Human Asset* or *Human Resource Accounting* (HRA). HRA involves, at its simplest, attempts to value the employees of an organisation. This is done for various reasons including (a) the recognition that employees may be the principal asset of an organisation and so should appear on the balance sheet; (b) accounting-driven arguments that expenditure on employees may often be in the nature of an investment and therefore, following the matching principle, should not all be shown as a cost of the period; (c) to attempt to assess the 'investment' in employees and whether or not the 'investment' is gaining or losing financial value to the organisation; and (d) as an element in the assessment of management performance in that a 'good' manager will manage the human resources as well and as carefully as other resources and not, for example, exploit them for short-term gains. The first recorded popular example of this was from the R.G. Barry Corporation, which was based on the pioneering work of Likert (1967) and Brummett *et al.* (1968) and attempted to measure and report on its human assets (see, for example, Flamholtz, 1974). The initiative was taken up with enthusiasm by the American Accounting Association (AAA, 1973b) and attracted considerable interest (see, for example, Brooks, 1980; Grojer and Stark, 1977; Groves, 1981; Preston, 1981) before seeming to come to an undignified halt. There are ethical and practical difficulties with the area but the subject still attracts interest (not just from football clubs attempting to value players!) and there are signs that the subject may re-emerge from the shadows in the 1990s. (This issue is re-examined in Chapter 7 and see also, for example, Roslender and Dyson, 1992; and Gray *et al.*, 1987, Chapter 8 for a summary.)

Reporting on the natural environment

The final area of development in CSR we wish to introduce in this chapter relates to the natural environment. As can be seen from the examples we provided in the 'total impact' section above, the physical environment was recognised as an important issue in the United States and parts of continental Europe throughout the 1970s. However, despite the seminal work undertaken by, *inter alia* Ullmann (1976) and Dierkes and Preston (1977), the focus in such reports tended to remain on specific issues and, in particular, levels of pollution. Figure 4.17 represents what was, until the early 1990s (see Chapters 5 and 6) still a major step in the reporting of a company's environmental interaction. In addition to its status as a useful example of the rare reporting about environmental matters, the Phillips Screw Report illustrates two useful elements. First, the report is of

Figure 4.15a *Report to employees: extract from Queens Moat Houses plc Financial Report to Employees, May 1992*

Opportunity knocks for staff

Left: Since Jürgen Schöndorf's arrival at the Queens Parkhotel, Velbert, the Union Jack has flown alongside the hotel's flag.

Above: Silke Jaeger

OPPORTUNITY Europe – that's what being part of Queens Moat Houses offers.

Jürgen Schöndorf and Silke Jaeger are just two of the employees in the Group who have chosen to develop their career along the European route.

Jürgen has already worked at five QMH hotels – with his latest move taking him to the top job at Queens Parkhotel, Velbert, one of the new hotels which joined the Group in 1991.

Previously he worked at the Holiday Inns at Frankfurt and Mannheim, the Moat House International at Stratford-upon-Avon and the Telford Moat House.

"Working in the UK was an excellent experience and it improved my English considerably," he said. "Speaking a guest's own language provides the basis for strong business relationships."

VALUE

Fellow German Silke Jaeger also appreciates the value of speaking another language. After four and a half years at the Holiday Inn, Dusseldorf, she transferred to the Elstree Moat House to improve her English, becoming part of the team before the hotel opened in September 1991.

The move also gave her an opportunity to extend her experience. In Dusseldorf she had worked as breakfast supervisor, assistant house-keeper, food and beverage secretary and conference and banqueting coordinator. But she was keen to have a spell in Front of House – which the job as receptionist at Elstree provided.

Silke was not the only non-British employee at Elstree when it opened: four staff came from The Netherlands and two from France.

"Being part of an international group made it easier to settle in," she said – but admits it was still difficult at times during the first few months.

Now, however, she has evidently made her mark, and taken the next steps along her career path. After just three months at Elstree, she was promoted to reception supervisor.

How the spending cake is divided. . .

THIS year the total sales by hotels in the Group increased again to £543 million – that's a 12% increase over last year.

The cake shows how this money was spent. The largest amount was accounted for by the purchases of goods, food, drink and services required for the day-to-day running of our hotels.

The next largest sum represents the amount paid to employees as wages, national insurance and other staff costs.

The other 'slices' of the total sales cake represent rent, interest, tax, dividends and profit.

Rent is the money payable on leasehold hotels. Interest is the money paid to the bank for borrowings to run the business. Tax is the amount paid to the government – calculated on profits. Dividends are paid to shareholders as a return on their investment in Queens Moat Houses PLC.

Finally, profit is the sum retained in the business as the basis for continued growth and prosperity.

WAGES & OTHER STAFF COSTS £148 million

GOODS, FOOD DRINK & SERVICES £238 million

RENT ON LEASEHOLD PROPERTIES £10 million

TAXATION PAID £12 million

SHAREHOLDER DIVIDENDS £34 million

PROFIT RETAINED IN QMH £44 million

INTEREST ON BORROWINGS £57 million

For each pound we earn in sales. . .

FIGURES in millions are impressive but mean a lot more when they're scaled down. For every pound of sales in 1991, this is where each of the 100 pennies went.

PROFIT RETAINED IN QMH	8p
SHAREHOLDER DIVIDENDS	6p
RENT ON LEASEHOLD PROPERTY	2p
TAXATION PAID	2p
INTEREST ON BORROWINGS	11p
WAGES & OTHER STAFF COSTS	27p
GOODS, FOOD, DRINK & OTHER SERVICES	44p

Queens ...lement ...ts of the ...opments 1991. ...statistics... compare to those of the previous four years.

These charts, which cover the period up to 31 December 1991, are based on information from the Queens Moat Houses PLC Annual Report & Accounts. If you would like to see a copy, please write or ...

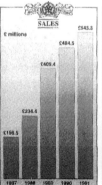

SALES
£ millions
£156.5 £234.4 £409.4 £484.5 £543.3
1987 1988 1989 1990 1991

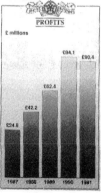

PROFITS
£ millions
£24.8 £42.2 £82.4 £94.1 £90.4
1987 1988 1989 1990 1991

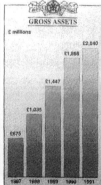

GROSS ASSETS
£ millions
£675 £1,035 £1,447 £1,868 £2,040
1987 1988 1989 1990 1991

Figure 4.15b Employment reporting: extract from Sevillana de Electricidad Annual Report 1993

Labor force

At December 31, 1993, the Company had 5,981 employees (6,102 in 1992).

The variation in the labor force follows the trend of previous years, since the reorganization of the distribution and hydroelectric plant areas, the automation of functions, etc. made it possible to improve the deployment of productive employees and to raise their efficiency.

The policy of upgrading employee skills continued in 1993. The breakdown of the labor force by years of service, working hours, age, professional category and activity is shown in the following tables:

Breakdown by category

Management	74
Technicians	1,289
Clerical staff	1,394
Clerical assistants	143
Craftsmen	2,874
Manual workers	51
Legal, healthcare and other employees	156
Total	5,981

Breakdown by working hours

Shift workers	2,226
Other	3,755
Total	5,981

Breakdown by operating area

Distribution and commercial	3,559
Production	870
Transmission and telecommunications	598
Economic and financial	186
Personnel	124
Research and development	120
Organization and systems	84
Coordination	22
Other	418
Total	5,981

Breakdown by years of service

0–5	506
6–10	964
11–15	1,211
16–20	931
21–25	1,047
26–30	409
31–35	395
36–40	352
41–45	124
46–50	39
over 50	3
Total	5,981

Breakdown by age

over 65	7
61–65	507
56–60	607
51–55	622
46–50	898
41–45	972
36–40	1,099
31–35	935
26–30	315
21–25	19
20 or under	–
Total	5,981

human resources

Figure 4.16 *A value-added statement: extract from ECC Group Report for Employees 1987*

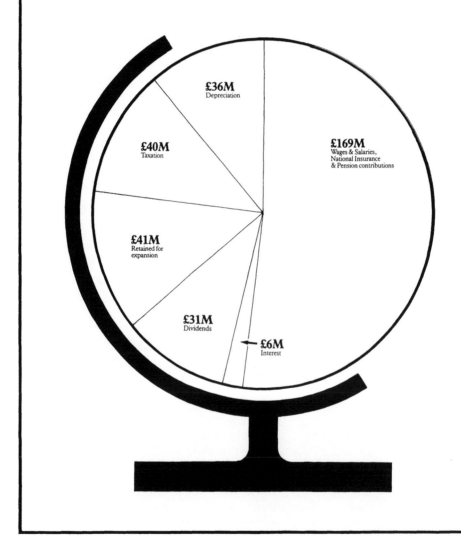

Financial
Achievements

£36M
Depreciation

£169M
Wages & Salaries,
National Insurance
& Pension contributions

£40M
Taxation

£41M
Retained for
expansion

£31M
Dividends

← £6M
Interest

Figure 4.16 *continued*

for the year

What is Added Value?

Added Value is the amount of value that we add to the materials, services and energy that we buy in. It is the difference between the amount we spend on these items and the amount that we sell our goods and products for. In 1987 Added Value was £323 million being the difference between sales of £762 million and expenditure on materials and services of £439 million.

Added Value differs from profit in that it can only arise at one level, whereas profit can be shown at several different levels. We talk about gross profit, operating profit, pre-tax profit, profit after tax, retained profit – all of them having different values.

The concept of Added Value is important if we wish to understand how our financial well-being affects the future. For it is only by the creation of sufficient Added Value that we can pay our way. The more value we add, the more successful we are and the more we can spend on expanding our operations and on replacing plant and equipment as they wear out. This is how we provide for our continued existence and success in the future.

Other items such as taxation and interest also come out of Added Value. What remains can be distributed to employees, in the form of wages and salaries, and to shareholders, in the form of dividends.

The Group globe is used to show how the 1987 Added Value of £323 million has been shared.

Turnover* (£M)

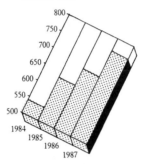

Profit after taxation (£M)

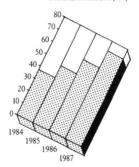

Profit before taxation* (£M)

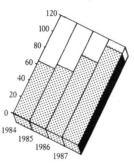

Profit attributable to shareholders (£M)

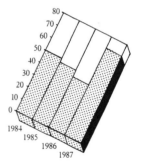

*Excluding discontinued businesses

Cash Flows

IN		OUT	
Profit before Tax and Depreciation	£148M.	Capital Spending and Acquisitions	£162M.
Issue of Shares	£40M.	Taxation	£38M.
Sales of Assets Grants and Other Receipts	£7M.	Increase in Working Capital and Other Payments	£40M.
Net Decrease in Cash Resources	£72M.	Dividends to Shareholders	£27M.

Figure 4.17 *Example of compliance with standard: extract from Phillips Screw Company Annual Report 1973*

Pollution Audit

The information herein has been extracted from a comprehensive pollution audit conducted by the undersigned on the Phillips Screw Company subsidiary Phillips Metallurgical, Inc. (PMI) and its subsidiary, Shell Cast Corp. (SCC). The audit included consideration of air, water, noise and solid waste effluents and consisted of engineering and economic segments. Preliminary technical equipment needs and costs were projected to provide management with parameters for determining the economic impact on the Company and its operations. Experience suggests that these preliminary cost estimates will prove to be within normally accepted deviation ranges.

Where required, effluent testing was conducted in accordance with standardized techniques applicable to the circumstances encountered at each site. For the business/economic analysis, not presented in the summary. Company financial data on PMI and SCC were provided and integrated with proposed abatement equipment capital and operating costs as estimated by the undersigned. Based upon our technical and economic analysis, the following significant conclusions have been drawn:

PMI has two effluent liabilities.

1.The plant exceeds Vermont air pollution standards – particulate emissions calculated at 7.0 lbs/hr compared to a maximum allowable level of 2.8 lbs/hr.

2.The plant exceeds Federal OSHA air contaminant standards – particulate concentration of at 25.2 mg/m3 compared to a maximum allowable level of 10.0 mg/m3.

SCC has two effluent liabilities.

1. The plant exceeds Connecticut air pollution standards – particulate emissions calculated at 3.0 lbs/hr compared to a maximum allowable level of 1.53 lbs/hr.

2. The plant emits at the Federal OSHA air contaminant standard – particulate concentration of at 10.0 mg/m3 compared to a maximum allowable level of 10 mg/m3.

No effluent liabilities in the areas of water, solid waste or noise pollution were observed.

Financial liabilities are as follows:

1. PMI to meet State and Federal air pollution standards requires a capital investment of $32,500 and annual operating expenses of $3,700.

2. SCC to meet State and Federal air pollution standards requires a capital investment of $25,500 and annual operating expenses of $3,200.

(These estimated costs are before tax and do not include amortization of capital equipment.)

In our opinion, expenditures of the levels cited for a remedial program of air pollution control will bring the current foundry operations into compliance with the respective State and Federal standards as they now exist. Furthermore, these expenditures are expected to provide sufficient margin to permit continued compliance in the event of any change in air pollution standards which we consider reasonably forseeable. Additionally, the nature and volume of solid waste effluents from current operations provide a sufficient margin for continued compliance in the event of reasonable changes to those standards.

Resource Planning Associates, Inc.

Cambridge, Mass.
June 1, 1973

environmental performance against regulatory standards; it therefore represents an example of the compliance-with-standard report that we argued (in Chapters 2 and 3) was an essential element in the discharge of social accountability. Secondly, the report is an 'audit report' from an independent attestor which we have seen is an essential element if the information reported is to have any credence.

4.6 Conclusions

In this chapter we have attempted to introduce the background to the more recent developments in CSR which we will be examining in later chapters. To do this, we have concentrated upon those examples of CSR from the mists of time and which represent milestones in the development of CSR. We emphasise these 'old' examples for three major reasons. First, with environmental reporting gaining such prominence, many companies, consultants and researchers are busy re-inventing wheels which have been tried and tested in the past. This seems to us a waste of valuable effort. Secondly, we do not come to CSR *ab initio*; there is a wealth of experience out there that has been hard-won and which it would be foolish to ignore; and, finally, with CSR once again gaining an increasing popularity we think it important that researchers, practitioners and consultants keep this past experience in mind — not least to avoid foolish comments such as suggesting that CSR is a recent phenomenon or that voluntary regulation is successful.

However, in attempting to provide such an introduction to the early developments of CSR we have tried to draw from the more recent developments in theorising about CSR that we met in Chapters 2 and 3 (see also, for example, Guthrie and Parker, 1989a; Patten, 1992; Roberts, 1992; Ullmann, 1985). This permits us to take what is variously referred to as a political-economy approach, a stakeholder perspective or a legitimacy theory approach to trying to understand the way CSR develops (or does not develop). Therefore we have provided a brief overview of the immediate context within which these developments have taken place. One thing becomes apparent. CSR, despite its crucial importance as a mechanism for developing the accountability and democracy of a society, ends up being treated like a fashion statement by the companies and the accounting profession. In virtually all cases, CSR is unregulated and voluntary and, as such, follows other trends in corporate and political concern. This leads us to the conclusion that *actual* — as opposed to moral — accountability has only developed slightly in the last three decades or so. Only when requirements for social and environmental disclosure enter the statute books does actual, discharged accountability change in any systematic and continuing way. In essence, the problem with 'market forces' as a determinant of CSR is that those with the power (in this case those with power over information, namely the State and organisations) have a disproportionate influence over those forces. If the accounting profession would take its 'public interest' duties more seriously it could offer some counter to these forces in the name of accountability and the public interest. We can live in hope.

Notes

1. Issues of responsibility in general and those of employers, owners and organisations in particular are major issues in the writings of Plato and Aristotle. A major feature of religious works such as the Bible and the Koran is the recognition of responsibility and the attendant accountability. Formal CSR, as we choose to understand it in this book, has a more recent history arising from the relatively recent development of modern organisations but, for example, Guthrie and Parker (1989a, b) clearly demonstrate that social reporting is much older than the three or so decades on which we shall be concentrating.
2. These were 'organisational focus' (often thought of as 'accounting entity'), 'economic events', 'financial description' and 'narrowly defined users' (Laughlin and Gray, 1988).
3. Just recall how many variants there are on conventional accounting despite this very careful restriction, its lengthy history and extensive regulation.
4. Figure 4.3 explicitly excludes the information already given to shareholders. As you are aware, the information disclosure by an organisation tends to be dominated by the, principally regulated, information provided to the owners and providers of funds in an organisation. While it is possible to trace the early motivations for this disclosure to what might be thought of as 'social' as well as economic reasons, most current discussion of conventional financial accounting tends to ignore the role and purpose of Companies Acts in favour of concentration on 'explaining' behaviour in terms of short-term self-interest gamblers in stock markets. This is one of the major reasons that CSR tends to place less emphasis on providers of financial funds (for a discussion see, for example, Cooper, 1988; Owen *et al.*, 1987).
5. Including 'quangos' — quasi-autonomous non-governmental organisations such as the Health and Safety Inspectorate in the United Kingdom or a country's Environmental Protection Agency.
6. As was the case with environmental consultants reports in the early stages of environmental debate of the late 1980s and early 1990s. In these cases, environmental consultants might help design waste-minimisation programmes, give guidance to the organisation on areas of toxic waste or contaminated land or, more proactively, help the company towards the establishment of environmental quality management or environmental audit and management systems (BS7750 in the United Kingdom, EMAS in the EU. See, for example, Gray *et al.*, 1993, for more detail).
7. It is worth mentioning at this point that the emergence of Freedom of Information Acts — initially in the United States and now elsewhere — have certainly exercised organisations which now know that outside bodies have access to some data that the organisation might prefer were kept from the public domain.
8. There are two major reasons for this. The first is that, although students of accounting need to be aware of development in political and social thought, this is a fairly recent development in accounting research and education (influenced by journals such as *Accounting, Organizations and Society, Accounting, Auditing and Accountability* and *Critical Perspectives on Accounting*) and this is not the right place to attempt to summarise this. The second reason is that it is not until business and governments explicitly recognise an issue that (a) the professional accountancy bodies are likely to respond and — although not necessarily related — (b) examples

of CSR are likely to emerge into the public domain.

9. Radical critique of business has a much longer history — at least as far back as social reformers such as the Webbs and the seminal work of Marx and Engels in the mid-19th century. However, the 'social responsibility of business' debate which Bowen is credited with originating was much less concerned with structural iniquities in society and more with recognition of the new power and ubiquity of corporations and the implications that this had for the way in which managers conducted the affairs of the organisation. For more penetrating analyses of these issues see, for example, Dickson (1974); Held (1987); Kapp (1950/1978); Neimark, 1992; Tinker (1984a, b, 1985).

10. Although in continental Europe — and most especially France — the debate often became more like open warfare. One should not forget the 1968 Paris riots which hindsight suggests came very close to bringing about the collapse of many of the institutions of capitalism in France and elsewhere.

11. For an alternative — and somewhat more penetrating — analysis of these events see, for example, Lehman (1992), Neimark (1992), Tinker (1985), Tinker *et al.* (1991).

12. If the very different cultural attitudes of (for example) African states, the Arab nations, China and Indonesia are added into the discussion it should be apparent that while international capital attempts (and often succeeds) in imposing its own culture on countries, there is a plethora of very different ways of conceiving of and articulating the complex issues arising from the social responsibilities of organisations.

13. It is worth noting that 'community' most realistically refers to the communities in which the corporation operates — especially including communities in the 'developing world' — lesser developed countries (LDCs). Despite significant steps taken by the United Nations throughout this period to offer a means whereby host countries could exercise control over multinational corporations it is not obvious that much was achieved. More especially, it is not apparent that impact on LDCs became a major issue in western consciousness until the late 1980s and early 1990s.

14. The United Kingdom, for example, saw the formation of Business-in-the-Community — a sort of business club founded by the Prince of Wales to encourage and help organisations to undertake their social responsibilities.

15. It may, of course, be that customer's information 'needs' are satisfied by other information channels such as advertising and the activities of consumer quality organisations. In modern societies in which high levels of consumption are almost a *raison d'être* the organisation's customer legitimacy may only need to be established via satisfying consumption wants, rather than by a wider range of concerns over the propriety of such consumptions and the implications of that consumption.

16. A considerable proportion of land which has been involved in industrial activity will be contaminated by the spillage, dumping and storage of toxic substances from waste oil to highly inimical chemicals. Increasing recognition that this contamination had enormous impact on natural habitats, frequently affected water tables and could so often affect human habitation and (for example) drinking water led to increasing worldwide attempts to clean up such land. The costs of doing so can be vast — thus presenting environmental and social problems as problems with very significant financial implications (for more detail see, for example, Gray *et al.*, 1993, Chapter 11; Tinker, 1985).

17. This issue of which perspective to take when constructing a social account is very important — although it may not be immediately obvious. It is a problem which has bedevilled attempts at CSR and, for an accountant, might be most easily thought of as the CSR analogue of the 'entity' versus 'proprietorship' concept in conventional financial accounting.

18. There is not the space to review these reports here but their wide-ranging analysis of the issues raised by such matters as social costs, environmental costs and the related concerns with human resource accounting demonstrated a more learned and thoughtful approach to a series of contentious accounting problems that you would be hard-pressed to find today in apparently 'authoritative' reports around this area.

19. For more detail on *The Corporate Report* see Gray *et al.* (1987, Chapter 3) and see also Chapter 6.

20. For more information on the Clarke C. Abt model and examples of the final published social accounts, see Belkaoui (1984); Epstein *et al.* (1977); Mueller and Smith (1976).

21. Naturally enough, the eventual collapse of apartheid in South Africa means that this is no longer the 'live' political issue it once was. This does not mean that such reporting is no longer necessary — simply, that CSR is once again responding to issues that arise and fall in the social and political environment.

chapter 5

Corporate social reporting practice
An international perspective

5.1 Introduction

Chapter 4 provided a broad overview of CSR and its development. We now attempt to build on this by looking in rather more detail at the international context of CSR. This has two distinct — although related — elements: the pan-national or global trends in and influences upon CSR; and specific national developments in various countries. Chapter 6 will examine CSR practice and developments in a western European context. This chapter offers a brief examination of both the global trends in CSR and the experiences of non-western European countries. These chapters are predicated on the belief that, to understand a practice (whether it be CSR or more conventional accounting) it is necessary to recognise:

> ... the specific cultural, economic, legal and political environments that helped to create and validate them and which they, in turn, helped to create and validate. (Adams and Roberts, 1994, p. 167).

In other words, accounting practices can only be understood if the context in which they develop is properly recognised (Burchell *et al.*, 1985; Hopwood, 1983, 1987; Hoskin and Macve, 1988; Laughlin, 1988; Loft, 1988; Roberts and Scapens, 1985). However, research into comparative social and environmental reporting has a much shorter history than (for example) comparative financial reporting. As a result our attempts in this area must be somewhat tentative. Nevertheless, the study of social reporting practices across different environments not only offers a rich illustration of the interdependence between accounting and the environment in which it operates (Adams and Roberts, 1994), but also aids understanding of recent and future influences on domestic social reporting practices.

Section 5.2 of this chapter examines the various supranational influences on corporate social reporting (other than those of the European Union and European Economic Area which are discussed in some detail in Chapter 6). Section 5.3 examines international survey data on corporate social reporting practices and sections 5.4, 5.5, 5.6 and 5.7 examine initiatives and developments in corporate social reporting practices in, respectively: United States and Canada; Japan; Australasia; and less developed and newly industrialised countries. The various sections are brought together in section 5.8 — the chapter's conclusion.

5.2 Supranational influences

It is unlikely that any nation or company[1] — regardless of its size — is entirely immune to external influences. It is, however, far from simple to identify those influences and any effects they may have had. Indeed, many of the most important global influences on CSR may have arisen from very broad pan-national trends such as the *relatively* recent growth of international capitalism, international business and international capital markets. For example, it may be that the growth of intrusive large organisations has imposed new cultures on nations and raised a new need for *formal* accountability as a means of assuring host nations of the legitimacy of the companies and their activities. Equally it might be that the increasing ubiquity of international capitalism has generated a new political economy in which the benign paternalism of companies had to be demonstrated — if only to reassure governments which no longer had the economic control of their countries. This is only speculation (but see, for example: Adams *et al.*, 1995a; Arnold, 1990; Gray *et al.*, 1995b; Tinker *et al.*, 1991) but it does counsel caution. That is, the greatest and subtlest influence on CSR may well be one which we have, as yet, been unable to identify.

That said, there seems little question that various initiatives from international governmental (e.g. the United Nations (UN)), international business (e.g. the International Chamber of Commerce (ICC)) and international non-governmental organisations (NGOs) (e.g. Amnesty International, Friends of the Earth, Greenpeace, Oxfam) have had a notable influence on developments in CSR over the years and across the globe. When one looks at these potential sources of influence, two things become apparent. *First,* the world is becoming an increasingly complex place. The need for international cooperation and regulation on corporate activity and reporting has never been greater; but, similarly, the difficulties of introducing such global agreement have never seemed so insuperable. *Secondly,* as we saw in Chapter 4, by the 1990s environmental issues were dominating the corporate/social agenda and, for the first time since the social responsibility debates of the 1970s, there appeared to be a will (within governments and business) to try and address the issues on a coherent basis. Consequently, much recent examination of corporate social responsibility and reporting is dominated by environmental concerns. This is illustrated by Figure 5.1, which summarises the reporting recommendations of various national and international codes of conduct.[2]

The remainder of this section examines a few of the more influential of these initiatives under the headings: *international government organisations, international business organisations* and *international non-governmental organisations.*

International governmental organisations

International governmental activity might be thought of as comprisinges two strands: meetings of national governments to make agreement between their members and supranational organisations in which a (potential) element of national sovereignty is sacrificed. Organisations such as the OECD (the Organisation for Economic Cooperation and Development) and GATT (General Agreement on Tariffs and Trade) are examples of the former while the European Union is the most obvious example of the latter (see Chapter 6). The United Nations may be thought of as falling somewhere between the two. Sadly, but unsurprisingly, while concern over the behaviour of multinational corporations (MNCs) has been a regular theme in the deliberations of these and similar bodies since the Second World War, their level of success and their attention to reporting and disclosure as such has been disappointing. Governments — especially in the so-called 'developed' countries — have generally appeared to be more concerned with establishing conditions for *increased* economic activity in the interests of the companies themselves rather than with control of the social and environmental behaviour of these entities. So while the UN has regularly attempted to encourage codes of practice (on such matters as conditions of employment, relationships with host-countries and the physical environment — see below) it has had no noticeable impact on CSR practice. The other supranational organisations, such as the World Bank, GATT and the International Monetary Fund have, if anything, encouraged the myths of 'free trade' and thus had a *negative* effect on CSR. There are some minor exceptions to this. Some of these we review below when we look at the lesser developed countries (LDCs) and the newly industrialised countries (NICs). The major exception, however, relates to corporate activity on the natural environment.

The United Nations has a long, and moderately successful, history of attention to the natural environment. Since the 1972 Stockholm Conference on the Human Environment,[3] when environmental issues were first brought to the centre of the world political stage, through to the influential Brundtland Report (UNWCED, 1987) and the 1992 Rio de Janiero Earth Summit, the United Nations has consistently attempted to encourage countries and MNCs to give serious attention to environmental regulation and disclosure. Of some importance here is the realisation that 'environmental' issues must, by definition, embrace other aspects of the human condition such as poverty, population, communities and so on and, equally, consideration of environmental issues raises broader ethical questions about corporate behaviour.

The principal sections of the UN concerned with issues raised by CSR are the United Nations Centre on Transnational Corporations (UNCTC)[4] and the United Nations Environment Programme (UNEP).[5] UNCTC has created a steady stream of research reports and disclosure proposals which have maintained a constant (but generally resisted) pressure on national governments and MNCs to improve their environmental (and environmentally related social) disclosures (for more detail, see, for example, Gray, 1990a; Gray *et al.*, 1993; UNCTC, 1984). If the UNCTC's attempts had been successful many of our present concerns with CSR and accountability would be redundant. UNEP, by contrast, has attempted to cajole MNCs into environmental (and related) disclosure. *Agenda 21* (the action programme adopted by governments at the 1992 Earth Summit) specifically called for business and industry to report annually on their environmental performance and on the implementation of codes of conduct promoting best environmental practice. UNEP's Technical Report No. 24, *Company Environmental Reporting* (UNEP IE, 1994) was partly a response to this and provides a proactive guide for companies. It addresses the question 'Why Report?' under three headings: responsibility, accountability and sustainability.

Figure 5.1 *Reporting ingredients and industry codes of conduct. Note that numbers refer to relevant principles in the codes of conduct and headings refer to the Coalition for Environmentally Responsible Economies (CERES), a US-based NGO, the ICC, the Japanese Keidanren's Global Environmental Charter, the WTTC and the International Iron and Steel Institute (ISSI). From UNEP IE, 1994*

REPORTING INGREDIENTS AND INDUSTRY CODES OF CONDUCT					
INGREDIENTS	CERES (1990)	ICC (1991)	K'ren (1991)	WTTC (1992)	IISI (1992)
I. MANAGEMENT & SYSTEM					
1 CEO Statement	✓ 9	✓ 1			
2 Environmental Policy		✓ 1	✓ 1	✓ 12	✓ 3
3 Environmental Management System		✓ 2&3	✓ 2	✓ 12	✓ 2&4
4 Management Responsibility	✓ 9	✓ 2	✓ 3	✓	
5 Environmental Auditing	✓ 10	✓ 16		✓	
6 Goals and Targets				✓	
7 Legal Compliance		✓ 16	✓ 3	✓	
8 Research and Development		✓ 9	✓ 4		✓ 5&9
9 Programmes and Initiatives		✓ 1&2			
10 Awards					
11 Verification					
12 Reporting Policy	✓ 10	✓ 16			
13 Corporate Context					
II. INPUT/OUTPUT INVENTORY					
Inputs	✓ 2	✓ 6&8	✓ 3		✓ 5&6
14 Material use	✓ 2				
15 Energy consumption	✓ 4	✓ 8		✓ 4	✓ 7
16 Water consumption	✓ 1			✓ 6	
Process Management	✓ 5	✓ 8		✓ 2	
17 Health & Safety	✓ 5				
18 EIAs & Risk Management	✓ 5	✓ 5		✓ 1	
19 Accidents & Emergency Response	✓ 5	✓ 12	✓ 6		
20 Land Contamination & Remediation	✓ 7	✓ 5			
21 Habitats	✓ 1	✓ 5&8		✓ 3	
Outputs	✓ 3	✓ 8,16	✓ 6		
22 Wastes	✓ 3			✓ 5	
23 Air Emissions				✓ 6	
24 Water Effluents				✓ 7	

Figure 5.1 *continued*

REPORTING INGREDIENTS AND INDUSTRY CODES OF CONDUCT					
INGREDIENTS	**CERES** (1990)	**ICC** (1991)	**K'ren** (1991)	**WTTC** (1992)	**IISI** (1992)
25 Noise and Odours				✓ 8	
26 Transportation					
Products	✓ 6	✓ 6&7	✓ 6	✓ 9	✓ 5
27 Life Cycle Design					
28 Packaging					
29 Product Impacts	✓ 6	✓ 6			
30 Product Stewardship	✓ 6	✓ 6			
III. FINANCE					
31 Environmental Spending					
32 Liabilities					
33 Economic Instruments					
34 Environmental Cost Accounting					
35 Benefits and Opportunities					
36 Charitable Contributions					
IV. STAKEHOLDER RELATIONS	✓ 8	✓ 14&15	✓ 7&8		✓ 8
37 Employees		✓ 4	✓ 7		
38 Legislators & Regulators		✓ 14	✓ 10		✓ 10
39 Local communities		✓ 15	✓ 8		✓ 8
40 Investors					
41 Suppliers		✓ 11	✓ 3		
42 Consumers	✓ 6	✓ 7	✓ 7		
43 Industry Associations		✓ 14 ·			
44 Environment Groups					
45 Science & Education ·					
46 Media					
V. SUSTAINABLE DEVELOPMENT		✓ 3			✓ 1
47 Global Environment	✓ 1		✓ 11		
48 Global Development			✓ 11	✓ 10&11	
49 Technology Cooperation		✓ 13	✓ 5		✓ 9
50 Global Standards		✓ 3.	✓ 9		

Figure 5.2 *The changing role of industry associations. From UNEP IE, 1994*

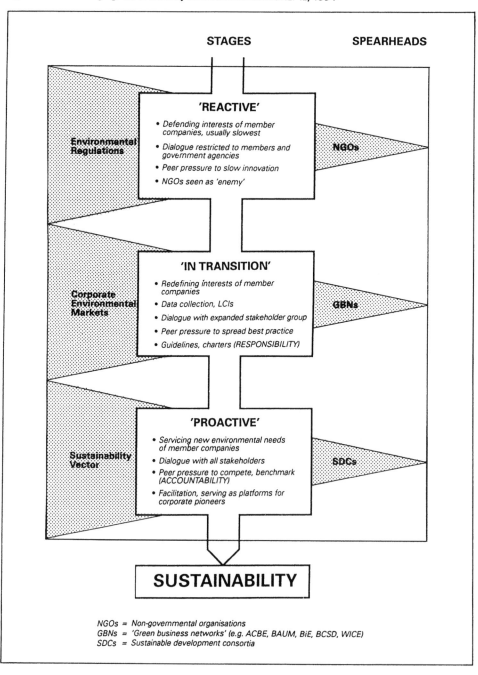

STAGES   SPEARHEADS

Environmental Regulations

'REACTIVE'
- *Defending interests of member companies, usually slowest*
- *Dialogue restricted to members and government agencies*
- *Peer pressure to slow innovation*
- *NGOs seen as 'enemy'*

NGOs

Corporate Environmental Markets

'IN TRANSITION'
- *Redefining interests of member companies*
- *Data collection, LCIs*
- *Dialogue with expanded stakeholder group*
- *Peer pressure to spread best practice*
- *Guidelines, charters (RESPONSIBILITY)*

GBNs

Sustainability Vector

'PROACTIVE'
- *Servicing new environmental needs of member companies*
- *Dialogue with all stakeholders*
- *Peer pressure to compete, benchmark (ACCOUNTABILITY)*
- *Facilitation, serving as platforms for corporate pioneers*

SDCs

SUSTAINABILITY

NGOs = Non-governmental organisations
GBNs = 'Green business networks' (e.g. ACBE, BAUM, BiE, BCSD, WICE)
SDCs = Sustainable development consortia

Figure 5.2 (reproduced from the report) illustrates the UNEP view as to how the social (but especially environmental) responsibility agenda has changed over time as a result of different influences. The agenda was first set in the 1970s by non-governmental organisations (NGOs). Industry associations were initially dismissive and then defensive. They moved to a more proactive role in the late 1980s eventually encompassing environmental accountability in the early 1990s. The UNEP diagram suggests that this evolutionary process is likely to continue moving towards a *sustainability* agenda (see particularly Chapters 3 and 10) in the late 1990s. The report goes on to identify five stages in corporate environmental performance (see Figure 5.3). These are used by UNEP to assess the degree of accountability of 100 pioneering corporate reporters (see section 5.3) and also serve as a template for the more innovative business seeking to undertake environmental reporting.

All in all, however, pan-national attempts to develop CSR have been desultory, scarce and fairly ineffectual. The power of the MNCs in influencing governments and, thereby, international governmental organisations has successfully prevented the development of any real international accountability. Despite the more recent (but still modest) advances achieved in environmental disclosure, there are few reasons to be optimistic about likelihood of significant developments in international regulation of CSR in the near future.

If, then, international business is largely responsible for preventing governmental developments in the field, what, if anything, are they doing themselves?

Figure 5.3 *Stages in corporate environmental reporting. From UNEP IE, 1994*

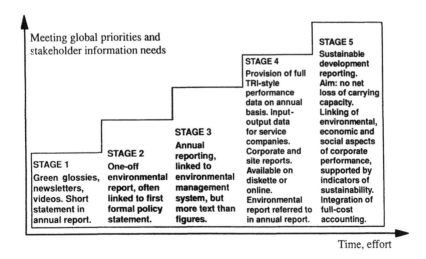

Time, effort

International business organisations

International business organisations — and, indeed, international business itself — has a long and desultory relationship with international self-regulation of social and environmental behaviour. As the power of international business has grown the range of its social and environmental impacts has similarly risen. However, ironically, that very growth in power has reduced the ability (and the willingness) of governments to attempt to control them and has reduced the need of business to legitimate its profit-seeking behaviours (see, for example, Bailey *et al.*, 1994a, b). Only in the more recent upsurge of environmental awareness has anything that might begin to look like real progress towards any form of social accountability been made.

This is not to say that international business has ignored entirely the wider social issues. The majority of large companies in the developed world have developed some sort of explicit statement of social responsibilities and/or ethics (Brooks, 1986; Maxwell and Mason, 1976). These statements serve three principal functions: they provide an expression of values to which the senior management of the organisation would wish to aspire; they help to legitimate the imbalance between the organisation's power and legal responsibility; and they provide a yardstick against which the organisation's performance can be judged — whether by employees, governments or NGOs. So there *has* been a history of voluntary attempts to self-regulate international business behaviour but, as with most voluntary approaches to self-regulation, it has more to do with form than substance. We return to this in later sections of this chapter.

As mentioned above, it is in the area of environmental reporting initiatives that international business organisations have made the most progress. These initiatives have been undertaken by a wide variety of business organisations and they come in a wide variety of formats. However, in general terms the initiatives can be thought of as combinations of (a) voluntary guidelines on issues such as environmental management and environmental reporting; and (b) encouragement, guidance and support on how to achieve those guidelines. The Chemical Industry Association's Responsible Care Programme is a good example of an industry-based code. It is explained in the extract from the Swiss company Ciba's 1992 corporate annual report in Figure 5.4.

A more widely targeted approach was that from the (modestly entitled) World Industry Council for the Environment (WICE). WICE was initiated in 1993 by the International Chamber of Commerce (ICC). Its membership comes from a wide diversity of industry sectors from countries inside and outside the OECD. WICE developed an Environmental Reporting Matrix (see Figure 5.5) which was intended to prompt companies to consider possible reporting items and audiences for them. The notion of accountability seems to have been missed. Indeed, the language used by WICE suggests that their efforts to improve reporting may be primarily motivated by corporations' desires to improve profitability, legitimate their actions and, perhaps, to avoid further mandatory reporting requirements. For example, the introduction to their 1994 publication *Environmental Reporting: A manager's guide* states: 'It is important to emphasize that it is up to individual enterprises to determine which of these suggestions are in *their best interests*' [emphasis

Figure 5.4 Extract from CIBA 1992 Report re Responsible Care

Ciba group companies are signatories to the the 'Responsible Care' programme developed by the chemical industry, and the company as a whole has declared its support for the International Chamber of Commerce's Business Charter for Sustainable Development. These initiatives are in line with our Vision 2000, our endeavours to achieve sustainable development and our open communications policy. For us, they have implications for all processes and products with respect to their research, development and manufacturing, sales and marketing, use by customers and final disposal.

Responsible Care

Responsible Care is a programme developed by the chemical industry for the chemical industry. It provides principles and guidance on being a 'responsible' industry with respect to employees, neighbours, the environment and other industries. The programme has been adopted by chemical industry associations around the world, each country adapting it to fit its culture, conditions, needs and priorities. While the actual programme varies from country to country, all programmes include certain basic features:

1. Guiding principles to which each company commits itself through the signature of the Chief Executive Officer.

2. Codes, guidance notes, and checklists to assist companies in implementing the commitment, as well as a variety of programmes for encouraging participation and communication between companies.

3. Indicators used to measure improvements in performance.

4. Communication with all interested parties on aspects of health, safety and environment. This includes activities such as community awareness programmes,

emergency response plans, and data about products and processes.

5. Ensuring worker safety by providing training and information appropriate for all levels of employee activities.

6. Stressing safety and protection of people and the environment as a major concern of the chemical industry.

As of April 1993, Ciba Group Companies in the following countries had become signatories to their local Responsible Care programme: Argentina, Australia, Brazil, Canada, Hong Kong, France, Germany, Italy, Japan, Mexico, Netherlands, New Zealand, Spain, Switzerland, United Kingdom, and the United States.

International Chamber of Commerce's Business Charter for Sustainable Development

The Charter consists of 16 principles which help to ensure that a business can operate in a 'sustainable', environmentally responsible manner. The principles cover virtually every aspect of a business's operations: establishing and integrating environmental management as among the highest corporate priorities; continuous improvement in all areas of environmental concerns; employee education; assessment and notification, before starting any activity; environmentally acceptable products and services, using a 'cradle-to-grave' approach; appropriate development, design, and operation of facilities; research; provision of customer advice; contractors and suppliers; emergency preparedness; technology transfer; contributing to public and private policies and programmes, as well as education; openness to concerns of all interested parties; and compliance and reporting.

5

Figure 5.5 *World Industry Council for the Environment (WICE) environmental reporting matrix. From WICE, 1994*

ENVIRONMENTAL REPORTING MATRIX

KEY AUDIENCES / CONTENTS	CUSTOMERS/ CONSUMERS	EMPLOYEES	ENVIRONMENTAL AND CONSUMER INTEREST GROUPS (NGOs)	FINANCIAL INSTITUTIONS AND SHAREHOLDERS	LOCAL COMMUNITIES	PRESS AND MEDIA	REGULATORS AND ENFORCEMENT AGENCIES, GOVT DEPTS. AND POLITICIANS	SCIENTISTS, ACADEMICS AND EDUCATIONAL INSTITUTIONS	SUPPLIERS, CONTRACTORS, JOINT VENTURE PARTNERS AND DEALERS	TRADE, INDUSTRY AND COMMERCE ASSOCIATIONS
QUALITATIVE										
FOREWORD										
PROFILE OF ENTERPRISE										
ENVIRONMENTAL POLICY										
ENVIRONMENTAL TARGETS AND OBJECTIVES										
VIEWS ON ENVIRONMENTAL ISSUES										
COMMUNITY RELATIONS										
MANAGEMENT										
ENVIRONMENTAL MANAGEMENT SYSTEMS										
MANAGEMENT OF ENVIRONMENTAL RISKS										
OFFICE AND SITE PRACTICES										
QUANTITATIVE										
ENVIRONMENTAL INDICATORS AND TARGETS : EMISSIONS, EFFLUENTS, ENERGY CONSUMPTION, TRANSPORTATION AND WASTE MINIMISATION										
USE OF ENERGY AND NATURAL RESOURCES										
COMPLIANCE WITH REGULATIONS AND PERMITS										
FINANCIAL INDICATORS										
PRODUCTS										
PRODUCTS, PROCESSES AND SERVICES										
GIVING MORE INFORMATION										

15

Figure 5.6 *The ICC* Business Charter for Sustainable Development

APPENDIX 2: THE ICC BUSINESS CHARTER FOR SUSTAINABLE DEVELOPMENT

PRINCIPLES FOR ENVIRONMENTAL MANAGEMENT

FOREWORD

There is widespread recognition today that environmental protection must be among the highest priorities of every business.

In its milestone 1987 report, 'Our Common Future', the World Commission on Environment and Development (Brundtland Commission), emphasized the importance of environmental protection in the pursuit of sustainable development.

To help business around the world improve its environmental performance, the International Chamber of Commerce established a task force of business representatives to create this Business Charter for Sustainable Development. It comprises sixteen principles for environmental management which, for business, is a vitally important aspect of sustainable development.

This Charter will assist enterprises in fulfilling their commitment to environmental stewardship in a comprehensive fashion. It was formally launched in April 1991 at the Second World Industry Conference on Environmental Management.

INTRODUCTION

Sustainable development involves meeting the needs of the present without compromising the ability of future generations to meet their own needs.

Economic growth provides the conditions in which protection of the environment can best be achieved, and environmental protection, in balance with other human goals, is necessary to achieve growth that is sustainable.

In turn, versatile, dynamic, responsive and profitable businesses are required as the driving force for sustainable economic development and for providing managerial, technical and financial resources to contribute to the resolution of environmental challenges. Market economies, characterised by entrepreneurial initiatives, are essential to achieving this.

Business thus shares the view that there should be a common goal, not a conflict, between economic development and environmental protection, both now and for future generations.

Making market forces work in this way to protect and improve the quality of the environment — with the help of performance-based standards and judicious use of economic instruments in a harmonious regulatory framework — is one of the greatest challenges that the world faces in the next decade

The 1987 report of the World Commission on Environment and Development, "Our Common Future", expresses the same challenge and calls on the cooperation of business in tackling it. To this end, business leaders have launched actions in their individual enterprises as well as through sectoral and cross-sectoral associations.

In order that more businesses join this effort and that their environmental performance continues to improve, the International Chamber of Commerce hereby calls upon enterprises and their associations to use the following Principles as a basis for pursuing such improvement and to express publicly their support for them.

Individual programmes developed to implement these Principles will reflect the wide diversity among enterprises in size and function.

The objective is that the widest range of enterprises commit themselves to improving their environmental performance in accordance with these Principles, to having in place management practices to effect such improvement, to measuring their progress, and to reporting this progress as appropriate internally and externally.

Figure 5.6 *continued*

PRINCIPLES

1. Corporate Priority

To recognise environmental management as among the highest corporate priorities and as a key determinant to sustainable development; to establish policies, programmes and practices for conducting operations in an environmentally sound manner.

2. Integrated Management

To integrate these policies, programmes and practices fully into each business as an essential element of management in all its functions.

3. Process of Improvement

To continue to improve corporate policies, programmes and environmental performance, taking into account technical developments, scientific understanding, consumer needs and community expectations, with legal regulations as a starting point; and to apply the same environmental criteria internationally.

4. Employee Education

To educate, train and motivate employees to conduct their activities in an environmentally responsible manner.

5. Prior Assessment

To assess environmental impacts before starting a new activity or project and before decommissioning a facility or leaving a site.

6. Products and Services

To develop and provide products or services that have no undue environmental impact and are safe in their intended use, that are efficient in their consumption of energy and natural resources, and that can be recycled, reused, or disposed of safely.

7. Customer Advice

To advise, and where relevant educate, customers, distributors and the public in the safe use, transportation, storage and disposal of products provided; and to apply similar considerations to the provision of services.

8. Facilities and Operations

To develop, design and operate facilities and conduct activities taking into consideration the efficient use of energy and materials, the sustainable use of renewable resources, the minimisation of adverse environmental impact and waste generation, and the safe and responsible disposal of residual wastes.

9. Research

To conduct or support research on the environmental impacts of raw materials, products, processes, emissions and wastes associated with the enterprise and on the means of minimizing such adverse impacts.

10. Precautionary Approach

To modify the manufacture, marketing or use of products or services or the conduct of activities, consistent with scientific and technical understanding, to prevent serious or irreversible environmental degradation.

Figure 5.6 *continued*

11. Contractors and Suppliers

To promote the adoption of these principles by contractors acting on behalf of the enterprise, encouraging and, where appropriate, requiring improvements in their practices to make them consistent with those of the enterprise; and to encourage the wider adoption of these principles by suppliers.

12. Emergency Preparedness

To develop and maintain, where significant hazards exist, emergency preparedness plans in conjunction with the emergency services, relevant authorities and the local community, recognizing potential transboundary impacts.

13. Transfer of Technology

To contribute to the transfer of environmentally sound technology and management methods throughout the industrial and public sectors.

14. Contributing to the Comon Effort

To contribute to the development of public policy and to business, governmental and intergovernmental programmes and educational initiatives that will enhance environmental awareness and protection.

15. Openness to Concerns

To foster openness and dialogue with employees and the public, anticipating and responding to their concerns about the potential hazards and impacts of operations,products, wastes or services, including those of transboundary or global significance.

16. Compliance and Reporting

To measure environmental performance; to conduct regular environmental audits and assessments of compliance with company requirements, legal requirements and these principles; and periodically to provide appropriate information to the Board of Directors, shareholders, employees, the authorities and the public.

Note: The term environment as used in this document also refers to environmentally related aspects of health, safety and product stewardship.

Figure 5.7 *The PERI guidelines on environmental reporting*

- **Company profile** so that the environmental data can be interpreted in context.
- **Environmental policy**
- **Environmental management** including a description of the environmental management structure and the level of organisational accountability for environmental policies.
- **Environmental releases** including **quantification** of emissions, effluent and wastes based on the **global activity** of the organisation. The inclusion of quantified data for the global activity of the organisation improves the accountability of many organisations which have tended to simply provide qualitative data concerning only some of the organisations' activities.
- **Resource conservation** efforts and activities including quantification of the reductions achieved in energy conservation and the consequent reduction in emissions.
- **Environmental risk management** including descriptions of environmental audit programmes, remediation programmes and environmental emergency response programmes.
- **Environmental compliance** with laws and regulations including information on significant fines or penalties incurred, the nature of non-compliance issues, the scope and magnitude of any environmental impact and the programmes implemented to correct or alleviate the situation.
- **Product stewardship** including descriptions of policies and programmes to support the organisation's commitment to reducing the environmental impact of its processes, products and/or services.
- **Employee recognition** such as information on education and reward programmes that encourage environmental excellence.
- **Stakeholder involvement** to include descriptions of the involvement of stakeholders such as research or academic organisations, policy groups, non-governmental organisations and/or industry associations on environmental issues.

added]. Indeed, in answering the question 'Why Report?' WICE lists reasons under the headings 'Business Benefit', 'Improved Performance' and 'Enhanced Reputation'.

Given WICE's relationship with ICC, it comes as no suprise to find considerable similarity between the WICE approach and that contained in the ICC's *Business Charter for Sustainable Development* launched in 1991 (Figure 5.6, p. 137). It is perhaps some consolation that the latter does at least recognise the importance of sustainable development and acknowledges the influence of the Brundtland Commission (UNWCED, 1987) in the development of its own Charter. WICE merged with the Business Council for Sustainable Development in 1995 to form the World Business Council for Sustainable Development.

A somewhat different initiative is that of the Public Environmental Reporting Initiative (PERI). PERI was formed in 1993 by nine North American multinational corporations[6] with the aim both to encourage environmental reporting and to develop a comprehensive and credible framework for environmental reporting. The PERI guidelines for reporting, published in 1994, were intended to allow maximum flexibility so that they could be applied by organisations of differing sizes operating in different industries and geographic areas. They are summarised in Figure 5.7.

Thus, with their call for information on the level of organisational accountability for environmental polices, the **quantification** of information for **global** activities, descriptions of environmental audit, remediation and emergency response programmes, descriptions of employee-related initiatives and stakeholder involvement and detailed environmental compliance legislation, the PERI guidelines go further than those of WICE. In particular they encourage companies to demonstrate accountability to other organisational stakeholders. They also recognise the importance of reporting on employee education and reward schemes as well as other environmental issues — not only for internal management purposes. Only time will tell how successful this voluntary initiative will be in genuinely developing accountability.

International non-governmental organisations

The theories that governments and companies respond to large changes in public opinion in order to maintain, among other things, their own legitimacy (see Chapter 2), suggest that the role of NGOs in the development of CSR may be very important.

NGO is a blanket term that covers a vast array of charities, protest groups, research institutes and so on, which are (directly) influenced by neither government nor business. They are manifestations of independent concerns. Groups such as Amnesty International, Friends of the Earth, Greenpeace and Oxfam have all played major roles on the international stage in raising awareness and touching the consciences of citizens and companies alike. The direct impact of these international NGOs is difficult to quantify. Circumstantial evidence suggests, however, that while some of these groups, typically Amnesty and the famine and child-relief agencies, have had impacts on corporate behaviour in areas such as dealing with repressive regimes and the more insensitive involvements with areas of poverty and deprivation, they have had little impact on social disclosure. There is suspicion that some issues (e.g. starvation, depravation, exploitation) are still too emotionally loaded for companies to deal with them within the public relations-orientated Annual Report. Not so the environmental movements, however. There is considerable circumstantial evidence (see, for example, Gray *et al.*, 1995a, b) that suggests that many major environmental reporting initiatives have arisen directly as a response to environmental NGO activity.

This said, however, it may well be that the real impact of the NGOs it at the national, rather than international, level. Thus, as we shall see, some national NGOs — most typically the Coalition for Environmentally Responsible Economies (CERES) and the Council on Economic Priorities (CEP) which are discussed later in this chapter — have had clear influence on corporate disclosure practices. The activities of the NGOs are increasingly important, not least because more of the NGOs are, themselves, either international in scope or are liaising with NGOs in other countries to seek to build up international pressure on governments and business. One area of particular NGO importance lies in the increasing use of external social audits — an important matter to which we return in Chapter 9.

5.3 International survey data on CSR practices

Chapter 4 provided a broad-brush overview of some of the strands in the history of CSR. From a variety of (mainly national) sources we could see that CSR varied over time; varied between countries; and tended to be related to both company size and industry. Detailed international comparative surveys of CSR have tended to be few and far between but have, nevertheless, tended to confirm these broad trends. We can put a little more flesh onto these bones before turning to look at the CSR practices of specific countries for the remainder of this chapter.

In general, international surveys of CSR have tended to concentrate on the (so-called) developed countries: United States, Canada, United Kingdom and Europe (see also Chapter 6), Australia, New Zealand and, latterly, Japan. This tendency arises, in part, from the national location and orientation of the researchers themselves. In part it arises, also, from the apparently greater importance given to CSR by the companies of these nations where external reporting is more widely practised and developed; the companies tend, on the whole, to be larger; and the complexity and ubiquity of the corporate systems require greater *formal* channels of accountability. Furthermore, there is some evidence to suggest that a company domiciled in a more developed nation is likely to report more extensively in the developed nations than it is to report in the lesser developed countries in which it operates (see, for example, United Nations, 1992). While companies in most developed nations place greatest emphasis on disclosure about human resources (see, for example, Guthrie and Parker, 1990; Roberts, 1990), countries vary in the types of human resource disclosures they give and their relative emphasis on other areas of CSR (see, for example, Preston *et al.*, 1978). Indeed, Roberts (1990) concludes that European, South African and, to a lesser extent, Australasian companies are more likely than companies in other parts of the world to disclose employment policies, health and safety information, or have separate sections on employment data or value-added. By way of contrast, the earlier study by Guthrie and Parker (1990) finds that American companies were more likely, in the early 1980s, to disclose information about products, energy usage and the environment than either UK or Australian companies. Perhaps the most striking finding is that the United States, which tended to lead the social disclosure revolution in the early 1970s, was being caught up by European countries by the early 1980s (see, for example, Guthrie and Parker, 1990) and overhauled by the late 1980s (Roberts, 1990).

A far more systematic picture emerges when we turn to international comparisons on environmental disclosures. Much of the credit for this goes to the United Nations which commissioned several studies on environmental reporting (see, for example, United Nations, 1991, 1992, 1994a, b, 1995). Indeed, the state of global environmental reporting in the early 1990s by industry is clearly shown in Table 5.1 reproduced from United Nations (1994a). It shows the results of the content analysis of 203 corporate annual reports with years ending in 1992 or 1993. The companies in the sample are all from *Fortune* magazine's 'Global 500' listing and represented a variety of industries. While 97 per cent of the sample reported some environmental information, it is clear from Table 5.1 that there are some very large industry differences — particularly with regard to the disclosure of capital investment activities and environmental policy statements.

Table 5.1 Environmental disclosures: overview of disclosures. From United Nations, 1994a

	All Corporations (203)		Chemicals (38)		Forestry (17)		Industrial Equipment (25)		Metals (40)		Motors (36)		Petroleum (19)		Pharmaceuticals (28)	
	No.	%	No.	%	No.	%	No.	%	No.	%	No.	%	No.	%	No.	%
Policies & views on environmental demands	121	60	35	92	11	65	10	40	20	50	16	44	14	74	15	54
Major environmental issues & programs	54	27	12	32	6	35	5	20	10	25	5	14	7	37	9	32
Targets, standards & output measures	92	45	21	55	10	59	7	28	20	50	10	28	12	63	12	43
Legal proceedings	50	25	14	37	3	18	5	20	3	8	6	17	8	42	11	39
Financial expenditures	57	28	19	50	5	29	3	12	14	35	2	6	7	37	7	25
Products & services	119	59	25	66	11	65	17	68	24	60	25	56	11	58	11	39
R & D activities	98	48	24	63	4	24	12	48	20	50	17	47	12	63	9	32
Capital investment activities	63	31	14	37	8	47	3	12	15	38	3	8	14	74	6	21
Operating & production activities	57	28	12	32	9	53	4	16	10	25	8	22	8	42	6	21
Remediation activities	29	14	4	11	3	18	4	16	6	15	4	11	7	37	1	4
Information in sales	54	27	13	34	2	12	5	20	7	18	7	19	11	58	9	32
Other information	57	28	18	47	10	59	3	12	7	18	7	19	6	32	6	11
Number of companies which disclosed some environmental information	196	97	38	100	16	94	24	96	38	95	33	92	19	100	28	100

Note: Figures in parenthesis below the column headings indicate total number of corporations responding to survey.

In a usefully complementary study, UNEP IE (1994) examined the *quality* of environmental reporting by 100 'pioneer' companies. Using their '5 stage reporting model' (see Figure 5.3), UNEP found that 39 per cent of these companies were still only at stages 1 and 2 while 25 per cent were at stage 3, with a further 11 per cent making the transition to stage 4. Only 5 per cent were actually at stage 4. No companies had reached stage 5 (see also Bebbington and Gray, 1995a). The report also notes that while more than 100 MNCs had issued separate environmental reports by the end of 1993, there were still more than 35 000 transnational companies that had not done so (although a significant minority included environmental information in their annual report). The message from this is a very clear signal about the very low level of environmental accountability — particularly with respect to sustainability — even among leading MNCs.

5.4 Corporate social reporting in the United States and Canada

Despite important differences between the United States and Canada, the close geographical and political ties have brought Canadian practice on CSR closer to the US pattern (at least as far as external reporting is concerned), thus weakening the historical UK and other Commonwealth influences (Maxwell and Mason, 1976, but see also Burke, 1980). The main historic difference between the two countries (with respect to CSR) is that the status of employees and their working environment has been given more emphasis in Canada than in the United States. The United States has historically given little consideration to these issues except in so far as they relate to race and sex equal opportunities (Preston *et al.*, 1978). Instead, US CSR practice has tended to be directed towards the interests of the general public and consumers and thus contrasts with the European and Canadian practice. In part this may be explained in terms of differing social concerns — consumerism, equal rights and the ecological movement in the United States have historically been high profile issues whereas, in Europe, the trade union movement has had the bigger historical impact.

Chapter 4 has already provided a broad overview of the historical development of CSR and we saw there the early dominance of the United States in the development of social disclosure. Indeed, more is probably known about US social disclosure practices during the 1970s than about any other country or time period (see, for example, Belkaoui, 1980; Belkaoui and Karpik, 1989; Chan, 1979; Cowen *et al.*, 1987; Estes, 1976; Freedman and Jaggi, 1988; Johnson, 1979; Nikolai *et al.*, 1976). In large part, this was due to the unique monitoring of US social disclosure by the accounting firm Ernst and Ernst (see, for example, Ernst and Ernst, 1978). This provided a database of broadly defined social disclosures by large US companies throughout the 1970s which has been widely used to identify and investigate patterns of CSR and changes therein. It is from this database that most of the dominating inferences about patterns of CSR (for example, its association with the larger companies, the influence of industry sector and the waxing and waning of issues of voluntary disclosure) are drawn. Despite this work, as we have already remarked, many of these inferences remain tentative because (a) the patterns rarely proved to be especially clear cut and (b) much has changed in the last two decades or so (see, for example, Ullmann, 1985).

Canadian research has tended to be less systematic (as a result of the lack of an equivalent to the Ernst and Ernst database) and, thus, detailed comparisons between Canadian and US CSR are difficult. Subject to the differences we highlighted above, it seems probable that Canadian CSR in the 1970s developed along the same broad — but tentative — lines we see in the United States (see, for example, Preston *et al.*, 1978; Maxwell and Mason, 1976). During the 1980s, however, there is some evidence that Canadian CSR began to develop in more creative and innovative ways that appear to reflect both a slightly less pressing concern with litigation over disclosure and an increasing reflection of a changing Canadian social hegemony (see, for example, Brooks, 1986; Zeghal and Ahmed, 1990 and see also Roberts, 1990); but these are tentative inferences on which more research is needed.

As we shall see below, the predominant emphasis in voluntary North American CSR in the 1990s has been environmental disclosure — in line with trends in the rest of the world. Research interest in CSR in the early to mid-1990s tended, equally, to move away from a concern with ethical, community and employee issues. As a result, the 1992 survey by Rivera and Ruesschoff, in focusing on the wider social disclosures by US companies, is both unusual and valuable.

Rivera and Ruesschoff (1992) examined ethical issues as disclosed in corporate annual reports of about 4000 US companies for the two accounting periods ending between July 1986 and June 1988. A search was made for the disclosure of ethics codes and policies and for the presence of key items such as 'illegal or unauthorised' acts, 'violations', 'conflicts of interest', 'discrimination', 'environmental' pollution, 'false information' and 'corrupt' practices. The authors found that, of the total sample, only 2.9 per cent and 3.7 per cent in the first and second years of the study, respectively, made any ethical statement disclosures in the management reports in the corporate annual reports despite the fact that most companies do have codes of conduct or ethics. The 'ethical statement disclosures' included any reference to a code of ethics, ethics policies or statements and any mention of, or comments on, ethical standards. In addition, the authors found that 3.6 per cent and 3.1 per cent of the total sample in the first and second years, respectively, made reference to ethical issues in the footnotes to the corporate annual reports. The majority of these were reporting violations of an ethical nature, for example with respect to securities regulations, racketeering-influenced acts, fair trade and business practices, environmental protection, personnel and employees and illegal acts of employees. The authors also found that the nature of ethical disclosures is related to the industry sector. A good example of reporting of violations which goes further than the legal minimum can be found in Figure 5.8.

Some North American companies continue to lead the way in the reporting of ethically responsible behaviour. The extract from Ben and Jerry's 1993 Annual Report shown in Figure 4.2c, for example, highlights that company's relatively radical equal opportunities policies. In a similar vein the extract from Timberland's 1993 corporate Annual Report in Figure 5.9 shows its famous advertisement used to combat racism. There was, by the mid-1990s, further evidence that the developing environmental agenda (see below) was creating a new climate in which wider social responsibility and reporting could be brought back onto the business agenda. For example, Businesses for

Figure 5.8 *Extract from Noranda Minerals Inc. 1991 Environmental Report, p. 7 and col. 1 of p. 8*

SPILLS

Although the mining industry has measures in place to prevent spills, incidents do occur. Spills can happen because of transportation accidents, operational errors and failures in pipelines that transport tailings and water to holding ponds.

Compliance

Noranda Minerals' operations are subject to federal, provincial and municipal regulations in Canada, depending on where they are located, and state agencies in the U.S. All spills have been reported in compliance with applicable laws and regulations.

Thirteen significant spills occurred at Noranda Minerals' operations in 1991.

- At the Heath Steele mine near Newcastle, New Brunswick a significant amount of untreated acidic mine water containing elevated levels of metal leaked from a broken, snow covered pipeline. The water entered a nearby river. A study involving Heath Steele, New Brunswick's Ministry of Environment and the Federal Department of Fisheries and Oceans is underway to evaluate the impact on fish and habitat, and possible mitigation.

- At our Bell copper mine near Granisle, B.C. water from the tailings pond leaked into Babine Lake through the dam. Biological tests confirmed that the water did not have an environmental impact. Repairs to the dam were completed.

- A seepage collection pond at our closed copper mine in Granisle, B.C. overflowed due to a frozen pipeline. The pipeline has since been insulated and covered with additional soil.

- At our closed copper-molybdenum mine near Peachland, B.C. water containing low concentrations of molybdenum from melting snow was pumped into a creek over several hours. Pumping was discontinued and the water was diverted to the tailings pond.

- Five incidents occurred at our copper refinery in Montreal-East in 1991. Three resulted in the discharge of a total of 425 kilograms of metal into the municipal sewer. In response, tank level alarms were relocated to the water treatment control panel, process treatment procedures were changed and operator retraining was carried out.

  Two atmospheric releases caused paint damage to neighbouring homes, cars and vegetable gardens. One involved the release of dilute selenious acid and the second, droplets of sulphuric acid. A team of four employees and specialists from two consulting firms has recommended new equipment, operating and maintenance procedures and instrumentation. Modifications costing more than $1 million have been approved and further expenditures are expected.

- Two incidents occurred at our zinc refinery in Valleyfield, Quebec. In the first, 120 cubic metres of solution containing sulphuric acid and zinc were released accidentally due to an operating error. New spill prevention procedures have been implemented.

- In the second, 600 cubic metres of residue containing zinc and copper leaked from a broken pipeline. Immediate clean-up action was taken and the recoverable material was removed for safe storage. The refinery has initiated daily inspections of the pipeline, and flow monitoring equipment will be installed during 1992.

- A break in a tailings pipeline at our Matagami zinc mine in northern Quebec resulted in the release of half a tonne of tailings containing zinc and copper. The pipeline system has been upgraded to prevent a similar incident.

- At Minnova's gold mine in Quebec a break in the tailings pipeline resulted in the release of approximately 18 tonnes of tailings containing cyanide. The tailings were contained and returned to the tailings dam.

Noranda Action

- Five of the 13 spills involved pipelines. An independent consultant has been hired to review and propose design, inspection, monitoring and operating procedures for our pipelines.

- Noranda is in the process of drafting a handbook of environmental management to improve performance. This handbook will provide guidelines on spill prevention and response procedures.

Figure 5.9 *Extract from Timberland 1993 Annual Report, p. 6*

City Year, an urban peace corps, is the foundation of our corporate citizenship.

Corporate Responsibility. In addition to making products to help individuals enjoy the outdoors, Timberland has remained a leader in corporate citizenship. In 1993, Timberland continued its focus on existing, long-term programs – the City Year youth service corps, "Give Racism The Boot" public service initiative, and employee community and environmental projects – all creating strength and added value for Timberland consumers, retailers, employees and shareholders.

It is Timberland's belief that today's consumer buys not only the product, but the company behind the product, linking positive financial results with community betterment. Therefore, Timberland has been able to advance its principles with discipline, while at the same time, infusing its discipline with better principles.

Table 5.2 *Surveys of corporate social reporting in North America*

Country	US	US	US	Canada
Survey	Ernst & Ernst (1978)	Guthrie & Parker (1990)	KPMG (1993)*	
Data year	1977	1983	1993	
Sample size	500	50	88	98
Sample criteria	Fortune 500 companies	Largest listed companies	In largest 100	
		Corporate annual report only	Questionnaire survey	
% of sample making disclosures on:				
Environment	50	53	67	68
Energy	53	43	—	—
Human resources	42	75	—	—
Products	29	35	—	—
Community involvement	29	63	—	—
Others	22	0	—	—
% of sample disclosing > 1 page	14	26	—	—
% of sample using separate booklet	1	10	16	23

* Figs are estimated from bar charts.

Social Responsibility in the USA, launched in 1992, committed member organisations to a social responsibility (encompassing the product — quality, environmental impact, etc. — the workplace and the community) which was to be treated as of equal importance to, and inseparably connected with, conventional profitability. The membership by the mid-1990s was more than 880 companies and growing (Stone, 1995).

As far as we are aware, there has been a lack of equivalent voluntary business initiatives conduct in Canada. At least one of the reasons is that there has not been the same volume of antitrust proceedings and corrupt foreign practices and, consequently, there has been less legal regulation than in the United States (see Brooks, 1986). Nevertheless, as can be seen from Table 5.2, it is environmental matters which increasingly dominate voluntary disclosure.

While the proportion of environmental disclosures shown in Table 5.2 is low when compared with global survey results (see Table 5.1 above), the disclosure of legal proceedings is relatively high in the United States. Of the 50 corporations disclosing any information on legal proceedings in Table 5.1, 76 per cent (36) were based in the United States (United Nations, 1994a).

This raises an important factor in the examination of environmental disclosure. Environmental reporting in North America (and to a lesser, but increasing, extent in the rest of the world — see below and Chapter 6) comprises three distinct elements: voluntary quantitative environmental reporting (in which the United States is relatively underdeveloped); *mandatory* environmental disclosure arising from an increasingly regulated business context with respect to the natural environment; and *mandatory financial disclosure* within the conventional financial statements.

The general encouragement of and guidance for broad environmental reporting has come from a variety of sources[7] and has been especially strong in Canada. Thus, not only did the Canadian Chamber of Commerce (CCC) issue *A Guideline on Corporate Environmental Reporting* in 1992, but the Canadian Institute of Chartered Accountants, the Canadian Standards Association, the Financial Executives Institute of Canada and the International Institute for Sustainable Development joined together to develop 'a comprehensive framework for environmental reporting' (CICA, 1993b). Examples of the sort of environmental reporting these initiatives were designed to achieve is shown in Figure 5.10.

However, environmental reporting in North America, and especially in the United States, was increasingly dominated in the late 1980s and early to mid-1990s by *mandatory* and *financial* disclosure. This centred around the potential environmental liabilities that companies might face under US (and Canadian) law — most especially the 'clean-up' (or *remediation*) of contaminated land under the Comprehensive Environmental Response, Compensation and Liability Act (CERCLA — commonly referred to as 'Superfund'). In addition, the US Financial Accounting Standards Board (FASB) together with the Canadian Institute of Chartered Accountants (CICA) required the disclosure of environmental liabilities. Further, the Securities and Exchange Commission (SEC) in the United States has issued guidelines concerned with the recognition, measurement and disclosure of environmental liabilities, while the Canadian provincial securities commissions require disclosure of the current and expected financial and operational impacts of environmental protection requirements on capital expenditure, earnings and competitive position (see, for example, United Nations, 1994b).

The SEC environmental disclosure obligations are fairly extensive (they are summarised in Figure 5.11). In addition, the SEC issued Standard Accounting Bulletin (SAB) No. 92 in 1993, which covers a variety of topics concerned with environmental accounting and reporting. In particular it requires the disclosure of judgements and assumptions underlying the recognition and measurement of liabilities to inform readers of the range of reasonably possible outcomes that could have a material effect on the registrant's financial condition, results of operations or liquidity.[8]

In addition to these government and professional body initiatives, NGO initiatives continue to be influential in the United States. For example, the Coalition for Environmentally Responsible Economies (CERES), an NGO, was launched after the *Exxon Valdez* tanker disaster in 1989. It is known for the 10-point CERES Principles (first adopted in 1992 and now signed by more than 50 companies) and the very comprehensive CERES reporting guidelines included in Figure 5.1 (Skalak *et al.*, 1993/ 4; UNEP IE, 1994). The Council on Economic Priorities (CEP), also an NGO, has a

Figure 5.10 *Extract from Shell Canada Ltd 1993 Annual Report, pp. 2, 3*

POLICY

SHELL CANADA IS COMMITTED TO THE INTEGRATION OF ECONOMIC AND ENVIRONMENTAL DECISION MAKING TO PROMOTE SUSTAINABLE DEVELOPMENT.

WE WILL:

- APPLY SUSTAINABLE DEVELOPMENT PRINCIPLES TO ALL SHELL ACTIVITIES.
- IMPLEMENT SUSTAINABLE DEVELOPMENT SELF-MONITORING MECHANISMS.
- EVALUATE PUBLIC OPINION ON SUSTAINABLE DEVELOPMENT.
- PARTICIPATE IN CONSULTATIVE PROCESSES ON SUSTAINABLE DEVELOPMENT.

PRINCIPLES

STEWARDSHIP will require that we design, build, operate and decommission our facilities in a safe, efficient and environmentally responsible manner—a life cycle approach. We will strive to produce and use products and packaging which reduce environmental impacts both as products and waste materials. We will work actively with our suppliers and customers to encourage the use and development of products and practices which are consistent with these principles.

SHARED RESPONSIBILITY entails support for the concept that all sectors of society must accept responsibility for sustaining the environment and the economy. It involves a recognition that consultation and co-operation are required from all sectors.

PREVENTION of potentially negative environmental, economic, social and cultural impacts arising from our development activities will be the focus of our policies, programs and decisions.

CONSERVATION AND RESOURCE MANAGEMENT will be practised in all our activities to protect people, plants, animals and the quality of air, water and soil. Energy conservation and efficiency will be promoted inside and outside the Company. We will enhance energy supply through technology and exploration and support developments that lower fossil fuel impacts.

WASTE MANAGEMENT will be pursued with elimination or reduction as our first priority. Reuse, recycling and by-product recovery will be promoted and disposal of remaining wastes will be done in an environmentally safe manner.

REHABILITATION AND RECLAMATION will involve consultation and co-operation with affected stakeholders to determine appropriate measures for repairing environmental damage resulting from our past and present operations.

SCIENTIFIC AND TECHNOLOGICAL INNOVATION will be supported to enhance environmental and economic well-being.

INTERNATIONAL RESPONSIBILITY. We recognize that all sectors within Canada must work co-operatively to achieve sustainable development at an international level and to find solutions for international problems.

2

Figure 5.10 *continued*

PROGRESS VERSUS 1993 PLANS

1993 COMMITMENT

STATUS

PLANNING
- Update sustainable development plans for all complexes and departments in the upstream

- Complete sustainable development plans for all downstream facilities including Shellburn terminal, national distribution department and Brockville lubricants plant

- COMPLETED

- SHELLBURN DEFERRED TO 1994; OTHERS COMPLETED

SUSTAINABLE DEVELOPMENT TRAINING
- Develop introductory and advanced training courses

- Deliver training to employees and management

- COMPLETED

- EMPLOYEE TRAINING COMPLETED; MANAGEMENT TRAINING DEVELOPED AND TWO PILOTS RUN

PERFORMANCE MEASURES
- Report key performance measures quarterly to senior management

- Develop additional indicators and targets

- IN PLACE

- BEING DEVELOPED

EMISSIONS INVENTORIES
- Complete inventories at all refineries and chemical plants

- COMPLETED FOR CHEMICAL PLANTS; WILL BE COMPLETED FOR REFINERIES, JUNE 1994

CALGARY OFFICES
- Reduce electricity consumption 10 per cent over 1992 levels

- Reduce solid waste by 50 per cent over 1992 levels

- REDUCED BY FIVE PER CENT

- REDUCED BY 24 PER CENT

SUSTAINABLE DEVELOPMENT AUDITS
- Complete six audits in the upstream

- Complete eight audits in the downstream

- THREE COMPLETED; THREE DEFERRED

- COMPLETED NINE

3

Figure 5.11 SEC environmental disclosure obligations

Regulation S-K requires disclosure of:

- the material effects that compliance may have upon capital expenditures, earnings and competitive position of the registrant and its subsidiaries;
- administrative or judicial proceedings arising under any environmental law if it is: material to the business or financial condition of the company; exceeds 10 per cent of current assets, involving a claim for damages, potential monetary sanctions, or capital expenditures; or a government authority is party to the proceeding and it involves monetary sanctions of $100 000 or more;
- commitments, events or uncertainties that are materially likely to affect the registrant's liquidity;
- material capital expenditure commitments and their general purpose;
- unusual or infrequent events or transactions or any significant economic changes that materially affected reported income; and,
- any trend, demand, commitment, event or uncertainty that is reasonably likely to occur.

longer history — and a wider remit than environmental issues. CEP is dedicated to evaluating corporate social performance and has carried out a number of studies on corporate social performance (see, for example, CEP, 1973). On the environmental agenda, as early as 1977 it published comparative environmental performance rankings by industry (CEP, 1977). It has, through its Corporate Environmental Data Clearinghouse Project, prepared detailed environmental reports on more than 100 US companies. In addition, reflecting the consumer orientation of the United States, it has published *Shopping for a Better World* which ranks companies on such factors as environmental and equal opportunities performance (Skalak *et al.*, 1993/4; Wiseman, 1982).

North America has a complex and rapidly changing business environment. While no longer the leader in broad social reporting, the United States looks set to continue to lead the world in financial environmental reporting and Canada, while not far behind on these issues, has been a consistent innovator in the broader approaches to environmental reporting (but see Chapter 6).

5.5 Corporate social reporting in Japan

By way of a complete contrast Japan, with its completely different social, political and economic structure, has demonstrated a quite different experience with CSR. Indeed, surveys have suggested that Japan is the laggard among the so-called developed nations in CSR (see, for example, Roberts, 1990; United Nations, 1992).

Most of the literature on Japanese social accounting has been published in Japanese accounting journals in the Japanese language. This brief summary of developments in Japan relies heavily on English language publications and working papers such as Kokubu and Tomimasu (1995), Kokubu, *et al.* (1994), Tokutani and Kawano (1978) and Yamagami and Kokubu (1991).

Corporate social accounting as we define it was first discussed and studied in Japan in the 1960s and 1970s (although the term had been used to refer to the application of accounting to economic analysis since the 1930s). It developed largely as a response to the growing anti-pollution movement (Tokutani and Kawano, 1978). In a note on the Japanese literature on the subject, Tokutani and Kawano (1978) identified three main categories of literature:

- **The cost approach to corporate social accounting** which focuses on the transfer of social costs from the public to the private domain in order to provide cost information useful to 'social decisions' of management or interested groups. This includes literature which considers classifications of social costs, where and how social cost information should be reported and management accounting for, and control of, social costs.
- **The responsibility approach to corporate social accounting** focusing on the role of accounting in measuring corporate social responsibility. This includes work describing the difficulties of defining social responsibility, work which attempts to develop accounting principles and work focusing on the need for disclosure of corporate social responsibility information.
- **The audit approach to corporate social accounting** which advocates a social audit.

Among the published work in this early period was a report published by the management committee of the Japanese Institute of Certified Public Accountants (JICPA) in July 1975 on social audit criteria and the means for institutionalising social responsibility accounting.

Unfortunately, however, this early interest of academics and the JICPA in the subject of corporate social reporting has not been matched by reporting practice as demonstrated by Kokubu (1993), Kokubu and Tomimasu (1995) and Yamagami and Kokubu (1991). The results of Kokubu's (1993) questionnaire survey show that while the majority of the 165 respondents carry out social activities in excess of the legal minimum (75 per cent, 79 per cent and 66 per cent with respect to environmental protection, employee relations and community involvement respectively), only a minority disclose in excess of the legal minimum (42 per cent, 44 per cent, 44 per cent and 42 per cent with respect to environmental protection, employee relations, community involvement and consumer relations, respectively). One of the reasons for the discrepancy between corporate social activities and disclosure practices would appear to be the Japanese cultural trait of being humble by concealing good conduct. Of further significance is the fact that, of those companies making social disclosures, very few choose the corporate annual report as a medium (25 per cent, 18 per cent, 18 per cent and 24 per cent with respect to environmental protection, employee relations, community involvement and consumer relations, respectively). This can be attributed to the *Keiretsu* relationship (see Lowe, 1990) whereby:

> corporate information is informally gathered and controlled mainly through the main-bank, and the stable and interlocking shareholders do not require corporate information to be disclosed in public because they can receive it informally and want to protect that relationship from outsiders. (Kokubu and Tomimasu, 1995, p. 9)

Table 5.3 *The practices of corporate social disclosure in Japan according to the type of report. From Yamagami and Kokubu, 1991*

	Environment		Community involvement		Employee relations		Research and development		International activity	
	No.	%	No.	%	No.	%	No.	%	No.	%
Operating Report (total: 49 companies)	0	0	6	12.2	21	42.9	38	77.6	23	46.9
English Version Report (total: 47 companies)	3	6.4	9	19.1	12	25.5	41	87.2	35	74.5
Public Relations Report (total: 49 companies)	13	26.5	25	51.0	17	34.7	41	83.7	39	79.6
Average percentage of the three reports		11.0		27.6		34.5		82.8		66.9

Yamagami and Kokubu (1991) studied the corporate social reporting of the top 49 publicly owned Japanese companies included in the *Fortune* 'Global 500' biggest industrial corporations outside the United States in 1985. Since the mandatory corporate reports required under the Commercial Code and the Securities and Exchange Law do not include any social information other than some trivial information about employees (such as average number employed and average age), the study concentrated on voluntary reports issued to external users, namely: the 'Operating Report' which is sent to shareholders after the annual general meeting; the English Language Version of the 'Annual Report' which is issued to raise funds on foreign capital markets; and the 'Public Relations Report', a general term for reports used to provide external interest groups with an outline of the company. Reports published in 1985 or 1986 were studied.

Corporate social disclosure practices were classified into five categories: environment (including energy and product safety); employee relations; community involvement; research and development (described as a 'quasi' corporate social disclosure because it makes contributions to society through the development of new products); and international activity (because it influences the social and economic states of foreign countries). The results, reproduced in Table 5.3, indicated that environment and community involvement disclosures in the most popular medium, the 'Public Relations Report', were made by only 26.5 per cent and 51.0 per cent, respectively, of the sample.

The growth in environmental reporting in Japan in the following 5 years was evidenced by the 1991 survey of Nishiguchi (1994) (reported in Kokubu *et al.*, 1994) who reported levels of environmental reporting of the 50 largest Japanese companies of 34 per cent, 34 per cent and 40 per cent in the Operations Report, English Version Report and Public Relations Report, respectively.

Two organisations concerned with environmental reporting in Japan are the Keidanren (Japan Federation of Economic Organisations) and the Valdez Society. The

Keidanren was established in 1946 through the merger of several economic and industrial organisations and currently has approximately 1000 corporate members (Keidanren, 1992). The Keidanren's Global Environment Charter (Keidanren, 1991) specifically calls for companies to publicise information and carry out educational activities on their measures for protecting the environment and to provide users with information on the appropriate use and disposal, including recycling, of their products. In its *Ten Points Environmental Guidelines for Japanese Enterprises Operating Abroad*, reproduced in Figure 5.12, it calls for companies to publicise the environmental activities of overseas operations both at home and abroad and provide the local community with information on environmental measures on a regular basis. The Japanese Keidanren makes very little reference to making information publicly available and makes little reference to the need for accountability. However, its concern for corporate responsibility overseas is unusual and should be applauded.

The Valdez Society (named after the CERES Valdez Principles) was conceived in 1990 and has a small but diverse membership including civic activists, employees, academics and journalists. Its aim is to increase the awareness of Japanese firms of the Valdez Principles and encourage them to be more environmentally responsible. The Society has three major subgroups: Green Consumer, Socially Responsible Investment, and Corporate Environmentalism. It is the Corporate Environmentalism Group, made up largely of company employees, which has the task of encouraging voluntary corporate environmental responsibility. In 1990 they issued 359 questionnaires to manufacturing companies listed on the Tokyo Stock Exchange with the aim of gaining a better understanding of corporate environmental performance. Of the 51 companies which replied, only 16 had a publicised environmental policy, 13 had a policy which was not publicised and a further 7 were in the process of formulating an environmental policy.

This survey precedes the passing of the Japanese Basic Environmental Law in 1993 which consists of a very broad policy statement — an earlier version of which was watered down by the Ministry of International Trade and Industry (MITI). It also precedes the production in 1991 of a policy statement by the Keidanren. However, neither of these are likely to have much impact on Japanese corporate social reporting practices, as both are very general and lacking in guidance as to how they should be implemented (see Figures 5.1 and 5.12 for the Keidanren's guidelines).

The more recent work of Kokubu and Tomimasu (1995) is particularly concerned with the *Voluntary Plan in Relation to the Environment* released by MITI in 1992. The plan has three chapters, the detail of which is set out in Kokubu and Tomimasu (1995):

- Basic policies for business activities.
- Items related to the environmental management system.
- Considerations for the environment in business activities.

Interestingly, the third chapter includes a section on public relations and social activities which incorporates, among other things, employee education and community involvement. In addition, it is unusual in that it calls for consideration of the environment in overseas business activities. Kokubu and Tomimasu (1995) studied the

Figure 5.12 *Extract from the Keidanren 10-point 1991 Environmental Guidelines*

TEN POINTS ENVIRONMENTAL GUIDELINES FOR THE JAPANESE ENTERPRISES
OPERATING BOARD

1   Establish a constructive attitude towards environmental protection and try to raise complete awareness of the issues amongst those concerned.
2   Make environmental protection a priority at overseas sites and, as a minimum requirement, abide by the environmental standards of the host country. Apply Japanese standards concerning the management of harmful substances.
3   Conduct a full environmental assessment before starting overseas business operations. After the start of activities, try to collect data and, if necessary, conduct an assessment.
6   Provide the local community with information on environmental measures on a regular basis
7   Be sure that when environment-related issues arise, efforts are made to prevent them from developing into social and cultural frictions. Deal with them through scientific and rational discussions.
8   Cooperate in the promotion of the host country's scientific and rational environmental measures.
9   Actively publicize, both at home and broad, the activities of overseas businesses that reflect our activities on the environmental consideration.
10   Ensure that the home offices of the corporations operating overseas understand the importance of the measures for dealing with environmental issues, as they affect their overseas affiliates. The head office must try to establish a support system that can, for instance, send specialists abroad whenever the need arises.

Source: Keidanren mimeo dated 23 April 1991.

environmental disclosures of electric power companies and automobile companies in relation to the plan. They found that the disclosures followed almost exactly the contents of the voluntary plan although the length and quality of the information varied considerably. The authors conclude that the reasons for these disclosures are found in legitimacy theory (see Chapter 2), rather than a desire to be accountable.

5.6 Corporate social reporting in Australasia

There has been a long-standing interest in CSR in Australia (see, for example, Gul *et al.*, 1984; Guthrie and Parker, 1990; Pang, 1982; Trotman, 1979; Trotman and Bradley, 1981) and New Zealand (Hackston and Milne, 1995; Robertson, 1978a). They have tended to follow the Ernst and Ernst (1978) disclosure categories and to have concentrated on large companies so their results can be relatively easily compared. Table 5.4 highlights relatively low — although increasing — CSR disclosure levels when compared with other countries (see, for example, Table 5.2 and Chapter 6). In particular, Table 5.4 indicates the general worldwide trend towards increased social and environmental disclosure (this is explored in more detail in Chapter 6).[9]

Table 5.4 *Surveys of corporate social reporting in Australasia*

Country	Australia					New Zealand	
Survey	Trotman (1979)			Pang (1982)	Guthrie and Parker (1990)	Robertson (1978a)	Hackston and Milne (1995)
Data year	1967	1972	1977	1980	1983	1975–6	1992
Sample size	100				50	100	47
Sample criteria	Largest			70 largest plus 30 at random	Largest	Largest	
% of sample making disclosures	26	48	69	79	56	54	83
% of sample making disclosures on:							
Environment	6	18	35	19	21	17	23
Energy	1	0	10	12	4	3	6
Human resources	17	30	43	61	93	50	79
Products	3	3	4	18	0	3	41
Community involvement	5	19	23	23	29	8	30
Others	5	13	34	20	18	2	19

Trotman and Bradley (1981) take this general observation further and, broadly in line with other national studies, reinforce the view that CSR tends to be associated with larger companies, those which take a longer-term view in their decision making and, in a less-commonly voiced conclusion, with companies which face a more active social environment and higher levels of risk.

Further insight into Australian[10] CSR is given in Guthrie and Parker's (1989a) relatively unique longitudinal analysis of 100 years of corporate annual reporting by BHP, a dominant corporation in the Australian mining/manufacturing industry. That study rejected legitimacy theory (see Chapter 2) as the primary explanation for social reporting in the Australian case. Total social disclosure levels over the period of the study varied considerably with peaks at intervals of 10–30 years. The patterns of disclosure in each of the categories of environment, energy, human resources, products and community involvement differed considerably with some being in focus at times when others did not appear at all. The authors compared the timing of observed peaks in each category of disclosure with any apparently related socioeconomic environmental conditions and BHP activities occurring immediately before and during the peak period. Little correspondence between the two was found and the authors concluded (p. 351):

A relationship between legitimacy theory and disclosure was only marginally supported for environmental issues, unconfirmed for energy and community issues, and subject to contradictory evidence for human resource issues.

The same authors later concluded (Guthrie and Parker 1989b) that 'critical accounting theory' better explained the patterns of disclosure by BHP. There was evidence that: management had a predisposition to establish management prerogatives and subscribed to the ideology of management's 'right to manage'; management had a hostile attitude towards labour and was prepared to promote conflict between capital and labour; and management had a predisposition towards selective disclosure policies, suppressing information on some major social impact events.

In a New Zealand context Robertson (1978a) reported that had been no previous surveys of CSR in corporate annual reports and that there were no mandatory CSR requirements. He also noted that the criteria for the Award for the best corporate annual report made by the New Zealand Society of Accountants did not explicitly include social reporting and that there were no mandatory social disclosures in the Companies Act. However, in addition to the general trend towards increased CSR in New Zealand noted by Hackston and Milne (1995) there have been other relevant developments since that study. Probably the most important of these is the Resource Management Act 1991 which aimed to promote the 'sustainable management of natural resources' by focusing on the environmental effects of new proposals (e.g. siting of new plants) by both public and private sector organisations (see Milne, 1993). The Act includes liability similar to the US Superfund legislation whereby land owners (corporate or individual) can be required to clean up any contamination, past or present. However, the professional accounting body, the New Zealand Society of Accountants — traditionally inactive in the field of CSR — has been slow to become involved with environmental concerns.

5.7 Corporate social reporting in other countries with especial reference to less developed and newly industrialised countries

The need for corporate social reporting in less developed countries (LDCs) and newly industrialised countries (NICs) is particularly acute given the existence of large numbers of developed country multinationals operating in these countries. Foreign-owned multinationals must be accountable for their social and environmental impacts if host governments are to have any hope at all of exercising some degree of control over them. The financial statements and regulations of their home countries are very largely investor-orientated and there is often an assumption that reporting which meets the needs of their home countries will also meet the needs of users in the host countries.[11] For example, Gray and Kouhy (1993) warn of the dangers of introducing western environmental accounting techniques to the different cultural and economic environments of LDCs. Gray *et al.* (1981) suggested that there was a need for improvements in information disclosure by MNCs and that market forces could not be relied upon to satisfy user needs.[12]

In considering the importance of host government control of MNCs, Briston (1984) considered the main activities which might have an impact on economic planning (using Hood and Young, 1979) and for which information is required for control purposes. Those for which social information is required include: purchase of inputs locally; profit and capital repatriation; extent of planned or actual local equity participation; local participation in top management; level of employment provided; obligation to train local personnel; environmental protection; construction of social overheads such as roads and housing; and use of locally owned transportation. Some of these items would not, of themselves, in a western domestic context be considered a necessary part of CSR, but considered in light of the increasing North–South divide most certainly are. To this list we would add information on environmental sustainability and community involvement and charitable activities in particular.

The United Nations Centre On Transnational Corporations develops this point:

> ... the very limited coverage of non-financial information constitutes an important gap in the existing reporting practices of transnational corporations. Non-financial reporting is as important as financial reporting in appraising the operations of transnational corporations and their contribution to the countries and communities in which they operate. Non-financial reporting is, furthermore, required by public authorities both at the national and regional levels and by labour and other interested parties, such as consumer groups and environmentalists concerned with specific aspects of the activities of transnational corporations ... There is evidence, nevertheless, that non-financial information has been increasingly reported by corporations, reflecting an awareness of their social responsibility. (UNCTC, 1982; p. 15)

In 1984, the UNCTC expanded its thinking on the issue and published a list of minimum items for disclosure in general purpose reports (UNCTC, 1984). It dealt separately with: financial and non-financial items, and items to be disclosed by either the enterprise as a whole or by individual member enterprises. The items in Figure 5.13 are the non-

Figure 5.13 *UNCTC's list of minimum disclosure of non-financial items in MNC General Purpose Reports*

● **Labour and employment**
Agreed to include: policies regarding corporate labour relations and recognition of trade unions; average number of employees broken down by geographic and line of business segment. For individual member enterprises only, a description of training programmes. Also recommended, although more tentatively: policy with regard to complaints and dispute settlement mechanisms; number employed by function broken down to show numbers of women and nationals; number of employees under contract and those hired as casual labour; average hours worked per week; labour turnover; absenteeism; accident rate; description of health and safety standards.

● **Production**
The UN recognised the following issues as important but could not get agreement on: reporting of physical output by line of business together with the market share for principal products; description of practices regarding raw materials acquisition; indication of average annual capacity utilisation; description of significant new products and processes; percentage of use of local materials and components.

● **Investment programme**
Agreed to include descriptions of major future capital expenditures; to give further consideration to including main projects together with their estimated effect on employment levels; and descriptions of announced mergers and takeovers.

● **Environmental measures**
The UN experienced some difficulty obtaining agreement on this area but recommends: environmental measures, together with cost data where available; information and policies concerning hazardous and toxic substances.

● **Transfer of technology**
The inclusion of policies, amounts, modalities and prices regarding transfer of technology to developing countries was considered, no agreement was reached.

financial elements recommended for inclusion in MNCs' general purpose Annual Reports. The UN met considerable difficulties in reaching consensus on these items and, unfortunately, did not develop these lists further.

Despite the value of corporate social disclosures to LDCs and NICs there are relatively few studies which have examined this important area.[13] The following brief review summarises the more notable findings from a selection of these studies.

Tanzania

A different approach needs to be taken when considering the quality of corporate disclosure in LDCs and NICs. Abayo *et al.* (1993) attempted to measure the quality of corporate disclosure in Tanzania. Although their study was concerned with all types of corporate disclosure in the corporate annual report, some of the general points are directly relevant to CSR. Abayo *et al.* conclude that, in LDCs and NICs the regulatory framework and/or enforcement mechanisms are inadequate. Thus users of corporate annual reports cannot assume that mandatory requirements have been complied with even when a clean audit report is given. They further argue that as many LDCs do not have stock exchanges or, where they exist, they are often new, small and underdeveloped, market pressures cannot be relied upon to ensure even a minimum level of reporting. Finally, Abayo *et al.* point out that given the widespread shortage of qualified accountants and auditors, it seems reasonable to assume that the internal accounting systems and audit quality are often poorer in LDCs than in developed nations. This leads Abayo *et al.* to conclude that we can expect to experience poorer quality disclosures, lack of quantitative data and the possibility of inaccurate disclosure in LDCs.

India

Singh and Ahuja (1983) examined CSR in the 1975/76 corporate Annual Reports of 40 Indian companies using a list of disclosure items derived by consulting foreign and Indian journals and corporate Annual Reports and by consulting financial, environmental and economic experts. Their list is therefore interesting in that it should comprehensively represent items for which companies could demonstrate social responsibility in India, a less developed country, at that time. Items included which were particularly relevant to that environment are: coordinating national projects; providing medical facilities to nearby villages; distribution of essential commodities; expenditure on township; establishment of educational institutions; donations (including flood/drought relief); expenditure on family planning programmes; maintenance of dairy and vegetable farms; and arrangement for adult education. There was a significant variation in the level of CSR between the sample companies. Approximately one-quarter of the sample disclosed less than 20 per cent of the information included in the index, half disclosed between 20 per cent and 40 per cent and approximately one-quarter disclosed more than 40 per cent.

Malaysia and Singapore

Andrew *et al.* (1989) carried out a content analysis on the corporate annual reports of 119 publicly listed Malaysian and Singaporean companies with years ending in 1983. They split disclosures into four themes, namely: human resources; community involvement; environment; and products. The study found that, while the overall number of disclosing companies was only 31 (26 per cent), the majority of which disclosed on one theme only, a higher proportion of large- and medium-sized companies made disclosures compared with small companies. While recognising that larger companies have more resources to engage in corporate social activities, the authors thought that:

> ... another plausible explanation relevant to developing countries was that generally these larger companies were foreign-owned and also, because of their greater visibility, they were more likely to be subject to scrutiny by the host government. A greater social

Figure 5.14 *The hierarchy of social objectives. From Teoh and Thong, 1984*

commitment and disclosure of this fact in the annual reports was one way of overcoming possible criticisms that these companies were only concerned with exploiting the economic resources of developing countries (p. 373).

Andrew *et al.* (1989) found that human resources disclosure represented 71 per cent of all social disclosures. They explained this as reflecting the concern by governments of less developed countries to improve the working conditions and living standards of the workers while the low level of other types of disclosures was explained by the relatively few powerful consumer and other interest groups.

Teoh and Thong (1984) carried out a personal interview questionnaire survey of mainly chief executive officers in 100 companies operating in Malaysia. They suggest that less developed countries could learn of the dangers of unrestrained and unregulated economic growth in terms of a deterioration in the quality of the environment and undesirable social outcomes (see Gray and Kouhy, 1993 for a critique of this attitude). The study examines the first three levels of the hierarchy of social objectives shown in Figure 5.14. Teoh and Thong found that by far the three most important factors leading to corporate social awareness were the philosophy of top management, legislation relating to social performance areas and alignment with parent company practice. It was also found that the country of major ownership has a bearing on the level of social awareness and the social issues that each company adopts. This would indicate that, for example, legislation adopted by the European Union to mandate corporate responsibility towards the environment will have a direct effect on corporate social responsibility and reporting practices in less developed countries. Multinationals originating in developed western nations had a broader view of their social responsibility than those originating in Singapore or Malaysia. When it came to measuring the degree of overall involvement in socially relevant areas, human resources and product/service to consumers were found to have considerably more coverage than community involvement and physical environment. This finding concurs with that of Andrew *et al.* (1989). Teoh and Thong conclude:

> Greater emphasis is thus given to social performance areas like human resources and product/service to consumers, where the potential impact from these activities can be associated, directly or indirectly, with the profitability of a company. Together with financial and physical resources human resources represent one of the most vital inputs in the economic production process. Hence interest in the welfare of employees is very much driven by a desire to develop a loyal, capable and dedicated work force that can demonstrate a high level of productivity, as it is motivated by a sense of social concern. In the same way, the survival of a company hinges very much on ensuring its products are relatively safe in application, of acceptable quality and reasonably priced. On the other hand, community involvement which can only be remotely related to profitability has been given the least consideration. The marginally higher overall mean score for the physical environmental activity is attributed to the effect of legislation which, as noted earlier, is an important factor in inducing social awareness. (1984, pp. 193–4).

Thus, despite the apparently greater awareness of social responsibility of western multinationals, their social disclosure practices in the LDCs appear to be motivated by self-interest. The low level of involvement in environmental protection measures is of particular concern. In addition, Teoh and Thong found that the level of corporate social reporting was much lower than the level of corporate social involvement. They identified the two main reasons as: (a) 'annual reports have always been kept very brief'; and (b), the 'company is active in social concerns but can see no reason for telling others what it is doing'. Companies with foreign ownership reported marginally more than Malaysian companies. This perceived lack of a need to be accountable is startling and may be a reflection of both the time period of the study or as noted in Andrew *et al.* (1989), the relatively small influence of consumer and other interest groups in LDCs.

South Africa

In a study of corporate social reporting by 54 of the 115 largest publicly listed companies in South Africa in 1992/93, Savage (1994) also found that human resources was by far the most dominant form of CSR. The percentages of the sample making human resources, community involvement and environmental disclosures were 89 per cent, 72 per cent and 63 per cent, respectively, with mean lengths of disclosure of 2.6, 0.8 and 0.5 pages, respectively. Human resources is a particular issue in South Africa where some companies at least want to appear to be taking some responsibility for the inequalities of society in the wake of apartheid (see also Bogiages and Vorster, 1994).

Poland

Similarly, Stepien (1994) reports that, like many of the other countries studied in this section, Poland has not seen environmental issues as a priority. Consequently, the systematic practice of environmental accounting is very rare — being dominated by 'more pressing issues' related to economic development. This may be a widely held view in many emerging economies.

Perhaps the final word in this section should be left, appropriately enough, to the United Nations. The United Nations (1995) reports on the results of a questionnaire survey of 18 transnational companies in the chemical industry and 8 in the food industry which focused on environmental reporting in India, Malaysia and the Philippines. All types of reporting media were considered. The results showed that the quantity and quality of environmental disclosures in the three host countries was disappointing and rarely covered aspects beyond stage 2 of the UNEP IE (1994) typology (see Figure 5.3 above), while environmental reporting in the home country had reached stages 3 and 4. This is despite the pledges given by international companies pledging (in their corporate reports, for example) worldwide environmental reporting (see United Nations, 1995, p. 8). The UN (1995) results suggest that we would be wise not to believe the statements from many MNCs.[14]

The UN (1995) report also found that corporations in the chemical industry were more likely to report on environmental issues than those in the food industry, concluding that public exposure is an important factor in determining disclosure practices.

5.8 Conclusion

While it is clear that CSR reflects — to a degree at least — the social and political context in which it takes place, we still know far too little about the relationship between the two. What does, however, seem clear is that a great deal depends on the relative power of the corporations *vis-à-vis* the pressure groups, stakeholders, NGOs and governments in the different countries. MNCs look like the clear winners at the moment (for further discussion see, for example, Bailey *et al.*, 1994a, b).

This chapter has also raised the interesting spectre of wider social, ethical and community issues being pushed from the social accountability by an (apparently) all-embracing concern with environmental issues. Given the relatively trivial nature of business' genuine interaction with sustainability issues (and it would be quite unrealistic to expect anything else) we should perhaps be more suspicious about why CSR so easily embraces 'environment' when it can ignore poverty and injustice.

The identification of differences in the nature and extent of CSR practice across countries highlights the need for further research on the extent and nature of reporting practices across countries. Such research should relate reporting practices to the particular characteristics of the countries studied. A fuller picture of the factors that influence social disclosure practices might then become apparent and there would be a greater awareness of what constituted 'good practice' — or at least, a greater chance to castigate 'bad practice'. This would be unlikely to aid the development of further voluntary reporting initiatives but it might raise the tone of the debate about whether such initiatives can ever work and whether, indeed, large companies can ever be genuinely motivated by accountability.

The low level of accountability can only be improved by increasing the number of mandatory requirements through greater governmental involvement. Given what is already known about why companies do or do not report (see also Chapter 2), the further development of mandatory social reporting requirements is essential.

We now turn to Chapter 6 which looks in detail at the regulation, and the extent and nature, of reporting practices in Western Europe and the European Union (EU) in particular. While progress is very slow, Chapter 6 highlights the EU's potential for improving corporate social accountability through legislation.

Notes

1. And note that many companies are a great deal bigger (economically and politically) than many nations.
2. It should be noted that, despite the heading on the table, specific parts of some of the codes of conduct do not refer to the reporting of information.
3. Related to the widely quoted and exceptionally influential Club of Rome Report *Limits to Growth* (Meadows *et al.*, 1972).
4. This was to fulfil UNCTC's objectives of: gaining a better understanding of the economic and social effects of transnational corporations; promoting the contribution of transnational corporations to national developmental goals while eliminating their negative effects; and, strengthening the negotiating capacity of less developed countries (UNCTC, 1982, p. 7). The work of the UNCTC is discussed in some detail in section 5.7 on corporate social reporting in less developed and newly industrialised countries.
5. The United Nations Environment Programme (UNEP) was created in 1972 and has, since the late 1980s, particularly concerned itself with environmental accounting for sustainable development (Ahmad *et al.*, 1989; UNEP IE, 1994).
6. The PERI initiative was founded by Amoco, Dow Chemical, Du Pont, IBM, Northern Telecom, Phillips Petroleum, Polaroid, Rockwell and United Technologies. It has since become an international concern.
7. Recall the early influence of the American Institute of Certified Public Accountants (AICPA) and the National Association of Accountants on the practising side and the American Accounting Association on the academic side, having sponsored research and publications in the field over the last two decades. Much of the early US research emphasised environmental initiatives. The more recent US initiatives have tended to be more closely focused — see below.
8. For more information on US disclosure requirements see Skalak *et al.* (1993/94).
9. Guthrie and Mathews (1985) also provide a useful review of the CSR literature in Australasia up to the early 1980s distinguishing between empirical work, normative work, attitude surveys and research on employee reporting including several unpublished working papers and dissertations.
10. In Australia, environmental issues fall under the control of each individual state government so that requirements on companies and consequences of non-compliance varies between states (see Gibson and O'Donovan, 1994).
11. For example, with respect to financial reporting, one of the stated objectives of the

International Accounting Standards Committee in 1983 (See Briston 1984)) read:

In some countries, where accounting standards have not previously been laid down, International Accounting Standards are adopted as the country's own standards. When this occurs, local accounting practices will be enhanced, and the financial statements prepared in that country should be internationally acceptable.

This was later updated with objectives for 1991–95 in IASC (1990): '. . . to ensure that International Accounting Standards meet the financial reporting needs of developing and newly industrialised countries and encourage the implementation of those Standards'.

12. Briston (1984) says: 'Little attention is paid to the fact that conventional financial statements are investor orientated and may well be inappropriate for an economy in which there are very few private investors, no stock exchange and very strong government involvement in the economy' (p. 14).

13. But see, for example, Abayo *et al.*, 1993; Andrew *et al.*, 1989; Chow and Wong-Boren, 1987; Marston, 1986; Savage, 1994; Singh and Ahuja, 1983; Singhvi, 1968; Stepien, 1994.

14. Examples of such pledges might include:

This report concerns all Rhône-Poulenc business worldwide. Every plant must also publish its own year-end results for the benefit of neighbouring communities, as well as its objectives for the following year. (Rhône Poulenc, 1993, p. 3)

Furthermore, all plants (high risk or not) are informing the public about the environmental impact of their activities (Rhône Poulenc, 1993, p. 24)

It is essential that Monsanto continue to be fully and publicly accountable . . . We chose to disclose Monsanto's data on emissions and releases directly to our communities . . . environmentalists and the media. (Monsanto, 1993, p. 3)

chapter 6

Corporate social reporting practice
Current trends in Western Europe

6.1 Introduction

This chapter focuses on social and environmental reporting in Western Europe. Europe is given special attention in this book for two main reasons. First, Europe has been the birthplace of many innovative developments in corporate social reporting. Secondly, the European Union's (EU) concern for improving social policy and environmental protection, together with its aim of achieving harmonisation of company law,[1] promises further developments in both policy[2] and reporting practices. Such developments are likely to influence not only the European Economic Area (EEA), but also Eastern European countries as they prepare to join the EU. These developments in the legal framework of corporate behaviour and reporting are important because, as noted in Chapter 2, the legal responsibility for action and the legal responsibility for accountability are unequal and the demands of accountability are rarely satisfied voluntarily. This chapter considers the extent and nature of voluntary accountability and the level of legal accountability.

The chapter is structured around the three themes of environmental reporting; reporting on employee issues; and the broad category, ethical reporting (ethical reporting is defined here as reporting of information concerned, directly or indirectly, with giving an impression of corporate ethical values: see Adams *et al.*, 1995b and Adams and Roberts 1995). Thus, section 6.2 looks at environmental reporting in Western Europe; section 6.3 at reporting on employee issues and section 6.4 at ethical reporting. Each section discusses the regulation of CSR; summarises surveys of social disclosure; and discusses the development of, and initiatives in, reporting practice. Illustrations of such practice are also provided. The chapter's conclusion discusses possible ways forward in the development of social reporting in Western Europe.

6.2 Environmental reporting

Environmental reporting in Western Europe has a long history (see, for example, Brockhoff, 1979; Lessem, 1977; Preston *et al.*, 1978; Schreuder, 1979). However, it was only during the late 1980s and early 1990s that it became widespread and came to overshadow the historic European emphasis on the provision of information to, and about, employees.[3] The 1990s saw a quantum increase in surveys and books on environmental reporting and accounting[4] and professional accounting bodies and firms paid the subject increasing attention (Butler *et al.*, 1992; Fédération des Experts Comptables Européens (FEE), 1993; Institute of Chartered Accountants in England and Wales, 1992; KPMG, 1993a, b, 1994; Tonkin, 1991; Touche Ross, 1990). The reasons for this increase in interest are many and complex (see, for example, Gray, 1990a; Owen, 1992). However, one of the major impetuses which ensured that the interest translated into action on the business agenda was the action by a variety of bodies that promised — and even sometimes delivered — to make environmental reporting part of conventional, regulated company reporting practice.

Regulation of environmental reporting

By the mid-1990s a regulatory framework for environmental reporting was beginning to emerge. While it still largely depended upon the sorts of voluntary initiatives we saw in Chapter 5 the EU, national governments, business organisations and professional accounting bodies were all beginning to lend their weight to the development of reporting about corporate interaction with the natural environment.

Significant developments of European Union regulation that had implications for environmental reporting began in the early 1990s with the development of an environmental policy in the European Economic Area (EEA) within the Agreement on the European Economic Area (1992). This required the signatory nations to preserve, protect and improve the quality of the environment; contribute towards protecting human health; and ensure a prudent and rational utilisation of resources.[5] The principles involved were that preventative action should be taken, environmental damage should as a priority be rectified at source and the polluter should pay. However, there were no mandatory rules concerning individual companies.

From this basis, the EU began to address more directly the environmental reporting issues. For example, the Commission's Fifth Action Programme on the Environment (European Commission, 1992; see, for example, Bebbington, 1993), entitled *Towards Sustainability*, called for enterprises to:

- disclose in their annual reports details of their environmental policy and activities, and the effects thereof;
- detail in their accounts the expenses on environmental programmes (this requires a clear definition of such expenses);
- make provision in their accounts for environmental risks and future environmental expenses. (EC, 1992, vol. II p. 67)

The 5th Action Programme also called for product pricing based on the 'full cost of a product' including the use and consumption of environmental resources (see chapter 7).

In contrast, the European Union's Environmental Management and Audit Scheme (EMAS) which was adopted in 1993 relied on 'market forces' to encourage businesses to improve their environmental protection measures. The idea was that companies who registered for the scheme and who, as a result, were permitted to use the eco-logo, were rewarded by the various corporate stakeholders. The main objectives of the scheme and its implications for reporting are summarised in Figure 6.1.

The EMAS regulations promised a significant increase in the environmental accountability of corporations if it could ever be made compulsory. However, one of its most interesting aspects from the accountants' point of view was its insistence on 'external verifiers' — in other words auditors.[6]

This terminology obviously made the accountants — in their guise as statutory auditors — sit up and take notice. It had the effect of combining with the increasing concern about the implications of the environmental agenda for company financial statements and placing accounting and accountants at the very heart of the environmental debate (we will look at the results of this below). If this message needed reinforcing, reinforcement indeed was emerging from some of the more far-sighted national governments. By the mid-1990s, regulations requiring corporate disclosure of both financial and non-financial details about the environment were emerging from Denmark, the Netherlands and the Scandinavian countries. This was providing an inexorable impetus to the inevitability of company environmental reporting.

Figure 6.1 *The principal features of the EMAS scheme*

Companies are encouraged to:

- set their own objectives for environmental performance and develop management systems which would achieve those objectives;
- initiate a pattern of eco-auditing to assess their environmental performance and to provide the information needed to develop their environmental management systems;
- show commitment to externally validated assessment of their progress in meeting these objectives; and make information available to the public in a '... concise, comprehensible form ...' [Article 5(2)].

As far as making information available to the public was concerned, the EMAS regulation required that the environmental statement should include, in particular:

- a description of the company's activities at the site considered;
- an assessment of all the significant environmental issues of relevance to the activities concerned;
- a presentation of the company's environmental policy, programme and management system implemented at the site concerned;
- the deadline set for submission of the next statement;
- a summary of the figures on pollutant emissions, waste generation, consumption of raw material, energy, water, noise;
- other significant environmental aspects as appropriate, as well as other factors regarding environmental performance; and
- the name of the accredited environmental verifier.

They were also required to draw attention to significant changes since the previous statement. All of this information had to be externally verified.

The real views of business in all of this remained unclear. While many leading companies proceeded to develop their voluntary environmental reporting (see below), mixed messages were being conveyed by those bodies ostensibly representing business. This confusion was especially strong in the United Kingdom. The environmental working party of the Hundred Group of Finance Directors of the UK issued a Statement of Good Practice concerned with environmental reporting in Annual Reports in 1992. It recommended that a minimum of one page of environmental information should be disclosed and gave some indication as to what it should cover.[7] The Advisory Committee on Business and the Environment of the UK's Department of Environment published a report in 1993 recommending (para. 11) that institutional investors call for the proposals of the Hundred Group of Finance Directors to be adopted. They further recommended that the London Stock Exchange adopt standards of environmental disclosure in its listing requirements and that the accounting professions provide guidelines on accounting for the environment. The Confederation of British Industry (CBI) launched its environment business forum with an *Agenda for Voluntary Action* in 1992 which required companies signing up to the Forum to publish their environmental policy and report progress towards meeting the targets and objectives for meeting the policy.[8] These initiatives were, however, usually accompanied by statements about how successful such voluntary codes were and why this was a good reason for governments to forebear from producing legislation on the issues. Some governments — notably in the United Kingdom — were persuaded by this nonsense with the consequence that something in the region of 90 per cent of European companies continued to refuse to produce environmental disclosure about their activities.

The professional accounting bodies were typically slow in responding to the rapidly developing agenda. The survey of current activities and developments in environmental accounting and auditing carried out by the FEE (FEE, 1993) reported that none of the accounting standard setting bodies in the countries reviewed was involved at that time in setting standards in relation to environmental accounting matters.[9] However, by the mid-1990s professional bodies in Belgium, Denmark, Germany, the Netherlands and the United Kingdom all had some relevant initiatives in hand. Furthermore, national accounting standards-setting bodies had begun the process of examining (i) the need for accounting standards on environmental issues and (ii) the need for guidance so that extant accounting policy could cope with the increasing financial impact of the environment on companies. It was all very slow and reactionary (see, for example, Bebbington et al., 1994) although the UK bodies — ICAEW, ICAS, ACCA and CIMA — had all sponsored research projects concerned with environmental accounting. Perhaps one of the most positive initiatives from the accounting bodies was the ACCA's Environmental Reporting Award Scheme (ERAS). This scheme was having a major influence on the direction of environmental reporting in the United Kingdom and elsewhere in Europe by highlighting 'good' and 'better' practices and publicising companies' attempts in the environmental reporting field.[10] None of this was, however, a substitute for firm, intelligent accounting standards and disclosure requirements within company law.

Surveys of environmental reporting in Western Europe

The early development of environmental reporting in Europe is well documented[11] and can be generally characterised as innovative but not widespread. This situation changed in the late 1980s. Table 6.1 summarises the results of two surveys (Adams *et al.*, 1995b and Roberts, 1991) of environmental reporting in selected countries in continental western Europe.[12] While the table shows an increase in the number of companies making any environmental disclosures in each of the countries studied it appears that, in all countries except Germany, there was actually a decrease in the *variety* of information disclosed during the early 1990s.[13] The results of both surveys indicate that German companies are leading mainland Europe in disclosing various types of environmental information followed by Swedish companies.[14] Less than two-thirds of the French or Dutch companies reported any environmental information in their corporate Annual Report. These apparent differences across countries could be due to the different industry compositions of the samples and/or the different pressures on companies to report resulting from the differing social, political, cultural and economic environments in which they operate.

As a result of both the lack of language barriers and the greater emphasis that the United Kingdom generally places on surveys, we tend to be better informed about environmental reporting developments in the United Kingdom than elsewhere. A selection of UK surveys are summarised in Table 6.2 (adapted from Gray, 1993). While there has clearly been a steady increase in the proportion of UK companies disclosing at least some environmental information over the early years of the 1990s, Table 6.2 should be read carefully as it strongly suggests that it is really only the very largest companies in the United Kingdom which give serious attention to this subject (see, for example, Gray, 1993; Gray *et al.*, 1993).

Such surveys do suggest that environmental reporting is, nevertheless, more widely adopted by UK companies than it is in the rest of Europe. However, Adams *et al.* (1995b) find that UK companies fall behind all but the Netherlands (see Table 6.1) in the *volume* of their disclosure.

Figure 6.2 (adapted from Gray *et al.*, 1995b) shows the general indifference that UK companies showed towards environmental issues until the late 1980s. From the late 1980s there has been a very clear rise in the proportion large UK companies disclosing environmental information. This increase in the *proportion* of companies was accompanied by a slight increase in the *quantity* of environmental information disclosed.[15] This increased attention — in the United Kingdom and elsewhere — encouraged innovation and experimentation with environmental reporting. It is to this that we now turn.

Developments in environmental reporting practice

As environmental reporting is not widely regulated, it came as no surprise that companies experimented with different approaches to presenting their environmental disclosures. These experiments in the early- to mid-1990s could be thought of as falling

Table 6.1 Surveys of environmental reporting in mainland Western Europe

Country	Germany		Sweden		France		Switzerland		Netherlands	
Survey	Roberts (1991)	Adams et al. (1995b)	Roberts (1991)	Adams et al. (1995b)	Roberts (1991)	Adams et al. (1995b)	Roberts (1991)	Adams et al. (1995b)	Roberts (1991)	Adams et al. (1995b)
Data year(s)	1988 or 1989	1992	1988 or 1989	1992	1988 or 19?9	1992	1988 or 1989	1992	1988 or 1989	1992
Sample	40	25	15	25	25	25	15	25	15	25
Any environmental disclosure	80%	100%	80%	88%	52%	56%	60%	76%	60%	64%
Policy statement	35%	80%	27%	48%	28%	40%	20%	36%	33%	52%
Targets/ standards	—	36%	—	20%	—	12%	—	8%	—	12%
Environmental impacts	—	56%	—	40%	—	16%	—	24%	—	24%
Product information	50%	72%	46%	44%	28%	32%	40%	32%	20%	16%
Process information	32%	36%	53%	20%	16%	8%	13%	12%	27%	4%
R & D activities	52%	80%	40%	24%	16%	12%	27%	20%	33%	12%
Expenditures incurred	—	36%	—	12%	—	4%	—	16%	—	8%
Investment information	42%	44%	46%	24%	4%	12%	27%	28%	7%	16%
Environmental audits	—	0%	—	20%	—	8%	—	16%	—	8%
Mean page length of disclosure	—	1.61	—	0.85	—	0.71	—	0.60	—	0.45

Note: Both surveys (Roberts, 1991 and Adams et al., 1995b) used the English language version of the corporate annual report only (i.e. they did not include any separate environmental reports). Use of English language reports results in only large companies being selected. Both surveys excluded the financial services sector.

Table 6.2 Surveys of environmental reporting in the United Kingdom

Survey	Roberts (1990)	Harte and Owen (1991)	Kirkman and Hope (1992)			Adams et al. (1995b)	KPMG (1993a)
Data year(s)	1987	1989 or 1990	1990, 1991			1992	1993
Sample size	15	30	78	125	34	25	100
	Large	Known good disclosers	Large	Medium	Unlisted	Large	Largest*
Sample criteria	CAR only	CAR only	Includes separate reports			CAR only	Includes separate reports
Any environmental disclosure	13%	100%	54%	23%	9%	80%	66%
Separate booklet	–	–	6%	0%	–	–	25%
Separate section	–	33%	32%	2%	–	32%	–
Financial information	0%	20%	9%	0%	–	**–	*–
Quantified information	–	10%	15%	1%	–	**–	**–
Policy statements	0%	40%	43%	12%	–	56%	70%
Targets/standards	–	–	–	–	–	16%	65%
Environmental impacts						28%	–
Product information	–	–	35%	9%	–	24%	–
Process information	–	–	43%	5%	–	8%	–
R & D activities	–	–	24%	2%	–	8%	–
Expenditures incurred	0%	–	–	–	–	12%	–
Environmental audits	–	–	13%	2%	–	24%	22%
Mean length of disclosure	0.50	–	–	–	–	0.59	–

* Results obtained by survey rather than content analysis of corporate annual reports.
** Information on financial and quantitative disclosures given by type of information rather than overall.
CAR corporate annual report

Figure 6.2a *Percentage of UK companies making voluntary and mandatory environmental and energy disclosures, adapted from Gray et al., 1995a*

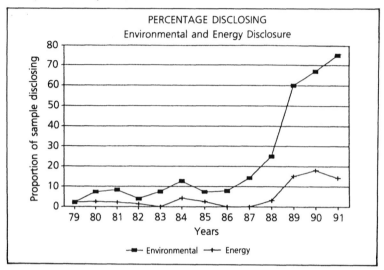

Figure 6.2b *Volume of environmental and energy disclosures, adapted from Gray et al., 1995a*

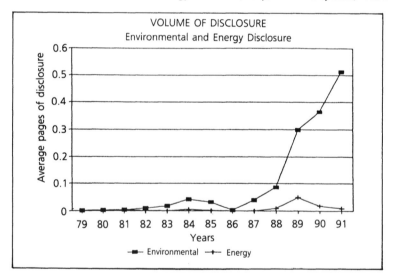

into three broad categories of environmental reporting: *descriptive and performance reporting; quantitative environmental accounts;* and *financial environmental reporting.* We deal with each of these in turn.[16]

UK companies tended to lead the development of the *descriptive and performance reporting* approach to environmental reporting. The production of a separate free-standing environmental report rapidly became accepted as 'best practice' (but see Gray *et al.*, 1995d).[17] These reports tended to include descriptions of environmental policies and corporate activity plus (frequently detailed) data on performance in such areas as emissions control and energy savings. The 1994 Environmental Performance Report of British Telecom (see Figure 6.3) is a useful example of this approach. The BT Report summarises the company's policies and the way in which it affects the environment. The policy identifies key environmental issues in most aspects of the company's operations — many of which are quantified later in the report. In addition, the BT Report quantifies many of its environmental targets and provides quantified progress against previous targets. While it appears to meet the requirements of the Hundred Group of Finance Directors (1992) — see Figure 6.4 — it still exhibits, as many 'state of the art' reports do, several weaknesses. Owen (1995, in press) notes, for example, that such reports often highlight inadequacies in target setting due to deficiencies in the company's environmental management system, as well as presenting over-aggregated or incomplete data. With regard to the descriptive content, he notes that it is often impossible to obtain a clear view of the company's strategic thinking, allowing information presented to be placed in context. In particular, the report user needs to know what the key environmental impacts are and how the company is going about tackling these issues. Nevertheless, BT is a past winner of the UK-based Certified Association of Chartered Accountant's (ACCA) Environmental Reporting Award Scheme (ERAS) and thus its report was considered to be one of the best examples of environmental reporting at that time. This approach to reporting was not, however, confined to the United Kingdom. Many continental European companies were also producing comparable reports at that time. The extract from Ciba in Figure 6.5 is one such example.[18]

The more innovative examples of environmental reporting which emphasise the *quantitative accounting approach to environmental reporting* have tended to come from mainland western Europe. These approaches tend to go a step further and provide a more *holistic* picture of the organisation's environmental interactions. As a result, such approaches might be thought of as first steps towards an understanding of the *sustainability* (or, more realistically, the un-sustainability—see Bebbington and Gray, 1995a) of a corporation. The most notable of these approaches was the *Ökobilanzen* (environmental report/eco-balance) developed by German, Austrian and Swiss companies and greatly influenced by the work of the Institutes of Environmental Research in Economics (IOW) of Germany and Austria (FEE, 1993; Jasch, 1993). The reports not only describe, for example, the company's environmental policy and the scope of its market share for 'environmentally friendly' products, but also show the resources used by a company and illustrate the efficiency with which these have been employed. Most of these reports include a form of a quantitative input–output analysis, known as an *Ökobilanz*, which is applied to a single product, division or entire company. The input side consists of all the inputs and energy used and the output side the products, emissions, etc. The Fédération des Experts Comptables Européens report that about 30 Austrian companies have prepared *Ökobilanzen*, though many of these are reported only internally for control purposes (FEE, 1993).

One of the earliest published examples of the *Ökobilanz* approach was provided by the Danish Steel Works Ltd (*Det Danske Stålvalseværk A/S*). The company's 23-page 1993 Annual Report included 6 pages of audited 'Green Accounts' — the centrepiece of which

Figure 6.3 *BT and the environment: 1994 Environmental Performance Report*

BT's Environmental Policy

BT is committed to minimising the impact of its operations on the environment by means of a programme of continuous improvement.

In particular BT will:

✚ meet and, where appropriate, exceed the requirements of all relevant legislation - where no regulations exist BT shall set its own exacting standards;

✚ seek to reduce consumption of materials in all operations, reuse rather than dispose whenever possible, and promote recycling and the use of recycled materials;

✚ design energy efficiency into new services, buildings and products and manage energy wisely in all operations;

✚ reduce wherever practicable the level of harmful emissions;

✚ market products that are safe to use, make efficient use of resources, and which can be reused, recycled or disposed of safely;

✚ work with its suppliers to minimise the impact of their operations on the environment through a quality purchasing policy;

✚ site its buildings, structures and operational plant to minimise visual, noise and other impacts on the local environment;

✚ support through its community programme the promotion of environmental protection by relevant external groups and organisations;

✚ include environmental issues in discussions with the BT unions, the BT training programmes and encourage the implementation by all BT people of sound environmental practices;

✚ monitor progress and publish an environmental performance report on an annual basis.

4

Figure 6.3 *continued*

How BT affects the Environment

Fuel and Energy

The combustion of fossil fuels generates emissions of carbon dioxide, sulphur oxides and nitrogen oxides. Increased atmospheric carbon dioxide is an important factor in global warming, while the latter two gases contribute to regional environmental problems such as acid rain.

Wastes

Significant BT wastes, in proportion to the UK totals, include telephones, exchanges, cable, batteries and PCB/PCN capacitors. BT acknowledges its responsibility to carefully manage its wastes in order to minimise any environmental impacts caused by their disposal.

Procurement

BT is the UK's largest civilian purchaser, and spends around £4 billion a year on goods and services. BT acknowledges its duty to practice environmentally responsible purchasing, a responsibility shared with its suppliers.

Emissions to Air

BT's fleet of vehicles is responsible for an estimated 0.2 per cent of the UK's total road vehicle-related VOC (volatile organic compound) emissions. These compounds affect local air quality. BT uses refrigerants, fire extinguishers and other materials whose emissions damage the ozone layer.

Product Stewardship

BT is the UK's principal supplier of telecommunications services and a major supplier of telecommunication equipment. BT acknowledges its responsibility to make them energy and resource efficient, safe in disposal, and to support their recycling or reuse.

Local Impacts

BT operates from more than 9,000 properties. In addition, BT's network includes 122,000 payphones, 4 million poles, 3.7 million covered manholes, 86 thousand roadside cabinets and 210 radio stations. Careful planning is required to minimise impacts on local communities.

Environmental Risk Management

BT is formalising the procedures for the assessment and management of the environmental risks posed by underground storage tanks, asbestos, holdings of potentially damaging chemicals and contaminated land.

Please see page 43 for a summary table of BT's main consumptions and emissions

5

was the eco-balance (or the 'mass balance' as they called it) shown in Figure 6.6. The *Ökobilanz* showed what inputs (materials supplied) had been converted into (finished goods, emissions, recyclable waste products and other waste products). The quantity of materials was reported in tonnes including water usage. The amount of electricity used was also reported (further details on how the data is collected can be found in Bank-Jorgensen, 1993). By way of explanation of the format, the Annual Report states:

> The circle illustrates the production area. Within the circle, the production units are shown separately. Volumes originating from transfer between the units are included in the mass balance, but are not shown in the circle in order to keep the illustration as simple as possible. As the volume of heavy metal is quite modest in relation to the total production volumes, a separate statement of additions and disposals of heavy metal has been prepared. Water, heavy metal and electricity are stated in proportions which cannot be compared with other figures. The volumes within the circle are of the same proportion. Volumes outside the circle are also of the same proportion.

A further unique aspect of the Danish Steel Works Report is shown in Figure 6.7 — the 'Environmental Declaration' from its 1993 Annual Report. The Report contains this explanation of the declaration:

> The objective of the 'environmental declaration' is to provide constructing engineers, using steel in a product, with a possibility of evaluating the total strain on the environment throughout the life cycle of the product in question. The values stated in the diagram are mean values for the product composition for plates and sections, respectively.
> In addition to values achieved for products, manufactured in 1993, the 'environmental declaration' contains goals for 1994 for selected areas. A *) in the goal column indicates that no goal has been set for 1994. The reasons for not setting goals are several, including dependence on circumstances that the company cannot influence and that the plans for 1994 do not include activities in these areas.

The 1993 Annual Report of the Danish Steel Works Ltd also shows: 'trend charts' in the form of line graphs for recycled waste products; heavy metal in scrap charged; noise emission; dust emission; dust and heavy metal immission; and accident frequency and number of absences due to accidents.

Figure 6.5 Extract from CIBA 1992 Corporate Environmental Report

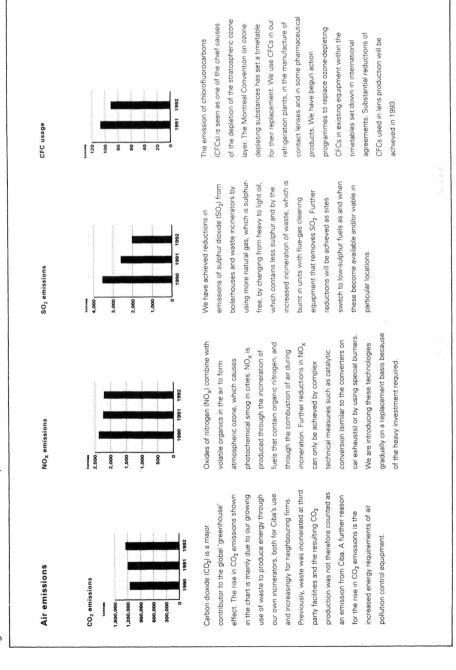

Air emissions

CO₂ emissions

NOₓ emissions

SO₂ emissions

CFC usage

Carbon dioxide (CO_2) is a major contributor to the global 'greenhouse' effect. The rise in CO_2 emissions shown in the chart is mainly due to our growing use of waste to produce energy through our own incinerators, both for Ciba's use and increasingly for neighbouring firms. Previously, waste was incinerated at third party facilities and the resulting CO_2 production was not therefore counted as an emission from Ciba. A further reason for the rise in CO_2 emissions is the increased energy requirements of air pollution control equipment.

Oxides of nitrogen (NO_x) combine with volatile organics in the air to form atmospheric ozone, which causes photochemical smog in cities. NO_x is produced through the incineration of fuels that contain organic nitrogen, and through the combustion of air during incineration. Further reductions in NO_x can only be achieved by complex technical measures such as catalytic conversion (similar to the converters on car exhausts) or by using special burners. We are introducing these technologies gradually on a replacement basis because of the heavy investment required.

We have achieved reductions in emissions of sulphur dioxide (SO_2) from boilerhouses and waste incinerators by using more natural gas, which is sulphur-free, by changing from heavy to light oil, which contains less sulphur and by the increased incineration of waste, which is burnt in units with flue-gas cleaning equipment that removes SO_2. Further reductions will be achieved as sites switch to low-sulphur fuels as and when these become available and/or viable in particular locations.

The emission of chlorofluorocarbons (CFCs) is seen as one of the chief causes of the depletion of the stratospheric ozone layer. The Montreal Convention on ozone depleting substances has set a timetable for their replacement. We use CFCs in our refrigeration plants, in the manufacture of contact lenses and in some pharmaceutical products. We have begun action programmes to replace ozone-depleting CFCs in existing equipment within the timetables set down in international agreements. Substantial reductions of CFCs used in lens production will be achieved in 1993.

Figure 6.6 *Det Danske Stålvalsværk A/S (Danish Steel Works Ltd), inside back cover*

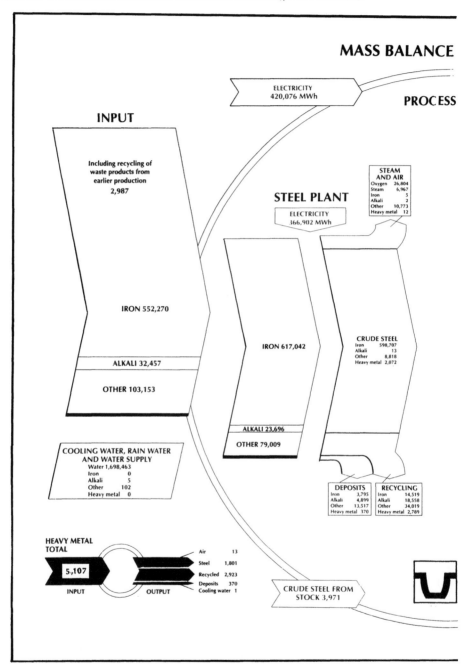

Figure 6.6 *continued*

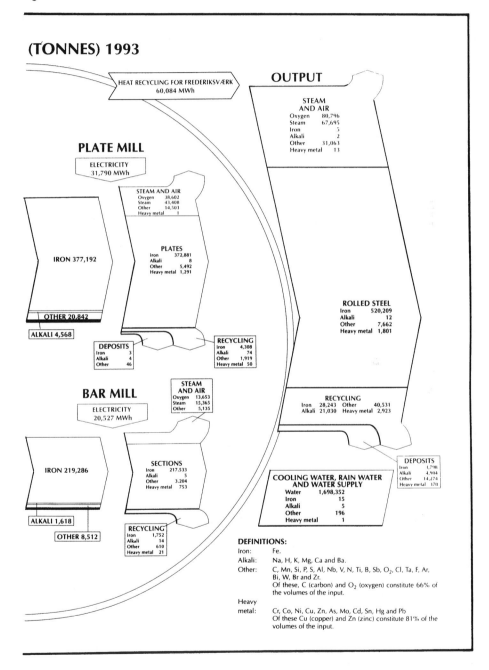

(TONNES) 1993

HEAT RECYCLING FOR FREDERIKSVÆRK
60,084 MWh

OUTPUT

STEAM
AND AIR
Oxygen	80,796
Steam	67,695
Iron	5
Alkali	2
Other	31,063
Heavy metal	13

PLATE MILL

ELECTRICITY
31,790 MWh

STEAM AND AIR
Oxygen	38,602
Steam	43,408
Other	14,503
Heavy metal	1

PLATES
Iron	372,881
Alkali	8
Other	5,492
Heavy metal	1,291

IRON 377,192

ROLLED STEEL
Iron	520,209
Alkali	12
Other	7,662
Heavy metal	1,801

OTHER 20,842

ALKALI 4,568

DEPOSITS
Iron	3
Alkali	4
Other	46

RECYCLING
Iron	4,308
Alkali	74
Other	1,919
Heavy metal	50

STEAM
AND AIR
Oxygen	13,653
Steam	15,365
Other	5,135

BAR MILL

ELECTRICITY
20,527 MWh

RECYCLING
Iron	28,243	Other	40,531
Alkali	21,030	Heavy metal	2,923

SECTIONS
Iron	217,533
Alkali	5
Other	3,204
Heavy metal	753

IRON 219,286

DEPOSITS
Iron	1,798
Alkali	4,904
Other	14,274
Heavy metal	170

COOLING WATER, RAIN WATER
AND WATER SUPPLY
Water	1,698,352
Iron	15
Alkali	5
Other	196
Heavy metal	1

ALKALI 1,618

OTHER 8,512

RECYCLING
Iron	1,752
Alkali	14
Other	610
Heavy metal	21

DEFINITIONS:

Iron:	Fe.
Alkali:	Na, H, K, Mg, Ca and Ba.
Other:	C, Mn, Si, P, S, Al, Nb, V, N, Ti, B, Sb, O_2, Cl, Ta, F, Ar, Bi, W, Br and Zr. Of these, C (carbon) and O_2 (oxygen) constitute 66% of the volumes of the input.
Heavy metal:	Cr, Co, Ni, Cu, Zn, As, Mo, Cd, Sn, Hg and Pb Of these Cu (copper) and Zn (zinc) constitute 81% of the volumes of the input.

Figure 6.7 *Det Danske Stålvalsværk A/S (Danish Steel Works Ltd), inside back cover*

"Environmental Declaration"
Net impact of 1 tonne of steel produced at Det Danske Stålvalseværk A/S

Type	Unit	Plates 1993	Plates Goal 1994	Sections 1993	Sections Goal 1994
Energy					
Electricity	kWh	829	829	749	710
Natural gas	Nm³	84	75	49	47
Oxygen	Nm³	41	40	16	16
Other gasses	kg	0.7	*)	0	*)
Metallurgic carbon (C)	kg	15	*)	14	*)
Recycled heat (52 8% of total consumption of Frederiksværk)	kWh	132	*)	86	*)
Air					
Dust emission	gram	153	143	152	142
Heavy metal emission (Ni, Pb, Cd, Zn and Hg)	gram	5	4.7	5	4.7
CO₂	kg	238	*)	156	*)
Water					
Tap water, consumption	m³	0.17	*)	0.17	*)
Cooling water, consumption	m³	3.8	*)	1.5	*)
Heavy metals discharged to water (Ni, Cr, Cu, Pb, Zn and Cd)	gram	1.5	*)	0.5	*)
Waste products					
Deposited waste products	kg	45	20	40	18
Recycled waste products	kg	186	233	161	205

	Unit	1993	Goal 1994
Number of industrial accidents	number/tonne	0.00012	0.00011
Hours of absence due to industrial accidents	h/tonne	0.0097	0.0090
Maximum immission, dust	µg/m³	149	136
Maximum immission, heavy metals (Ni, Pb, Cd, Zn and Hg)	µg/m³	39	32
Recycling of waste products (recycled/produced)	%	82	98

*) no goal

A contrasting approach to quantitative environmental reporting has been taken by the Eni Enrico Mattei Foundation (FEEM), a non-profit organisation based in Italy. FEEM has developed an environmental 'balance sheet' (see Bartolomeo, 1994) in liaison with the Instituto Nazionale di Statistica (ISTAT). In addition to providing information for corporate management, the standardised format of the 'balance sheet' allows it to provide a link between the micro- and macro-levels in that the 'balance sheets' of different companies can be consolidated to provide local, regional or national data on industrial impact on the environment together with environmental expenditures to reduce that impact.

Figure 6.8 shows the format of the environmental 'balance sheet' of EniChem, one of Italy's largest chemical companies. As well as linking quantitative data on inputs with those for emissions, as the Danish Steel Works Ltd mass balance approach does (see Figure 6.6), it also provides information on current and 'investment' expenses for environmental protection and provides a link between the monetary values of inputs and products.

The attempt to link the micro- and macro-levels of economic and environmental activity has attracted considerable attention in Europe. In addition to the Italian ISTAT/ FEEM approach, France (see, for example, Christophe and Bebbington, 1992) and the Netherlands have both given the matter serious investigation. For example, the Netherlands Central Bureau of Statistics developed an extension to the existing national accounts (the usual way of measuring Gross Domestic Product — GDP) in a matrix format in order to derive what has been called 'Environment Satellite Accounts' (see Keuning and Bosch, 1993). They record information on emissions and waste and the information aids Dutch ministries to demonstrate how branches of industry and households contribute to environmental problems. This sort of reasoning has then been taken further — especially in the Netherlands — to develop a sensible means of calculating a 'Green' GDP as a better measure of an economy's 'performance' than existing national accounts (for more detail see, for example, Ahmed et al., 1989; Anderson, 1991; MacGillivray, 1993).

Since the early attempts at financially derived CSR in the early 1970s (see, for example, the references to Abt and Linowes in Chapter 4) there has been a fascination with trying to produce 'financial accounts of society' or, in the present case, *financial environmental accounts*. The most adventurous (and widely reported) example of attempts in this direction in the 1990s was the attempt by BSO/Origin (see Figure 6.9). BSO/Origin (a Dutch consulting and electrical engineering company) attempted to financially quantify its environmental impacts (or 'environmental value lost' as it was termed) and *deduct* this number from its financial gain arising from economic activities (i.e. its profit) using a value-added statement. While as an experiment it should be applauded, it is seriously flawed in that the valuation approach used is inconsistent. As noted by Gray *et al.* 1993, p. 225): 'On the downside, the company recognises that the accounts are partial, subjective and, in effect, add possible apples to approximate pears and subtract the results from hypothetical oranges.' On the upside, of course, are the lessons learnt from the process of undertaking this kind of analysis and the possible benefits of such experiments in contributing to sustainability (see Gray, 1995a; Gray *et al.*, 1993; Huizing and Dekker, 1992 for more information on the approach used).

Figure 6.8 Format of environmental balance sheet for EniChem (reproduced from Social and Environmental Accounting (1994) 14(1))

Social & Environmental Accounting

Vol.14 No.1 April 1994

THE COMPLETE ENVIRONMENTAL BALANCE-SHEET

Data collection units	RESOURCES		GOODS AND SERVICES		POLLUTANT AND ENVIRONMENTAL EXPENSES																	
	Produced	Non-Produced	Prod1	Prod2	Air (quantity of pollutants and expenses)				Water (quantity of pollutants and expenses)				Wastes (quantity and expenses)				Soil and underground water protection (expenses)	Noise (quantity and expenses)		Other exp.	Total ce	Total ie
					Group 1		Tot ce	Tot ie	Group 1		Tot ce	Tot ie	Group 1		Tot ce	Tot ie	ce	ie				
	1	1			1.1	1.2			1.1	1.2			1.1	1.2				n1	n2			
	1.1	1.1			ce	ie			ce	ie			ce	ie			ce	ie		ce	ie	
	q	q	v	av	q	v	v	v	q	v	v	v	q	v	v	v	v	q	v	v	v	v
Unit 1																						
Unit 2																						
Unit 3																						
TOTAL COMPANY																						

ENI ENRICO MATTEI FOUNDATION, Milano, 16/07/93

SYMBOLS:
1.2 code of the family of product or pollutant   1.1, 1.2, 2.1, 2.2 = code of the single product or pollutant

ce= current environmental expenses   ie=investments expenses

v= monetary value   q= physical quantity   av= added value

8

Figure 6.9 *Extract from BSO/Origin 1991 Annual Report*

Costs of environmental effects in thousands of Dutch guilders				1991		1990*
Atmospheric emissions	Emission	Unit cost	Total			
Natural gas consumption						
NO$_x$	468 kg	10 NLG/kg	**5**		5	
CO$_2$	496 t.	100 NLG/t.	**50**		48	
Total				**55**		53
Electricity consumption						
SO$_2$	7.595 kg	14 NLG/kg	**106**		111	
NO$_x$	5.803 kg	10 NLG/kg	**58**		62	
Dust	640 kg	10 NLG/kg	**6**		7	
CO$_2$	2.342 t.	100 NLG/t.	**234**		252	
Total				**404**		432
Traffic by road						
NO$_x$	47.486 kg	40 NLG/kg	**1.899**		1.048	
HC	36.600 kg					
CO	181.436 kg					
CO$_2$	10.442 t.	100 NLG/t.	**1.044**		764	
Total				**2.943**		1.812
Traffic by air						
NO$_x$	1.409 kg	10 NLG/kg	**14**		12	
CO$_2$	385 t.	100 NLG/t.	**38**		32	
Total				**52**		44
Waste incineration						
SO$_2$	326 kg	14 NLG/kg	**5**		4	
NO$_x$	401 kg	10 NLG/kg	**4**		4	
Dust	276 kg	10 NLG/kg	**3**		3	
HCI	753 kg	13 NLG/kg	**10**		9	
CO$_2$	301 t.	0 NLG/kg	**0**		0	
Total				**22**		20
Sub total atmospheric emissions				**3.476**		2.361

* The figures shown for road traffic emissions have been
recalculated to business kilometers traveled in private
cars, in contrast to the figures published in the 1990
annual report.

61

Figure 6.9 *continued*

	Emission	Unit cost	1991 Total	1990
Subtotal atmospheric emissions			**3.476**	2.361
Waste water				
Water treatment	377 inh.eq.	048 NLG/i.e.	**18**	13
Transportation	377 inh.eq.	12 NLG/i.e.	**5**	3
Residual water pollution			**36**	27
Total			**59**	43
Waste				
Waste produced by company				
Collection	409 t.	80 NLG/t.	**33**	30
Incineration	251 t.	100 NLG/t.	**25**	23
Residual waste after incineration				
Heavy ash	25 t.	100 NLG/t.	**3**	2
Fly ash	8 t.	200 NLG/t.	**2**	1
Total			**63**	56
Waste produced by electricity power stations				
Fly ash	60 t.	200 NLG/t.	**12**	13
Waste produced by water treatment				
Sludge	5 t. dry matter	500 NLG/t. dry matter	**3**	2
Total			**3.613**	2.475

62

Figure 6.9 *continued*

Environmental expenditure in thousands of Dutch guilders	**1991**	1990
Fuel levy in The Netherlands		
Natural gas for heating purposes	**1**	1
Liquid gas for cars	**20**	18
Fuel for electricity	**5**	8
Total	**26**	27
Purification levies, garbage collection rates, sewerage tax and other environmental taxes	**147**	138
Private waste processors	**81**	51
Total	**254**	216

Net value withdrawn in thousands of Dutch guilders		
Costs of environmental effects	**3.613**	2.475
Environmental expenditure	**(254)**	(216)
Total net value withdrawn	**3.359**	2.259

Net added value in thousands of Dutch guilders		
Value added	**377.298**	255.614
Value withdrawn	**(3.359)**	(2.259)
Net added value	**373.939**	253.355

63

While developments in the EU's environmental policy, together with the initiatives of business, the accounting profession and some companies have led to a general increase in accountability for the environment, the current level of accountability is clearly inadequate. In addition, while the EU provisions are to be applauded, in that they cover accountability as well as responsibility, the voluntary nature of much of them makes potential benefits questionable. Unless mandatory requirements for accountability are forthcoming, the moral responsibility felt by some companies to account may wane.

6.3 Reporting on employee issues

Regulation of employee-related reporting

The European Union has a long history of concern with the conditions of employees and their rights within organisations. This history both reflects, and provides an impetus to, the historical emphasis placed on employee-related CSR in Europe. From the Treaty of Rome (1957) through the Single European Act (1986) to the Community Charter of Fundamental Rights of Workers 1989 (the Social Charter) and the Treaty on European Union 1992 (the Maastricht Treaty) the EU has provided a steadily increasing bed of recommendation and regulation covering such matters as working conditions; health and safety; training; collective bargaining; equal pay; and initiatives directed to encourage full employment and the protection of those outside the labour force.[19]

These developments in European social law provide a base for the further development of reporting on employee-related matters in two ways. *First*, they provide directly for employee-related CSR. As an illustration, the European Works Council Directive[20] requires more than 1000 European multinational companies to consult employees on a wide range of issues and disclose information on corporate performance (see Carlin, 1995 and Cressey, 1993 for more information). *Secondly*, they highlight areas of concern over corporate responsibility. Indeed, it is likely that future legislation will specifically require further reporting on employee-related matters such as, for example, disclosure as part of the process of employee consultation.

Such reporting may also aid the achievement of the European Union's goal of harmonisation of employment conditions across the EU. Indeed, one of the indirect effects of EU regulation in the employee field has been the use made by a variety of European companies of their corporate Annual Report to highlight areas where harmonisation has not been achieved. For example, the 1992 Annual Reports of the German companies BMW, RWE and Deutsche Babcock highlighted the drawbacks of locating industrial units in Germany arising from, *inter alia*, the shorter working hours in that country. In an extension of this, the BMW Report provides a bar chart depicting the standard yearly working time in the metal-working industries of Germany, France, Italy, Great Britain, Spain, United States and Japan and comments on the resulting relatively high cost of labour in Germany. This is not only a relatively novel example of CSR but also illustrates one example of how companies might use disclosure to attempt to manage

Figure 6.10 *Standardised structure for social reporting: UEC, 1983 Strasbourg Congress*

1. **A summarized statement** An outline of the most significant aspects of the social performance of the enterprise over the year together with a statement of principal objectives and review of prospects for the following year.
2. **A social report** To be composed solely of quantitative indicators, the precise nature of which is not specified, in the following nine areas;

    (a) Employment levels
    (b) Working conditions
    (c) Health and safety
    (d) Education and training   The relationship between the
    (e) Industrial relation   enterprise and the workforce
    (f) Wages and other employee benefits
    (g) Distribution of value added
    (h) Impact on the environment
    (i) The enterprise and external parties
         (shareholders and other providers of   The relationship between the
         capital, local and national government,   enterprise and society
         customers and suppliers)

3. **Notes to the accounts** Explaining where necessary the methods and principles used in calculating the figures appearing in the social report, giving full information on any changes of method and indicating the effect of the change on the results shown, and defining terminology used.

their legitimacy or the political economy of the environment through attempting to influence perceptions of the corporate climate.

However, pan-European EU legislation is, clearly, not the only influence on employee reporting. National governments throughout Europe have given considerable legislative attention to the area. As we shall see below (and see also Chapters 7 and 9), whether it be the *bilan social* in France or the United Kingdom's Annual Report disclosure requirements, corporate information to and about employees has been central to any study of CSR at both national and international levels (for more detail see, for example, Gray *et al.*, 1987; Roberts, 1990).

Similarly, the European accounting profession is not without influence in this field — if, sadly, it is an influence it rarely chooses to exercise. A rare example of an initiative by the accounting profession in Europe came in a report of the social reporting working party of the *Union Européene des Experts Comptables, Economiques et Financiers* (UEC), forerunners to the FEE, to its 1983 Congress in Strasbourg, which concentrated largely on the relationship between the enterprise and the workforce suggesting a standardised structure for social reporting outlined in Figure 6.10.

New ground was also broken in the report with the suggestion that social accounts should be subject to independent audit. In particular, it was argued that the auditor should be able to: ensure that a satisfactory system of internal control is in existence to safeguard the quality and reliability of social information produced; confirm that the definitions and methods of calculation used are acceptable; verify that the figures used in the social report agree with those in financial and technical reports; and certify the truth and fairness of any financially quantified information.

The overriding theme of the UEC report was that to gain credibility, the production of social information must be tackled with the same degree of rigour as that applied to the more traditional financial statements; hence the emphasis on formal structure and the audit function. Although the formalised structure would go a long way to ensuring the harmonisation of social reporting practice in Europe, it has not been widely adopted. The use of quantitative indicators in corporate annual reports, as suggested by the UEC, is minimal.

Surveys of reporting on employee issues in Western Europe

Table 6.3 summarises the results of three surveys of reporting on employee issues in Western Europe (Adams *et al.*, 1995b; Roberts, 1990, 1991). The surveys show the main areas of disclosure to be pay and benefits, breakdown of numbers, recruitment/ redundancies and training. Information on communication/consultation, health and safety and trade unions is much less frequently disclosed. German companies disclosed by far the most information with a mean length of 3.36 pages, the United Kingdom followed with 2.04 pages, while Swiss, Swedish, Dutch and French companies disclosed an average of between 1.41 and 1.68 pages of employee information in the English language version of their corporate Annual Report.

Adams *et al.* (1995b) indicated that within each of the categories of information in Table 6.3 there was a broad divergence on what was disclosed. For example, whereas 74 per cent of the total sample gave at least some information on pay/costs and 79 per cent gave some information on pensions, only 25 per cent gave any information at all regarding conditions of employment (see Table 3.2, Adams *et al.*, 1995b). When it came to reporting breakdowns of employee numbers, Adams *et al.* (1995b) reported that German, Swedish and Swiss companies provided the most informative examples. The extract of Atlas Copco's (Swedish) 1992 corporate Annual Report in Figure 6.11, for example, used a map of the world to show the geographic distribution of its personnel and used tables to show the percentages of women and men in each geographic region and the average number of employees in each business sector. It also disclosed the sales, net profit and value added per employee. The German group RWE's 1992 corporate Annual Report, an extract of which is reproduced in Figure 6.12, provided a very detailed breakdown of employees and included information on the percentages of foreigners employed in Germany, women, part-time employees, disabled employees and 'temporarily interrupted working relationships'. Also disclosed were the employee turnover rate, average age of employees and average length of service. Another example worth commenting on is that of Veba (Germany), which used bar charts in its 1992 corporate Annual Report to show the analysis of employees by business sector and the analysis of trainees between office and trade/technical trainees and female and male trainees.

Despite these examples of quantified information, the usefulness of much of the reporting on employee issues in the corporate Annual Report is called into question when it is realised that most of the disclosures are qualitative. For example, Adams *et*

Table 6.3 Surveys of reporting on employee issues in Western Europe

Country	Germany		Sweden		France		Switzerland		Netherlands		UK	
Survey	Roberts (1991)	Adams et al. (1995b)	Roberts (1991)	Adams et al. (1995b)	Roberts (1991)	Adams et al. (1995b)	Roberts (1991)	Adams et al. (1995b)	Roberts (1991)	Adams et al. (1995b)	Roberts (1990)	Adams et al. (1995b)
Data year(s)	1988 or 1989	1992	1988 or 1989	1992	1988 or 1989	1992	1988 or 1989	1992	1988 or 1989	1992	1987	1992
Sample size	40	25	15	25	25	25	15	25	15	25	15	25
Any employee disclosure	95%	100%	60%	100%	76%	100%	60%	100%	53%	100%	—	100%
Separate employee section	—	92%	—	24%	—	52%	—	44%	—	36%	53%	20%
Employee appreciation	—	88%	—	36%	—	84%	—	92%	—	88%	73%	88%
Pay and benefits	—	100%	—	96%	—	96%	—	84%	—	100%	—	100%
Breakdown of numbers	—	100%	—	100%	—	92%	—	96%	—	96%	—	88%
Recruitment redundancies	—	100%	—	88%	—	64%	—	84%	—	84%	—	80%
Training	—	88%	—	40%	—	76%	—	56%	—	76%	40%	60%
Communication/consultation	—	64%	—	24%	—	36%	—	28%	—	60%	80%	96%
Health and safety	40%	64%	0%	24%	12%	32%	20%	16%	33%	52%	33%	56%
Trade unions	—	36%	—	0%	—	16%	—	16%	—	32%	0%	16%
Mean page length of disclosure	—	3.36	—	1.56	—	1.68	—	1.41	—	1.65	—	2.04

Note: The Adams et al. (1995b), Roberts (1990, 1991) used the English Language version of the corporate annual report only resulting in only large companies being selected. Both surveys excluded the financial services sector.

Figure 6.11 *Extract from Atlas Copco's 1992 Corporate Annual Report*

PERSONNEL

	Average number of employees* 1992	1991
Compressor Technique	7,481	7,790
Construction and Mining Technique	5,369	5,902
Industrial Technique	6,170	5,573
Others	175	279
Total	19,195	19,544

*) A detailed presentation showing the average number of employees, and wages, salaries and other remuneration paid, prepared in conformity with the Swedish Companies Act, is included in the Annual Report filed with the National Patent & Registration Office in Sweden and may be obtained free of charge from Atlas Copco's headquarters in Nacka, Sweden

SEK thousands	1992	1991
Sales per employee	834	769
Net profit per employee	3†	26
Value added per employee	336	311

The average number of employees in the Atlas Copco Group decreased by 349 persons during 1992 to 19,195 employees (19,544). The proportion employed in Swedish companies was 15 percent (19) and 42 percent (35) in companies within the EC. Salaries, wages and other remunerations totaled SEK 4,781 m. (4,536), of which SEK 1,227 m. (1,233) represented social welfare costs.

The distribution of women and men is shown below.

	Distribution as % Women	Men	Total number
Europe	19	81	11,448
of which Sweden	18	82	2,907
of which EC	19	81	7,975
North America	14	86	2,604
South America	12	88	1,504
North Africa/Middle East	26	74	235
Southern Africa	18	82	465
India/East Asia	7	93	2,464
Oceania	18	82	475
	16	84	19,195

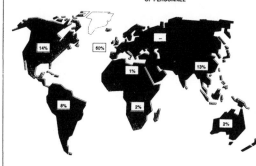

GEOGRAPHIC DISTRIBUTION OF PERSONNEL

Value added and interested parties
The value added corresponds to the Group's total invoicing, SEK 16,007 m., reduced by costs for the purchase of raw materials, wholly and partially finished goods as well as services, SEK 9,565 m. The figure obtained is a measure of the company's productive contribution, i.e. the value added through processing etc.

In 1992, the value added amounted to SEK 6,442 m. (6,073), an increase of approximately 6 percent.

The value added is distributed among interested parties, i.e. employees, creditors, government, municipalities and shareholders. Remaining funds are retained in the company to cover costs for wear on plants and equipment (depreciation) and to provide for continued expansion of operations (retained in the business).

DISTRIBUTION OF VALUE ADDED	1992 SEK m.	%	1991 SEK m.	%
Wages and salaries	3,554	55	3,303	54
Social costs	1,227	19	1,233	20
Depreciation	527	8	482	8
Capital costs, net	107	2	153	3
Corporate and municipal taxes	412	6	392	6
Dividends paid	288	5	284	5
Retained in business	327	5	226	4
Value added, total	6,442	100	6,073	100
Value added per employee, SEK thousands	336		311	

54

Figure 6.12 *Extract from RWE's 1992 Corporate Annual Report*

Personnel structure	1991/92	Previous year
Proportion of total workforce		
– Domestic	91.3%	91.7%
– Foreign	8.7%	8.3%
– Foreigners employed in Germany	5.9%	5.9%
– Salaried employees	40.8%	40.3%
– Wage earners	55.1%	55.4%
– Trainees	4.1%	4.3%
– Women	12.4%	12.3%
– Part-time employees	2.3%	2.1%
– Disabled employees	4.3%	4.6%
Turnover rate	8.7%	7.2%
Average age	39.7 years	39.7 years
Average length of service	13.3 years	13.5 years
– Proportion with over 10 years of service	57.1%	57.7%
Temporarily interrupted working relationships	1.0%	0.8%
– Leave to look after young children	0.4%	0.3%
– Military/alternative civilian service	0.6%	0.5%

al. (1995b) found that while 83 per cent of the total European sample provided some information regarding recruitment and redundancies, only 35 per cent of the sample (or 42 per cent of disclosing companies) provided quantitative or financial information (see p. 33, Adams *et al.*, 1995b). Similarly, while 66 per cent of the sample disclosed some information on training and career development, coverage of the issues was haphazard and scant. Only 46 per cent of the total sample gave their policy on training, 52 per cent described activities and only 8 per cent gave any information regarding training outcomes. Other areas were covered by even fewer companies. In particular, the level of disclosure on health and safety was disappointingly low with only 19 per cent and 11 per cent of the total European sample giving accident and sickness rates, respectively. Figure 6.13 showing BMW's line graph of its accident frequency and severity is one of the better examples of disclosure in this area.

This broad overview now provides us with a basis from which to examine the practice of reporting on employee issues in a little more detail. While reporting on employee issues has a much longer history in Europe than environmental reporting, it appears to be subject to 'fashions' in that subjects, emphasis and focus change over time (see also Chapter 4). In order to get a flavour of European reporting practice, we will look at the historical development of reporting on employee issues in the United Kingdom, Germany, France and Sweden.

Figure 6.13 *Extract from BMW's 1992 Annual Report*

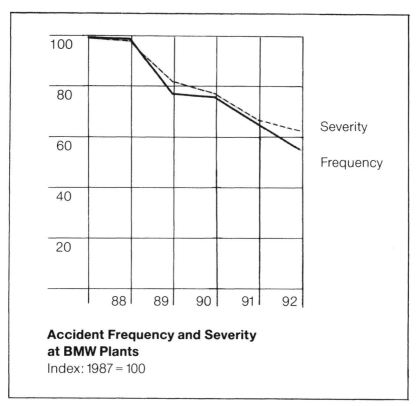

Developments in reporting on employee issues: United Kingdom

Hussey (1981) pointed to a few examples of companies giving information to employees in the first half of this century and to a quickening interest in employee reporting in the 1940s, but such practice did not become widespread until the 1970s. This coincided with the appearance of a growing literature in the subject area in the United Kingdom, some of which discussed the potential benefits to companies of issuing separate reports to employees. For example, Parker (1977) points to the role of reports to employees in developing favourable employee impressions of the company and reducing resistance to change, as well as their educative function in broadening employee perspectives away from matters merely affecting their own particular part of the shop floor, developing an awareness of company finance and explaining the role of the shareholder to employees. Our concern in this book, however, is with accountability and it is to the issue of accountability to employees to which we shall turn in discussing the reporting of information to employees.

A study by Lyall (1982) based on 60 employee reports received from a random sample of companies chosen from the *Times 1000* largest UK companies, indicated that generally only a very small amount of information was disclosed in the Annual Report to employees, which was generally insufficient to meet employees' basic information needs. The most frequent disclosures were profitability (57 companies), value-added (43 companies), divisional information (29 companies), financial resources (21 companies) and capital investment (21 companies). None of the reports contained information on budgets or future cash flows, which are relevant for determining job security, nor did they include information on production, selling and administration costs which aid the assessment of company performance. On weighting the information, to take account of the fact that the level of provision under the various headings varied considerably (ranging in the case of profit, for example, from a comprehensive profit statement to a single profit figure), value-added replaced profitability as the item receiving most attention in the reports. Lyall (1981) argued that the value-added statement can be unhelpful and misleading. He pointed to the common practice of showing both company retentions and distributions to shareholders net of tax while the amount paid to employees is shown inclusive of tax, thus effectively overstating by a considerable amount the employees' share of value-added measured in terms of take-home pay. Furthermore, the practice of including pension contributions, national insurance contributions, sickness benefits and other welfare expenditure in the employee share of value-added also tended to overstate their position. Indeed, an apparent increase in the employees' share may have been due to an increase in national insurance contributions, which of course really represents an increase in the Government's share of value-added.

In 1974 the United Kingdom Accounting Standards Steering Committee (the forerunner of the United Kingdom Accounting Standards Board) set up a working party (the Boothman Committee) to re-examine the scope and aims of published financial reports and to concern itself with public accountability, identifying people or groups for whom financial reports should be prepared and the information appropriate to their interests. In its discussion paper, *The Corporate Report*, published in 1975, the Boothman Committee illustrated its concern for the lack of accountability to the workforce by stating:

Nothing illustrates more vividly the nineteenth century origin of British Company Law than the way in which employees are almost totally ignored in the present Companies Acts and in corporate reports. (para. 6.12)

It was recommended (para. 6.19) that special purpose employment reports should be published. The Committee's recommendations as to the contents of these reports is shown in Figure 6.14.

In addition, *The Corporate Report* recommended the provision of a value-added statement (para. 6.7) (see Chapter 4 for a discussion about value added statements and Figure 4.7 for other recommendations in *The Corporate Report*).

The Corporate Report proposals were endorsed by the publication of the Department of

Figure 6.14 The Corporate Report's recommendations on the content of the Employment Report

1. Numbers employed, average for the financial year and actual on the first and last day.
2. Broad reasons for changes in the numbers employed.
3. The age distribution and sex of employees.
4. The functions of employees.
5. The geographical location of major employment centres.
6. Major plant and site closures, disposals and acquisitions during the past year.
7. The hours scheduled and worked by employees giving as much detail as possible concerning difference between groups of employees.
8. Employment costs concerning fringe benefits.
9. The costs and benefits associated with pension schemes and ability of such schemes to meet future commitments.
10. The names of unions recognised by the entity for the purpose of collective bargaining and membership figures where available or the fact that this information has not been made available by the unions concerned.
11. Information concerning safety and health including the frequency and severity of accidents and occupational diseases.
12. Selected ratios relating to employment.

Trade's discussion document *Aims and Scope of Company Reports* in 1976, which was met with hostility. Both the Stock Exchange and the Confederation of British Industry (CBI) expressed their profound disapproval of any move away from the 'traditional stewardship' concept, with its narrowly acknowledged obligations towards shareholders, in favour of a more public form of accountability. For example, the CBI expressed the view that whereas user groups other than shareholders had a right to ask for information, they had no general right to expect it to be provided, and it would certainly be wrong to impose such a legal duty upon companies (CBI, 1976). This view was reinforced by the election of the Thatcher Government in 1979 which signalled a strong lurch to the right and a return to the more 'traditional stewardship' (*sic*) form of financial reporting. Accountability to employees was no longer a matter of concern.

Figure 6.15 is adapted from Gray *et al.* (1995b) and shows the proportion of the sample of UK companies disclosing various types of information on employees together with the average volume of such disclosures for a sample of UK companies since 1979. The graphs show that reporting on employee issues such as health and safety, pensions and employee share ownership schemes (ESOPs) has increased in frequency since the late 1980s.[21] However, the volume of disclosure on specific issues such as health and safety and consultation has remained very low.

Developments in reporting on employee issues: Germany

German companies also have a long tradition of reporting on employee issues. In a survey of 296 1973–74 corporate Annual Reports, Brockhoff (1979) found that as many as 205 companies published a clearly identifiable 'social' section (*sozialbericht*). Even at

Figure 6.15a *Percentage of UK companies disclosing information on pensions, value-added, ESOPs, consultation, health and safety, employee other, adapted from Gray et al., 1995a*

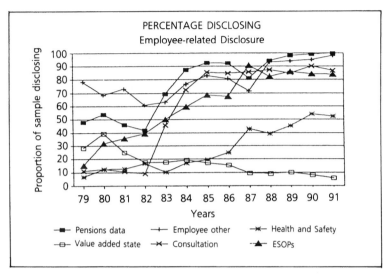

Figure 6.15b *Mean length of disclosure of information on employment data, pensions, consultation, ESOPs, health and safety, employee other, adapted from Gray et al., 1995a*

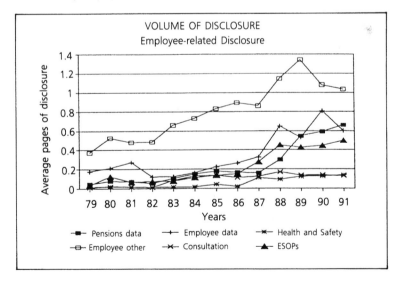

this early stage, 28 per cent of this large sample of corporate Annual Reports provided a breakdown of the workforce with respect to salaried versus hourly paid personnel; 22 per cent of the sample gave data for German versus foreign personnel working in Germany; 17 per cent for female versus male employees; and, 14 per cent for age. Further, 97 per cent of the sample reported information on pensions and retirement benefits, 47 per cent on apprenticeship programmes, 43 per cent on other training programmes, 21 per cent on employee housing, and 20 per cent on the security of the workplace. Thus German employee reporting in the early 1970s was more detailed than employee reporting in some European countries in the early 1990s. Schoenfeld (1978), in a survey of the 1972–74 reporting of known 'good disclosers' (16 German, 9 Swiss and 6 Austrian), also noted the particular concern for, and high level of, employee reporting and its regulation in Germany. His argument that level of disclosure reflected public concern at the time would suggest that stakeholder and/or legitimacy theory could help explain these findings on employee issues.

Three different approaches towards the production of early German social reports can be clearly identified:

1. A broadly based and partially integrated cost–benefit reporting system. Reports of this type, notable examples of which are STEAG (first published in 1973) and Saabergwerke AG (in 1973),[22] attempted to relate corporate expenditure to specific societal benefits. However, whereas private corporate costs can be stated with precision, societal benefits cannot be satisfactorily quantified. They are therefore stated verbally only, while societal costs themselves are completely omitted.

2. An extension of the traditional employee-orientated social report, by the inclusion of more information, largely descriptive, on the wider social aspects of the company's activities. Notable examples were Rank Xerox Gmbh and Bertelsmann AG.

3. Corporate goal accounting and reporting in which quantitative indicators are used wherever possible to describe the attainments of corporate objectives in areas of social performance and promotion of general public welfare. This particular concept was championed by Deutsche Shell AG (see Chapter 4 for a further discussion and Figure 4.11 for extracts from the 1975 report).

The climate for the development of social reporting in Germany has probably been aided by institutions such as the Business and Society Foundation (established by business leaders to study important social developments affecting the business community); the Social and Behavioural Science Division of the Battelle Institute; and the government-sponsored International Institute for Environment and Society. It is also interesting to note that in Germany, unlike the United Kingdom, businesses themselves have shown great interest in the development of social reporting. A particularly influential group were the Study Group on Practical Aspects of Social Reporting (*Arbeitskreis Sozialbilanzen Praxis*), established by seven leading companies in the field. Recognising a need for standardisation in social reporting, they developed the following formal structure and content of such reports in 1977:

- A social report, providing primarily verbal descriptions of goals, actions taken and achievements in area of social concern.
- A value-added statement, indicating the company's contribution to GNP and its distribution among the various stakeholders.

- A social account, providing a quantitative presentation of all measurable societally orientated corporate expenditures and revenues.

Despite the active involvement of business enterprise in the practical and theoretical development of social reporting in Germany, Ullmann (1979) reports that there was little interest among accountants, shareholders and citizen action groups, with only trade union organisations making their views known. Interestingly enough, initial union reaction to social reports was hostile. For example, the published opinion of the German Federation of Trade Unions (Deutsche Gewerkschaftsbund) in 1977 was that social reports were merely corporate public relations exercises disclosing inadequate information while using pseudo-objective terminology. Since then the unions have shown some interest in entering into a dialogue with management as to the objectives of social reporting. A publication by a social reporting working party of the Deutsche Gewerkschaftsbund in 1979 developed a set of indicators for inclusion in social reports which, while mainly concerned with employment issues, also dealt with factors such as environmental pollution and corporate contribution to societal goals such as regional development (Ullmann, 1979).

Developments in reporting on employee issues: France

Following a period of widespread strikes and plant occupations in France in the late 1960s, the French Employers National Council (CNPF) officially acknowledged in 1970 that the management of human resources could not be neglected further (Rey, 1978). Following this decision, a growing number of companies began the practice of issuing voluntary social reports, largely concerned with employment issues, on a regular basis. President Valery Giscard d'Estaing set up a working party chaired by Pierre Sudreau to generate proposals for the reform of the enterprise. The Sudreau Report, published in 1975, made recommendations covering a wide range of matters but their main thrust concerned the relationship between the enterprise and employees. In particular, much

Figure 6.16 *Summary of the requirements for France's bilan social. From Christophe and Bebbington (1992, p. 284)*

(1) Details of employees by physical characteristics category such as gender and age . . .
(2) Levels of employee remuneration and other expenses which provides information regarding the firm's remuneration policy.
(3) Hygiene and security conditions (health and safety standards) . . .
(4) Other working conditions which impact on workers' conditions such as hours of work, night-work, and noise levels at work.
(5) Staff development and training records . . .
(6) Information regarding the relationship between firm and employees which provides an indication of the internal social climate . . .
(7) Other employment-related factors . . . such as initiatives in the participative management or employer subsidies to staff facilities.

Figure 6.17 *Extract from Total's 1993* bilan social

② rémunération et charges accessoires

②1 montant des rémunérations — 1993

	Cadres	Agents de Maîtrise 290 et +	Agents de Maîtrise 215/270	Employés, Techniciens et Ouvriers 185/200	Employés, Techniciens et Ouvriers 120/170	TOTAL
211 Masse annuelle totale*	655.658.815	42.631.988	74.144.948	30.564.745	9.557.467	812.557.963
Effectif mensuel*	1.530 = 428.535	172 = 247.860	393 = 188.664	206 = 148.373	78 = 122.532	2.379 = 341.554
Hommes	607.088.183	31.484.865	28.196.246	5.870.703	4.313.290	676.953.287
	1.380 = 439.919	124 = 253.910	143 = 197.177	39 = 150.531	33 = 130.706	1.719 = 393.806
Femmes	48.570.633	11.147.123	45.948.702	24.694.042	5.244.177	135.604.676
	150 = 323.804	48 = 232.232	250 = 183.795	167 = 147.869	45 = 116.537	660 = 205.462
212 Rémunération moyenne du mois de décembre** Ensemble	33.211	19.209	14.621	11.499	9.496	26.470
Hommes	34.093	19.678	15.281	11.666	10.130	30.520
Femmes	25.095	17.998	14.244	11.460	9.032	15.923
213 Grille des rémunérations et traitements mensuels minima au niveau de la profession	1 : 13.390 3A1 : 20.672 3B : 29.238 SUP : 38.660	290 : 13.390 340 : 15.532	215 : 10.178 270 : 12.534	185 : 8.893 200 : 9.536	120 : 6.109 170 : 8.251	

1992

	Cadres	Agents de Maîtrise 290 et +	Agents de Maîtrise 215/270	Employés, Techniciens et Ouvriers 185/200	Employés, Techniciens et Ouvriers 120/170	TOTAL
211 Masse annuelle totale*	621.866.710	46.878.801	78.808.426	32.634.088	11.694.741	791.882.756
Effectif mensuel*	1.501 = 414.302	191 = 245.439	429 = 183.703	224 = 145.688	98 = 119.334	2.443 = 324.144
Hommes	576.469.542	36.499.507	30.514.810	6.590.156	4.940.257	655.014.272
	1.357 = 424.812	146 = 249.997	158 = 193.132	45 = 146.448	40 = 123.506	1.746 = 375.151
Femmes	45.397.168	10.379.293	48.293.607	26.043.931	6.754.485	136.868.484
	144 = 315.258	45 = 230.651	271 = 178.205	179 = 145.497	58 = 116.457	697 = 196.368
212 Rémunération moyenne du mois de décembre** Ensemble	32.121	19.029	14.243	11.295	9.252	25.131
Hommes	32.936	19.382	14.974	11.354	9.575	29.086
Femmes	24.442	17.882	13.816	11.280	9.029	15.224
213 Grille des rémunérations et traitements mensuels minima au niveau de la profession	1 : 13.024 3A1 : 20.105 3B : 28.436 SUP : 37.601	290 : 13.024 340 : 15.106	215 : 9.899 270 : 12.190	185 : 8.650 200 : 9.275	120 : 5.942 170 : 8.025	

Masse salariale de référence composée des salaires des effectifs, évalués au 1er janvier de l'année et réputés fixes pendant toute l'année. Compte tenu de cette définition de la masse salariale figurant au numérateur, l'effectif moyen figurant au dénominateur est celui du personnel sous contrat au 1er janvier de l'année considérée. Cet effectif est réputé invariable au cours de l'année.
Rémunération moyenne du mois de décembre calculée sur la base de l'horaire légal de travail et ne comprenant pas les primes à périodicité non mensuelle, soit 1/13e de la rémunération annuelle.

8

Figure 6.17 *continued*

1991		Cadres	Agents de Maîtrise		Employés, Techniciens et Ouvriers		TOTAL
			290 et +	215/270	185/200	120/170	
211 Masse annuelle totale*		678.108.453	57.239.555	95.547.997	38.809.548	17.523.326	887.228.879
Effectif mensuel*		1.692 = 400.773	239 = 239.496	529 = 180.620	273 = 142.160	149 = 117.606	2.882 = 307.852
	Hommes	634.265.471	44.874.617	39.150.514	7.423.955	7.740.451	733.455.008
		1.549 = 409.468	184 = 243.884	207 = 189.133	52 = 142.768	66 = 117.280	2.058 = 356.392
	Femmes	43.842.982	12.364.937	56.397.382	31.385.593	9.782.875	153.773.871
		143 = 306.594	55 = 224.817	322 = 175.147	221 = 142.016	83 = 117.866	824 = 186.619
212 Rémunération moyenne du mois de décembre**	Ensemble	31.500	18.824	14.197	11.174	9.244	24.197
	Hommes	32.184	19.169	14.866	11.221	9.218	28.012
	Femmes	24.098	17.670	13.766	11.162	9.264	14.668
213 Grille des rémunérations et traitements mensuels minima au niveau de la profession		1 : 12.667 3A1 : 19.554 3B : 27.657 SUP : 36.570	290 : 12.667 340 : 14.692	215 : 9.628 270 : 11.856	185 : 8.413 200 : 9.020	120 : 5.779 170 : 7.805	

22 hiérarchie des rémunérations

		1993	1992	1991
221 bis RAPPORT ENTRE LA MOYENNE DES RÉMUNÉRATIONS DES CADRES Y COMPRIS CADRES SUPÉRIEURS ET DIRIGEANTS ET LA MOYENNE DES RÉMUNÉRATIONS DES OUVRIERS OU ÉQUIVALENTS (calculé à partir des moyennes de rémunérations du 1er janvier de l'année considérée)	Ensemble	32.461 10.702 1 à 3,03	31.240 10.381 1 à 3,01	30.184 10.054 1 à 3
	Hommes	33.324 10.714 1 à 3,11	32.032 10.229 1 à 3,13	30.839 9.679 1 à 3,19
	Femmes	24.528 10.697 1 à 2,29	23.772 10.435 1 à 2,28	23.091 10.199 1 à 2,26

23 mode de calcul des rémunérations

	1993	1992	1991
231 POURCENTAGE DES OUVRIERS DONT LE SALAIRE DÉPEND EN TOUT OU PARTIE DU RENDEMENT	0	0	0
232 POURCENTAGE DES OUVRIERS PAYÉS AU MOINS SUR LA BASE DE L'HORAIRE AFFICHE	100	100	100

24 charges accessoires

	1993	1992	1991
242 MONTANT DES VERSEMENTS EFFECTUÉS A DES ENTREPRISES EXTÉRIEURES POUR LA MISE A DISPOSITION DE PERSONNEL :			
Entreprises de travail temporaire	8.890.000	9.639.000	14.681.000
Autres Entreprises	–	–	–

9

attention was directed towards improving working conditions and the introduction of employee consultation and information rights. It was recommended that each enterprise produce an annual social balance sheet, the *bilan social*, based on indicators of its social and working conditions. This particular recommendation was taken up by the French government and a bill was passed in 1977, requiring companies with more than 250 employees to publish social balance sheets in 1979. This requirement was changed to companies employing more than 300 employees in 1982. The *bilan social* includes non-financial quantitative information as well as financial information covering the seven areas, which are itemised in Figure 6.16, p. 199.

An illustration of this approach is shown in the 1993 *bilan social* of the Total company. The report was a 22-page document with sections covering each of the areas in Figure 6.16 and providing detailed quantitative and financial information covering a 3-year period. Of the first six areas, the one covering levels of employee remuneration and other expenses was the shortest and is reproduced in Figure 6.17, p. 200.

Developments in reporting on employee issues: Sweden

As in France and Germany, corporate reporting in Sweden has historically focused almost exclusively on the areas of industrial relations and employee welfare. However, unlike those countries the focus in Sweden has been on reporting for internal decision-making areas. Companies such as AB Volvo, Astra AB and ASSI (part of the stateholding group Statsforetag AB) have been particularly active in developing administrative systems which attempt to integrate personnel reporting into the rest of the management information system (Burchell, 1980). Allied to this development has been the incorporation in co-determination agreements of provisions giving trade unions the right to use employee consultants (*Arbeitstagarkonsulter*), accountants working on behalf of unions, who have rights of access to corporate financial and economic information similar to those of the auditor in the United Kingdom. Such agreements were entered into in the public sector, banks and insurance companies in the late 1970s (Kjellen, 1980).

A particularly interesting example of the use of social information for managerial decision making was developed by AB Volvo, which developed a social accounting model capable of providing a preliminary account of the economic and social effects of personnel turnover and absenteeism. The work of Volvo was based on the premise that priorities for investment should take into account investments in a better physical and mental working environment (see Jonson *et al.* 1978 for a fuller account of the work carried out by AB Volvo). The need became apparent after observing particularly high rates of personnel turnover in the most rapidly expanding production units. Recognising that high rates of personnel turnover resulted in increased costs for the company, efforts were made to quantify financially such effects and similarly to quantify savings that could be achieved if investment in preventative measures designed to improve working conditions and eliminate monotonous tasks was undertaken. These calculations were extended to include the consequences for the community and the state of the reductions in personnel turnover and absenteeism in terms of savings in governmental and community spending to alleviate resultant social problems, and additional tax revenue (Jonson *et al.*, 1978).

In conclusion, the trends in reporting on employee issues are particularly disappointing in Europe. There have been few significant developments since the 1970s beyond the potential offered by initiatives such as the Social Charter and the Agreement on Social Policy. Voluntary initiatives such as the value-added statement have been transitory and appear to be subject to fashions. Only the French *bilan social* and other mandatory requirements (for example in UK reporting) are guaranteed to stay with us for some time since they are not subject to short-term changes in the social and political environment. Further developments in reporting on employee issues in Western Europe are unlikely to be significant or long-lasting unless the EU social policy law specifically covers accountability as well as responsibility.

6.4 Reporting on ethical issues

'Ethical issues' is used here to cover issues concerned, directly or indirectly, with giving an impression of corporate ethical values (see Adams *et al.*, 1995b, Adams and Roberts, 1995). This will embrace issues relating to, especially: community and community welfare; equal opportunities issues; customer and socially beneficial products and services; and host government issues. Such issues are high on the ethical investment trusts' agendas (Harte *et al.*, 1991 and Rockness and Williams, 1988). It is a relatively underdeveloped area of social reporting (but see Chapter 4) to which attention was drawn in the 1980s by, *inter alia*, the rapid rise in both ethical investment trusts and their criteria for selecting investments (see Chapter 8) and the widening role of the NGOs — especially in the area of the 'social audits' (see Chapter 9). Given the nature and number of ethical conflicts businesses can face (see Chapter 1, Figure 1.4 for examples), it is an area which deserves more attention.

Regulation of reporting on ethical issues

With the exception of a concern for consumers and the dealings of companies with operations in South Africa, there has been little apparent concern at the EU level with ethical business practices. Legislation has been limited and has tended to concentrate on consumer protection. For example, the preamble to the Agreement on the European Economic Area (1992) stated that the contracting parties were to promote the interests of consumers and to strengthen their position in the marketplace, aiming at a high level of consumer protection. In addition, the Treaty on European Union 1992 has possible implications for corporate social reporting on product safety and testing in providing that the Community should contribute to the attainment of a high level of consumer protection through specific action which supports and supplements the policy pursued by the member states to protect the health, safety and economic interests of consumers and to provide adequate information to consumers.[23] The corporate Annual Report, being the main publicly available formal corporate document, would be an obvious place for the provision of such information.

The European Community's (now EU) EC Code of Conduct applying to companies with operations in South Africa required that information on consultation and collective bargaining, pay, trade union rights, migrant labour, equal opportunities, fringe benefits and desegregation should be submitted to the appropriate government department (the Department of Trade and Industry in the United Kingdom) and a statement that this report is available had to be contained in the corporate Annual Report.[24]

In the United Kingdom, the Companies Acts only required disclosure on 'ethical issues' with respect to disabled employees, donations to political parties and charitable donations.[25]

Surveys of ethical reporting in Western Europe

Given our earlier comments it should come as no surprise to learn that there have been few detailed, comparative, surveys of reporting on ethical issues in Europe. Table 6.4 reproduces one such survey (Adams et al., 1995b) which covers most of the elements conventionally understood to be part of CSR but which do not fall into the categories of environment or employee.[26] (It thus compares reasonably directly with the subject column of Figure 4.1 in Chapter 4 above.)

Of the items surveyed, Table 6.4 shows that the only items disclosed by the majority of the sample were customer relations (63 per cent) and political donations, activities and statements (51 per cent). Surprisingly few companies made any comment at all about community involvement and public welfare activities (27 per cent); equal opportunities (31 per cent of non-UK sample where disclosure concerning disabled employees is compulsory); sponsorship and advertising (18 per cent); product safety and testing (16 per cent); and charitable donations and activities (2 per cent of the non-UK sample).[27]

Figure 6.18, by way of contrast, focuses on the United Kingdom and takes a longitudinal perspective over 13 years. Taken from Gray et al. (1995b), Figure 6.18 shows that although the frequency of voluntary disclosures in this area had increased significantly over the period,[28] the actual volume of those disclosures remained very low.

Remaining with the United Kingdom, Adams et al. (1995a) undertook a more detailed study of just one area — equal opportunities disclosures — in the corporate annual reports of the top 100 UK companies listed in the *Times 1000*. The average space given to these disclosures by the United Kingdom's largest companies was just one-tenth of a page. The study went further and focused on the *mandatory* disclosure of employment conditions for disabled employees. Here also, the study found a low level of reporting — even with respect to mandatory compliance. Only 34 companies complied fully with the legislation, 52 provided partial compliance and 14 made no mention at all of disabled employees. Even where disclosure took place, the disclosures were little more than brief policy statements or discursive disclosures regarding the company's equal opportunity activities. Only six companies made quantitative or financial disclosures in this area. In contrast to some other European companies where an analysis of employees by gender, race, etc. is frequently provided (see Adams et al., 1995b) only three of the top 100 UK companies provided a breakdown by gender and one by race.

Table 6.4 Surveys of ethical reporting in Western Europe. From Adams et al. (1995b)

	Netherlands		Sweden		Switzerland		France		Germany		UK		Total	
	No.	%	No.	%	No.	%	No.	%	No.	%	No.	%	No.	%
Number cos. giving any information	19	76	22	88	18	72	20	80	25	100	25	100	129	86
of which:														
Customer relations	14	56	18	72	15	60	14	56	18	72	16	64	95	63
Political donations, activities and statements	10	40	12	48	6	24	7	28	19	76	22	88	76	51
Equal opportunities	3	12	19	76	3	12	–		14	56	25	100	64	43
Community involvement and public welfare	3	12	–		7	28	3	12	7	28	20	80	40	27
Sponsorship and advertising	3	12	–		4	16	6	24	3	12	11	44	27	18
Charitable donations and activities	1	4	–		1	4	–		–		23	92	25	17
Product safety and testing	1	4	3	12	2	8	5	20	9	36	4	16	24	16
Foreign corrupt practices/ethical business practices	1	4	3	12	3	12	4	16	5	20	4	16	20	13
Legal proceedings, litigation and liabilities	2	8	2	8	–		2	8	2	8	4	16	12	8
Investment policies	–		5	20	–		2	8	3	12	–		10	7
Length (pages)	0.26		0.32		0.40		0.25		0.93		0.81		0.50	

Figure 6.18a *Percentage of UK companies disclosing information on customers, community, charity, disabled, South Africa, adapted from Gray et al., 1995a*

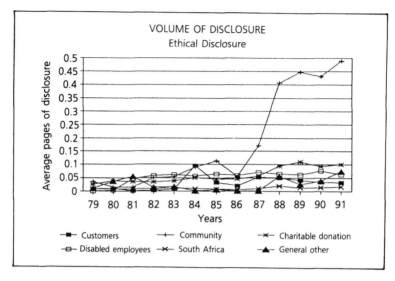

Figure 6.18b *Volume of such disclosures, adapted from Gray et al., 1995a*

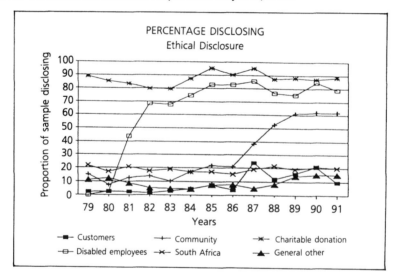

Developments in ethical reporting

It would now be appropriate to turn our attention to examine some of the detail of the practice of reporting on ethical issues. However, as reporting on ethical issues is particularly undereveloped, there are no clear trends in reporting practice. As such,

Figure 6.19   *Extract from Valeo 1992 Annual Report*

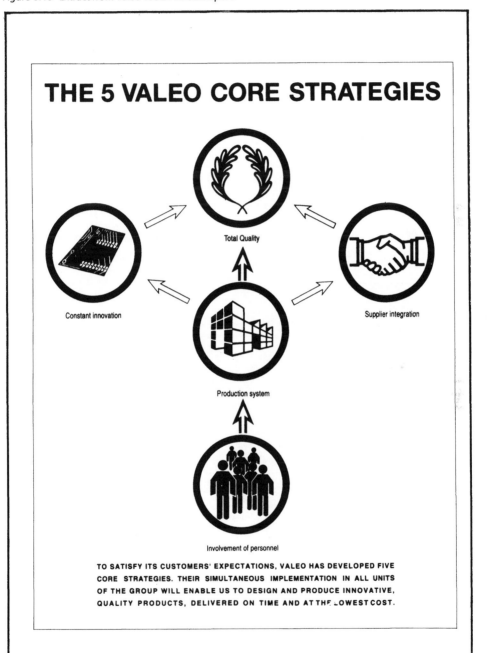

THE 5 VALEO CORE STRATEGIES

Total Quality

Constant innovation

Supplier integration

Production system

Involvement of personnel

TO SATISFY ITS CUSTOMERS' EXPECTATIONS, VALEO HAS DEVELOPED FIVE
CORE STRATEGIES. THEIR SIMULTANEOUS IMPLEMENTATION IN ALL UNITS
OF THE GROUP WILL ENABLE US TO DESIGN AND PRODUCE INNOVATIVE,
QUALITY PRODUCTS, DELIVERED ON TIME AND AT THE LOWEST COST.

Figure 6.20 Extract from Grand Metropolitan's 1992 Annual Report

COMMUNITY

Partnership With The Community
GrandMet's commitment to the communities in which
it operates is built on a conviction that, in helping to
develop healthy communities, the group is also
developing a prosperous market for potential
consumers and future employees. In short, it sees its

The principle of helping people in need to help themselves is a fundamental part of GrandMet's culture and strategy.

*Volunteers from Burger King (UK) decorated classrooms
at Chasebridge School, Twickenham – their 'adopted'
school – during National Volunteer Week.*

involvement in the community as an investment rather
than a cost. GrandMet's investment in worldwide
community activities, including sponsorships,
donations in kind, secondments and direct donations
to charity, is approximately £20 million.

To ensure that this investment is made wisely, the
group applies the same professional techniques and
accountability to managing its community activities
that it employs in the rest of its business operations.

As an international company, GrandMet also
extends to its community initiatives the guiding
principle that it follows in all other business pursuits –
that of "thinking globally" and "acting locally".
Thinking globally, because many of the social issues
confronting society do not recognise national
frontiers. Acting locally, because the group can address
these issues most effectively by concentrating
resources in the communities where it does business.

During the past year, the group has adopted a
community strategy that sums up the group's
fundamental aim in these terms: "GrandMet will
contribute actively to the prosperity of the
communities in which it operates, seeking to
demonstrate a leadership role in helping others to
help themselves."

To fulfil this aim, GrandMet follows a carefully
planned course of action: concentrating the majority
of initiatives in its defined area of community focus;
developing partnerships with selected external
agencies; sharing expertise and resources; directing

GRAND METROPOLITAN

Figure 6.20 *continued*

COMMUNITY

the group's charitable donations to the selected community focus area; encouraging employee volunteerism and ensuring total commitment from GrandMet management to the global communications strategy.

Community Focus

The focus of GrandMet's community strategy is to develop programmes that empower individuals, particularly young people, to achieve self sufficiency. This emphasis on enabling people to realise their potential is well illustrated by GrandMet's training and education programmes:

• The GrandMet Trust is one of the largest providers of training and job counselling for unemployed youth and adults in the United Kingdom. In 1992, over 20,000 individuals received assistance and 75 per cent went on to full time employment or further training.

• In the United States, KAPOW (Kids And the Power Of Work) enlists the energies of GrandMet employee and retiree volunteers, who meet with students in elementary school classrooms once a month to discuss the adult world of work – familiarising youngsters with the skills and attitudes conducive to success later in life.

• More than 1,700 high school dropouts in the United States have resumed their education through GrandMet's Burger King Academies programme, which is now being extended to the United Kingdom. A Burger King Academy will open in East London early in 1993.

Partnerships

Joining in partnership with major charities, civic associations and similar bodies helps GrandMet to secure maximum impact for its initiatives and ensures that all resources are deployed effectively. Among GrandMet's many community partners are:

• More than 100 employment centres and over 30 Training and Enterprise Councils in the UK;

Students from Wilder Elementary School, Minneapolis, on a KAPOW field trip to Pillsbury's R&D Centre, with Pat Hahn, Senior Research Scientist.

Heublein President and CEO Bob Furek visits "Building Blocks", a company sponsored early intervention programme for a group of pre-school children.

Figure 6.20 *continued*

COMMUNITY

- Teachers and educators who contribute to the success of KAPOW; and
- The Cities in Schools organisation, which supports the Burger King Academies programme.

Charitable Donations

In the United Kingdom, the GrandMet Charitable Trust is the primary vehicle for the group's philanthropic giving. Donations are channelled to UK charitable organisations that are principally concerned with helping individuals achieve self-sufficiency. Major recipients include the British Sports Association for the Disabled, Cities in Schools, the Civic Trust and the Prince's Youth Business Trust.

In the United States, recipients include The United Way, Second Harvest Foodbank and Boys' and Girls' Clubs.

Brian Stack, Training Advisor, assists young people at GrandMet Trust's Job Club at the Centrepoint Hostel for homeless youth, London.

Employee Volunteerism

Even more effective than the group's substantial financial aid towards meeting community challenges are contributions of individuals' talent and energy. For that reason, volunteerism plays a central role in GrandMet's community efforts, with an emphasis on programmes that are company-sponsored but employee-led.

Volunteering programmes have been particularly extensive in the United States, which has a strong tradition of volunteerism. Besides KAPOW, major initiatives include REACH (Recognising Employee Actions in Community Help) and Golden Ambassadors, a programme for Pillsbury retirees. Through these endeavours, current and past US employees contribute to their communities – tutoring young students, delivering meals to the housebound and numerous other ways.

GrandMet's volunteering initiatives have earned it recognition as a "leadership company" by the Points of Light Foundation, America's leading exponent of corporate volunteerism. GrandMet is the only foreign owned company to have received this honour.

The group recently appointed a UK Volunteerism Manager to help adopt its US programmes to meet UK needs and to share GrandMet's experience with other UK firms.

Management's Role

Recognising that the task of setting a good example must begin within the organisation itself, GrandMet's senior managers see personal involvement in community programmes as a key measurement of corporate leadership. GrandMet's operating companies have long standing commitments to local community programmes that directly complement their business objectives.

Throughout the group, GrandMet is committed to strengthening its worldwide community activities to generate thriving communities and a prosperous market for potential consumers and future employees.

'ethical reporting' is entirely piecemeal with no consensus on what should be reported or how it should be disclosed. Even the dominance of customer-related disclosure found by Adams *et al*. (1995b) followed no clear pattern.[29] Only 30 per cent of the sample had any kind of a policy statement in connection with customers. One example of such a policy statement is provided in Figure 6.19 (p. 207) from the French company Valeo .[30]

Even disclosures regarding product safety and testing were scarce.[31] One rare example in this area is provided in the 1992 corporate Annual Report of the German company Volkswagen which uses narrative, photographs and graphics to explain safety features, such as the airbag system. The motive behind such disclosure is apparent from the statement: 'The safety aspect is increasingly becoming a major criterion influencing a customer's decision on whether or not to buy a particular model.'

Looking beyond customers and products, the level of reporting aimed at stakeholders in the wider community in which companies operate is particularly low — although a few companies do stand out as especially innovative disclosers in this area. One such example is provided by Grand Metropolitan (UK) in Figure 6.20, p. 208.

The lack of detailed attention given to community and ethical reporting by companies speaks of the relative lack of power wielded — or lack of interest exhibited — by non-environmental and non-employee stakeholders. As a result the greater developments in reporting practices in public sector through performance measures and other measures of service and product quality is all the more striking (see Chapter 4). At a time when local accountability is so widely threatened more developments in this field are sorely needed.

The level of reporting on ethical issues is particularly low demonstrating a lack of corporate responsibility and accountability for the social impact of business on the whole community in which it operates. In pointing to the potential of political economy theory (see Chapter 2) to explain the lack of equal opportunities disclosure in UK corporate Annual Reports, Adams *et al*. (1995a) note that where disclosure is either voluntary, or mandatory without penalties for non-disclosure, companies may selectively fail to communicate information which is inconsistent with business self-interest. As with reporting on employee issues, it is an area of increasing EU legislation, particularly with regard to responsibility to consumers. However, without the development of mandatory accountability disclosures, even the low level of momentum gained in recent years is likely to be lost.

6.5 Summary, conclusions and the future

Although still largely voluntary, the frequency and volume of social reporting in Western Europe has increased over the last two decades. However, corporate social reporting in Europe is still generally sketchy, the interests of many stakeholders being either completely ignored or inadequately addressed. The voluntary nature of much of social reporting has resulted in some innovative developments in the field of environmental reporting, but this has not been mirrored by developments in either reporting on employee issues or in ethical disclosures in the last decade or so. Even with regard to environmental disclosures reporting, where voluntary, is still very haphazard.

For example it is impossible, in the large majority of cases, for readers to determine whether or not they are being given an adequate picture of, for example, environmental impacts, or whether they are being given examples only. In addition, readers often cannot ascertain whether information applies to the whole organisation or just one particular segment of the business.

We believe that environmental reporting in western Europe is close to its voluntary peak (see Gray 1995) in terms of both its extent and the development of innovative methods of reporting. As far as reporting on employee issues, which has a stronger history, is concerned we have seen developments (such as value-added statements) come and go with changes in the social, political and economic environment. We fear that voluntary reporting on ethical issues will similarly be dependent, to a greater or lesser extent in different time periods, on the strength of various stakeholder groups (stakeholder theory), the social, political and economic climate (legitimacy theory) and what companies perceive to be their own self-interest (political economy theory).[32] We therefore believe that it is essential that further developments in European social policy address the issue of accountability.

Although mandatory social reports may stop companies viewing social reporting as some kind of public relations exercise (Dierkes, 1980), they are unlikely to be effective unless they can be, and are, verified. Even with the application of penalties for non-disclosure, quantitative social reports will have little more value than qualitative or discursive reports unless they are audited. The extent of non-compliance with UK law regarding disclosure of information concerning disabled employees illustrates these points (see Adams *et al.*, 1995a). It seems, then, that the most appropriate solution for Europe is to go down the route of making social reporting mandatory, but to do so by a process which can quickly reflect innovations and developments in practice.

Notes

1. Article 54(3)(g) EC required the Council and Commission of the EC to harmonise company laws as necessary to the achievement of the freedom of establishment of businesses in any member state.
2. The basis for a common social policy law in Europe was set by the Treaty of Rome (1957) which established the European Economic Community (EEC), now the European Union (EU). Its area of impact was extended by the Agreement on the European Economic Area (EEA) (1992) made between the European Community (EC) (now European Union) countries of Belgium, Denmark, Germany, Greece, Spain, France, Ireland, Italy, Luxembourg, the Netherlands, Portugal and the United Kingdom and the European Free Trade Association (EFTA) countries of Austria, Finland, Iceland, Liechtenstein, Norway and Sweden. Three of the EFTA countries, Austria, Finland and Sweden, have now joined the European Union. Switzerland is considered in this chapter although it did not ratify the Agreement on the European Economic Area, since the Preamble to the Protocol Adjusting the Agreement on the European Economic Area (1994) makes reference to the wish that Switzerland be able to participate in the EEA in the future. Although slow

progress was made initially, the development of social policy law in Europe has recently been progressed by the EU. See Nielson and Szyszczak (1993) for further information on the development of the EU's social policy.

3. The historical emphasis on employees related principally to the dominance of the Trade Union movement in Europe as the most visible and powerful of corporations' non-financial stakeholders.

4. See, for example, Adams *et al.*, 1995b; Freedman and Stagliano, 1992; Gray, 1990a; Gray *et al.*, 1993; Harte and Owen, 1991; Owen, 1991; Roberts, 1990, 1991 .

5. Article 73.

6. The verifiers had to consult with the company on the detail to be made public and were required, among other things, to check the accuracy and coverage of the contents of the environmental statement (see, for example, Barnes, 1994). In the initial formulation, compliance with EMAS is voluntary and rather than applying to companies it applies to any sites where industrial activity is carried out. It therefore remains to be seen not only whether the attraction of being awarded the eco-logo was and is sufficient to encourage companies to apply for registration to the scheme (from April 1995), but also whether there will be any consequent effect on CSR.

7. Subsequent surveys strongly suggest that no signatory companies actually complied with their own code! (see below). This can be taken as yet another piece of evidence about the inefficacy of voluntary initiatives.

8. See Gray *et al.*, 1993 for details of the CBI's Environment Business Forum's other requirements and other related initiatives.

9. The large accounting firms — typically through their consultancy arms, however — were very active in moving the environmental reporting debate along and in sponsoring and undertaking surveys of practice and attitudes. It is worthy of note that Touche Ross (1990) noted that a number of UK companies claimed that their activities had no environmental impact at all and stated (p. 22): 'In only one instance *outside* UK did we find a public relations department with any environmental involvement (and it was peripheral to an environmental department), while in the UK quite a few firms leave environmental issues entirely to public relations departments' [emphasis added].

10. ACCA were also a major founding patron of The Centre for Social and Environmental Accounting Research (CSEAR).

11. For example, Brockoff (1979); Dierkes (1979); Grojer and Stark (1977); Jaggi (1980); Lessem (1977); Preston *et al.* (1978); Roberts (1990); Schreuder (1979); and see also Meek and Gray (1989) and early issues of *Social Accounting Newsletter* (eds J. Guthrie and M.R. Mathews) which chronicled much of the early development.

12. There is also a study by Freedman and Stagliano (1992). This was excluded since it looked at a total of only 24 corporate Annual Reports in total from 12 EU member states.

13. However, this might reflect differences in sample size and selection procedures rather than decrease in interest in environmental reporting. See, for example, Cowen *et al.* (1987) and Trotman and Bradley (1981) for empirical evidence regarding the effect of firm size on social disclosures.

14. It should be noted that while the number of Swiss companies disclosing environmental information was high (76 per cent in 1992), the mean length of disclosure at 0.60 pages was low.

15. Some of the increase is due to a change in the sample — see Gray *et al.*, 1995b for details of the sample selection.

16. *Social and Environmental Accounting*, the newsletter of the Centre for Social and Environmental Accounting Research at the University of Dundee provides useful and informative updates of developments in environmental (as well as social) reporting around the world. Material in this chapter and Chapter 5 is taken from that newsletter.

17. At the forefront of UK environmental reporting were such household name companies as British Airways, British Gas, British Petroleum, British Telecom, ICI, Thorn EMI, the Body Shop and National Power.

18. The Swiss company Ciba published its first Corporate Environmental Report in 1992 which included: a statement of corporate responsibility; descriptive statements concerning resource consumption, waste reduction, the 'eco-efficiency' of products, safety, managing for sustainability; a list of milestones in the development of Ciba's environmental responsibility; information on the group wide standardised 'Safety, Energy and Environmental Performance' (SEEP) reporting system; and a question and answer section including questions about environmental performance from members of the public and employees. Quantitative information, covering a 3- or 4-year period, includes: bar charts showing purchases of different forms of energy; water usage; solvent usage; emissions to the atmosphere from production; methods of disposal of hazardous waste; and discharges to the Rhine. Examples of these disclosures are provided in Figure 6.5. In addition, Ciba published a separate 36-page document in 1993 entitled *A Matter of Principle: Ciba's Commitment to Safety and Environmental Protection*.

19. The historic concern with employee issues was reflected in the Treaty of Rome (1957) which stated: 'Member States agree upon the need to promote improved working conditions and an improved standard of living for workers, so as to make possible their harmonisation while the improvement is being maintained' (Article 117, EEC). The Treaty further gave the Commission the task of promoting close cooperation between member states in matters relating to: employment; labour law and working conditions; basic and advanced vocational training; social security; prevention of occupational accidents and diseases; occupational hygiene; and the rights of association and collective bargaining between employers and workers (Article 118, EEC). It established the principle that women and men should receive equal pay for equal work and provided an explanation as to what that meant (Article 119, EEC). This provision was repeated in Article 69 of the Agreement on the European Economic Area (1992) and so now applies to all European Economic Area countries. Later, the Single European Act 1986 which amended the Treaty of Rome (Article 22 of the Single European Act 1986 added Articles 118A and B, EEC) granted express power to the Community to enact legislation concerned with the health and safety of workers (Article 118A, EEC). (There were, however, certain provisos designed to protect the interests of small and medium-sized companies). In addition, it also required the Commission to take a role in institutionalising collective bargaining (Article 118B, EEC). Many of these provisions were included in the preamble to the Agreement on the European Economic Area (1992) which specifically required the contracting parties (i.e. all countries in the EEA) to take a high level of protection concerning health, safety and the environment as a basis in

the further development of rules. It also emphasised the importance of the further development of the social dimension, including equal treatment of women and men, to ensure economic and social progress and to promote conditions for full employment and an improved standard of living and improved working conditions. In the EU itself, further developments came in the form of the Community Charter of Fundamental Social Rights of Workers 1989 (the Social Charter). While outlining 12 fundamental social rights (*Freedom of movement; freedom to chose and engage in an occupation and to be fairly remunerated; improvement of living and working conditions; social protection; freedom of association and collective bargaining; vocational training; equal treatment; information, consultation and participation; protection of health and safety at the workplace; protection of children and young persons; protection of the elderly*), it did not have a binding effect. It was endorsed by all but one member state, the United Kingdom, and was seen by some commentators as a negative step in the development of social policy law: 'the concept of a European Social Area has been abandoned for the present; in its place has been substituted that of the social aspect of the Internal Market' (Vogel-Polsky, 1990, p. 75 quoted in Nielsen and Szyszczak, 1993, p. 28). The Treaty on European Union 1992 (Maastricht Treaty) which further amended the Treaty of Rome 1957 placed a greater emphasis on education and vocational training. The Chapter on Social Policy (which was taken out of the Treaty on European Union and annexed as a Protocol and Agreement to the Treaty — the United Kingdom is not party to the Agreement), stated that the Community should support and complement the activities of Member States in the fields of: improvement in workers' health and safety; working conditions; the information and consultation of workers; equality between women and men with regard to labour market opportunities and treatment at work; and the integration of persons excluded from the labour market (Article 2 of the Agreement on Social Policy). It also required that the Council act unanimously in the following areas: social security and social protection of workers; protection of workers where their employment contract is terminated; representation and collective defence of the interests of workers and employers; conditions of employment for third country nationals legally residing in community territory; and financial contribution for promotion of employment and job-creation. The Agreement is also concerned with promoting consultation between management and labour (Article 3).

20. The European Works Council Directive (Council Directive 95/45[1994]O.J. L254/64) does not apply to the United Kingdom. All other member states were required to incorporate it into their national law by 22 September 1996.

21. Some of the increase is due to a change in the sample — see Gray *et al.*, 1995b for details of the sample selection.

22. Extracts and summaries of various early German social reports can be found in Schoenfeld (1978).

23. Article 129A, EEC.

24. Enacted in the United Kingdom through Cmnd 7233, 1978, replaced by Cmnd 9860, 1986.

25. Companies Act 1989, s234; Companies Act 1985, Shed 7.

26. The list of ethical items included in the Adams *et al.* (1995b) survey, reproduced in Table 6.4, was derived from the literature on ethical investment trusts such as Harte *et al.* (1991) and Rockness and Williams (1988) (see Chapter 8) to which was added

any other information which the authors considered was concerned, directly or indirectly, with giving an impression of corporate ethical values.

27. Recall that disclosure of charitable donations is covered by legislation in the United Kingdom.

28. But see Gray *et al.*, 1995b regarding sample selection.

29. Adams *et al.* 1995b. Note, for example, that with regard to the most frequently disclosed ethical issue, customer relations:

> Most of these disclosures were descriptions of activities designed to improve customer service in some way. For example, 16 companies described new information systems or networks, 14 described changes in organisational structure to enable a better focus on customer needs, 16 referred to reduced delivery times or improved reliability of delivery and 9 specifically referred to a product/counselling service to customers. (p. 46).

30. See Chapter 4, Figure 4.2 for further examples of corporate social reporting on this matter.

31. Product safety and testing, specifically referred to as an item on which customers should be provided with adequate information in the Treaty on the European Union (1992),[28] were made by only 16 per cent of the Adams *et al.* (1995b) sample.

32. See Chapter 2 for a full discussion of these theories.

chapter 7

Social accounting and the management information system

7.1 Introduction

The principle focus of this book — and, indeed, of most social accounting — is the provision of information about accounting entities to parties external to that entity — the external participants or external stakeholders. In this sense, social and environmental reporting is broadly analogous to financial reporting by organisations. However, social and environmental data is not always only prepared for external participants. There is a 'management accounting and information systems' equivalent for social and environmental accounting. This refers to social and environmental data collated by the organisation, *not* for external consumption, but for use by the management of the organisation and, to a lesser extent, by other employees and employee groups within the enterprise. This is the focus of this chapter.

It is this dominance of internal social reporting by management that has both driven most of the developments in this field and, ultimately, imposed the limitations on the types of internal social and environmental information which organisations have compiled. In this context it is possible to identify four major themes in internal social accounting:

a First, any management undertaking *external* social disclosure — whatever the drivers for that might be — will need an *internal* information system to support that disclosure. That is, if an organisation is to systematically report on (for instance) its level of health and safety infringements, its involvement with communities or its environmental performance, it can only do this if the information is available in the organisation.

b Secondly, management will be aware that control of certain social and environmental factors is actually compatible with the private efficiency of the organisation. Thus, for example, the monitoring of employee absenteeism, the identification of energy usage or waste disposal costs, or a reduction in the costs incurred by the organisation in managing external social pressures can all be seen to be in the financial interests of the organisation and, thus, compatible with the objectives of the conventional management accounting and control systems. Thus there are areas where *social and environmental* accounting and *economic* financial and management accounting are complementary aspects of conventional profit-seeking behaviour.

c Thirdly, management will have short- and long-term strategic objectives to manage the external environment of the company. This may involve such matters as monitoring stakeholder concerns, attitudes and preferences in order to both maintain control of the organisation in the face of changing preferences or, even, stakeholder pressure and to ensure that the organisation is not 'surprised' by new issues (e.g. animal testing or employee health and safety) which could damage the economic success of the organisation. Social accounting can provide mechanisms for monitoring and reporting data which will be useful to management on such issues.

d Finally, internal social and environmental information systems, if properly integrated with the conventional economic systems, may lead to changes in the organisational culture. This is a somewhat contentious area (see, for example, Newton and Harte, 1994) but it does seem to be the case that attempting to ensure a more socially and environmentally aware culture in an organisation — a greater emphasis on a 'values-based' culture or a more ethical organisation — cannot be achieved unless the 'new' (human-centred) values are in some way internalised in the organisation and integrated into the existing performance appraisal systems (Pomeranz, 1978; Ramanathan, 1976). There does, however, also seem to be some circumstantial evidence that in values-based organisations the conventional accounting system is much less dominant than in conventional success-orientated, non-values-based organisation (see, for example, Gray and Bebbington, 1994).

These themes parallel much discussion in the more conventionally orientated management and accounting literature. That is, it is a basic axiom of financial reporting that it must be supported by the financial bookkeeping system and, further, there is increasing concern that external reporting may actually *drive* internal accounting and information systems. It is also increasingly obvious that management accounting is generally a very reactionary activity which has failed to innovate in order either to provide more useful financial information to management or to expand in order to recognise the new exigencies which companies face in an increasingly dynamic world (see, for example, Kaplan, 1984). Finally, writers such as Kaplan and Norton (1992) have argued that successful organisations move away from immediate cost-saving/profit-seeking behaviour to incorporate wider, softer criteria (such as quality, customer satisfaction, employee innovation) into the heart of their decision making.

Social accounting clearly has a role in each of these areas. However, while the management of an organisation may look to social accounting only in terms of its contribution to conventional organisational behaviour, social and environmental accounting has wider objectives than this. Indeed, internal social and environmental accounting and information systems may have the important quality of attempting to *subvert* the organisation's conventional goals and helping re-introduce normal human and environmental values back into a system which explicitly excludes most of the values and principles which human activity admires and holds to be worthy of civilised human pursuit.

There will often be a tension in the discussion of internal social accounting that rises, principally, from the potential contradiction between conventional management goals and broader social and environmental aspirations. The historical analysis of the examination of internal social and environmental information systems reflects this. While the careful — and pathbreaking — analyses from the National Association of Accountants (Nikolai *et al.*, 1976), the American Accounting Association (1973a, 1974, 1975b) and other writers (see, for example, Anderson, 1978; Burck, 1973; Gray *et al.*, 1993; Sethi, 1972; Stone, 1994) has usually been couched in terms of the contribution that social information can play in supporting management objectives, underlying it is always a sense that management must seek to 're-invent' more ethical, socially just and environmentally responsible organisations. This is an objective which raises increasing conflicts as we shall see.

This chapter will therefore be hung around these different — often implicit — objectives behind internal social and environmental accounting and information systems. The chapter broadly follows the structure employed in the preceding chapters. We will first examine the environmental issues as they apply to internal social accounting. We will then move onto an examination of the wide-ranging and substantial issues that arise with employees. This includes accounting for and to labour, collective bargaining and human resource accounting. Finally, there are some less well-developed issues surrounding the 'ethical' aspects of internal social and environmental accounting which lead into the more comprehensive attempts to devise a full social accounting system and the development of social bookkeeping systems.

7.2 Management accounting and information systems and the environment

The 'polluter pays' ethos driving much environmental legislation throughout the industrialised world has been instrumental in focusing business attention on adopting a more proactive environmental stance, with environmental protection issues being increasingly addressed at the design stage of products and industrial processes. The emphasis on the development of environmental management systems, whereby progress towards implementing corporate targets in the environmental sphere can be objectively measured, within the European Union's EMAS regulations (which we outlined in the previous chapter) are symptomatic of this trend. A similar emphasis is apparent in the British Standards Institute's Environmental Management Standard BS7750 introduced in 1992. The latter document stresses, among other things, the necessity for companies to develop a coherent environmental policy, appoint senior personnel to implement environmental programmes, establish fully documented environmental management systems to ensure that objectives and targets are systematically achieved and to undertake regular environmental audits in order to ascertain that the systems laid down are operating effectively and company policy is being adequately carried out. Taken together the EMAS regulations and BS7750 provide a demanding framework for the management of corporate environmental performance, and raise major implications for the management accounting system in its role as a support mechanism in the realisation of environmental policy objectives.

The wide-ranging nature of the challenge posed to management accounting systems design by the ever-developing environmental agenda is clearly spelt out in Gray *et al.*'s (1993) analysis.[1] Initially, systems are in need of modification so that environmentally related areas of expenditure (and revenue) may be identified separately. Beyond that, even more fundamental change is called for in ameliorating the environmentally negative elements of existing systems, in particular the restrictive, short-term 'bottom line' perspective adopted, and introducing a more forward-looking focus whereby potential environmental threats and opportunities can be taken into account. Ultimately, completely new information systems will need to be developed, probably employing both physical and financial measures, which are of a status equal to the present management systems.

The modification of existing management accounting systems

In considering the issue of the modification of existing management accounting systems, initial areas to address are probably those of energy and waste, not least because environmental sensitivity and financial benefit are here closely related. Minimisation of energy usage and waste production clearly makes sound economic sense, particularly with some form of energy taxation continually mooted as a means towards meeting commitments to reduce greenhouse gases and waste disposal costs, together with penalties for infringements of regulations, rising steadily and significantly. As Gray *et al.*'s (1993) analysis indicates, in accounting for both energy and waste there is a need to maintain accounting systems based on both physical and financial units.[2] In the case of energy in particular, reductions in cost incurred may arise through changes in the nature of the business or production process, or perhaps through switching between fuels, and hence not measure adequately changes in energy efficiency. Furthermore, accounting in physical units facilitates the setting of energy targets and subsequent assessments of volume variances.

In accounting for energy the essential aim is to identify where, and how, energy is used and to identify inefficiency and wastage, thus focusing attention on the areas where savings may be made. Similarly for waste production, the aim is to identify its major sources, and hence costs incurred, within the organisation and to hold particular managers accountable. As far as the financial accounting system is concerned the overriding aim is to charge all identifiable costs to the cause of their creation and ultimately to allocate them to products. Clearly here the 'new' management accounting techniques such as activity-based costing (ABC) and life-cycle costing have much to offer.

Activity based costing (ABC) seeks to allocate costs to products on the basis of the individual product's demand for particular activities. Whereas traditional costing systems allocate overheads to products on the basis of simplistic volume-related bases such as direct labour hours, ABC systems recognise that different products make different demands on organisational resources for reasons that are not necessarily related simply to production volume. Initially ABC systems focused on factors such as size of production orders, number of machine set-ups required and number of subcomponents in seeking to differentiate between the demands generated for particular activities by individual products. However, as Kreuze and Newell (1994) point out, product specific environmental costs may require the use of ABC costing to an even greater extent than the perhaps more obvious factors listed above. In addition to operating costs such as energy usage and waste disposal, and regulatory compliance costs being important components of a full environmental costing analysis, future costs also have to be considered. In calling for the use of life-cycle costing as an extension of ABC systems Kreuze and Newell point to the growing importance of both contingent liability costs and the intangible benefits resulting from achieving higher environmental performance standards, with enhanced profits arising from improved customer satisfaction, employee relations and corporate image.

A particularly sophisticated environmental costing system framework which employs ABC and life-cycle concepts is that developed by the US Environmental Protection Agency (EPA) (Tellus Institute, 1992a, b).[3] The framework developed consists of four ascending tiers, with each offering greater sophistication, and subjectivity, in terms of information supplied:

Tier 0 Includes only direct environmental costs associated with a particular product or process.
Tier 1 Includes indirect costs, or overheads such as would be captured in an ABC system, in addition to direct environmental costs.[4]
Tier 2 Encompasses an estimate of future legal liability costs in addition to the actual costs currently incurred addressed by the two lower tiers.
Tier 3 Goes further still in taking into account the intangible benefits (including costs saved) arising from environmentally responsible business practice.

While acknowledging that the EPA's framework is a pioneering piece of work which incorporates many of the financial dimensions of corporate environmental performance, Bennett and James (1994) also point to a number of limitations in the model. In particular, they argue that insufficient emphasis is placed on the (potentially considerable) benefits of environmentally responsible behaviour which are only considered at Tier 3 — the highest tier with the greatest level of subjectivity and uncertainty attached to it. Additionally, they consider the model to be too firmly bounded by current market and legislative circumstances. Hence it pays too little attention to the dynamic nature of environmental issues, as evidenced by a highly volatile regulatory background, the probability of major future shifts in the market prices of environmental resources and the likelihood of technological innovation radically changing the relative costs of different environmental control options. It is suggested that environmental costs which are at present externalities as far as the company is concerned, being borne by society rather than entering internal cost structures, may be particularly useful in providing an indicator of future actual costs. Incorporating such costs into the company's decision-making procedures does, of course, raise a number of severe practical problems associated with the need to employ what are essentially non-market-based valuation techniques.

Further reform: the issue of non-market valuation techniques

Milne (1991) argues that in addressing the issue of the measurement of non-market environmental resource values, accountants can learn much from recent work on extended cost benefit analysis appearing in the environmental economics literature. While pointing to reliability and cost-effectiveness problems in using techniques such as dose–response models, hedonic pricing, travel cost and contingent valuation methods, and acknowledging their hitherto exclusive employment in public decision-making settings, Milne nevertheless considers them to provide a potential means of incorporating environmental concerns into the corporate accounting framework. In developing private decision-making applications of the above techniques Milne suggests a need for further research directed towards:

- classifying companies according to the type and significance of their environmental impacts;
- matching available and appropriate non-market valuation techniques to those environmental impacts;
- systematically cataloguing previous value estimate studies;
- exploring means by which non-market valuation techniques may be used, modified or adapted for the corporate framework.

The need for research along the lines outlined by Milne is clearly underlined by the emphasis placed on full cost pricing as a key measure in promoting environmental protection within the European Commission's Fifth Action Programme on the Environment (European Commission, 1992). The development of a full cost pricing mechanism, or 'getting the prices right', entails the internalisation of external costs through valuation and costing methods and, as such, clearly poses a major challenge to accountants and the accounting profession. The magnitude of the task is indeed indicated by the Commission's statement that what is needed is a: 'redefinition of accounting concepts, rules, conventions and methodology so as to ensure that the consumption and use of environmental resources are accounted for as part of the full cost of production and reflected in market prices' (European Commission, 1992, Vol.II, section 7.4, p. 67).

There is increasing evidence that the accounting profession on both sides of the Atlantic is beginning to acknowledge that present accounting systems are inadequate in terms of their ability to incorporate the full financial effects of corporate environmental impacts (see, for example, FEE, 1993; ICAEW, 1992; Gray *et al.*, 1993; Stone, 1994). A particularly clear endorsement of the need for change in management accounting practices has been forthcoming from the Society of Management Accountants of Canada:

> The role of the management accountant must change to support an organisation's obligation to be environmentally accountable. The management accountant should take a leadership role in developing environmental reporting mechanisms and internal standards . . . Furthermore, they must consider new regulatory controls and market-based incentives in the assessment of project feasibility. They must develop new financial and non-financial

measurements for valuing environmental assets and provide information and environmental reports. (Society of Management Accountants of Canada, 1992, p. 22)

The accounting function's contribution towards eco-efficiency

Despite the above apparent support from professional bodies for developing more environmentally sensitive accounting information systems, studies by Bebbington *et al.* (1994) and Gray and Bebbington (1994) suggest that the involvement of accountants, and the accounting function, in corporate environmental activity is generally at a very low level. Bebbington *et al.*'s survey of the United Kingdom's top 1000 companies indicated that only in the areas of accounting for energy and waste and investment appraisal could any discernable accounting input be observed, with more than 20 per cent of respondents currently undertaking such activity. Significantly, only a small number of responding companies anticipated implementing further environmental accounting initiatives in the future. Initial returns from the later international survey conducted by Gray and Bebbington broadly confirm the impression that accounting is one of the least developed areas of corporate response to the environmental agenda.[5] Identification of various costs appeared to be the most favoured use of accounting systems with, in addition to waste and energy, EMAS costs, investment procedures, compliance costs and packaging and retrieval costs being mentioned by a majority of respondents. It is, however, significant to note here that fewer than one-third of respondents were using accounting information to help allocate environmental overheads. Therefore, it comes as little surprise to learn that the more sophisticated environmental accounting approaches we have recently outlined, which employ full cost accounting (EPA/Tellus Institute) or full cost pricing (EU Fifth Action Programme) methodologies, were only being used by 11 per cent and 7 per cent of responding companies, respectively. Furthermore, more than half the respondents, which include in their number some of the world's leading companies, admitted to being unfamiliar with these latter accounting initiatives.

Gray and Bebbington's study also draws attention to the fact that while accounting is of marginal relevance at the present time in the context of corporate environmental management, the accounting system still clearly dominates traditional areas of decision making such as medium- and short-term planning, capital expenditure and divisional performance evaluation. There is therefore a clear danger that the short-term, restrictive focus adopted by traditional accounting systems, which ignore the environmental dimension, may be transmitting signals that encourage environmentally malign behaviour and offer resistance to initiatives designed to encourage more environmentally sensitive behaviour. The capital budgeting system offers one example here where the conventional approach to discounting handles uncertainty by employing short-term payback criteria and inflated discount rates, thus discriminating against giving a fair weighting to long-term environmental factors.[6] Even more fundamentally, as Gray *et al.* (1993) point out, while systems which lie at the heart of the organisation — notably budgeting and performance appraisal systems — emphasise conventional financial factors and remain largely untouched by the changing environmental agenda, the former are always likely to dominate the latter.

The modifications to traditional management accounting systems we have considered thus far in this chapter — accounting for energy and waste; activity-based and life-cycle costing; full cost accounting; and full cost pricing — point the way towards more sustainable business activity. Used as support mechanisms for corporate environmental management systems they promote environmental efficiency by focusing management attention on environmental protection at the design stage of products, processes and systems rather than 'end of the pipe' preoccupation with liability for past environmental transgressions (Stone, 1994). Also, in signalling a move away from short-term financially driven decision making they are very much in harmony with evolving Total Quality Management Systems (TQM) in their emphasis on continuous improvement in performance (see Bennett and James, 1994). Indeed, as Gray *et al.* (1993) point out, increasingly good environmental management is seen as an essential component of TQM as:

> The organisation has to seek, in all dimensions, to be the best. This leads organisations to consider anything other than (for example) zero complaints, zero spills and accidents, zero pollution and zero waste as fundamentally unacceptable. (Gray et al., 1993, p. 93)

Introducing the eco-justice dimension

In terms of the terminology we introduced in Chapter 3, the reforms to management accounting systems discussed thus far in this chapter are essentially concerned with issues of eco-efficiency. However, as we noted in Chapter 3, the concept of sustainability is not just confined to eco-efficiency elements but also entails a recognition of inter- and intragenerational eco-justice issues. Gray *et al.* (1993) address at some length the intergenerational aspect of accounting for sustainability. Three approaches are outlined, these being the inventory approach, the sustainable cost approach and the resource flow throughput/input–output approach.

The first two are based round a categorisation of capital into critical natural capital (such as the ozone layer or the rainforests) that can only be expended with the direst consequences, other natural capital (such as agricultural products or minerals) which may be substitutable or renewable and artificial, or man-made, capital. This categorisation is then employed to highlight the fact that the creation and expansion of artificial capital, which our economic and accounting measurement systems focus upon, is only achieved at the expense of a declining stock of natural capital. The inventory approach is concerned with identifying, recording (in non-financial units) and monitoring the depletion and/or enhancement of the different categories of natural capital utilised by the organisation. The sustainable cost analysis approach takes the process a stage further by attaching a financial (replacement) cost figure to the natural capital used up.[7] This sum represents the money the organisation would have to spend at the end of the accounting period to leave the planet no worse off as a result of its activities. For many organisations this figure would wipe out any reported profit, and hence indicate the unsustainable nature of its operations.

The final suggested approach, resource flow/input–output, seeks to catalogue and (non-financially) quantify the resources flowing into the organisation, the losses, or leakages, from the production process (wastes, emissions, etc.) and the resources flowing out of the organisation. As we noted in Chapter 6, such an 'eco-balance' approach is being used by a number of European companies for external reporting purposes. However, the confidentiality of much of the information utilised in preparing a comprehensive eco-balance statement suggests that the method is more suitable for internal reporting as the experience of Austrian companies appears to indicate (see, for example, Jasch, 1993).

In focusing upon the organisation's utilisation of natural capital, the above (highly exploratory) models can be considered as true attempts to begin to account for sustainability as they give clear indications of the extent to which corporations are reducing the options available to future generations as a result of their activities. All, of course, give rise to many complexities in terms of practical utilisation. In the case of the first two approaches, considered identifying, and then measuring, the organisation's impact on the natural capital stock is a highly complex process. For example, as Milne (1995) points out, such broad, eco-based methodologies require an understanding of cumulative environmental change and particularly a recognition of the fact that changes may be non-linear, discontinuous, synergistic and, beyond certain thresholds, irreversible. Therefore, measuring at the level of the individual firm may be insufficient, as for many natural resources the key variable is not the cumulative impact of one firm but that of all firms using the resource. In Milne's analysis, recognition of this fact gives rise to a questioning of the validity of project and firm-based assessments of environmental impact and he goes on to suggest the need for research into possibilities for integrating firm-based information with community or regionally developed ecological information systems. While the resource flow/input–output approach perhaps avoids some of these measurement difficulties it also raises many practical difficulties in implementation. In particular, placing manageable boundaries around the product life cycle (from raw material acquisition to final disposal) presents a major stumbling block.[8]

The analysis presented in this section of the chapter has indicated the immense difficulties faced in developing management accounting systems that are capable of incorporating the environmental performance dimension and, more particularly, addressing the concept of sustainability. Tentative steps taken thus far in separately identifying environmental costs — particularly those of waste and energy — merely scratch the surface of eco-efficiency issues and certainly do not address the eco-justice dimension of sustainability. Furthermore, the inventory, sustainable cost and resource flow throughput/input–output approaches, while attempting to engage the complexities of intergenerational equity, largely ignore questions of intragenerational equity, or social justice.

In addition to discounting the needs of future generations, traditional accounting systems with their capital-orientated bias emphasise shareholder returns at the expense of other stakeholders. Most notably, the interests of employees are subordinated to that of generating short-term profit, while transfer pricing is used as a potent mechanism for establishing the control of multinational companies over third world economies. It is to these wider issues of eco- or social justice that we now turn our attention.

7.3 Accountability to the workforce

Our discussion of emerging social legislation and regulation within the European Union in the previous chapter clearly suggests that the employee is regarded as a key stakeholder in the enterprise. However, a number of critical accounting theorists have suggested that corporate management accounting systems, despite claims to 'objectivity' and 'neutrality', routinely express and further the perceived priorities of capital while neglecting labour interests (see, for example, Hopper *et al.*, 1987; Kern, 1975). In effect, accounting is used to discipline rather than empower labour (Knights and Collinson, 1987).[9] Nevertheless, there would appear to be some potential for accounting systems to play a role in developing the concept of accountability to the workforce in view of Shanks' (1978) remark that: 'Objectives of a social nature can be set, and some . . . can be quantified, particularly those that deal with relationships with employees' (p. 4).

A key mechanism for providing quantified measures of the human resources in an enterprise is that of human resource accounting (HRA) to which we alluded briefly in Chapter 4. Our purpose here, in keeping with the theme of this particular chapter, is to assess the role of HRA as an input into management social reports, rather than as a means of 'putting people on the balance sheet' for external reporting purposes. Such an emphasis accords with the original intentions of the 'founding father' of HRA, the American social psychologist Rensis Likert (Roslender, 1992), and other early researchers such as Brummet *et al.* (1968) who saw HRA as a managerial tool not constrained by accounting conventions and legal restrictions.

Human resource accounting (HRA)

Human resource accounting has been defined as:

> the process of identifying and measuring data about human resources and communicating this information to interested parties. (American Accounting Association, 1973b, p. 169)

As noted above, the concept was originally popularised by Likert, who adopted a behavioural science approach to human resource measurement in investigating the relationship between the system of management used and productivity of the organisation. Likert (1967) went on to advocate incorporating human resource accounting into the formal organisational accounting system. The challenge set for accountants, to develop suitable measurement methods for evaluating the human resource, was rapidly taken up, although Likert's broad definition of the term 'human resources', which included the value of assets such as a firm's human organisation, customer loyalty and reputation in the local community, was also narrowed down to a concentration on the valuation of the firm's human capital, i.e. its workforce.

The pioneering work of Likert

Likert's work arose from a concern that traditional accounting systems with their emphasis on short-term profit maximisation tended to encourage managers to misuse human resources by ignoring factors such as the need for employee participation in decision making and for more training of subordinates. He argued that short-term profit increases generated in this way were largely illusory, as the resultant increases in employee turnover and consequent additional spending on hiring and training more than offset the immediate savings. Likert's study of management styles and their effect on the achievement of organisation goals led to the development of a behavioural model of management which identified four basic management systems:

System 1 exploitive authoritative
System 2 benevolent authoritative
System 3 consultative
System 4 participative group

The first three systems represent varying degrees of authoritarian management, while the fourth involves the type of supportive and participative management recommended by many modern organisation theorists. Likert suggested that an organisation's management style can be classified into one of the above systems through the observation of certain variables consisting of three broad classes:

a Causal variables, which include organisational structure, managerial leadership styles and organisational policies, are independent variables which can be directly or purposely altered by the organisation and its management and in turn determine the quality and capabilities of the human organisation.

b Intervening variables which reflect the internal state, health and performance capabilities of the organisation, for example the attitudes, motivations, perceptions and performance goals of the members of the organisation.

c End result variables which are dependent variables and reflect the results achieved by management such as productivity, costs, scrap loss, growth, market share and earnings.

Briefly, Likert argued that changes in causal variables would produce, after a time lag, changes in the intervening variables, which again after a time lag produce changes in the end result variables. His basic thesis is that a firm in which the causal variables display system 4 characteristics will generate more effective intervening variables and therefore more desirable end result variables in the long term. However, management accounting systems which overemphasise short-term profits and cost reductions may penalise the manager who is making the greatest long-term contribution to the organisation and reward the manager who achieves impressive short-term results at the cost of using up human assets. To correctly evaluate the performance of a system 4 manager the causal and intervening variables must be measured and periodically reported so that their impact may be considered, at least subjectively. One suggested way of measuring intervening variables is by means of employee attitude surveys, covering items such as job satisfaction levels. Experiments have been conducted in this area in the United States (Preston, 1981), Canada (Brooks, 1980) and Sweden (Gröjer and Stark, 1977). Ultimately Likert believed that human resources could be measured by predicting a firm's future earnings, based on the current status of causal and intervening variables, and then discounting to a present value, a portion of which is allocated to human assets.

Later developments in HRA

The complexity of behavioural relationships tends to limit the practical value of Likert's model, and it has indeed proved impossible to model accurately his organisational psychology approach to human resource valuation (Groves, 1981; Harte, 1988). However, the decade from the mid-1960s to the mid-1970s saw many researchers attempting to develop more practical accounting centred methods for measuring human resource values. The models developed can be conveniently classified as cost-based and value-based. In the case of the former costs incurred in, for example, recruiting, training and developing or replacing employees instead of being written off immediately as an expense are capitalised and then amortised over the expected useful working life of the employee (or human asset). By contrast, value-based methods adopt a more forward-looking economic income approach whereby an attempt is made to value the future contribution that the employee will make to the firm. Among several possible suggested approaches here are models based on discounting future salaries (Lev and Schwarz, 1971) or future forecast earnings of the firm (Brummet et al., 1968).[10]

Despite the ingenuity of the researchers concerned, significant practical applications of human resource valuation techniques failed to materialise, with the result that interest in the area faded rapidly in the latter part of the 1970s. However, the issue has never entirely left the accounting research agenda. Flamholtz, an indefatigable champion of HRA, has continued to pursue practical, field-based studies (see, for example, Flamholtz, 1987) while occasional evaluative survey papers have served to keep interest in the area simmering (Harte, 1988; Sackmann et al., 1989; Scarpello and Theeke, 1989).

Indeed, the move towards a post-industrial knowledge-based economy supporting a growing service sector, together with the suggestion that lessons may be learnt from Japanese human resource management techniques, has led some writers to suggest that the time is now ripe for a resurgence in HRA research endeavour (Roslender, 1992; Roslender and Dyson, 1992; Sackmann et al., 1989).

A particularly interesting pointer towards a future research agenda is provided by Roslender and Dyson (1992). They suggest that instead of seeking further measures of cost or value what is now needed is a somewhat different emphasis which focuses on the 'worth' of employees. Essentially this requires estimates to be made of the retention value of employees which is arrived at by assessing the loss to the organisation arising through being without the services of the employee.[11] Thus:

It requires employers to be in a position to know the value of the best efforts at the organisation with the individual employee in post and the value of the best efforts of the organisation without the individual in post, perhaps replaced by a substitute who would need to be recruited for this purpose. By comparing the two valuations it will be possible to arrive at a measure of the cost of being without an individual employee, their worth to the organisation. (p. 325).

It is particularly stressed that such an approach calls for the use of 'soft' accounting information which entails seeking out the views of senior management as to what constitutes worth in their employees and acquiring knowledge of the labour markets in which the organisation operates. Hence, it is argued, accounting for human worth follows the emerging trend in strategic management accounting, where the focus is on information which management may find useful in pursuing competitive advantage rather than simply on conventional hard accounting numbers.

HRA: a brief critique

There has been much debate in the literature concerning the role HRA may play in promoting a greater level of corporate accountability to the workforce, and indeed whether the subject belongs at all in the realm of social accounting.

Among proponents of HRA, Bauer and Fenn (1972) feel that human valuation is naturally included within the scope of a corporate social audit, while Wright (1970) argues that it leads the way to a more humanistic treatment of employees. In particular:

Greater attention may be given to individual selection, development, placement, advancement, incentive and redevelopment. Greater care may be taken to avoid overtaxing man, under-utilising his talents and allowing managerial obsolescence. (p. 298)

Certainly Likert's pioneering work was greatly motivated and influenced by similar thoughts. Giles and Robinson (1972) also believe that the dignity of the employee is enhanced by being recognised as a vital asset of the organisation, and that the personnel manager is equipped with powerful new arguments, based on financial quantification, to justify the expense of training and development programmes and to indicate the contribution of personnel expenditure to corporate success. Similarly, Mirvis and Macey (1976) see a role for HRA in providing relevant cost–benefit data justifying human resource development programmes designed to provide the employee with opportunities for personal development and improved quality of working life.

Despite arguments such as those presented above, there seems little doubt that the major impetus for the development of HRA has been a desire to improve managerial decision making (Harte, 1988). In particular, the aim of developing measures has been to provide the data necessary to convert 'qualitative' decision making, inherent in the management of human resources, into a more quantitative framework (American Accounting Association, 1973b). One can see in this development the influence of scientific management principles which seek to make the most efficient use of all resources, including human resources, employing quantitative methodology. Even later work, such as that of Roslender and Dyson (1992), while claiming to represent a shift from the narrow economic-accounting of past efforts towards a broader social scientific perspective, with the 'soft' accounting information produced being easier for the workforce and trade unions to identify with, still acknowledges that, '... in the first instance the principal beneficiaries will be those responsible for the effective management of human resources' (p. 321). Perhaps most significantly, as Harte (1988) points out, hardly any attention has been paid by researchers in the HRA field to the impact of proposed measures on the workforce itself, despite Glautier's (1976) observation that a study of the internal social effects of organisational decisions should be a key focus of research endeavour.

Glautier indeed provides a particularly damning critique of HRA research. He points out that the accounting models suggested have been concerned essentially with the problem of economic, as opposed to social, efficiency and further highlights the influence of powerful user groups in this development. Glautier argues that consideration should be given to the wider social-economic goals that may be served by HRA, and suggests that non-monetary measures may provide a better indication of social effectiveness. He further feels that the potential of HRA in promoting social effectiveness, for example in eroding the classical view that gives all advantages associated with capital to shareholders and in ensuring that individuals are placed in organisational tasks to which they are best suited, is not being realised.

Other writers such as Marquès (1976) and Cherns (1978) have also pointed to the fact that most human resource accounting research implicitly presumes classical capitalistic objectives, which means essentially maximisation of shareholders' return. Marquès goes on to pose the question 'are people a resource for the enterprise or is the enterprise a resource for people?'. Research in the HRA field thus far, particularly in the United States, appears to favour the former view, and therefore it has tended to develop as a manipulative management tool rather than a vehicle for extending accountability to the workforce.

Of course, such a narrow focus for HRA research is by no means inevitable, as our earlier discussion makes clear. Indeed, both Glautier and Roslender and Dyson draw attention to the potential usefulness of the disclosure of data on the value, or worth, of employees in the context of collective bargaining between management and trade union representatives. Significantly, this latter arena provides a clear channel of accountability whereby employees, through the medium of the trade union, may seek to actively influence decision making rather than simply acting as passive recipients of corporate information. It is to the role that trade unions may play in enforcing a wider social accountability that we now turn our attention.

Collective bargaining

Trade unions are vitally concerned with many aspects of an organisation's social performance. For example, Pope and Peel (1981) have suggested that the union may be regarded as an organisation attempting, under conditions of uncertainty, to maximise an objective function having as key components the employment and real wages of its members. Support for the inclusion of the employment factor in this function is provided by Daniel (1981) who points to the high priority union negotiators attach to the avoidance of any redundancies arising from pay settlements reached. Indeed other writers such as Cooper (1984) have argued that unions take a far broader social perspective still, as in striving to improve the welfare of their members, union officials are concerned not only with wage levels and job security but also working conditions, industrial and community health, industrial democracy, national income and quality of life.

Trade unions and financial information

The issue of the disclosure of *financial* information to trade unions for collective bargaining purposes was the subject of much public policy debate throughout the 1960s and 1970s, with an apparent measure of consensus emerging across the political spectrum that information disclosure had an important role to play in promoting more informed and 'rational' bargaining. A particularly significant development was the enactment of the Employment Protection Act of 1975 which, among its provisions, obliged companies to disclose to trade unions:

a information without which trade union representatives would to a material extent be impeded in carrying out collective bargaining; and
b information which it would be good industrial relations practice to disclose.

Interestingly, despite the changed industrial relations climate dating from the election of the first Thatcher government in 1979 the above provisions have been retained in subsequent legislation.

Trade unions themselves appeared to respond with enthusiasm to the encouragement given them to add a concern with the financial circumstances of the company to their more traditional emphasis on cost of living changes, productivity and comparability with other groups of workers when conducting wage negotiations. For example, certain unions, notably the General and Municipal Workers Union (GMWU) began to seek, as a matter of policy, to secure information agreements with companies and indeed published advice for their shop stewards on what types of information to ask for (GMWU, 1978). Other unions such as the Transport and General Workers Union began to adopt the practice of using detailed financial arguments in pursuing certain 'prestige' national wage claims (e.g. TGWU, 1971, 1977). Furthermore, early evidence produced by researchers suggested that changes in union attitudes towards the importance of corporate financial information as an input into the negotiating process were being reflected at local, individual company and plant levels (Daniel, 1976; Cooper and Essex, 1977).

These early indications of there being the potential for accounting information to be of increasing relevance in the collective bargaining arena gave rise to a great deal of interest on the part of the academic community. One major strand of research focused on the construction of theoretical models of trade union decision making which generally implied a major role for corporate financial information (see, for example, Climo, 1976; Foley and Maunders, 1977; Pope and Peel, 1981),[12] while other researchers embarked on further empirical investigation of the use actually being made of financial information by trade unions. Significantly, these latter studies contradicted earlier work in producing little evidence of union interest in the acquisition and use of financial information (Jackson-Cox et al., 1984; Mitchell et al., 1980; Moore and Levie, 1981; Reeves and McGovern, 1981).

The empirical studies are particularly interesting in that they foresee a wider role for financial information acquisition than its use merely in wage bargaining. For example, they regard such information as being useful in order to arrive at an understanding of the rationale underlying management decisions, obtaining advance warning of issues or decisions, particularly those having repercussions on job prospects which may need to be negotiated, and furthermore in enabling unions to question the validity of certain management decisions or propose alternative courses of action. In other words, they see an important role for information acquisition in extending collective bargaining beyond the traditional areas of concern, terms and conditions of employment. Obviously trade unions need to seek such an extension of collective bargaining if they are to participate meaningfully in corporate decision making in the area of social, as opposed to merely financial, performance.

A further important contribution of the empirical studies is, as noted by McBarnet et al. (1993), that they identify a host of specific problems in the use of corporate information by trade unions.[13] Among issues drawn to our attention are:

- A large difference in the degree of expert power in the use of information operates in favour of management, with union research departments being small and overworked while education services are overstretched and underfinanced.
- The potential for mobilising membership support behind demands based on detailed financial arguments appears very limited compared to support that could be mobilised behind comparability or cost of living claims.
- Management controls the communication process, thus giving them a wide discretion over what to disclose or not to disclose. It is significant to note here that employers have frequently resorted to taking advantage of the generous exemption clauses to the main disclosure provisions of the Employment Protection Act. In particular, recourse is often made to the 'substantial injury' clause, which exempts firms from having to disclose information that would cause substantial injury to the enterprise for reasons other than its effect on collective bargaining (i.e. generally information that is regarded as being of a sensitive commercial nature).[14] Furthermore, this reluctance to disclose significant financial information also appears to apply to firms which have established profit-sharing schemes in the 1980s, with a clear detrimental effect on the motivational benefits which may otherwise have been realised (see Ogden, 1993).
- Management possession of the means of production enables them to command decision-making procedures. In particular, empirical research has highlighted managerial control of strategic decision making with the union side being restricted to a reactive stance, enabling them to merely impede implementation of decisions with no power to initiate and influence decision topics.

The latter issue is of particular significance. As Ogden (1986) points out, the whole *raison d'être* for unions to pursue the disclosure issue is for them to be in a position to pursue *extended* collective bargaining. The distinctive feature of extended collective bargaining is that it focuses on questions of strategic decision making and corporate control. Merely accepting at face value routine, non-sensitive, information that management chooses to disclose while being excluded from key policy making networks leads to the union side absorbing managerial values and imperatives, or being 'sucked into management'. In order for this not to happen Ogden and Bougen (1985) point to the need for unions to generate and develop alternative criteria to those used by management for assessing organisational performance.[15]

Extending collective bargaining

A number of empirical studies have indicated that one noticeable exception to the general pattern of overall union disinterest in financial information at the domestic bargaining level occurs when security of employment becomes a major issue (see, for example, Jackson-Cox *et al.*, 1984; Reeves and McGovern, 1981; Sherer *et al.*, 1981). In particular, unions appear willing to abandon their traditional stance of merely reacting to managerial initiatives in favour of using information to positively extend collective bargaining in cases of threatened plant closure. However, a common feature of these efforts is that they tend to come too late to have any real effect. This is hardly surprising, for, as Jackson-Cox *et al.* indicate, union representatives are at a major disadvantage in dealing with non-routine issues, of which redundancy questions are a prime example, as they only become involved after management has taken the vital initial decisions. Bryer *et al.* (1984) have suggested that unions can only begin to grapple with this problem when they undertake sophisticated financial analysis exercises on a consistent basis or, in Bryer *et al.*'s terminology, engage in 'shadow planning', which would enable them to understand and challenge management's plans.

A particularly rigorous analysis of how the union side can use corporate information in such a fashion in order to extend collective bargaining is provided by the work of Roy Moore and his colleagues at Ruskin College (Moore *et al.*, 1979; Moore and Levie, 1981). It is suggested that ambitiousness of union demands is a key factor in combating constraints imposed on the union's use of information arising from both managerial attitudes and actions together with deficiencies in union organisation such as poor levels of inter union cooperation and inadequate technical back-up. The basic thesis adopted is that as union demands become more ambitious in the context of developing collective bargaining the union moves along an 'information scale'. Starting at the bottom of the scale, with an acceptance of company information as it comes, the union moves through points such as asking for additional information, seeking access to the management information system and changing the system towards the ultimate point of developing its own trade union information system.

The level of democracy in the union is considered to be the yardstick of its ability to improve its use of company information. Whereas formal democracy can be said to exist in all unions, the relationship between union officials and the membership resting ultimately on a voting nexus, decision making within the union in many cases has become an autocratic one-way process. Moore and Levie, in their use of the term democracy, are referring to the need for active, as opposed to merely formal, democratic procedures.

This requires:

> . . . a much higher level of involvement of the members and their representatives. It means a bargaining structure that is present at every level of the company. It implies a high level of co-operation, or at least discussion between and within unions. It means creating a new role for full-time officers who no longer have to solve members problems, but who enable them to solve their problems themselves. It means an active education and research programme that changes as collective bargaining develops. It means a flexible organisation that is capable of re-organising itself as the needs and problems of the members change. (p. 29)

Moore *et al.*'s analysis clearly indicates the magnitude of the challenge facing unions in trying to extend collective bargaining. Interestingly, work by McBarnet *et al.* (1993) paints a less pessimistic picture than the empirical work we considered earlier in suggesting that unions are beginning to use financial information strategically in order to critique and challenge management's plans. They suggest that:

> According to our pilot study, trade unions use financial information for a range of purposes, some more predictable than others: for wage bargaining, for negotiation and takeover and merger situations, in relation to closure or redundancy proposals, to argue the ability of management to improve health and safety conditions; they use it to negotiate over profit related pay and in arguing against tenders for public contracts; they use it for recruitment campaigns and in wider propaganda battles with the public or in the political arena more generally. (p. 87)

While McBarnet *et al.* present a persuasive case suggesting that unions can successfully employ what they term 'adversary' accounting techniques in order to avoid being sucked into management, their analysis places the union very much in the position of reacting to management plans whilst confining the debate to purely financial dimensions of performance. However, there are clear signs that union ambitions extend to influencing corporate social (as well as financial) objectives and performance, an area which, as we noted earlier, comes very much within their ambit of concern.

In particular, recent years have seen the trade union movement taking an increasing interest in the environmental dimension of corporate performance. The Trades Union Congress (TUC), for example, established an Environment Action Group in 1989 which has been particularly active in developing a policy framework for future action while encouraging individual unions to negotiate 'Green Agreements' with employers and to seek active involvement in corporate environmental initiatives. Figure 7.1, an extract from the TUC's 1991 publication *Greening the Workplace*, provides a cogent justification for union involvement in the greening of industry and indicates clearly why green issues are central to union aims and objectives.

The TUC's proactive stance has been enthusiastically followed by several individual trade unions. Significantly, however, employers have in many cases exhibited a profound

Figure 7.1 Why be green?

- Because trade unionists are concerned and affected as workers, consumers and local citizens.
- Because each of us has a responsibility to minimise the damage our work causes to fellow workers and future generations.
- Because environmental pressures impact on decisions about employment, pay, training, workloads, health and safety, and workforce cooperation.
- Because union involvement and experience can improve environmental performance and thereby best protect jobs, pay and conditions.
- Because in practice successful environmental protection at work begins with sound health and safety performance.
- Because unions are uniquely placed to identify and articulate worker concerns and practical ideas and solutions.
- Because unions have the structure and machinery to raise awareness and facilitate change.
- Because involvement in joint strategies with the employer can create opportunities for discussing other corporate policy issues.
- Because it can help raise the unions' profile, aid union recruitment and facilitate closer links with outside groups.

Source: Greening the Workplace (TUC, 1991)

reluctance to involve trade unions fully in discussions concerning the environmental aspects of corporate performance (see, for example, Benn, 1992; Jackson, 1992). Indeed, this apparent desire on the part of management to exclude trade unions from any participation in environmental decision making is symptomatic of a long-standing resistance to union attempts to extend collective bargaining into the social domain.

This perhaps becomes particularly apparent when one considers that lack of employer support was also a major factor in thwarting what was probably the most ambitious attempt yet by trade unions to extend collective bargaining into the realm of the social — the Lucas Aerospace Corporate Plan of 1976.[16]

Produced against a background of 5000 job losses in the company over a 5-year period by the combined shop stewards committee (made up of stewards representing some 14 000 union members from 13 different unions at 17 sites) the objectives of the plan were:

1. To protect jobs by proposing a range of alternative products in the event of further cutbacks in the aerospace industry.
2. To ensure that among the alternative products were a number that would be socially useful to the community.

Backed by impressively detailed technical and economic supporting information, proposals were put forward for the development of approximately 150 products in 6 major technological areas. The criteria of social usefulness were that:

- The product must not waste energy and raw materials, either in its manufacture or use.
- The product must be capable of being produced in a labour intensive manner so as not to give rise to structural unemployment.
- The product must lend itself to non-alienating forms of production with work organised so as to link practical and theoretical tasks and allow for human creativity and enthusiasm.

In addition, a proposed Employee Development Programme was outlined which called for retraining and re-education schemes for both blue and white collar employees.

Whereas press reaction to Corporate Plan was generally very favourable (the *Financial Times* (23.01.76), for example, calling it 'one of the most advanced yet prepared in the UK by a group of shop stewards. One of the most radical alternative plans ever drawn up by workers for their company . . .') the reaction of company management was not equally enthusiastic. The combine intended to put the plan forward in a negotiating framework in order to promote an extension of collective bargaining. In the event, management refused to even discuss the plan with the combine, insisting instead that local consultative machinery be used, regarded by the union side as a normal divide and rule tactic (Lucas Aerospace Combine Shop Stewards Committee, 1979). With sustained support also not being forthcoming from the official trade union movement and the then Labour government the Corporate Plan was doomed to failure, although 'mini' versions were (temporarily) successfully introduced at a handful of sites.

Despite its fate, the Lucas Plan is worthy of particular attention in that it represents a rare attempt to undermine in a practical, rather than purely theoretical, way the legitimacy of a system of production that gives priority to competitive success and profitability while ignoring matters such as the social costs of unemployment, the consequences of the productive process on the environment and people's health and safety. It also challenged management's right to manage without accountability to the workforce. At the same time it all too clearly demonstrates the major problems facing trade unions, or indeed other stakeholders, seeking to introduce human-centred values into commercially orientated organisations whose performance appraisal systems privilege the financial dimension to the virtual total exclusion of the social, environmental or ethical.

7.4 Social bookkeeping systems

As we noted in the introduction to this chapter, for a more socially and environmentally aware culture to be introduced into an organisation it is necessary to integrate new values centrally into the existing performance appraisal system. In other words, organisations which truly wish to embrace the concept of social accountability will need to specifically design *social* bookkeeping and information systems which enable them to assemble and collate the data necessary for preparing a 'social account'.

With the possible exception of environmental reporting by certain European companies focused upon in the previous chapter, it would appear that companies generally do not produce systematic social (or environmental) accounts derived from fully developed internal management information systems. However, a new wave of social audit activity being undertaken by 'values-based' organisations, which we shall look at in Chapter 9, is beginning to point the way towards change. The experiences of one such organisation, Traidcraft, which imports third world products for sale in the home market, provide pointers as to the degree of change in organisational culture called for in developing systematic social bookkeeping systems.[17]

At the outset it should be noted that while social bookkeeping systems can be utilised for the purposes of internal control, for social accountability to be truly established 'transparency' must be a key objective. As Dey *et al.* (1995) emphasise:

> ... the accountability and transparency objective is concerned with exposing the organisation as a whole to a potentially 'confessional' experience through attempting to make the organisation more transparent and to satisfy the information rights of stakeholders. (p. 11)

Thus a clear link is established between the internal information system and the public accountability, or external reporting, function. To this end, the organisation has to identify systematically all its stakeholders and define the nature of the social relationship together with the information rights and needs of each stakeholder group. Moral as well as legal rights are involved here and stakeholders will in all probability have to be consulted in depth.

Turning to the data collection exercise itself, while certain information, for example relating to employees and environmental emissions, may already exist in the information system much of it will not be systematically collated and most will require re-arrangement and/or adjustment. Other information, for example on the product life cycle or employee motivations and attitudes, will have to be collected from scratch. Finally, a significant proportion of the data particularly relating to aesthetic or value issues will be in a qualitative, or 'soft' form.

Given the range of social issues and stakeholder concerns to be addressed, completeness of information provision is perhaps an impossible objective. Certain data may simply be unobtainable while some, for example on customer and supplier satisfaction levels, too cumbersome to collate on a regular basis. Clearly, important decisions have to be made on what to leave out of the social account and it will be necessary to be explicit about what is missing and why. As Dey *et al.* point out, the design of a social bookkeeping system is likely to be an interactive exercise, over several cycles of the social accounting process, with feedback from stakeholders being an important influence in refining and developing the approach adopted. Indeed, such feedback can itself be part of the social information system. A particular problem to be faced here is that the specificity of the data being collected draws attention to a more exact expression of the social dimensions of the organisation than would be found in a simple 'mission statement' and hence increases the conflict between competing stakeholder groups over the way such dimensions are expressed.

While space constraints have not permitted us to undertake an in-depth coverage of the practical problems inherent in the development of social bookkeeping systems, hopefully some indication of the degree of change called for in management information systems design has been conveyed. Indeed, the major change is not simply a practical one but is essentially cultural — an acceptance on the part of corporate management of the need for transparency and the central involvement of all stakeholders in defining the objectives of the organisation and evaluating its success in achieving them.

7.5 Summary and conclusions

Our review of the internal reporting dimension of social and environmental accounting in this chapter has clearly indicated that in the cases of both environmental accounting and information systems and accounting for and to labour the imperatives of private efficiency have prevailed over objectives of transparency and accountability in much research and practical endeavour. The continued dominance of conventional management goals is apparent in the lack of attention paid to the eco-justice dimension in the development of environmental accounting systems, the narrow focus on economic efficiency in the development of HRA and continued managerial resistance to trade union attempts to extend collective bargaining into the realm of the environmental and social. Given this state of affairs, the widespread adoption of social bookkeeping and information systems which encompass the eco- or social justice dimension appears to be a very remote possibility.

This having been said, there are pressures for change. Trade union concerns with issues of industrial democracy and social justice are unlikely to go away and may be given fresh impetus and encouragement from developments within the European Union. Further pointers towards change are provided by developments in social investment practice and the social audit movement, of which newly emerging 'values-based' organisations are an increasingly important part. It is to these latter developments we turn our attention in the following two chapters.

Notes

1. Gray et al. (1993) (chs 3–9) provide a comprehensive overview of the practical implications for management accounting systems of the introduction of environmental concerns into organisational activity. Issues addressed at length include environmental auditing, accounting for energy and waste, investment, budgeting and appraisal and life-cycle analysis.
2. See Gray et al. (1993) (chs 6 and 7) for detailed discussion of this issue.
3. See Bennett and James (1994) for a fuller description and critical analysis of the Tellus Institute methodology.
4. As Bennett and James (1994) point out, the distinction between tier 0 and tier 1 depends largely on the sophistication of the accounting system employed in terms

of which costs are capable of being traced directly to products.

5. Gray and Bebbington's (1994) survey is part of the United Nations Conference on Trade and Development's (UNCTAD) project to examine the development of environmental accounting and reporting in Transnational Corporations. Questionnaires were directed to 10 companies in each of 21 different countries. The initial analysis described here is based on returns from companies in the United Kingdom, Italy, Austria, Denmark, Sweden, the Netherlands, Finland, Korea, Japan, Switzerland, South Africa, France, Hong Kong and Spain, with response rates varying from a low of one (Denmark) to a high of ten (South Africa).

6. For example, the future cost of safe disposal at the end of an asset's useful life may not be taken fully into account, while environmental projects with long gestation periods and low values in current prices are undervalued (see Gray *et al.*, 1993, pp.153–60 for an extended discussion of such issues).

7. Critical natural capital being by definition irreplaceable and non-substitutable would have to be 'included' at infinite cost.

8. See Gray *et al.* (1993, ch. 9) for further discussion of this issue.

9. For a fuller discussion of this issue see Colwyn Jones (1995), particularly chapter 7.

10. For extended discussion and analysis of the various cost and value based measurement approaches see Harte (1988).

11. In other words, an opportunity cost approach is suggested which draws on earlier work by Hekimian and Jones (1967).

12. For a particularly comprehensive discussion of the theoretical role of information into models of the collective bargaining process see Foley and Maunders (1977).

13. For a fuller discussion of these issues see Gray *et al.* (1987, ch. 9).

14. For a comprehensive analysis see McSweeney (1983).

15. Ogden and Bougen (1985) present a detailed critique of the disclosure models appearing in the accounting literature which we mentioned earlier. They point out that these tend to be concerned solely with the costs and benefits of disclosure as they affect management, and in so far as the interests of labour are considered they are assumed to be consistent with those of management. Thus the models only reflect a partial analysis of the disclosure issue from a societal viewpoint.

16. For a comprehensive, and highly readable, account of the full story behind the Lucas Aerospace Corporate Plan see Wainwright and Elliott (1982).

17. See Dey *et al.* (1995) for a fuller description of the Traidcraft initiative.

chapter 8

Social investment

8.1 Introduction

A major theme in the development of CSR has been to view the disclosure of social information as essentially an extension of financial reporting to profit-seeking investors. Indeed, over the past 20 years a burgeoning research literature has appeared which focuses on the relationship between social responsibility measures of various types and the economic or stock market performance of companies. We begin the chapter with a brief review and critique of this literature, drawing particular attention to its narrow interpretation of CSR, posited on a restricted user needs perspective as opposed to the broader and richer 'accountability framework' introduced in Chapter 2.

The essential point, of course, is that purely profit-seeking investors are likely to be almost entirely uninterested in CSR except in so far as it influences their financial position. However, a number of writers have argued the necessity to distinguish investors aiming simply for short-term, speculative profit from those who seek to practice more responsible share ownership involving long-term commitment (see, for example, Charkham, 1990; Church of Scotland, 1988; Moore, 1988). It has been suggested that the latter group may have a significant role to play in the development of CSR and an associated widening of corporate accountability (Owen, 1990). It is with this issue that the current chapter is largely concerned.

A particularly noteworthy feature of the investment scene in recent years is the rise to prominence of the 'ethical', or social, investor. The most visible manifestation of the development of a socially responsible investment movement, on both sides of the Atlantic, has been the proliferation of ethical and, more recently, environmental mutual funds/unit trusts which seek to base their investment portfolios on a number of social criteria (typically environmental performance, enlightened personnel policies, avoidance of relations with repressive regimes and absence of involvement in armaments manufacture, alcohol or tobacco products). While amounts invested in the funds are relatively modest[1] their high profile and pioneering work in introducing an explicit social dimension into the investment decision-making function is beginning to attract a wider institutional response, notably among pension funds.

Our task in this chapter is not merely to trace the development of the ethical and environmental unit trusts, and the social investment movement in general, but to appraise critically their potential as a potent force for imposing a wider social accountability on business enterprise. In doing so we raise serious reservations as to the efficacy of the movement as an agent of social change, centring particularly on the eco consumerist, free market ideology espoused together with the absence of an explicit theoretical, or conceptual, basis underpinning its activities. Nevertheless, we also acknowledge that the existence of a small, but growing and increasingly vociferous, group willing to undertake investment on other than purely financial grounds is a matter of some significance. In particular, there are clearly implications for the corporate reporting function which are addressed in the final substantive section of the chapter.

8.2 Social reporting and the profit-seeking investor

As we have already noted, a major theme in the CSR literature has centred on empirical enquiry as to whether firms exhibiting better social performance gain any economic advantage over their competitors, and hence should prove more attractive to the profit-seeking investor. A major problem confronting researchers in this area is the lack of agreement as to what constitutes a suitable measure of social performance. The following three measures constitute those most predominantly employed.[2]

Social disclosures made by the firm itself

Research into whether social disclosure is related to a company's economic performance is generally inconclusive, whether performance is measured by accounting or stock market variables. In the former category for example an early study by Bowman and Haire (1975) of 88 firms in the food processing industry suggested an association between degree of social disclosure and return on equity, with medium disclosers (as opposed to high or low disclosers) producing the highest returns. However, a later study by Abbot and Monsen (1979) of 450 firms drawn from the *Fortune* Global 500 could discern no significant differences in returns to investors from high and low disclosers. A number of later studies similarly failed to uncover any consistent relationship between social disclosure and accounting return.

Turning to studies employing market variables as a measure of economic performance, the general conclusion is that such disclosures have economic content, giving rise to investor reaction in terms of changes in share price (Anderson and Frankle, 1980; Belkaoui, 1976) or increased trading volume (Patten, 1990). However, some studies failed to find a link between disclosure and market return (Mahapatra, 1984) while there is far from universal agreement concerning the direction of any change in share price (see Freedman and Jaggi, 1988). The picture is further complicated by the fact that the disclosure–performance relationship would appear to be influenced by factors such as the size of the firm and the market segment within which it operates (Freedman and Jaggi, 1988; Ingram, 1978). Finally, and perhaps most significantly in terms of the implications arising from these studies for CSR practice, Freedman and Jaggi (1986,

1988) have suggested that the *extent* of disclosure, as opposed to disclosure *per se*, appears to have little effect upon investor reactions.

The diversity of the findings of researchers investigating the relationship between corporate social disclosure and economic performance should cause little surprise when viewed in conjunction with another strand of research suggesting that social information provided in annual reports bears little relationship to actual social performance, and can indeed be positively misleading (Ingram and Frazier, 1980; Rockness, 1985; Wiseman, 1982). Using the techniques of content analysis and indexing procedures, respectively, to measure the extent of disclosure of environmental information by a sample of US companies both Ingram and Frazier and Wiseman failed to find any meaningful positive association between such disclosure and available objective measures of environmental performance for the same companies. (The latter measures were compiled by the Council on Economic Priorities (CEP), an independent, non-profit-making organisation dedicated to evaluating corporate social performance.) Indeed, Ingram and Frazier found that the Annual Reports of the poorer social performers per the CEP indices, generally contained *more* environmental disclosures than the better performers! Equally damning, in the context of the user needs perspective adopted by the strand of research we are considering, is Rockness's finding that whereas environmental disclosures in a selected sample of corporate Annual Reports were indeed sufficient for statement users from diverse backgrounds[3] to form consistent comparative evaluations of firms environmental performances, such evaluations were inaccurate interpretations of actual performance as measured by the CEP.

Independent measures of corporate social performance

As an alternative to using the apparently unreliable disclosures made by firms themselves, some researchers have employed independently produced social data in order to investigate possible links between social and economic performance. The most widely employed measures are derived from the pollution data base generated by the CEP in the 1970s in its analyses of the pollution performance of US firms in the steel, oil refining, pulp and paper and electric utilities industries.

An early study by Bragdon and Marlin (1972) of 12 companies in the paper and pulp industry indicated that those having a good record on pollution tended to turn in a better profit performance. Later studies performed on firms in the same industry broadly confirmed these findings. However, the pattern is far from clear-cut. For example, Bowman and Haire (1975) detected a 'U'-shaped correlation in that middle level polluters outperformed both worst and best polluters, while Spicer (1978) indicated a discernible 'size' effect, with the most profitable larger companies having the best pollution control record. Indeed, a replication by Chen and Metcalf (1980) of Spicer's study suggested that firm size, rather than pollution performance, was the key explanatory variable.

Turning to studies using financial market variables as a measure of economic performance, a highly inconsistent pattern of results is produced. Thus, for example, Shane and Spicer (1983) indicate a positive relationship between environmental and economic performance, Stevens (1984) a negative one, while Folger and Nutt (1975) could find no significant correlation at all between the two dimensions of performance.

Use of reputational scales and opinion surveys as a measure of corporate social performance

Perhaps not surprisingly, studies over the years have utilised a great variety of opinion survey data on perceived corporate social responsibility and have produced widely divergent results when seeking correlations with economic performance, particularly when the latter is represented by financial market variables (see Herremans *et al.*, 1993). Thus, for example, a study by Sturdivant and Ginter (1977) employing opinion scale data derived from early work by Moskowitz (1972) found a positive association between economic and social performance, while other studies by Vance (1975) and Alexander and Bucholz (1978) utilising ratings from a 1972 *Business and Society Review* survey indicated a negative relationship, and no relationship respectively. A major weakness of this approach is, of course, that individuals' opinions concerning the degree of social responsibility exhibited by a particular company are likely to be heavily influenced by the social disclosures made by that company. As we noted earlier, there is a considerable body of evidence to suggest that such disclosures bear little relationship to actual social performance.

Herremans *et al.* (1993) argue that in order to counteract this particular problem reputational evidence should be constructed from data which are both broadly assimilated in the public domain and appraised by people with relevant expertise in the salient issues and experience of the firms being rated. To this end their study, in common with other relatively recent work in the area (see, for example, McGuire *et al.*, 1988), employs data from the annual survey of corporate reputations conducted by *Fortune* magazine since 1982. This survey elicits the opinions of a large sample of senior executives, outside directors and financial analysts, all of whom are well acquainted with the industries and companies they are evaluating.[4]

The research design employed by Herremans *et al.* is explicitly informed by methodological lessons from previous studies. In particular the mediating effect of structural factors, such as industry and firm size, together with key financial variables such as gearing, on corporate social performance are taken account of (see Belkaoui and Karpik, 1989). Additionally, a 6-year time period of observation is used in order to counteract volatility in the variables and relationships being studied. The results obtained indicated corporate social responsibility to be positively associated with higher corporate profitability, lower risk and, during the period studied, higher stock market returns.

The profit-seeking investor and the development of CSR

The above review is far from comprehensive and is designed simply to give the reader a brief flavour of the literature investigating the link, if any, between corporate social and economic performance. While the overall picture is complicated and, at best, inconclusive, at least some evidence has been produced which suggests there may be a tenuous link between the two performance dimensions. The link is indeed tenuous when one bears in mind that: (i) the studies are careful to refer only to *associations* between economic and social variables and do not claim *causal* relationships (see Mathews, 1993, ch. 2); (ii) the results produced by each study are only applicable to the particular sample of companies analysed in the particular time period chosen; and (iii) the influence of intervening structural and financial variables is crucial.

Nevertheless, the suggestion that data on corporate social performance may have 'information content' for the profit-seeking investor cannot be dismissed out of hand. Indeed, support for such a suggestion is forthcoming from a further strand of decision-usefulness research in which particular user groups are asked to rank various accounting data, which may or may not be currently supplied in corporate reports, in order of perceived importance. The general picture emerging from these studies indicates that the financial community find corporate social information at least of some use in their decision-making processes (see, for example, Benjamin and Stanga, 1977; Firth, 1984). One may expect investor interest in such information to increase as the financial costs to companies of social irresponsibility, particularly environmental irresponsibility in the emerging climate of 'polluter pays' driven legislation, become ever greater.[5]

In the context of this latter issue it is significant to note that stock market interest in environmental performance data appears to be far lower in Europe and Japan than in the United States, where environmental legislation is more advanced, and the issue of potential liabilities under the legislation crucial in appraising the financial health and prospects of companies (Deloitte, Touche Tohmatsu International, 1993). At a practical level this would appear to suggest that concentrating exclusively on the apparent information needs of the profit-seeking investor is unlikely to get us very far in terms of advancing CSR practice, at least as far as Europe is concerned. More fundamentally, however, the financial consequences of corporate social irresponsibility are but a small part of the potential domain for reporting practice. For many stakeholders essentially non-financial issues such as clean air, community health and workplace safety are of far more vital importance.

Such an observation raises fundamental questions concerning the strand of research we have been considering: in particular, the primacy given to those who possess wealth and the focus on investor preferences, as reflected in stock market prices and accounting profit, as the basis on which to assess social and environmental disclosure. As Cooper and Sherer (1984) point out, it is highly unlikely that capital market reactions tell us anything about the social value of information, or indeed have any implications for the desirability or otherwise of alternative accounting measures and disclosure practices. In particular:

> focussing an informational efficiency in the capital market may contribute towards an efficient allocation of resources from the perspective of the shareholder class, but the resulting equilibrium may not be efficient for other members of society. (p. 211)

It is also important to note that despite its pretensions to 'positivism' such research is not value free. As Cooper (1988) reminds us, concentrating on the interests of the economically powerful simply endorses the *status quo* in terms of the power relations in, and social functioning of, society. Furthermore, the decision-useful, investor-needs approach adopted is culturally specific in being located in a society (predominantly the United States for much of the research in this area) that places great reliance on market forms of regulation. It does not necessarily follow, of course, that this form of regulation is the most efficient or desirable on wider social grounds.

Similar reasoning has, as the reader will recall from Chapter 2, led us to adopt an accountability framework as the theoretical 'anchor' for the analysis undertaken in this book. Such a framework is broader, in terms of issues addressed and wider, in terms of constituencies to whom moral accountability is acknowledged, than that employed in the investor-needs studies.[6] For us, CSR possesses the potential to make organisational life more visible and organisations themselves more transparent through developing the democratic functioning of information flows. Therefore, in our analysis the most significant finding to emerge from the investor needs studies is that corporate social disclosure bears little relationship to actual performance. By contrast, for researchers such as Herremans *et al.* this appears to be of little consequence. In their study (1993), incidentally one of the most impressive of the genre in terms of sophistication of technical analysis, the finding that corporate social responsibility, measured by reputational indices rather than disclosure, appears positively associated with accounting and stock market returns is all that matters. Indeed, the fact that investors are apparently sophisticated in using social responsibility information, and are not dependent on corporate disclosure, is employed to caution against trying to alter the accounting model in order to carry more information of a social nature. Nothing, surely, could better illustrate the narrowly focused, essentially anti-democratic nature of the investor studies that this!

A final major flaw with the investor studies lies in the lack of any explicit theory underpinning the analysis performed, which may go a long way towards explaining the very mixed results obtained. This is particularly apparent in the case of those studies which focus on investor reactions to corporate social **disclosure**, which are also of most interest to us in terms of their implications for developments in CSR. As Cooper (1988) points out, equally plausible arguments can be advanced for profit-seeking investors preferring any one of the whole range of possible combinations of social expenditure and disclosure. Thus, at one extreme the investor may prefer high expenditure and maximum disclosure in order to minimise the possibility of future liability and to secure maximum public relations benefits. At the other extreme, minimal expenditure and no disclosure may be preferred in order to maximise both short-term financial returns and the chances that corporate social irresponsibility remains undiscovered.

A further, and vital, theoretical issue concerns the (largely implicit) assumption that shareholders can be considered to be a homogeneous grouping, concerned solely with financial returns. As we noted in the introduction to this chapter, recent years have witnessed the appearance of so-called 'ethical' investors who are apparently seeking to introduce an explicit social dimension into the investment decision-making process. To the extent that non-financial returns are desired by this group in addition to, or indeed instead of, financial returns the implications for developments in corporate social accountability, and associated CSR, are likely to be very different from those derived from the studies we have just been considering. It is to these issues that we turn our attention in the remainder of this chapter.

8.3 The 'ethical' investor or the 'concerned owner'

The whole ethos of ethical, or socially responsible, investment is rooted in the notion of individual responsibility. As Miller (1992) notes, 'Any individual or group which truly cares about ethical, moral, religious or political principles should in theory at least want to invest their money in accordance with their principles' (p. 248). Indeed, the social investment movement, with its emphasis on saver sovereignty and personal commitment towards companies or projects in which one is investing, may be viewed at least in part as a reaction to the growing impersonality of the savings function consequent upon the post-war boom in institutional investment (Cadman, 1986).

In seeking to use the investment function in order to pursue social goals the social investment movement largely appears to adopt the objective of keeping within the capitalist 'rules of the game' in order to achieve evolutionary change in society. As such it has much in common with the longer established consumer movement which has been so influential in contributing to the increased level of green awareness prevalent in western economies in recent years (see, for example, Elkington, 1987; and Elkington and Hailes, 1988). That consumer (or investor) pressure should play such a central role in attempts to impose new social controls on business enterprise is hardly surprising, for, as Craig-Smith (1990) points out, consumer sovereignty provides the essential rationale for capitalism and in employing market forces it is particularly appropriate to what, in Britain at least, may be described as a post-socialist society.

Social investment has, in fact, a long history. Miller (1992) traces its origins back to Victorian England and to social reformers such as Octavia Hill, whose espousal of 'five per cent philanthropy' was designed to provide good standard housing for the poor while offering acceptable financial returns to those providing funds for this purpose. A prominent early role was also played by religious groups, notably the Quaker movement with its traditional antipathy towards investing in areas such as armaments and alcohol production. The movement reached new levels of prominence in the late 1960s and early 1970s as the social proxy movement in the United States spawned an increasing number of shareholder resolutions on various social issues.[7] Prominent among early resolutions were those filed with Dow Chemicals in 1969, which questioned the morality of producing napalm, and nine resolutions submitted to General Motors annual meetings addressing the needs of minorities, workers and consumers under the umbrella title 'Campaign GM'. By 1983 the social proxy movement had grown to the extent of proposing more than 200 social responsibility resolutions in that year, covering such issues as weaponry, anti-union activities and South Africa, compared with just two resolutions in 1973 (Domini and Kinder, 1984). As was the case in the United Kingdom, once again religious groups were to the fore in the growth of the social investment movement in the United States.

A more recent manifestation of an increased interest in the concept of socially responsible investment has been the successful launching of a rapidly growing number of ethical mutual funds/unit trusts, dating from the early 1970s in the United States and the mid-1980s in the United Kingdom and continental Europe. The high profile assumed by these organisations makes them an excellent vehicle by which we can investigate the conceptual foundations of social investment in general, and in particular examine its potential as a mechanism for imposing a wider social accountability on business enterprise.

8.4 The ethical and environmental unit trusts

Funds focusing on socially responsible investment were launched in the United States in the early 1970s. By the late 1980s asset figures had risen to something in excess of $50 billion (Rockness and Williams, 1988). A further boost to the market, evidenced by the launch of a number of new funds, was provided in 1989 in the aftermath of the *Exxon Valdez* Alaskan oil-spill incident (Brown, 1990). Within the United Kingdom and continental Europe developments have been of a more recent nature,[8] although growth rates, at least in percentage terms, have been equally impressive. For example, in the United Kingdom the first fund to enter the field was the Friends Provident Stewardship Fund in June 1984. By the end of 1988 14 funds were already in existence reporting total assets of £144 million, with a growth rate in money invested of approximately 50 per cent during that year (EIRIS, 1989). Latest figures available at the time of writing indicate there to be more than 20 funds now in operation, with total sums invested in these funds and related ethical products, such as pension funds and personal equity plans (PEPs), in excess of £600 million. A similar pattern is discernible in continental Europe with 31 funds being launched between 1987 and the beginning of 1993 attracting an investment of over £334 million. This represents a 500 per cent increase in terms of sums invested since 1987, when only four funds were in existence (Campanale *et al.*, 1993).

Turning to the investment policies pursued by the funds, Rockness and Williams (1988) identified an emerging consensus on the primary characteristics of corporate social performance looked at by US fund managers. They list six performance factors — environmental protection; equal employment opportunity; treatment of employees; business relations with repressive regimes; product quality and innovation and defence contracting — as investment criteria for a majority of managers. Research conducted by Harte *et al.* (1991) and Perks *et al.* (1992) indicates a broadly similar set of issues concerning UK fund managers, although markedly greater importance appears to be placed on avoiding companies involved in the alcohol, tobacco and gambling industries, together with, in the Harte *et al.* study, considerably more emphasis on animal rights issues.[9]

Such differences in emphasis should perhaps cause little surprise. As Harte *et al.* point out, the 'ethical' agenda changes over time and attitudes, and concerns, can vary between different countries and situations. In the former context, some commentators (see, for example, Lamb 1991) have drawn attention to the fact that, originally, ethical funds in the United Kingdom were set up to avoid investment in companies operating in certain areas (usually particular products such as tobacco and alcohol or trading with repressive regimes) while the more recently launched 'green' funds tend to look for more positive criteria, notably in the area of environmental sensitivity. Similarly, Campanale *et al.* (1993) have suggested that funds in continental Europe launched predominantly in the late 1980s tend to be more 'positive' in focus than their UK equivalents. However, one must be careful not to make too much of such distinctions, for as Lamb (1991) acknowledges, there has been a gradual blurring of the distinction between green and ethical funds, with both now adopting positive and negative criteria (see also Harte *et al.*, 1991).[10]

Indeed, as the research unit attached to the United Kingdom's first avowedly ecological, or green, fund has stressed:

> The terms 'green investment' and 'ethical investment' are often considered to have very different meanings. However, such terms begin to blur on closer inspection of either the green or ethical case. The ethical norms which characterise a company are fundamental to any green investment analysis. They include the integrity of the vision and leadership of top management, and a company's openness and accountability to its employees and to the outside world. Company policies towards animal testing and overseas trade, as well as management attitudes towards women, minorities and the community are therefore important indicators to consider. Without the presence of at least some of these elements, the potential for excellence in environmental management is minimal. (Merlin Research Unit, 1993, p. 3)

A more meaningful distinction between the various funds, rather than relying simply on the above differences in terminology, is drawn to attention in the annual guide to ethical and green investment funds published by independent financial advisers Holden Heehan. Among other features, the funds are assessed by reference to both the degree of rigour with which ethical and environmental criteria are applied and the resources devoted to research. In both areas quite noticeable differences in ranking are apparent. In the former these differences arise due to both a lack of precision in defining investment policies on the part of the funds, thus giving managers considerable freedom in their choice of investments, and differing extents of avoidance being applied in the case of negative investment criteria. Thus, to take but one example, some funds may exclude companies both producing and selling alcohol products, others may simply regard production, and not retailing as a no-go area, while yet others may regard a 'major' interest in production and/or retailing (where major may or may not be defined as a percentage of total business) as the key avoidance issue (see Perks *et al.*, 1992).[11]

Turning to the issue of research it is particularly noticeable that very few funds directly employ specialists to provide advice on environmental and social performance issues.[12] The most common practice is for external expert advice to be sought, predominantly utilising the services of the independent Ethical Investment Research Service (EIRIS) and, in addition, appointing an independent ethical committee to ensure that the social credentials of the portfolio are checked on an ongoing basis (see, for example, EIRIS, 1993; Holden Meehan, 1994). However, not all funds have recourse to independent advice, and for those that do there are clearly major differences in both the extent of advice sought[13] and, in particular, the role played by the ethical committee.

Despite differences between the various funds in terms of the degree of rigour with which both ethical or environmental criteria are applied and supporting research utilised, broadly they share a common aim of introducing an explicit social dimension into the investment decision-making process. This has led Rockness and Williams (1988) to suggest that: '... an understanding of the actual investment policies, information needs and information sources of these funds is an essential step in the development of social accounting' (p. 398).

Significantly, empirical research in both the United State (Rockness and Williams, 1988) and the United Kingdom (Harte et al., 1991) has drawn attention to the fact that corporate annual reports and accounts are a primary source of information for fund managers. This raises important issues relating to the current adequacy, and future potential, of these documents for purposes of making decisions on the non-financial aspects of corporate performance, which we will address in the final substantive section of this chapter. However, equally important questions are raised concerning the efficacy of the funds as an agent of social change and the role they play in sensitising the investment community in general to the ethical and social dimensions of corporate performance. It is to these issues that we now turn our attention.

Ethical investment: a potential agent of social change?

The ethical trusts operate in the financial market place and therefore compete for funds. Indeed, much has been made of the financially prudent nature of a socially responsible approach to investment (Ward, 1991). Thus the Merlin Research Unit (1993) unequivocally states that: 'The purpose of green investing is to make money in the short and long term ...' (p. 2). Similarly, Franklin Research and Development Corporation, a leading US social investment portfolio management company, have as their acknowledged primary goal: '... to achieve superior results for our clients on two bottom lines — financial and social' (undated, advertising material).

Due largely to their relatively recent appearance on the investment scene there has actually been little market-based research on the performance of ethical investments in the United Kingdom (Perks et al., 1992). However, Luther et al. (1992) have suggested that ethical investment could conceivably offer inferior financial returns because of factors such as increased monitoring costs and, due to restrictive avoidance criteria, a smaller investment universe with reduced potential for portfolio diversification.[14] Such research as there is in fact indicates that ethical investment portfolios, whether hypothetically constructed on the basis of particular criteria (EIRIS, 1989) or comprising the actual shareholdings of the ethical trusts themselves (Luther et al., 1992; Luther and Matatko, 1994), broadly produce returns in line with the market as a whole. Equally, however, it must be noted that in the case of the latter, performance varies substantially between different funds. Significantly, in this context, strictness of ethical criteria is identified as a financially detrimental factor — to be solved by being less ethical (see Gray et al., 1993, p. 194)). Clearly, such a 'solution' would appear to contradict the very concept of ethical investment which, in Moore's (1988) analysis, entails sharing in success and failure — and seeing that reflected in the return obtained. Indeed, Moore goes on to suggest that:

> Ethical Unit Trusts, by their very nature, seek, by speculation, to extract maximum profit from their portfolio of shares, and cannot again by their nature, take the responsibility of ownership seriously. As such they, and other forms of speculating in shares, cannot fall within a definition of ethical investment. (p. 13)

A further problem in regarding ethical funds as involved owners, rather than mere speculators, lies in the equivocal attitude they adopt towards seeking to influence the policies of companies in which investments are held. In Simon *et al.*'s (1972) analysis, the basing of portfolio purchases on maximum return principles *can* be regarded as compatible with an ethical approach to investment, but only if the individual shareholder actively seeks to bring about corrective action on discovering a corporate wrong: 'The shareholder's own vote or voice may well have been ineffective, but to fail to use it at all — to fail to test it — amounts to participation in the injurious practice' (p. 57). It is significant in this context to note that fewer than half the UK funds surveyed by EIRIS (1992) stated that they tried to directly influence the activities of company groups in which they invested. Even among the more active funds, such activism was largely confined to private discussion with corporate management, particularly when a decision to disinvest had been taken.

Essentially, the ethical funds can be considered a prime example of the eco-consumerist approach towards imposing a wider social accountability on business enterprise. Eco-consumerism, as Pepper (1989, p. 18) points out: '... aims to change society through changing spending habits, towards products and services considered "environment-friendly" and "ethically sound" '. An integral feature of this approach rests on a desire to accommodate problems arising within the prevailing sociopolitical system, utilising a free market economy approach or via gradualist liberal reform of the market system (Pepper, 1984).

The eco-consumerist strategy has been fundamentally questioned by radical ecologists (or 'deep greens'), the main tenets of whose position were discussed in Chapter 3. The central point of departure for a prescriptive analysis of society's current environmental and social malaise from this latter perspective, it will be recalled, lies in a rejection of the pursuit of economic growth as an essential societal goal. Furthermore, integral to such analysis is the necessity to make a sustained assault on the market system, which is regarded as having an ineluctably expansive tendency (see, for example, Gorz, 1989; Ryle, 1988; Seabrook, 1990). In addition to their reliance on market forces, issue is also taken with the eco- consumerists' emphasis on individual action in order to secure social change. Pepper (1989), for example, argues that such a view underrates the power of opposing vested material interests, as well as effectively disenfranchising the poor where the power of the purse is taken to represent the quintessential vote in a capitalist world economy.[15] The ethical funds strategy of stock market investment in order to pursue social and environmental goals is further questioned by the radicals' emphasis on the need for direct investment in local economies and the role of central planning in giving vital coherence to national investment strategies which seek to allocate resources to areas of need (Frankel, 1987).

At root, radical ecologists take serious issue with the basic belief underpinning the ethical trusts, that one can successfully pursue social and traditional growth-orientated, economic values largely simultaneously within the workings of the market economy. Furthermore, they indicate the dilemmas that can be introduced into the concept of ethical investment when it is no longer conveniently equated with notions of financial self-interest.[16] On the other hand, while a fundamental critique of current patterns of consumption and production is offered, very little serious thinking seems to have gone into developing actual strategies for change (Dobson, 1990; Frankel, 1987). A pragmatist may argue that by starting to move away from the exclusive short-term financial interest prevailing at the moment in western economies the ethical funds at least point a way towards practical change. The reader is invited to come to his or her own conclusions in this respect!

8.5 The wider field of social and environmental investment

Institutional investors

Given their small size relative to the stock market, and indeed unit trust market as a whole, the ethical and environmental funds can achieve little directly in bringing about practical social change. However, there is now some evidence that the concerns they espouse are attracting a supportive response from other institutional investors. Particularly prominent among this latter group are pension funds, which have witnessed a remarkable increase in the market value of their assets over recent years on both sides of the Atlantic.

In the United States a number of trade unions are showing an increased interest in the social ramifications of pension fund investment, most notably the Central American Union Federation AFL-CIO which some years ago established a national committee to develop social criteria for investing its pension funds. Additionally, a growing number of states have undertaken socially targeted investment. Particularly active among the state pension funds is the California Public Employee Pension System, with assets exceeding $50 billion, which has been prominent in recent moves to force a stronger environmental commitment on the part of the directors of the Exxon Corporation in the wake of the *Exxon Valdez* disaster.[17] In all, it has been estimated that around $650 billion of investment on Wall Street was subject to some form of social responsible screening by the early 1990s (Lamb, 1991).

Similarly, within the United Kingdom trade union and local authority pension funds have been at the forefront of developments in socially responsible investing. In the case of the latter, more than half the funds covered in a 1987 Local Government Chronicle Survey had established investment policies on non-financial matters (Keenan and Miller, 1988). Increasingly, local authority pension funds are demonstrating a willingness to actively lobby companies in which they hold shares on issues of social and environmental concern. One particular example here was the campaign led by the South Yorkshire Pensions Authority, with the support of other funds coordinated under the auspices of Pensions and Investments Research Consultants Ltd (PIRC) concerning Fisons peat-stripping activities, which had long been criticised by the environmental lobby for the damage done to rare habitats. Interestingly, more than a dozen other substantial institutional investors, including the Norwich Union, Commercial Union and Clerical Medical, subsequently took up the issue of peat extraction with Fisons following the PIRC initiative (see PIRC, 1991).

Some estimates suggest that the amount of investment in the United Kingdom now ethically screened to some extent stands at over £10 billion (Holden Meehan, 1994). However, a major obstacle to the continued growth of socially directed investment is presented by legal restrictions on institutions operating non-financial investment criteria. Particularly significant here was the failure of trustees appointed by the National Union of Mineworkers to gain legal backing for an attempt to promote social objectives (namely restricting investments made overseas and in directly competitive energy industries) within the investment plan of the Mineworkers Pension Fund (*Cowan* v *Scargill*, 1984). More recently, the Bishop of Oxford was similarly rebuffed by the courts in a 1991 case brought against the Church Commissioners in which he challenged their view that Church of England investments should be made entirely on financial, and not ethical, grounds. Whereas legal restrictions on how local authority pension funds may be utilised appear less onerous (Murray, 1983), considerable difficulties still lie in the path of such funds seeking to utilise social criteria in decision making. These difficulties centre particularly on the control of funds by trustees and advisers from financial institutions (Minns, 1980; Schuller, 1986) and problems encountered in obtaining information on potential investments which does not rely on 'city' assumptions concerning what represents a good investment (Moore and Levie, 1981). Additionally, as Perks *et al.* (1992) suggest, it may well be that investment decisions are seen to be the prerogative of specialists, so that those who could exert influence in an institution in which they have an interest are reluctant to do so.[18]

The legal position concerning institutions investing on social, in addition to financial, grounds is far from clear-cut. However, there appears to be a strong suggestion that if the prime purpose of the investment is to provide financial benefits for the beneficiaries (as is the case with pension funds) then such investment must be made in their best financial interest (Perks *et al.*, 1992). More particularly, **short-term** financial interest would seem to outweigh all other considerations. That such an emphasis may well not accord with the **long-term** interests of beneficiaries is brought to our attention in a report published by the Ecumenical Committee for Corporate Responsibility (ECCR), a research organisation concerned with the social and moral issues raised by church investment in transnational corporations.

> On the matter of the financial advantage of beneficiaries, there seems to be a failure to make connections and see the picture whole. For example, many 'beneficiaries' in the current recession have lost their jobs. Companies are reducing their costs wherever they can, especially with regard to labour. Fear of poor performance leading to loss of investor

confidence and possible takeover has led companies to seek out low-waged areas for placing new plant and closing old plant. Consequently, a beneficiary may be made redundant from the firm s/he works for because her/his pension fund's investment has encouraged this same company (for fear of otherwise losing it) to establish a new plant somewhere else. (ECCR, 1989, p. 2).

The need to 'see the whole picture' when making investment decisions similarly points to the long-term relevance of social factors as far as local authority pension funds are concerned. For example, local authorities have statutory responsibilities for, among other things, waste collection and disposal, monitoring of air emissions and water pollution. Therefore it would not seem unreasonable for special attention to be paid to the environmental performance of companies operating in the waste, water and chemical industries in making investment decisions (see PIRC, 1991). More generally, the essential point is that the interest of beneficiaries cannot simply be equated with short-term financial gain, particularly when this is achieved via social and environmental degradation. It is this simple proposition that provides the *raison d'être* for the social investment movement as a whole.

The banks

As a major supplier of both short- and long-term loan finance to industry, the banking community clearly has the potential to play a major role in the promotion of corporate social and environmental accountability, should it so wish. Initially their attention has been exclusively focused on issues of loan security and the potential for lender liability arising from the enactment of ever stricter environmental legislation, particularly in the United States (see Gray *et al.*, 1993, ch.10). An apparently somewhat less narrow approach was heralded by 'The Statement By Banks on Environment and Sustainable Development', supported by 31 banks and the United Nations Environment Programme (UNEP), presented to the 1992 Earth Summit. The statement declares that:

We the undersigned, believe that human welfare, environmental protection and sustainable development depend on the commitment of governments, businesses and individuals. We recognise that the pursuit of economic growth and a healthy environment are inextricably linked. We further recognise that ecological protection and sustainable development are collective responsibilities and must rank among the highest priorities of all business activities, including banking. We will endeavour to ensure that our policies and business actions promote sustainable development: meeting the needs of the present without compromising those of the future. (UNEP, 1994)

The statement goes on to address a number of key issues, such as the importance of environmental criteria in lending decisions and the need to promote employee, customer and general public awareness of the developing environmental agenda. Furthermore, the obligation to ensure best practice in the banks' own environmental management systems is acknowledged and support given to the conduct of periodic environmental reviews and public disclosure of progress made in implementing environmental policy. Conspicuous by its absence, however, is any mention whatsoever of the issue of third world debt, regarded by many environmental groups as the major factor preventing developing countries addressing environmental concerns as the pressing necessity to earn foreign currency outweighs all other considerations. Equally significant is the unquestioning acceptance of the efficacy of market mechanisms in promoting environmental protection.

Within the United Kingdom the National Westminster Bank has been at the forefront of moves towards placing environmental considerations on the banking agenda. In addition to being a leading signatory of the UNEP Statement,[19] National Westminster was the first UK bank to establish an environmental management unit and in 1993 published the results of its first environmental audit. The latter was the result of 2 years' work examining every aspect of the business from 'housekeeping' issues, such as energy consumption and waste disposal, to lending policy. It must be pointed out, however, that the approach adopted is very much one of 'enlightened self-interest', with great emphasis placed on the financial benefits accruing from the bank's environmental initiative.

By contrast, the Cooperative Bank has taken a more explicit moral stance with the recent publication of its ethical policy (reproduced in Figure 8.1). In addition to spelling out the bank's commitment to community development, environmental responsibility, equal opportunity in the workplace and customer rights, a number of activities of which the bank disapproves are identified, and an undertaking made not to engage in any form of business with organisations involved in these activities. Interestingly, a similar explicit ethical stance has been undertaken by the Danish Sbn Bank (Sparekassen Nordjylland). In this case, however, major emphasis is placed on the interests and needs of employees, customers, shareholders and the local community with detailed feedback from these stakeholder groups concerning the banks' performance in the area of a mutually agreed code of values, utilised in producing what is termed an 'ethical accounting statement'. A brief extract from the 1993 statement is reproduced in Figure 8.2.

The initiatives described above represent examples of all too isolated moves by the banking community towards addressing issues of social and environmental concern. In the main banks, as Gray *et al.* (1993) point out, still tend to see themselves as amoral, or environmentally and socially neutral in their adherence to 'sound financial practices'. However, as Bruyn (1987) among others argues, investment inevitably has a social factor which is intricately intertwined with economic development issues. Failure to acknowledge this in the context of third world investment has played a large part in the imposition of unsuitable patterns of economic development, generally based on western models, together with the unleashing of a debt crisis which has placed intolerable social and environmental burdens upon the poorest of the world's population (see, for example, George, 1988; Mayo, 1993). In the United Kingdom the degree of social responsibility exhibited by the high street banks is increasingly called into question as soaring profits (and executive compensation levels) are accompanied by staff redundancy programmes and an ever-growing volume of customer dissatisfaction.[20] Clearly, the banking community has a long way to go before it can be regarded as an integral part of the social investment movement.

Figure 8.1 *The Cooperative Bank Social Policy Business Advantage (1), 1994*

Our *Ethical* Policy

The Bank's position is that:

1 **It will not invest** in or supply financial services to any regime or organisation which oppresses the human spirit, takes away the rights of individuals or manufactures any instrument of torture.

2 **It will not finance** or in any way facilitate the manufacture or sale of weapons to any country which has an oppressive regime.

3 **It will encourage** business customers to take a proactive stance on the environmental impact of their own activities.

4 **It will actively** seek out individuals, commercial enterprises and non-commercial organisations which have a complementary ethical stance.

5 **It will not speculate** against the pound using either its own money or that of its customers. It believes it is inappropriate for a British clearing bank to speculate against the British currency and the British economy using deposits provided by their British customers and at the expense of the British tax payer.

6 **It will try to ensure** its financial services are not exploited for the purposes of money laundering, drug trafficking or tax evasion by the continued application and development of its successful internal monitoring and control procedures.

7 **It will not provide** financial services to tobacco product manufacturers.

8 **It will continue** to extend and strengthen its Customer Charter, which has already established new standards of banking practice through adopting innovative procedures on status enquiries and customer confidentiality, ahead of any other British bank.

9 **It will not invest** in any business involved in animal experimentation for cosmetic purposes.

10 **It will not support** any person or company using exploitative factory farming methods

11 **It will not engage** in business with any farm or other organisation engaged in the production of animal fur

12 **It will not support** any organisation involved in blood sports, which it defines as sports which involve the training of animals or birds to catch and destroy, or to fight and kill, other animals or birds.

We will regularly re-appraise customers' views on these and other issues and develop our ethical stance accordingly.

GEN 2024

The **COOPERATIVE BANK**

Figure 8.2 *Extract from the 1993 Ethical Accounting statement of the Sparekassen Nordjylland Bank*

Contents

Sbn Bank is a regional bank.
Our vision is:

**"To be the power centre for
economic and human resource
development in North Jutland"**

Our vision emphasizes that economic
and human development are vital to
the bank as well as to the region of
which the bank is a part.

Sbn Bank, the seventh largest
bank in Denmark, is a decentralized
organization with 71 branches in 19
regional areas.

Over and above serving the region
North Jutland, the bank has
additional branches in the major
cities, Copenhagen and Aarhus. In
1993, the bank had 1300
employees, and every third resident
in North Jutland is a customer.

Headquarters, located in the
largest city in North Jutland, Aalborg,
includes administration as well as
several customer services such as
stocks and bonds and foreign
business.

Sbn Bank/
Sparekassen Nordjylland
P.O. box 162
DK-9100 Aalborg
Denmark
Phone: +45 98 18 73 11
Fax: +45 98 18 91 03
Interpretation and Commentary
Keld Gammelgaard
Coordination
Karen Bagge
Company Reg No. 180 030 Aalborg

2

Figure 8.2 continued

Report from the Management

The Financial Accounting Statement for 1993 was satisfactory, but the Ethical Accounting Statement showed that we made heavy demands on our staff.

Recent hard times have perhaps caused us - briefly and unconsciously - to tone down the basic values of the bank. It is therefore now that the concept of Value-Based Management must prove its worth. It is precisely in difficult times that we must stand firm and act to remedy our performance where we have failed to live up to our stakeholders' expectations.

The development since 1992, particularly with respect to the employees, is unsatisfactory. Time after time, we have emphasized that the Ethical Accounting Statement must be taken just as seriously as the financial results. This commits us!

One of the strengths of Ethical Accounting is that it enables us to quickly register changes in attitude among our customers, employees,

shareholders and the local community. We can thereby be sensitive to both positive and negative signals before they become apparent in the financial accounting statement and, via our dialogues with the stakeholders, we are in a better position to react.

The trends revealed by the Ethical Accounting Statement for 1993 were as follows:
- Customers give by and large high scores to Sbn, but they want more information, particularly as to our fees.
- The general evaluation by the staff is not as positive as in previous years and some clear signals have been sent to management. There is, however, an important exception; the feeling of job security is back at the same level as before major staff reductions were carried through at Danish banks.

- Shareholders show signs of dissatisfaction with the financial development up to 1993.
- Non-customer residents of the region tell us that we have spent so much time and effort concentrating on ourselves that we have become less visible in the local community.

In 1993 we initiated a research project, which will shed light on the connection between the Ethical and Financial Accounting Statements. It will also explore the consequences of supplementing management based on profitability, rules and regulations with value-based management.

The Ethical Accounting Statement was something of an experiment when it was launched in 1990. It has now become part of our daily lives. Our departments pay just as much attention to our ethical performans as measured in the Ethical Accounting Statement as to purely financial matters.

The Ethical Accounting Statement also improves management options within the bank. The information collected provides us with the opportunity to see the results of each individual organizational unit. It allows us to initiate a dialogue and to act promptly should we become aware of developments which are contrary to the values shared by the stakeholders and Sbn.

An overall evaluation of Sbn's Ethical Accounting Statement for 1993 is that there is a need for improvement. There are areas where we have not been sufficiently active in promoting the shared values we have committed ourselves to support. If we are on the wrong track, it cannot be concealed. It is precisely here the Ethical Accounting Statement must demonstrate its effectiveness: now is the time to act.

3

Community-based and 'alternative' social investment

A particular problem faced in many poorer communities is that of 'capital flight' — the process by which savings with commercial banks by residents of low income neighbourhoods rather than being used to fund local development projects are reinvested elsewhere by the banks on maximum return principles. The scale of this phenomenon is indicated by Dauncey's (1988) observation that: 'In the whole of the USA, only one out of 14,500 commercial banks ... puts more money back into low-income neighbourhoods than it takes out' (p. 185).

For Dauncey and other writers such as Bruyn (1987) and Ekins (1992b) the promotion of local economic autonomy is a major task for the social investment movement. Community banks, credit unions and development loan funds, based on the principle of members' control, are put forward as key mechanisms for achieving such an end. Perhaps the most well-known example here is at Mondragon in the Basque country of north-east Spain where the local credit union, the Caja Laboral Popular, channels the savings of some 400 000 members into more than 100 cooperatives employing 20 000 people.[21] While being most prevalent in the United States (see Bruyn, 1987) community-based investment is very much a worldwide phenomenon. Dauncey (1988), for example, points to thriving initiatives under way in Britain, Germany, New Zealand and, most particularly, Canada. One final example worthy of special note is the Grameen bank in Bangladesh which by October 1990 had lent $278 million to its 830 000 members, all classified as very poor, and predominantly female, with a repayment rate of 98 per cent (see Ekins, 1992b, p. 37).

The unifying principle behind the numerous, generally small-scale, community banking initiatives taking place around the world is the notion of saver sovereignty, or personal commitment towards the project or community one is investing in that we introduced earlier. This principle is further evident in the growing volume of 'alternative' social investment practice becoming observable in Europe, coordinated by the International Association for Investors in the Social Economy. This organisation, launched in Brussels in 1989, seeks to promote social banking initiatives across Europe by connecting investors directly with social projects (Campanale et al., 1993).

A similar approach is adopted in the United Kingdom by Mercury Provident, a small licensed deposit-taking institution founded in 1974. In addition to investors being able to direct their funds to individual projects of their own choice, they may also choose the interest rate they wish to receive. This principle of sacrificing financial returns in order to achieve greater social returns is a fundamental feature of the 'alternative' investment scene, and stands in clear contrast to the notion promoted by the larger, more conventional, institutional social investors that both values may be maximised together. A further example is provided by the Cooperative Bank's ethical savings account, paying 1.5 per cent less than the rate of return on the bank's ordinary account with the difference going to the Industrial Common Ownership Finance (ICOF) organisation which helps to set up worker cooperatives. Share flotations in the late 1980s by Traidcraft, the third world trading organisation, and the Centre for Alternative Technology (CAT) in Wales give additional interesting illustrations of the social dimension of investment outweighing the financial return. Traidcraft's prospectus, for example, clearly states that:

> Dividends will be low . . . and the directors do not envisage a substantial appreciation in the share price. If, however you are interested in the well-being of the weak and disadvantaged and feel that changes in our own lifestyle and attitudes are necessary we invite you to read the following details and subscribe to Traidcraft's work.

Information intermediaries and research organisations

A final feature of the social investment scene worthy of brief mention is the ever-growing number of support groups established to provide information and research back-up for social investors. Such groups have been prominent on the US investment scene for many years now.[22] For example, the Council on Economic Priorities (CEP), of which mention has already been made earlier in this chapter, commenced publishing the results of its research into various aspects of the social performance of business corporations in the early 1970s. More recently two organisations, Franklin Research and Development Corporation (FRDC) and Kinder, Lyndenberg, Domini (KLD) have achieved particular prominence by developing scoring systems for measuring a company's overall social performance based on their own in-house analysis. The move to scoring from a more simple screening system employed by the ethical trusts in operating the avoidance criteria described earlier indeed has significant ramifications for the development of the corporate reporting function, which we shall shortly address.

Within the United Kingdom, the Ethical Investment Research Service (EIRIS), established in 1983, is extremely influential. In addition to advising a number of the ethical and environmental unit trusts and publishing the annual guide *Choosing an Ethical Fund*, EIRIS undertakes a myriad of other activities. These include publication of a quarterly newsletter together with briefing notes on various issues of interest to the ethical investor, portfolio screening services and the drawing-up of acceptable lists of companies based on criteria supplied by the individual investor as well as the organisation of regular conferences and seminars, the proceedings of which are generally published. Pensions and Investment Research Consultants Ltd (PIRC) undertake a similarly wide range of activities in providing advice and assistance to local authorities concerning the social implications of pension fund investment decisions. A particular feature of PIRC's work is their commitment to shareholder activism as an integral part of the long-term investment approach, as opposed to short-term speculation, which they espouse. In addition to coordinating action against specific companies, of which the Fisons case mentioned earlier is but one example, PIRC launched the UK Environmental Investor Code in 1990. A number of their local authority clients have subscribed to the code which outlines key steps, such as a commitment to regular monitoring and reporting of environmental impacts, that companies should be taking in order to demonstrate a positive response to environmental concerns.

Significantly, the emergence of an explicit campaigning role is becoming a central feature of the activities of a number of prominent social investors and support groups.

Church groups such as the Interfaith Centre on Corporate Responsibility, which has coordinated many shareholder campaigns in the States on issues of social concern, have been well to the fore in this respect. A particularly well-known recent example of activism is the development of the Valdez Principles by the US Social Investment Forum in the wake of the *Exxon Valdez* disaster. Now administered by the Coalition for Environmentally Responsible Economies (CERES), whose membership comprises leading social investors, environmental groups, religious organisations, public pension trustees and public interest groups representing more than $150 billion in invested assets, and renamed the CERES Principles, signatory companies commit themselves to abiding by a strict charter of environmental responsibility (see Gray *et al.*, 1993, pp. 63–7). Additionally, a system of annual reporting by signatories has now been established so that adherence to the Principles may be monitored. However, it is particularly noticeable that whereas dozens of private and publicly held corporations have endorsed the Principles, these are in the main relatively small concerns with signatories from among the *Fortune* Global 500 companies largely conspicuous by their absence (CERES, 1993).

The latter point raises major questions concerning the degree of influence that the social investment movement may be able to exert on large and powerful business organisations. The preceding overview of the activities of the movement has highlighted the fact that essentially it is made up of many different strands expressing a wide range of concerns. Other than an implicit reliance on the power of the 'consumer' in the marketplace, there appears little agreement on a coherent set of theoretical aims and objectives. Perhaps the one area of emerging consensus is that there is a need for more rigorous and reliable information on corporate social activity to be made available to the investment community. It is to this issue that we now breifly turn our attention.

8.6 Social investment and the corporate reporting function

Surveys of the ethical investment scene in general identify the availability of relevant information as the key to effective action (Domini and Kinder, 1984; Ward, 1991). Indeed, Rockness and Williams's (1988) study of US ethical funds suggested that availability of appropriate information on social performance, rather than frequency of negative criteria, is the main reason for excluding firms from ethical portfolios.

Of particular relevance to accounting policy makers is the fact that ethical fund managers on both sides of the Atlantic apparently place heavy reliance on company annual reports for investment decision making, despite their awareness of major deficiencies in the provision of data on corporate social performance within these documents (Harte *et al.*, 1991; Rockness and Williams, 1988). Deficiencies in information provision are particularly highlighted in a study by Perks *et al.* (1992) which, from a scrutiny of portfolios, identified 17 companies most frequently invested in for environmental reasons by UK ethical trusts, and then extracted information from those companies annual reports that was relevant to environmental investment decisions. Their analysis indicated that:

... the annual reports of those companies shows that the information required to establish compliance with environmental investment criteria was generally not provided. Although company annual reports may be presented as meeting the information needs of investors in general terms, they are clearly lacking in relation to the specific needs of ethical investors who are concerned with environmental issues. (p. 55)

Additional areas identified by ethical fund managers as being currently inadequately addressed in corporate annual reports are those of animal experimentation, community and social issues and trading interests in companies with oppressive regimes (Harte *et al.*, 1991) together with equal opportunities, employee welfare and product quality (Rockness and Williams, 1988). When considered in conjunction with earlier research suggesting that such social information as is provided within annual reports tends not to be directly related to actual social performance, and indeed at times appears positively misleading (Ingram and Frazier, 1980; Rockness, 1985; Wiseman 1982), corporate reporting practice is clearly indicted as a major constraint facing the ethical investor.

Significantly, respondents in the studies carried out by Rockness and Williams and Harte *et al.* called for accounting policy makers to give a higher priority than they do at present to issues of ethical information disclosure.[23] Bruyn's (1987) analysis suggesting that the information needs of fund managers can be generalised to larger groups of social investors indicates that the social investment movement has the potential to become an important lobby group for improved corporate social reporting (see Owen, 1990).

Demands for a greater degree of rigour in information provision are likely to become more pronounced as the screening approach to portfolio selection (by which firms are simply excluded on the basis of negative ethical criteria) is supplanted by scoring. An early exponent of this latter technique has been Franklin Research and Development Corporation (FRDC) in the United States, which has developed a five-point numerical rating system covering eight different social performance dimensions. Wokutch and Fahey (1986) argue that a scoring approach is superior to the ethical investors typically implicit and intuitive decision-making process in:

forcing ethical investors to identify ethical investment guidelines, and to identify, measure and evaluate social performance dimensions resulting in an overall value weighted corporate social performance rating. It facilitates reflection by providing the decision maker with an analytical frame of reference through which a priori or 'gut feel' beliefs or expectations can be critically examined. (p. 211)

As Harte *et al.* (1991) indicate, the implications for accounting of a move towards scoring corporate social performance are significant since more detailed information is required to arrive at an assessment, and companies would necessarily be reviewed in more depth as potential investments. Our review of the current state of corporate social reporting practice at both domestic and international levels in Chapters 5 and 6 highlights the nature of the challenge facing the accounting profession should the social investment movement become a more sophisticated, and powerful, information user group.

8.7 Summary and conclusions

Whereas the overview of the social investment movement presented in this chapter largely suggests there to be a multiplicity of disparate organisations seemingly pulling in different directions, there does seem broad agreement among those adopting a 'market centered' investment philosophy (perhaps most notably the ethical and environmental unit trusts) that both social and economic returns can be pursued simultaneously. Significantly, one rare and notable attempt to develop a conceptual framework for social investment practice, that of Bruyn (1987) is based upon just such a premise.[24] However, in equating social advancement with financial self-interest one avoids facing the key ethical and moral dimensions of the investment decision process. In particular, omitted from consideration is any analysis of the role that 'inner directed' ecological, humane or spiritual values may play in changing the very concepts of 'economic' and 'uneconomic'. By contrast, the work of writers such as Schumacher (1973) and Moore (1988) who bring inner-directed perspectives, derived from the tenets of Buddhism and Christianity, respectively, to bear on questions of investment and economic development enable us to discern the elements of just such a challenge to prevailing notions of simple materialism. Most fundamentally, questions are raised concerning whether objectives such as ever-increasing levels of material consumption and maximising financial returns can be morally equated with the notion of investing ethically.

Such questions are increasingly being addressed by the rapidly growing community-based and 'alternative' social investment organisations that we briefly drew attention to. The degree of challenge being mounted to traditional economic values is most graphically illustrated by the emergence of local exchange (LETS) systems, originating in Canada but now taking off in the United Kingdom, under which people in a community come together to exchange a wide range of goods and services with money itself playing no part in proceedings.[25] More generally, it is being increasingly recognised that the community-based 'social' economy with its explicit value base and emphasis on social participation is very much distinct from government or business and hence calls for a very different approach to investment (see Sattar, 1995). Significantly, Bruyn's (1987) attempt to develop a theoretical framework for social investment practice, despite its adherence to the notion of economic gain as a key investment objective, pinpoints the local community as the ultimate focus for decision making. Indeed, Bruyn unequivocally states that 'At every level the question arises as to how investment decisions will affect the local community, which is where the philosophy underlying social investment is finally judged' (p. 183). We are very much in agreement with this view and would tend to look towards community-based investment as the arena in which future social investment questions are explored and the dilemmas and contradictions of the concept itself most directly addressed.

Notes

1. See the annual guides to ethical and green investment funds published by the Ethical

Investment Research Service (EIRIS) and Holden Meehan for details of amounts invested in the various UK funds. In total, funds currently under management in the United Kingdom amount to no more than 1 per cent of the entire unit trust market.

2. For a more detailed analysis of empirical work in the area see, for example, Belkaoui and Karpik (1989), Herremans *et al.* (1993) and Mathews (1993).

3. Participants in the study included financial analysts, members of environmental protection organisations, environmental regulators and MBA students.

4. Companies are rated on eight dimensions of performance one of which is 'responsibility to the community and the environment'. Herremans *et al.* compared companies' ratings on this dimension to responsibility ratings from a study conducted from the perspective of consumers (Lyndenberg *et al.*, 1986) and found a broad level of consistency between the two.

5. See Gray *et al.* (1993, ch. 10) for an extended discussion of this issue.

6. For an extended discussion concerning the major differences between the 'accountability' and 'decision usefulness' perspective see Gray *et al.* (1991, pp. 3–7).

7. See Domini and Kinder (1984, ch. 13) and Bruyn (1987, chs 2 and 3) for further discussion of the social proxy movement and other US initiatives from the late 1960s onwards.

8. An intriguing exception was the launch by Ansvar Fund Management in Sweden of the Ansvar Sverige Aktiefunds, an ethical fund avoiding investment in companies engaged in the production of tobacco and armaments or with operations in South Africa, as early as 1965 (see Campanale *et al.*, 1993).

9. Significantly, in view of the point made earlier that the social investment movement has much in common with the consumer movement, a very similar set of criteria is employed by the campaigning journals, *New Consumer* and *The Ethical Consumer* (see Chapter 9).

10. Both green and ethical funds with their focus on non-financial dimensions of corporate performance should, however, be clearly distinguished from environmental *opportunities* funds which focus exclusively on the *financial* returns obtainable from companies in certain industries benefiting from current concerns with environmental issues.

11. These differences are reflected in the analysis of the funds portfolios presented by EIRIS in its annual guide *Choosing an Ethical Fund*. An avoidance score is calculated for a wide range of ethical and environmental issues, which measures the tendency of each fund to avoid companies identified by EIRIS as poor performers on that issue. Wide divergences are apparent between the funds in key performance areas.

12. A major exception is provided by the Merlin Jupiter Ecology Fund which employed an in-house Environment Research Unit. On 1 August 1994 the unit was acquired by a rival institution, NPI.

13. Poor levels of research support are particularly apparent in the case of European based funds (see Campanale *et al.*, 1993).

14. Luther *et al.* (1992) point out, for example, that adopting the simple criterion of avoiding companies paid more than £5 million in any one year (from 1984–87) by the Ministry of Defence would exclude almost one-quarter of the value of the *Financial Times* All-Share Index. Furthermore, also excluded would be companies comprising more than half the market capitalisation of the telephone network, the

electrical, the electronics and the oil and gas sectors.

15. This attack on marginalist economic analysis, with its focus on individualism, has much of the flavour of Tinker's (1985) analysis and leads to a similar damning indictment of conventional accounting theory and practice (see Gorz, 1989; Ryle, 1988; Seabrook, 1990).

16. For further analysis of this issue see Harte *et al.* (1991), particularly pp. 245–51.

17. For further details of US initiatives see Bruyn (1987) and Miller (1992).

18. Interestingly, Perks *et al.* (1992) single out universities as institutions that one may expect to be concerned about social responsibility issues in making investment decisions but in practice appear to show little interest. Furthermore, they produce evidence to show that students may have the potential to influence investment policy, but, in general, have made little attempt to do so!

19. The four other leading signatories were the Royal Bank of Canada, Deutsche Bank AG, Germany, Hong Kong and Shanghai Banking Corporation and Westpac Banking Corporation, Australia.

20. The social and environmental performance of UK banks in particular has been subjected to highly critical scrutiny by the Bankwatch project initiated by the New Economics Foundation (see Mayo, 1993).

21. See Dauncey (1988, ch. 7) for an extended discussion of the Mondragon initiative.

22. See Bruyn (1987) for an in-depth analysis of the history and activities of these groups.

23. See also the 1993 report from the Merlin Research Unit outlining changes in reporting practice necessary for improving the quality of environmental performance analysis.

24. See Owen (1990) for an analysis and critique of Bruyn's work.

25. See Dauncey (1988, pp. 52–69) for a fuller analysis of the history and operations of LETS systems.

chapter 9

The social audit movement

9.1 Introduction

The social audit movement has essentially concerned itself with constantly challenging and extending the actual recognised responsibilities and discharged accountabilities of business and other organisations. Perhaps the movement's greatest achievement has been in demonstrating that an alternative does exist to the 'New Right' project indicated by the Thatcher and Reagan governments (Geddes, 1992), and that promotion of personal greed and callous indifference to the plight of the financially and socially disadvantaged is not an essential ingredient in the establishment of economic and industrial policy.

The nature and central concerns of the social audit movement are neatly conveyed by Geddes (1992) who suggests that:

> Social audit is best understood as a reaction against conventional accounting principles and practices. These centre on financial viability and profitability of the individual economic enterprise, paradigmatically the capitalist firm. By contrast, social audit proposes a broader financial and economic perspective, reaching beyond the individual enterprise, for example to the local economy of which it is a part or to different types of organisation such as state agencies. Relatedly, social audit posits other goals as well as, or instead of, financial profitability . . . Moreover, social audit attempts to embrace not only economic and monetary variables but also — as its name suggests — social ones, including some which may not be amenable to quantification in monetary terms. (p. 216)

A further essential feature of a social audit lies in the active involvement of external participants (or stakeholders) in the preparation and evaluation of the published report. Initially, in the United Kingdom at least, compilation of the reports was solely the province of external participants.[1] More recently in both the public sector and private sector active collaboration of internal participants has been forthcoming. This latter development is potentially significant for, as we shall see throughout this chapter, any individual or group seeking to collect social data on an organisation without the cooperation of the organisation concerned is faced with very real, and at times almost insurmountable, difficulties (see, for example, Stephenson, 1973).

Our purpose in this chapter is to chart the development of the social audit movement in the United Kingdom from its beginnings in the early 1970s, to critically evaluate the progress it has made and to provide pointers towards future developments. Our reason for adopting a largely UK perspective lies in a desire to paint a coherent picture of how the concerns of the movement and methodologies employed have evolved over time. Furthermore, notable developments such as attempts to reach beyond the boundaries of the organisation and hence adopt a community or local economy perspective (particularly in the case of local authority initiatives) are to the best of our knowledge largely a UK phenomenon.

Nevertheless, it is necessary at the outset to acknowledge developments in the United States which, just as was the case with the emergence of social and ethical investment practice considered in the previous chapter, have had an undoubted influence on events in the United Kingdom. To this end we would recall to the reader's attention the early, and rare, examples of both independent attestation of corporate social reports (Atlantic Richfield) and external-to-the-organisation preparation of such reports (Phillips Screw) appearing in Chapter 4, together with the discussion of the activities of the Council on Economic Priorities in Chapter 8. Indeed American influence is clearly apparent in the first example of early social audit activity within the United Kingdom to which we now turn our attention, that of the organisation Social Audit Ltd, one of the leading figures of which, Charles Medawar, had previously gained considerable campaigning experience with Ralph Nader, the doyen of the US consumer movement.

9.2 Social Audit Ltd[2]

Of early British attempts in the field of CSR the work of Social Audit is probably the best known. The organisation was formed in 1971 by Michael Young, the Founder of the Consumer's Association (CA) and has maintained a particular interest in the effects of corporate behaviour on consumers (Medawar, 1978).

Social Audit describe themselves as: 'an independent non-profit-making body concerned with improving government and corporate responsiveness to the public generally' and initially defined their aims thus: 'it will be one of our objectives to illustrate the feasibility of progress towards the day when reasonable safeguards for economic democracy will be embodied in law and social audits universal' (*Social Audit* No. 1, 1973, p. 3). Their work conveniently splits into two, the *Social Audit Quarterlies*, published between 1973 and 1976 and containing , among other things, social audits of specific organisations and the later (post-1976) books and pamphlets. The *Social Audit Quarterlies* contain general articles reviewing such items as armaments and industry, the social cost of advertising and company law reform as well as their best-known work — the social audits of Tube Investments Ltd, Cable and Wireless Ltd, Coalite and Chemical Products Ltd, Avon Rubber Co Ltd and the Alkali Inspectorate (no longer extant).

The latter organisation, now subsumed within Her Majesty's Inspectorate of Pollution, was at the time a government body appointed under statute to monitor air pollution emissions in cooperation with local authorities. The *Social Audit Report* of

1974 was an attempt to answer the perennial question *quis custodiat custodians* (who guards the guards)? The report, almost entirely narrative, is an analysis of the history of the Inspectorate, their *modus operandi* and their effectiveness and fairness in controlling air pollution. The Inspectorate did not fare well in the investigation. Social Audit found them ineffective and, most importantly, secretive and unaccountable. The difficulties of extracting information from government bodies, such as the Alkali Inspectorate (who purportedly monitor social activities on behalf of the public), was central to much of Social Audit's work and is indeed a continuing, and growing, problem today.

Later work of the organisation can again be conveniently split into that intended to help others perform social audits; for example, handbooks on pollution and consumer audits and a guide to chemical hazards (Frankel, 1978, 1982; Medawar, 1978) and detailed investigation of various social issues, for example chemical suppliers' health and safety information (Frankel, 1981), various aspects of pharmaceuticals (Blum *et al.*, 1983; Medawar, 1984; Medawar and Freese, 1982) and the marketing and advertising of food and drugs in the third world (Medawar, 1979).

The reports on specific organisations produced by Social Audit Ltd are highly detailed, lengthy documents. The report on Tube Investments, for example, is about 60 pages long (about 30 000 words) and that on Avon Rubber is about 90 pages long (about 100 000 words).

The reports are mainly narrative although photographs, cartoons, statistical summaries, compliance with standard and financial data are also employed. We can only give the briefest of reviews of the work of Social Audit here, but the following description of the salient points of the Avon Rubber Report, the most substantial and famous (or infamous) of the organisation's investigations, gives the general idea.

Avon Rubber

The Avon Rubber Report is unique in that, in the initial stages at least, it was carried out with the full cooperation of the management of the company (this cooperation was later withdrawn with a number of consequences which are discussed below). The Report reflects both this cooperation and the experience gained by Social Audit from their previous investigations. Figure 9.1 indicates the areas covered by the Report. The introduction to the Report contains the objectives Social Audit set for themselves.

> The aim of the report goes beyond a description of what a single company has done, at a certain point in time. The report has been prepared also: (i) to show to what extent it may be possible to assess what, in social terms, a company gives to and takes from the community in which it operates; (ii) to advance understanding about the practical problems and possibilities that may be involved in making assessments of this kind; and (iii) to establish precedents for the disclosure of more, hard information about what companies do, why they do it, and to what general effect. (p. 2)

It then reviews their experiences of the company's cooperation together with the problems of extracting information from government bodies. The Report makes fascinating reading in its attempts both to catalogue Social Audit's attempts to gain

Figure 9.1 *Avon Rubber: the Social Audit Report 1976*

Social Audit on Avon

> Most sections of this report have been organised into
> three parts: an introduction, which includes details of
> yardsticks of performance used; a report, which includes
> statements (or representations) of fact; and a discussion,
> which summarises and comments on the main findings.

Contents

Figure 9.1 *continued*

Participation and Alienation	24		86
Consultation			
Union facilities		RESPONSE FROM AVON	88
Industrial relations			
Health and Safety	29		
Frequency of accidents			
Safety organisations			
Relations with Factory Inspectorate			
Noise			
Chemical hazards			
List of hazardous chemicals in use			

Source: Social Audit, Spring 1976, p. 1.

access to information held by public bodies and, in a genuine attempt at frankness, to communicate the biases that Social Audit perceived as informing their work.

The review and analysis of Avon's business which follows is a useful background to the social audit of the company. In a general sense this section amounts to a simplified interpretation of the Annual Report and accounts for the previous few years. One notable inclusion is the analysis of value-added.

As with other reports from Social Audit there is extensive and thorough analysis of employees and employment conditions. The Report examines problems of motivation and productivity, the effectiveness of union representation and the extent and effectiveness of employee participation. There is also a useful analysis of safety. The description and analysis of Avon's products and services which follows seems to show the company as one of the 'better' organisations in their industry, although industry-wide practices with regard to advertising and keeping consumers informed about the products they buy are heavily criticised.

The section of the Report on the environment uses statistical summaries and compliance with standard approaches as a major theme and to good effect. Figure 9.2a shows the results of Water Authority analysis of effluent from one plant. Social Audit point out, however, that the use of independent figures is essential — the company's figures cannot necessarily be trusted (Figure 9.2b).

The Report also examines noise pollution, reporting Avon's performance against government standards, then setting the standards in context for the lay person by reference to the noise levels typically generated by everyday things.

The Avon Rubber Report concludes with a summary of the problems that resulted from the company's withdrawal of cooperation. The company's response to the draft report was:

Figure 9.2a Extract from *Social Audit Report 1976* showing effluent discharge reporting and the sample problem.

Results of sampling of trade effluent discharged into sewers from the Bradford-on-Avon factory.

(Results of 9 analyses between November 1974 and August 1975; together with conditions of consent issued in March 1975.)

Parameter	Limit imposed (parts per million, unless indicated)	Range of samples
pH	6–10 pH	3.2–9.5 pH
Temperature	43.3°C	—
Volume	100 cu.m/day	—
BOD	—	4–70
COD	—	28–432
Phenols	—	3–8
NH_3	200	1.5–224
Suspended solids	400	49–220
SO_3	500	21–970
Cl	—	8.4–294
Total Heavy metals	20	< 1.5–12.1
Zinc	10	0.4–10.5

Figure 9.2b

Effluent discharges from Avon Medicals

Date of sampling	Source	pH (limit 6–12)	Suspended solids (limit 400 ppm)	Chemical oxygen demand (limit 600 ppm)
15.7.74	Avon	8.5	6	0
8.8.74	**Water Authority**	**7.9**	**72**	**5,735**
25.10.74	Avon	8.3	5	5
19.12.74	Avon	7.7	2	0

> Having read the draft copy of the *Social Audit of Avon Rubber Company Limited*, the reaction of the Management and most of the Trade Union Representatives in the Avon Companies involved in the Audit is one of acute disappointment and concern at the enormous number of inaccuracies and misinterpretations that it contains. This, in spite of the very considerable assistance given to the Social Audit researchers and the many hundreds of hours of interview time and volumes of correspondence.
>
> A detailed correction of the report would in our opinion result in a document as voluminous as the draft report itself.
>
> In these circumstances, and whilst appropriate action has and will be taken on any criticisms which we believe are justified, both Management and most Union Representatives in the Avon Companies concerned feel they must disassociate themselves from the general contents of the report and do not wish to have any further discussions or correspondence on it.
>
> Having received and considered these reactions from our Subsidiary Companies, the Board of Avon Rubber Company Ltd, endorses their viewpoint.

Social Audit amended the draft report in the light of such comments as they did receive and conclude: 'this report on Avon represents what we believe to be an accurate and fair record of some of the Group's principal activities, as they were observed over the Winter of 1974 and 1975' (p. 89).[3]

This aspect of the Avon Report does raise the important practical problems of how to avoid bias (through providing partial information) and inaccuracy (through difficulties of measurement and monitoring). It seems highly unlikely that an outside body without the full cooperation of the organisation concerned and the appropriate government bodies can realistically hope to produce a wholly 'accurate and unbiased' report. In addition, of course, every 'social auditor' is likely to bring his or her own personal values and bias to all matters of selection and description. It is likely, therefore, that an objective such as 'freedom from bias' is little more than a pious hope.

Despite the problems with production and interpretation of the Report outlined above there was some encouraging response to it, albeit from abroad rather than at home.

In the United Kingdom the publication of the Avon Report has certainly not gone unnoticed, even if it has failed to provoke the discussion in public we might have hoped for. Possibly, this lack of an open response is indicative of the kind of cover-up with which British business (and other) establishments characteristically seek to hide their embarrassment, confusion and dismay. Alternatively, the Report may simply have been published in the wrong place and at the wrong time. In Sweden, by contrast, the Report has led to extensive and continuing discussion about social accountability which has been evident to us, not least through the arrival of several delegations from 'big business' (Volvo and two state-owned manufacturing concerns among them) from across the North Sea (Medawar, 1976, p. 391).

Critique of Social Audit Ltd

A major strength of the reports produced by Social Audit is that all include a statement of objectives, with the overriding objective being the pursuit of the discharge of accountability. Assessing how well the reports relate to their objectives is, however, less easy. A comprehensive range of major constituencies and issues are addressed but difficulty in acquiring information has often led to uneven treatment of the different categories. In addition, whether deliberately or not, Social Audit did not specify the exact range and type of information they intended their reports to include and therefore assessment of completeness of information provision by the reader is difficult. The information is generally in the form of raw unmanipulated data, although the *ad hoc* use of anecdotal evidence and the frequent expression of writers' opinions could be viewed as defects in the communication process. This, together with the difficulties of gathering information and the inevitable lack of any general independent attestation of the Report mean that the Report's 'correspondence with reality' cannot be wholly relied upon. The reports are eminently readable and no expert knowledge is required. A variety of presentations are used — photographs, narrative, etc. The length of the reports raises problems however. First, as a basis for the development of CSR the production of reports such as that of Avon Rubber is clearly impracticable — the Avon Rubber Report took something in the region of 5 staff-years to prepare, not including the time given by Avon personnel. Secondly, the length of the reports has been referred to by many commentators as a negative element — being too long to read and digest. Given the complexity of the issues underlying CSR, however, whether length is a critical advantage or disadvantage is clearly a debatable point.

Some 20 years on, the work of Social Audit Ltd remains among the most thorough and important examples of independently produced CSR in the United Kingdom. Unfortunately, the very independence of Social Audit Ltd, and consequent lack of wider economic or institutional involvement with the organisations concerned, both limited their power and made articulation of a framework of accountability involving them impossible. The inevitable result was that the reports produced were, apparently, ignored in the main by company management, particularly where the message conveyed was a largely unpalatable one. Furthermore, an attempt to mobilise shareholder opinion behind various recommendations made in the Tube Investments social audit met with scant response, even from supposedly socially concerned groups such as clergymen and charities.[4]

Similar problems in making a lasting impact, beyond providing a 'toolbox' of information and ideas, have generally bedevilled other early social audit initiatives conducted by bodies independent of the 'audited' organisation to which we now briefly turn our attention.

9.3 Other early social audit initiatives

Defined broadly enough, social audits can encompass anything from *ad hoc* or more systematic analysis of specific and general issues of social accountability to investigative journalism.

In the former category, some of the best-known examples of less systematic social audits, generally concentrating on particular aspects or consequences of organisational performance, are those conducted by special interest groups. The leading environmental groups Greenpeace and Friends of the Earth have, for example, from their earliest days mounted investigative campaigns largely concentrating on the environmental ramification of the activities of companies operating in particularly sensitive industrial sectors. Gray *et al*. (1993) indicate that for a number of organisations they worked with in the course of their research the 'external shock' produced by such campaigns has provided the stimulus for corporate management to take a serious and hard look at their environmental activity. This external pressure towards 'transparency' and accountability in respect of corporate environmental performance has indeed heightened in recent years with the trend towards more regularity in the provision of environmental campaigning information (see, for example, the monthly publications *Greenpeace Business* and the longer established, and widely respected, *ENDS Report* published by Environmental Data Services).

An early example of systematic social auditing from a consumerist perspective is provided by the Consumers Association. Best known for their magazine *Which?*, this private sector body initially concerned itself with quality and value for money together with ethical issues relating to the supply of goods and services to the public. Gray *et al*. (1993) consider the work of the Consumers Association to be: 'an important early example of the social audit as a mechanism for challenging the passivity of the individual in the face of the growing power of organisations and their capacity to exploit advertising and the nature of choice' (p. 263). They do, however, go on to point out that commercial pressures in the late 1980s reduced this campaigning dimension, leading to a much narrower focus upon questions of product cost and efficiency (see also Geddes, 1992). Despite this, the issue of social accountability to consumers remains alive with journals such as *New Consumer* and *The Ethical Consumer*, both launched in the late 1980s on a surge of interest in 'green' consumerism, taking up the social auditing torch apparently abandoned by the Consumers Association. We shall discuss further these more modern manifestations of consumer-orientated social auditing later in this chapter.

Another organisation concerned directly with one particular constituency, or stakeholder group, in this case labour, was Counter Information Services (CIS). This Marxist collective of journalists was dedicated to seeking radical changes in society,[5] as Ridgers (1979) makes clear when outlining the goals of the organisation as: 'providing information resources for workers engaged in specific struggles and exposing the nature of the social and economic system which is the cause and content of these struggles' (p. 326).

The CIS reports, issued throughout the 1970s, covered a wide variety of topics — including, for example, South Africa, nuclear technology and the position of women in society. Their best-known reports which can be considered to be broadly in the CSR field are, however, the 'Anti Reports'. These focused on, among other organisations, Lucas, Ford, Unilever, RTZ, Consolidated Gold Fields, Courtaulds, GEC and the NHS. The reports are deliberately undated and Gray (1980), from an interview with CIS members, identified the priorities of the reports as being: 'a good story', readable, and encouraging to employees. As a result the reports are quite deliberately selective and biased.

The reports are largely of a narrative format with tables of financial and statistical data as available. The effects of redundancies, strikes and working conditions are given high priority although other dimensions of social performance are frequently touched upon (the first Anti Report, that on RTZ, for example, made a number of observations concerning environmental performance utilising material culled from *The Ecologist* magazine).

The power of the reports lies in the use of photographs, frequent quotations and vivid, emotive phraseology. For example, in one report we are told that: 'The history of Consolidated Gold Fields is one of brutal and inhuman exploitation which still continues. It is a case history of our current economic system operating in its purest form' (*Anti Report* No. 3, p. 35 *c.* 1973). Photographs are frequently used in direct appeal to the emotions: a portrait of Franco, 'fascist dictator of Spain', appears in the *Ford Anti Report* (p. 9, *c.* 1978), Hitler graces the *Lucas* and *Unilever Anti Reports* (p. 11, *c.* 1976 and p. 81, *c.* 1976), while a caption reading 'the effects of bombing in Vietnam' appears over the picture of a burnt-out hospital in the *GEC Anti Report* (p. 31, *c.* 1973).

The Anti Reports clearly have little relevance to CSR as a form of 'objective', 'balanced' and 'unbiased' communication. They are, however, important as a particular, and somewhat rare, example of a 'radical' approach to reporting produced on a regular basis. As such, they provide a critical contrast to what could be seen as the more conventional CSR we have largely concerned ourselves with in earlier chapters.

A further example of social audits conducted from a labour perspective worthy of brief mention are isolated attempts at auditing the economic and social effects of plant closures conducted by trade union and worker groups (Institute for Workers Control (IWC) 1971, 1975) and academic economists (Rowthorn and Ward, 1979). These reports adopted a macro-economic, as opposed to simply an organisational, perspective towards the issue of plant closure in analysing GDP and balance of payments consequences in addition to employment effects. They are particularly significant in being a forerunner to more sustained local authority activity in this area in the 1980s , a consideration of which we turn to in the next section of this chapter. The 1971 IWC report (on Upper Clyde shipbuilders) is also of some historic interest, being one of the earliest published works in the United Kingdom to actually use the term 'social audit' (Zadek and Evans, 1993).

The few illustrations touched upon above give but a flavour of the whole range of social audits that have been conducted from an environmental, consumer and labour perspective, respectively. Other initiatives have been yet more narrowly defined. To give but one example, the End Loans to Southern Africa Organisation produced a series of 'Shadow Reports' on Barclays Bank during the 1980s (see Wells, 1985); interesting in particular for being modelled loosely on the bank's own annual report and accounts, the Shadow Reports aimed to 'provide a substantial dossier exposing the bank's support for apartheid'. The contents of the reports are *ad hoc*, vary from the simply provocative to the apparently factual and had the sole aim of attempting to embarrass Barclays into withdrawing from South Africa and Namibia.

As may be seen, the term 'social audit' has from the outset embraced a wide range of aims and perspectives which encompasses investigative journalism, commissioned research, special interest group campaigns and the efforts of self-appointed 'watchdog' organisations. The common thread is that all are part of the broad, if usually partisan and *ad hoc*, process of opening up, exposing, explaining, developing and attempting to control the myriad aspects of organisational activity in modern society.

9.4 Local authority social audits

Plant closure audits

Rapid large scale de-industrialisation within the UK economy and the attendant dramatic rise in unemployment levels, particularly in regions dependent upon traditionally labour-intensive manufacturing activity, gave rise to a new manifestation of social audit activity in the early to mid-1980s. The prime movers this time were local authorities facing both declining income and a deteriorating industrial infrastructure as Thatcherite 'new right' economic policy took a grip. Plant closure social audits (or 'social cost analyses') were carried out by a number of local authorities in the hardest-hit areas, with Merseyside leading the way.

The plant closure audits, drawing upon work done at the macro-economic level which sought to quantify the exchequer, or public, costs of unemployment (CAITS, 1984a; House of Lords (Select Committee on Unemployment), 1982), exhibit two major features. First, an estimate of the total impact on employment in the locality of the plant closure is made. In addition to highlighting direct job losses consequent upon the closure decision, this entails making an estimate of the number of indirect redundancies occurring in local firms supplying materials and services to the affected plant and induced job loss in retailing and other firms serving the local market, due to decreases in purchasing power. The latter impacts are generally arrived at by utilising employment 'multipliers', which may be standard industrial or regional multipliers or alternatively specific figures derived from specially commissioned surveys. Additionally, a number of the reports made an attempt to estimate the likely duration of unemployment which largely hinges on factors such as the age and skill composition of the workforce together with the pattern of local job opportunities.

The above information is then utilised in deriving the second major feature of the reports, an estimate of the public costs of unemployment imposed on local government and the national exchequer by companies implementing closure decisions. The costs focused upon in the reports are predominantly those arising from redundancy payments made from public funds, income tax and national insurance contributions forgone, social benefits paid (funded both nationally and locally) and loss of local tax revenue.[6]

Plant closure audits: a critique

Two common criticisms of the approach adopted in the plant closure audits centre on the subjectivity of the analysis and the reactive one-off nature of the exercise.

Turning to the first criticism, it must be acknowledged that there are obvious practical problems inherent in the audit exercises. There is, for example, some disagreement over what costs should be considered. Thus, certain categories of cost considered in the macro-economic studies referred to earlier (CAITS, 1984a; House of Lords, 1982) such as loss of indirect tax revenue and costs of ill health consequent upon increased unemployment levels are largely ignored in the local authority reports. Also generally omitted is any consideration of both balance of payments implications (Rowthorn and Ward, 1979) and loss of output (Glyn and Harrison, 1980) resultant upon closure. Additionally, costs reported are estimated on a uniformly conservative basis with a tendency to exclude welfare items such as free school meals and other education and health benefits together with associated administrative costs (Harte and Owen, 1987). Further subjectivity is inherent in attempting to measure the full impact of plant closure on employment, particularly in estimating indirect and induced effects, together with specifying the likely duration of unemployment in deciding the time horizon to adopt in the report.

While the above questions raised over the methodology employed in the reports are sufficient to indicate that there is no 'uniquely right' figure that can be produced to represent the cost of unemployment, at least an indication of the order of the cost to the public purse of lost jobs is conveyed. Thus, rather than a detailed, accurate figure, an intimation is given of whether the cost is, for example, of the order of £3million, £30 million or £300 million (CAITS, 1984b).

The criticism that plant closure audits are one-off affairs that simply promote the retention of decaying industries is forcefully put forward by Anell (1985), in reviewing 12 Swedish exercises concerned with the investment/disinvestment decision. The basic thesis she advances is that it is only by abandoning unprofitable business that resources can be set free to seek better uses, and that closure audits merely obstruct this necessary change. However, this criticism surely loses much of its force in a situation of continuing mass unemployment, such as that experienced in the United Kingdom in recent years, and where more modern production methods are a less labour-intensive than displaced methods. As Glyn (1985) puts it:

> Installing the most up-to-date system of production so that one worker can do the work of five is of no benefit to society as a whole if the four whose jobs are lost are unemployed. (p. 11)

Furthermore, one might point out that quantifying the costs of unemployment resulting from a plant closure does not, of course, necessarily indicate that the plant should be kept open. Rather, important information concerning a vital aspect of corporate performance or non-performance is presented which, if nothing else, illustrates the dimensions of a problem that has to be confronted by society.

It is also of some interest to note that the multiplier methodology adopted in the closure reports has also been utilised in other situations. Examples include studies of the potential effects of privatisation (SCAT, 1985) and council spending (Sheffield City Council, 1985) together with two exercises designed to highlight the importance of specific industries to particular regions — these being steel (County of Cleveland, 1983) and coal (Barnsley Metropolitan Borough Council, 1984). There does indeed seem scope for further developing such a regular monitoring approach towards strategic industries. Other situations in which social audit techniques developed in the context of plant closures may be employed are in examining the public interest implications of takeover and merger activity (Transport and General Workers Union (TGWU), 1986) and, perhaps more fundamentally, as a forward appraisal technique in evaluating new expansionary projects (Haughton, 1988).

Two further issues of note concerning the closure audits are their implications for corporate accountability and the particular conceptualisation of social welfare employed.

Harte and Owen's (1987) analysis of a number of local authorities' closure audit initiatives seeks to articulate a framework of accountability between business corporations and local government. It is suggested that the relationship between the parties, based on local government's support of business via provision of infrastructure, financial aid and the purchasing function together with the community's dependence on business for employment provision and economic health, is such that a 'social contract' can be said to exist.

A particularly useful mechanism for operationalising such an accountability relationship would be the institution of a public inquiry whenever a closure having significant impact in a particular locality is proposed. One such initiative was that of West Lothian District Council (1985) following the decision taken by the (then) National Coal Board (NCB) to close Polkemmet Colliery due to water damage caused to the pit during the coal strike of 1984–85. In addition to attempting an assessment of the pit's technical and economic viability the inquiry report included an analysis of the economic and social implications of closure. Significantly, the inquiry was conducted without the two (then) public sector organisations concerned in the closure decision, the NCB and British Steel (BSC), which provided the main market for Polkemmet's output, feeling it incumbent on them to attend and give evidence. The conclusions of the inquiry panel, made up of a prominent accounting academic together with a local church minister and industrialist, draw particular attention to this failure to provide information while at the same time cogently justifying the legitimacy of such exercises.

> As nationalised industries we believe the BSC and NCB should be accountable to their shareholders, the British public, and respond to requests for information from democratically elected public bodies. West Lothian District Council have, we suggest, a legitimate right to know the basis of decisions taken by another public body, particularly one which has been the second largest employer in the area. (West Lothian District Council, 1985, para. 5.17)

It is indeed a stark feature of plant closure audits, whether focused on private sector or public sector organisations, that they have had no apparent effect in reversing closure decisions. This simply illustrates the fact that no matter how persuasive the social audit may be, or how strong the arguments for developing accountability might appear, without the support and involvement of central government local authorities are unable to enforce their views. Far from supporting local authorities in their attempts to adopt a responsible attitude towards the needs of their communities, central government has rather in recent years emasculated local government (Puxty, 1991). Indeed, the Thatcher and Major governments have seemingly adopted a stance of indifference to community hardship imposed by plant closures or, in the case of the mining industry, actively promoted a policy of job losses and community breakdown.

In the face of such government indifference it is perhaps unsurprising that business corporations in the United Kingdom have been unwilling to accept the principle of accountability to the community. This lack of accountability is clearly reflected in the absence of any reference to the public's costs of unemployment imposed by companies implementing closure and run-down decisions in corporate reports, with only redundancy costs to the company being reported.

The unpromising reaction of both government and business, together with something of a slow-down in closure activity in the second half of the 1980s has, with the exception of isolated initiatives in response to particularly major disinvestment such as that of British Aerospace (see Geddes, 1992), caused a considerable fall-off in plant closure audits. However, the community perspective they adopted has continued in further local authority social auditing activity, which we shall shortly consider briefly.

Significantly, the need to focus collective action at the level of the community is also a major feature of green political critique (see, for example, Dauncey, 1988; Porritt, 1984). Indeed, there is a strong political tradition emphasising collective action going hand-in-hand with decentralisation that can be traced back to the work of the 'utopian' socialist William Morris in the 19th century, which has led a number of writers to point to a degree of convergence between green and socialist thought (Dobson, 1990; Ryle, 1988). Thus, there are grounds for believing that the issue of corporate accountability to the community may at some point in the future again feature centrally on the political and economic agenda. This in turn may cause some re-examination of the corporate reporting function and particularly the lack of both social and financial information provided by local economic entities which are divisions as branches of corporations and hence not legally required to report separately.

The run-down of UK manufacturing industry in the 1980s can at least be partly attributed to accounting calculations grounded in criteria reflecting short-term profitability and financial viability (Williams *et al.*, 1983). Furthermore private profit, rather than any notion of the social value of production, is used as the criterion for employment provision. Thus there is a failure to consider the possibility that while a plant is not profitable for an employer to operate, it may still be in society's interest for it to continue in production (Glyn and Harrison, 1980). A significant feature of the local authority plant closure reports lies in the use of a fundamentally different conceptualisation of social welfare than that of private wealth maximisation, to which traditional accounting techniques address themselves, in measuring organisational performance. The alternative employed, that of employment and consequent spending power is, it must be acknowledged, undoubtedly a crude one. For example, little attention is paid to qualitative factors such as quality of employment or social usefulness of production. In essence, the reports tend to consider productive activity *per se* as beneficial, which in itself poses an interesting contrast to much social accounting theory and practice which focuses on costs imposed on parties external to the organisation arising from such activity.

A further difficulty arises in the reports' focus on financial quantification. This leads inevitably to the use of market data, such as level of redundancy payments made together with state benefit and taxation payment levels prevailing. Of course, such data is open to government manipulation as well as failing to capture the full effects of the various social stresses, for example strains placed on family life or increased incidence of ill health emanating from unacceptably high unemployment levels in particular localities.[7] This shortcoming is indeed highlighted in one of the reports which states:

> Yet it is this human cost that is perhaps the most important cost; this ghost can be seen lingering between many of the lines of this report, yet it will not appear in any of the figures. (City of Edinburgh District Council and Lothian Regional Council, 1985, para. 2.4)

Later local authority social auditing initiatives which move beyond the reactive, single entity focus of the closure audits have signalled something of a shift away from crude financial quantification in seeking to address more qualitative and less tractable issues. It is to a brief consideration of these later initiatives that we now turn.

Later local authority social audit initiatives

Two local authority social audit reports published in the mid-1980s marked a major step forward from the limited methodology and focus of the plant closure audits.

The Newcastle upon Tyne Social Audit (Newcastle City Council, 1985) outlined the results of an inquiry into the impact of government policy on the welfare of residents of the city over the time period 1979–84. This indicated that residents suffered a net reduction in disposable income of some £70 million (or £700 per household per annum) compared to that which would have been available had policies and conditions remained unchanged. Pointing out that the impact was not evenly spread over all residents, the report went on to identify major gainers and losers. The former comprised a relatively small number of very high earners, while prominent among the latter were the newly unemployed, pensioners and those on below average earnings. Detailed analysis was presented indicating the relative importance of reductions in disposable income consequent upon unemployment, changes in the system of welfare benefits and social security provision and cost increases for fuel, rates and rent in contributing to overall income reduction. The latter part of the report went beyond simply figures in order to highlight less quantifiable reductions in the overall quality of life, represented by diminution in sundry public service provision and higher incidences of ill health, crime and family stress, with case studies drawn from welfare rights work being effectively used to illustrate the human effects of policy change.

A yet more detailed exercise was the Sheffield Jobs Audit (Sheffield City Council, 1985) which adopted a similar regional perspective in attempting to assess the volume and, equally significantly, quality of direct and indirect employment created by council expenditure as well as studying the impact of rates and other charges on local jobs. The audit runs to some 260 pages set out in eight sections which examine:

- The council's spending and how it is financed.
- The general trends of employment in Sheffield and the contribution of council employment to the overall picture.
- Total jobs supported by council spending, comprising direct employment and that generated by council employees, spending and placing of council contracts.
- The jobs effect of council capital and housing revenue expenditure.
- Quality of council employment, examining how pay and conditions compare with those of other workers.
- The impact of rates and charges levied to finance council spending on local employment levels.
- The employment, wage level and public expenditure effects of the threatened privatisation of a number of council services.
- The impact of Dudley Council's policies of spending cuts, privatisation and establishment of an Enterprise Zone in order to provide a contrast with Sheffield's very different policies.

For Geddes (1992) these latter two initiatives are particularly important; not only in that they are positive and forward-looking, rather than simply reactive, but also in the community perspective adopted which goes far beyond the confines of a single economic entity. Essentially they are concerned with defending the principle of public sector provision at the level of the community and pose an alternative to the ubiquitous 'value for money' approach towards State services with its emphasis on efficiency and cost savings rather than the satisfaction of human need.

A similar concern with satisfying needs is at the forefront of the activities of a number of community groups which in recent years have conducted social audits of local public service provision. Writing of one such exercise, the Leeds Urban Audit of 1990, Geddes (1992) points to this as an example of:

> ... a community-based initiative designed to make information about local state decisions and processes accessible, to enable local people to exercise greater influence and control over local state policies, and to bring the concept of need back into determination of policy priorities and resource allocation. (p. 222)

Community audits seem to be very much a growth area in the 1990s and are particularly interesting in that, while seeking to defend public provision, they by no means adopt an uncritical attitude towards current local government activities, as the above quote makes clear. As such their conceptual underpinnings are probably more in tune with the 'external pressure group' approach of organisations such as Social Audit Ltd than the 'in-house' approach of the Sheffield and Newcastle upon Tyne initiatives. A particular problem they face, however, is that despite a growing literature in the area it is probably true to say that at the present time we lack a sufficiently rigorous theoretical framework for distinguishing real 'needs' from mere 'wants' (Dobson, 1990).[8]

As may be seen from this section of the chapter, social auditing at the level of the local economy has been, in manifestations ranging from plant closure to community audits, a major growth area from the early 1980s onwards. As such it has presented probably the only truly coherent challenge to prevailing 'new right' economic orthodoxy throughout that time in its championing of the cause of social accountability as opposed to the 'me' and 'now' society so beloved of the Thatcher and Major governments. The ever-increasing involvement of local governments in the field of environmental reporting and auditing suggests that community-based initiatives will continue to be at the forefront of developments in social auditing practice. Indeed, it is of some significance to note that Friends of the Earth's *Environmental Charter for Local Government* (1989), in calling for regular audits of the local environment; expressed the belief that '... the enhancement of local democracy must form a fundamental element of any attempt to increase environmental sustainability' (p. 8).

9.5 Green consumer 'audits'

Despite the fundamental questions concerning the efficacy of green consumerism as a social change agent which we raised in the previous chapter it must nevertheless be acknowledged that campaigning consumer groups have taken on a primary role in supplying corporate social information in recent years. As Adams (1992) puts it: 'Social reporting enables the public to relate their personal values to their everyday expenditure' (p. 107). Thus the activities of such groups can be regarded as a new, and very buoyant, manifestation of social audit activity. This is particularly apparent when one considers the approach adopted by two campaigning journals launched at the end of the 1980s, *The Ethical Consumer* and *New Consumer*.

Noting the wide set of assessment criteria employed by *The Ethical Consumer*, which are far more extensive than simply traditional 'green' issues, Gray *et al.* (1993) suggest that their approach is: '... a serious attempt to link the consumer with the people, countries, processes and effects that produced the product now being purchased and consumed' (p. 269).

The Ethical Consumer assesses, and displays graphically in a simple table format, companies' policies and past records in the areas of animal testing; involvement in armaments manufacture; environmental impact; irresponsible marketing practice; land rights of indigenous peoples in the countries of operation, involvement with nuclear power; associations with repressive regimes; investment in the South African economy; trade union relations; and wages and conditions. For each of these issues degree of approval is signified by awarding a full mark, a borderline half-mark or a blank.

The journal's editors stress that the evaluation performed is purely relative, in that one company's record is judged against another's, rather than the absolute moral worth of a company being pronounced upon. Furthermore, for reasons of practicality, relative judgements are confined to comparison with other firms in the same report, which are generally drawn from the same product grouping, and the reader is counselled not to compare evaluations between reports (*SANE*, No. 2, January, 1990).

In common with a number of other external social audit initiatives considered in this chapter, acquiring information on corporate activities is a major problem area for *The Ethical Consumer* researchers. Heavy reliance has to be placed on publicly available

Figure 9.3 *Extract from Exxon Corporation 1989. From Adams et al., 1991*

EXXON CORPORATION

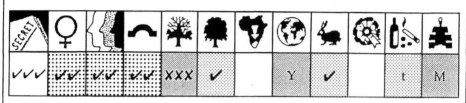

Exxon Corporation is one of the five largest industrial companies in the world. In the USA it is second only to General Motors, and stands right behind Royal Dutch Shell as the world's second biggest oil refiner and producer. Exxon's 1989 profits of over £3bn were greater than the GNPs of many of the 80 countries in which it operates. The company's principal business is energy, involving exploration for and production of crude oil and natural gas, manufacturing of petroleum products, and the transport and sale of crude oil, natural gas and petroleum products. Exxon Chemical Company is a major manufacturer and marketer of petrochemicals. Exxon is engaged in exploration for, mining and sale of coal and other minerals.

Exxon began life as Standard Oil in 1882, the first oil company in the USA. Its British arm, Esso UK, was launched in 1888 under the name Anglo-American Oil company. The parent company changed its name to Exxon in 1972. In 1989 Exxon's 70%-owned Canadian affiliate Imperial Oil Ltd acquired Texaco Canada for $2.3bn. In the UK, where Exxon has had an operation since 1888, Esso UK, a wholly-owned subsidiary of Exxon Corporation, is a major company in its own right with a considerable degree of autonomy from its parent company. There are two operating subsidiaries in the UK: Esso Exploration and Production UK Ltd, responsible for the exploration and production of crude oil and natural gas, and Esso Petroleum Co. Ltd, responsible for refining, distribution and marketing of petroleum products. The company's refinery at Fawley near Southampton is the largest in Britain.

Financial data for the year ending 31 December 1989

Turnover	£54,076m
Profit before tax	£3,147m
Turnover by business:	
Petroleum	£47,690m
Chemicals	£5,233m
Other/eliminations	£1,153m
Turnover by region:	
Petroleum and chemicals	
USA	£13,082m
Other western hemisphere	£9,245m
Eastern hemisphere	£30,595m
Other/eliminations	£1,153m

In 1988 Esso UK made a pre-tax profit of £468.2m on a turnover of £3,242m.

Exxon responded to CEP's survey and commented on the draft profile. Esso UK answered the New Consumer UK subsidiaries questionnaire and provided significant additional information.

At the end of 1989 the number of Exxon employees worldwide was 104,000, with some 4,000 in the UK. In the USA Exxon offers a high standard of benefits. Exxon reimburses employees for up to 100% of costs for courses that help directly or indirectly with job development. The company gives all new employees a pamphlet entitled *Ethics and*

Source: Adams R. et al. *Changing Corporate Values* (London: Kogan Page, 1991)

Figure 9.3 *continued*

Responsible Behaviour.

Exxon, like other oil companies, pays its employees extremely well. Esso in the UK provided New Consumer with a copy of its employee handbook: employee benefits appear excellent. In 1989 the highest paid employee of Exxon was the chairman, who received £787,000. This figure included all cash and cash equivalents including salaries, bonus awards in cash or shares of equivalent value, and other compensation for service. The 1988 emoluments (excluding pension contributions) of the chairman of Esso UK, who was also the highest paid director, were £238,000 (an increase of 20.8% on the £197,000 paid in 1987). In 1989 Esso Petroleum Company Ltd negotiated a basic pay increase of 7% with maintenance workers at its Fawley refinery effective from 1 April (4.6% in 1988). A Craft 1 maintenance worker was then paid £15,501 for a 37.5-hour week.[1] A base rate process worker would be paid £13,669 per annum under the new arrangements (excluding a £3,400 shift allowance), illustrating the generous level of pay in the oil industry.

Exxon has an employee stock ownership plan and a thrift plan. The thrift plan is a savings plan whereby the company also makes contributions to a savings trust fund on top of each participant's contributions. The majority of the company's full-time employees in the USA are eligible for the scheme. Exxon matches up to 6% of an employee's salary in contributions to his or her savings plan. The company stated that the thrift plan was an alternative to profit-sharing. In 1990 it offered thrift plan participants a leveraged employee stock ownership plan as an additional investment option. Employees choosing this option have their contribution matched seven for six. In the UK, employees have a share ownership sceme with the company matching employee contributions up to 5% of annual compensation. 3,600 of the 4,000 UK employees hold shares in the company through the share schemes. Exxon also operates incentive pay schemes which make payments in cash or in the form of options to purchase shares. These appear to apply only to senior executives.

Esso stated that a quarter of its employees belong to trades unions, with whom the company negotiates for collective bargaining purposes. The company provided material illustrating well-developed employee communications and involvement processes. In particular it operates a number of advisory forums which give employees the opportunity to engage in 'a free exchange of information and discussion of matters of mutual interest, and the airing of local issues and difficulties'.

One woman and one member of an ethnic minority sit on the 15-person main board of directors. No women or members of ethnic minorities are among the top 20 executives. In 1989 the overall participation of women in Exxon's US workforce increased from 25.9% to 26.7%. Managerial jobs held by women rose from 10% to 10.4%, while those in professional assignments increased from 19.5% to 20.5%. Exxon's employment of members of ethnic minorities in managerial posts advanced from 11.4% to 11.6% and those in professional jobs increased from 11.7% to 12.2% of US employees. In 1989 *Black Enterprise* magazine cited Exxon as one of the 25 best places for black employees. The Upward Mobility Taskforce encourages the wellbeing and promotion of women within the corporation. Programmes such as Early Minority Identification and Inroads find and encourage ethnic minority students to work for Exxon. In the United States, Exxon operates an affirmative action programme for people with disabilities. Family-related benefits in the USA are also good, including up to six months' unpaid post-maternity parental leave for both women and men. An equivalent job, however, is not guaranteed for returning men.

In the UK in 1990 the four-person board of directors contained no women or members of ethnic minorities. Of the top 60 managers in the UK, one was black and none were women. Half of Esso's 80-strong graduate intake in 1989 were either women or members of ethnic minority communities. The company offers a career break scheme.

information for, as the editors point out: 'The Co-operative that researches for the magazine is small and low budget, and cannot spend much time on "primary research" which is often slow and, more importantly when companies are uncooperative is frequently unproductive as well' (*SANE*, No. 2, January, 1990, p. 14). Thus, certain issues have to be excluded due to lack of publicly available information. One such is that of equal rights for women for, as is pointed out, no company admits to practicising discrimination and the only relevant facts generally obtainable are company directors' names which provide but scant evidence of overall company policy in the area. Furthermore, while some issues such as exposure in South Africa or armaments manufacturing activity are essentially factual and 'on the record', others, for example trade union relations and environmental impact, are more difficult to evaluate as although companies do provide information in these areas, what is available is heavily influenced by a desire to be seen to have a good record.

New Consumer operates in a similar way, utilising much the same criteria and faces similar problems in acquiring information on corporate activities. This was particularly apparent in a comprehensive survey undertaken of the social and environmental policies operated by 128 companies, covering some 35–40 per cent of the UK consumer goods market (*New Consumer*, 1991). A ratings system, backed up by detailed written analysis, was applied to the following areas:

- Industrial democracy
- Employment issues
- Equal opportunities
- Community involvement
- Environment
- Third world impact and policies
- Animal testing and factory farming
- Political involvement
- Alcohol, tobacco and gambling links
- Oppressive regime links
- Military sales
- Marketing policy
- Disclosure of information

Figure 9.3 gives an indication of the style of reporting employed. Significantly, a very patchy response was forthcoming from companies. For example, only 32 even returned the full questionnaire, or part questionnaire with supporting information, with the response from UK firms being significantly lower than that from American or other foreign-owned companies (Adams, 1992).

The new wave of consumer-orientated social audits, despite being clearly directed towards one particular stakeholder group, does address, as may be seen, a wide range of social and environmental issues. Thus we can trace their lineage right back to early pioneers such as Social Audit Ltd. The reports succeed in conveying information both clearly and succinctly, and hence may be considered more 'user friendly' than the earlier initiatives. Furthermore, in the case of *New Consumer* at least, the intention is apparently not to simply carry out one-off reporting exercises but to maintain a permanent, continually updated, database. Indeed, *New Consumer* claim this to be the most comprehensive archive of information about the social and ethical performance of companies in Britain. However, despite the power of the consumer lobby, which Adams (1992) for example considers has yet to be seriously explored, consumer audits share one major problem with many of their predecessors. That is, they are conducted by external participants or self-appointed 'watchdogs' to whom corporate management are reluctant to acknowledge accountability and hence to supply information.[9] Arguably, more could be achieved in terms of developing public accountability if internal, as well as external, participants are involved in the audit exercise. It is to this issue we now turn our attention.

9.6 Involving internal participants in the social audit exercise

Zadek and Evans (1993) suggest that because many of the social audit initiatives considered so far have been undertaken by outsiders, and not generally validated by 'neutral' auditors, they tend to be confrontational in nature. Hence they have not been accepted by the organisation concerned and have, as a result, largely been marginalised or ignored. In an intriguing analysis, Puxty (1991),[10] drawing upon the work of Habermas, argues that they therefore cannot be regarded as attempts to develop a discursive dialogue. That is, they are not designed to reach an understanding through working with the organisation concerned. A further problem with audits conducted solely by external participants is that they tend to be restricted to either a limited range of social issues (for example the local authority plant closure reports overriding focus on the costs of unemployment) or stakeholder groups. A new approach to social auditing pioneered by the third world trading organisation Traidcraft, by involving internal as well as external participants and addressing itself to a wide range of issues and constituencies, appears to avoid the above pitfalls. As such, it may provide a valuable pointer as to the further development of social auditing practice.

The Traidcraft social audits[11]

The Traidcraft approach to social auditing may be understood as: 'a process of defining, observing and reporting measures of an organisation's ethical behaviour and social impact against its objectives, with the participation of its stakeholders, and the wider community' (Zadek and Evans, 1993, p. 7). Participation of stakeholders is, as will be recalled from Chapter 7, a vital ingredient in the establishment of a systematic social bookkeeping system which itself underpins the preparation of the social accounts being audited.

Two perspectives on performance are adopted — an internal one which assesses performance against stated organisational objectives, and an external one which utilises comparisons with other organisations' behaviour and social norms. The approach adopted also places particular emphasis on external verification of the audit report and disclosure of results to all stakeholders.

Four key stakeholder groups are identified:

- Producer partners (i.e. overseas producers supplying the goods marketed by Traidcraft in the United Kingdom);
- Consumers and the wider public;
- Traidcraft community (i.e. staff and volunteer workers); and
- Shareholders.

Particular stress is laid on consulting all stakeholders in formulating performance indicators and, in the interest of process transparency, explaining decisions made to use specific indicators. The aim is to make the audit report reflect the views of stakeholders as well as the company and the external auditors. Thus it is not intended to present a 'universal' view of performance. Rather, the audit is regarded as a social document, 'one that reflects the reality of diversity that is intrinsic to any living community' (Zadek and Evans, 1993, p. 29).

The participatory nature of the audit exercise, involving both internal and external participants, is highlighted in the development of the methodology employed. This draws on the work of:

- An **internal reference group**, comprising Traidcraft staff with expertise in marketing, personnel, product selection and producer support; an audit consultant from the New Economics Foundation (NEF), a charitable body responsible for external validation of the report;[12] the director of a consumer organisation; and an academic having previous experience of working with the organisation on social responsibility issues. This group has responsibility for assessing, commenting and offering direction on aspects of method and process.
- An **external advisory group** made up of people with expertise in social audit and related areas.
- An **NEF Audit Group**. In addition to having final responsibility for approving (or otherwise) the social accounts produced by Traidcraft in conjunction with researchers from NEF, this group has the duty of establishing the adequacy of treatment of information produced in the audit process.

In establishing performance indicators the major criteria are that the social and ethical implications of the organisation's aims be taken fully into account, key stakeholders be consulted and external comparisons, as well as comparisons over time, can be made. A number of indicators employed are financial. For example, the proportion of third-world-sourced turnover actually paid to third world producers is employed as a measure of financial efficiency in relation to that stakeholder group. However, it is stressed that although financial measures may be possible, 'this does not obviate the need to look behind the numbers to understand the non-quantifiable ethical issues at stake' (Zadek and Evans, 1993, p. 25). Indeed, much use is made of qualitative data as well as quantitative, non-financial indicators, such as results of attitudinal surveys conducted among employees, shareholders and customers. Finally, it should be noted that no attempt is made to add up the various indicators employed in order to arrive at an overall figure for social profit or loss. It is argued that such a figure would be meaningless as 'it is not possible at least in quantitative terms — to judge the relative importance of costs and benefits to different stakeholders, or even arguably to the same stakeholder over time' (Zadek and Evans, 1993, p. 26). Figure 9.4, which is an extract from the producer's perspectives' section of the 1994/95 social audit, illustrates the wide-ranging reporting methodology employed.

Traidcraft's 1994/95 audit was only the fourth of what is intended to be an annual exercise. It is anticipated that the methodology and style of reporting will continue to evolve as feedback is forthcoming from the various stakeholder groups. A further aim is to develop a method of auditing that is relevant to a wide range of business organisations. However, it is accepted that different organisations may focus on very different social and ethical interests, hence giving rise to the need to utilise a wide variety of methodologies and indicators.

In this latter context, it must be borne in mind that while Traidcraft is a business organisation and operates as a public limited company it is hardly the archetypal commercial concern. Its social and ethical perspectives, which incorporate values that relate to the needs of peoples in the third world rather than centring on the shareholders' desire for financial gains, are enshrined in its Memorandum and Articles of Association. This provides a coherent focus for the audit exercise which more commercially orientated firms are unlikely to possess.[13] Furthermore, the degree of involvement of its external 'auditors' which encompasses assisting in the development of the audit methodology and overseeing, and in part implementing, the accounting itself, in addition to performing the validation function, is something many companies would be unwilling to contemplate. Not only is the comprehensive nature of the exercise an onerous task to be conducted on an annual basis, but also there is a distinct paucity of independent organisations with adequate resources and expertise to enable such work to be undertaken.

Despite the above reservations there are undoubtedly lessons to be drawn by others from the Traidcraft initiative. In particular, auditing progress made towards clearly defined objectives, making comparisons with the performance of other organisations and involving stakeholders centrally in the audit process offer pointers towards much-needed further development in social auditing practice. The latter aspect is particularly innovatory as far as the United Kingdom is concerned and indeed contrasts somewhat starkly with current corporate environmental reporting and auditing practice considered in Chapter 6. In sum, the Traidcraft approach shows what is possible given a commitment to systematic, comprehensive and regular social accounting and auditing.

9.7 Summary and conclusions

A particularly significant feature of the development of the social audit movement lies in the diversity of groups and individuals undertaking such exercises and, relatedly, the range of issues addressed. However, what the various initiatives do have in common is

Figure 9.4 Traidcraft social audit 1994–95, pp. 4–5

Key Performance Indicators

Sales of "third world" goods

TARGET   1991-1995 Business Plan set a target of 25% volume increase during the plan.

OUTCOME   23%   (5.7% IN 1994/95)

% of total sales from "third world" goods

TARGET   minimum 66%

OUTCOME   67%   (93/94-68%, 92/93-67%)

Income to "third world" partners[2]

TARGET   Continuous growth - no quantitative target.

OUTCOME   10% IN 94/95 £2.2 million
(93/94 £2.0 million)
(92/93 £1.6 million)

Fig 1. Sales Sourced from "Third World"

Fig 2. "Third World" Purchases 93-95

Figure 2 shows significant growth in Gifts (13% in 1993/94 and 31% in 1994/95). Crafts and fashion have the highest added value for Traidcraft's producers.

PRODUCERS' PERSPECTIVES

Objectives

Traidcraft's Foundation Principles state the mission of the organisation.

To establish a just trading system which expresses the principles of love and justice fundamental to the Christian faith.

Traidcraft plc is a business based on the common goals and shared action of its stakeholders. Its primary business objective is to increase the volume, value and quality of fair trade with primary producers in the "third world".

Scope of the Producer Accounts and Consultation Process

Each year Traidcraft has undertaken an intensive consultation with producer partners in one country or region - 1993 The Philippines, 1994 Kenya, Tanzania and Zimbabwe, and in 1995 Bangladesh. The selection has been made by Traidcraft with the aim of building a balanced and inclusive view over time of the company's relations with its "third world" suppliers.

Richard Evans, Traidcraft's Director of Social Accounting visited Bangladesh in March. The producers organisation ECOTA helped organise visits to producers and suppliers. Structured interviews based on a list of topics identified by producers as key determinants of fair trade during the consultation process for previous Social Accounts were recorded by Traidcraft and checked, amended and endorsed by the senior manager present for the discussions in each of the organisations visited.

In addition, there is an overall analysis of Traidcraft's performance in 1994/95 in relation to the issues its producers have identified, and short reports on the producer group selection reviews referred to in the Directors' Response to last years' report on page 22.

The report has the following sections:

Key performance indicators
Producer perspectives - Bangladesh
Review of craft sourcing
A new food sourcing policy

Key Performance Indicators

We have used the same indicators for growth as in previous years to measure performance against the key objective of expanding fair trade for our "third world" partners.

We have continued to monitor payments in advance to suppliers and the amount of contact time with producers spent by Traidcraft's product development and design staff. This year we have introduced an overall review of the company's performance in terms of the continuity of orders. Producers have emphasised the importance they attach to continuity as a differentiating characteristic of fair trade.

Commentary on continuity of orders

Traidcraft emphasises continuity of relationship in its Purchasing Policies, but has not systematically monitored changes in order values at the year end. The new social bookkeeping system (see p22) will facilitate monitoring of year on year order variations for individual partners, as well as country and regional changes. Year on year comparisons will not take account of distortions arising from changes in ordering or delivery patterns. Changes in value may reflect changes in currency values as well as changes in order volumes.

Key Performance Indicators

- 21 of the 26 'third world' countries supplying Traidcraft had increases in the value of goods shipped to Traidcraft in 1994/95.

- Africa (60% increase) and Latin America (100% increase) benefited mostly from direct sourcing of teas and coffees. The African result also includes a £92,000 (90%) increase in shipments of T-shirts, cards and papers from Dezign Inc in Zimbabwe received during the year.

- 5 countries had falls in the value of goods supplied: Indonesia down 44% (a reduction of £63,000), Zambian Cashew Company delivered one sixth of previous year's value (a reduction of £16,000); Bangladesh deliveries were down 5% (a reduction of £8,000); Nepal down 39% (a reduction of £2,000) and there was no order to the Nicaraguan instant coffee processor Encafe.

4

Figure 9.4 continued

5

The positive outcome for the majority of countries where Traidcraft has supplier partners disguises large variations for individual suppliers. In discussions with producers in Africa for the 1993/94 social accounts, and this year in Bangladesh, producers were not generally aware of Traidcraft's longer term marketing plans and none had been given forecasts to indicate what continuity of business might mean for them. In Bangladesh, Kumudini and Aarong had been forewarned about reductions in specific clothing lines, and seemed satisfied with the explanation. Heed were not satisfied that they had been warned about the loss several years ago of their shipping contract with Traidcraft for Swallows Thanapara.

BANGLADESH PRODUCERS SUPPLYING TRAIDCRAFT 94/95

Aarong*
Ayesha Abed Centre   Fashions & accessories
                                  Gifts and interiors crafts
                                  Gift wrap
BRAC Printers   Cards

MCC*
Action Bag *   Bags & soft toys
Eastern Screenprinters   Cards & stationery
& Letterpress *   Stationery
Shukhara Paper *   Paper products
Biboton   Desiccated coconut
Surjosato   Twine & skipping rope
Bagdha   Greetings cards
Mirpur Wheatstraw

Jute Works*
Chandpur Cottage Industries *   Jute Handicrafts
Many other producer groups   Jewellery
                                  Ceramics

Kumudini*   Fashion & accessories
                                  Textile furnishings

Ideas
International*   Wide range of crafts
Thanapara*   Traidcraft buys cards
                                  Clothing, bags and
                                  nakshi kantha

EDM*   Baskets, brass & ceramics
Valerian*   Palm leaf products
HEED*   Handloom, accessories
                                  candles

Aranya*   Natural dyed textiles
Rishilpi   Jute & leather bags

Producers marked * were visited.

Producer's perspectives in Bangladesh

Bangladesh was selected for the 94/95 accounts for three reasons. First it has a national producers' organisation - ECOTA - which was willing to assist in the consultation process[4]

Second, Bangladesh was the first country Traidcraft bought from and has consistently been one of the biggest supplier countries.

Thirdly, there continue to be particular vulnerabilities for craft producers in Bangladesh because of poor resources, lack of product diversity, and a general lack of exposure to European markets for consumer goods. Bangladesh faces increasing competition from suppliers in other countries, even in the "fair trade market".

The sections below are based on the issues identified by producers themselves, in earlier Traidcraft social accounts, as essential determinants of fair trade.

Continuity

All producers identified continuity of their relationship with the company and continuity of orders as the key factor in assessing Traidcraft's performance. The only new partner this year is Aranya, although Rishilpi had a first small trial order after a considerable gap. The other suppliers have been Traidcraft partners for at least ten years.

Figure 4 shows the pattern of purchases over the last three years. Most noticeable is the dominant position of Aarong supplying 60% of Traidcraft's purchases. Paper purchases have had a very significant impact for Aarong, MCC and Ideas, but the picture for crafts and clothing suppliers is mixed with a long term decline in traditional products like jute and basketry.

Aarong were concerned about losing Traidcraft's orders for blank T-shirts and the fall in orders for its machine printed gift wrap and cards. Traidcraft had been selling "fairly traded" T-shirts to campaigning organisations in the UK for screen printing, but the price was uncompetitive. Aarong said they understood that problem but were nervous about the simultaneous decline in paper orders, when they know Traidcraft's fashion business, for which they are a main supplier, has a record of poor profitability and growth.

Key Performance Indicators Continued

Advances[3]

AIM — To meet producers' requirements for advance payments, a major benefit of dealing with fair trade buyers.

OUTCOME 94/95 45 out of 106 received advances. Average amount outstanding £117,000. Cost to Traidcraft £9,000 in interest. (52 suppliers had advances in 93/94 at a similar cost to Traidcraft.)

Contact time with producers

AIM To provide product development, business management and market intelligence inputs to producers.

OUTCOME The actual time spent by Traidcraft staff visiting producers to work on product development and production monitoring in 94/95 was 311 days. [93/94 - 223, 92/93 - 233]

Continuity of orders

AIM Producers have repeatedly emphasised continuity as a key characteristic of a fair trade relationship.

OUTCOME 94/95 106 producers supplied orders. Including 10 new suppliers and 3 where Traidcraft sourced directly where previously it had sourced through a third party. 36 established partners saw order values INCREASE by more than 20%. 23 established partners saw order values FALL by more than 20%. 8 established partners did not deliver any orders during the year.

Fig 3. Shipment Values Compared 93-95

a desire to increase the public accountability of powerful economic organisations and, to varying degrees, a questioning of the desirability of unfettered market capitalism. As Geddes (1992) puts it: 'conventional accountancy attempts to reduce the social to the economic and the economic to the cash nexus. The importance of the social audit movement ties in its commitment to the restoration of social and political control over the economy' (p. 237).

While falling short of essaying a coherent, systematic critique of the capitalist economy, the initiatives we have been considering clearly share a belief in change. The belief in change lies in a faith about the effects of an increase in information. The reluctance of both private and public sector organisations to share information, which has been the case in the overwhelming majority of audit exercises we have considered, raises a fundamental question as to the true extent of democracy prevailing in our supposedly 'democratic' society. The Traidcraft initiative with its overriding commitment to openness and 'transparency' provides both a welcome exception to the code of secrecy subscribed to by all too many organisations and a way forward for those truly wishing to exhibit *public* accountability.

Notes

1. See Figure 4.4 in Chapter 4.
2. The name 'Social Audit', while being the title by which the organisation is best known, strictly speaking refers to the publishing arm of the Public Interest Research Centre (PIRC) — a registered charity, and is the title given to their early periodic publications. We will use 'Social Audit' as a general reference to both Social Audit Ltd and PIRC.
3. The similarity to a standard audit report is probably not coincidental.
4. Medawar, however, has argued that the audits had at least an indirect effect with, for example, the Tube Investments report contributing to the decision of several other companies to pre-empt possible outside interference by carrying out enquiries of their own (Medawar, 1976).
5. See Figure 2.2 in Chapter 2.
6. For more detailed descriptive analysis of the content and methodology of plant closure social audits see Harte and Owen (1987).
7. A number of non-quantified social factors are, in fact, briefly referred to in most of the reports. However, the overriding emphasis is on financial quantification and generation of a 'bottom line' figure for the 'cost' of unemployment (see Harte and Owen, 1987).
8. For a fuller discussion of this issue see Geddes (1992). The reader is also referred to the biannual newsletter *Social Audit Network News (SANE)*, published under the auspices of the Policy Research Unit (Leeds Metropolitan University) and the University of Warwick's Local Government Centre, which carries regular updates on community-based social auditing practice.
9. One exception here is the growing practice of 'supplier' auditing, pioneered by IBM and the DIY group B&Q among others, whereby companies seek to satisfy themselves as to the environmental credentials of those supplying them with

products and services (see Gray *et al.*, 1993, pp. 98–9).

10. Puxty's analysis specifically refers to the local authority plant closure audits. It would, however, appear to apply more generally to the range of social audits considered so far.

11. This section of the chapter draws heavily upon the work of Zadek and Evans (1993).

12. NEF took the significant step of deciding to subject its own activities to annual social audit scrutiny in 1993. This rare example of 'auditing the auditors' contrasts starkly with the far more secretive processes underpinning financial audits! (See Raynard, 1995.)

13. A possible exception here are 'values-based' commercial organisations that expose wider aims and objectives than simply generating profit. In this context it is interesting to note that The Body Shop has recently instigated a social auditing programme based on consultation with a wide range of stakeholder groups.

chapter 10

Accountability, transparency and sustainability
The future for CSR?

10.1 Introduction

In this final chapter we return to where we started. Although the world's leading companies have brought enormous benefits to a small and privileged proportion of the human race (i.e. you and us) it has only been achieved at an increasingly unacceptable cost. Some of this cost arises from the financial scandals that accounting has been unable to prevent — the Maxwells, Nadirs, Boerskys, De Loreans, etc., of the corporate world. Some arise from the increasing social and environmental disasters — Bhopal, *Exxon Valdez*, British Petroleum's alleged involvement in displacing Amazon peoples, Shell's alleged involvement in community dislocation in Nigeria, Proctor and Gamble's alleged implication in the disruption of the Sami, mining companies' disruption of the Australian Aboriginals, and so on. These and many other violations (alleged or real) point to a system with a less-than-perfect track record. Something is not quite right and demands our attention.

Despite its undoubted achievements there are also increasing doubts about the corporate capitalist system as a whole. It is increasingly evident that the gap between the richest and poorest is widening — both within nations and between nations.[1] The exploitation of the LDCs (lesser developed countries) is looking less and less acceptable as a source of a western affluence for a decreasing proportion of the population. Added to this, there is also an increasing concern that even we in the West are *not* any better off. Certainly, those with decent jobs have more to consume and more toys to play with, but when western GDP (gross domestic product) is adjusted for social dislocation — freedom, crime, insecurity, environmental quality, etc. — it looks increasingly likely that western 'wellbeing' reached a peak some time around the mid-1960s, and has been declining ever since (for more detail see, for example, Anderson, 1991; Ekins, 1992a, b; MacGillivray, 1993).

Something is sick — what can we do about it? Well, the idea that accountants can solve the world's problems is clearly ludicrous. However, it *is* clear that accounting is increasingly failing to act as a control on companies (see, for example, Lindblom, 1984) and accounting is ever more closely implicated in a range of the less attractive manifestations of corporate and political life (see, for example, Briloff, 1986; Cooper and Hopper, 1990; Hopwood and Miller, 1994; Laughlin *et al.*, 1992; Tinker, 1985).

Even if accounting were perfect — and it clearly is not — there would still be an information vacuum arising from the increasing complexity and power of large corporations in comparison with the increasingly irrelevant financial information they produce and the increasingly irrelevant control exercised (or, rather, not exercised) by shareholders. The once-powerful voice of labour is heard less and less frequently as unions lose power and labour becomes increasingly casualised. States — especially in the Anglo-Saxon world — seem increasingly unable and unwilling to offer any source of control over economic growth, expansion and the pursuit of profits.

It may be that all this points to a systemic problem (see, for example, Marcuse, 1955/ 1986, 1964). One characteristic that *may* influence the direction of such a problem is accountability and transparency. That is, while it *may* change nothing, we believe that increased formal accountability with an attendant increase in the transparency of organisations offers a morally sound demand that at least allows the polity to observe the consequences of their voting, employment and consumption decisions.

Accountability *is* a profoundly moral concept. In an increasingly amoral (or immoral?) world, dominated by explicitly amoral (immoral?) disciplines of thought such as conventional economics, accounting and finance, the call for morally based development seems highly attractive. This chapter will attempt to summarise what this morality is and what the consequential accountability and transparency mean to us and, we hope, may come to mean to you.

This chapter is brief and is organised as follows. The next section proposes that a new paradigm is emerging in the form of a re-conceptualisation of human interaction with the planet. This 'new' paradigm is sustainability. Section 10.3 explores what is meant by sustainability in a little more detail. Section 10.4 then explores in some detail what CSR, which responded to both the demands of accountability and the imperatives of sustainability, might look like. The final section considers briefly what the principles explored in this book might mean for each of us.[2]

10.2 An emerging new paradigm?

A number of themes have emerged from the foregoing nine chapters. We can see that CSR has been a lively and widespread activity spanning more than three decades. While much of this activity has been both marginal and has ebbed and flowed with fashion it has demonstrated a wide range of experimentation and, most particularly, that CSR is practicable. Admittedly, much of what organisations do will normally be in their own economic interests. Given the way in which we as a species currently choose to organise our economic, social and political life that should come as no surprise to anyone. CSR can be in the organisation's own interests. Much more importantly, however, we hope that we have shown that CSR is in the species' own interests. This brings us to a crucial point.

Over the decades we have reviewed in this book it has become apparent that we — whether as voters, politicians, employees, shareholders, accountants or consumers, for example — have managed largely to ignore the consequences of our wellbeing. Looking on the favourable side of this, it is never *entirely* clear that our consumption, economic decisions or voting choices, for example, have been directly responsible for the exploitation of others. Similarly, we have to recognise that for many of us in the West it will probably always remain a matter of debate as to whether or not (for example) labour has a generalised right to employment with decent pay and conditions, whether third world poverty is a consequence of a non-western culture, whether communities bring destruction on themselves, and so on. But something very important changed in the early 1990s. This was the environmental debate.

The environmental debate did not permit us to ignore any longer the consequences of our choices and actions. This was not a matter of simple political ideology but a matter of fact. If the species failed to manage the global ecology sensibly, then, as a species, we would have no future.[3] Ecological desecration would be no respecter of national boundaries because it is not a social, but a physical, issue. There is some evidence from which we take comfort that globally people are increasingly willing to consider the state of the natural environment and do something about it. Whether environmental awareness arises from immediate self-interest, moral outrage or a more atavistic concern for our planetary home is difficult to assess, and perhaps does not matter too much. What matters is that morally driven concerns are beginning to influence thinking on all matters related to global ecology.

As soon as one starts to consider such matters, then it rapidly becomes apparent that environmental issues as they relate to the human species are inseparable from social, economic and political issues — all the issues over which CSR and this book have been exercised. Recognition of this has led to a new concept (new to the West, at least). This 'new' concept is that of **sustainability** and this, we believe, will be the basis upon which CSR — and all organisational–society relationships — will be founded in the future.

10.3 Sustainability

We met (and defined) sustainability in Chapter 3. We saw that it comprised two elements: *eco-justice* (which was the domain of social accounting) and *eco-efficiency* (which was the domain of environmental accounting). Sustainability has opened up a whole new range of debates which fundamentally address the way in which we organise ourselves, treat each other and interact with the planet. It is almost certain to become the guiding principle of most areas of policy in the coming decades.

Some of the important matters which have emerged from the debates on sustainability are that it is a profoundly difficult idea which challenges conventional economics and many of our taken-for-granted assumptions in the West: so much so that it does not seem likely that it can be safely left in the hands of vote-hungry politicians and/or hard-pressed (or profit-hungry) businesses. For sustainability to have any realistic chance of being achieved, society must make many judgements about the choices that govern our current ways of life, for this society needs information — information on accountability and transparency. This is an important task for CSR and social and environmental accounting. A sustainable society is going to need a plethora of information about the environmental impacts of its choices and actions. Environmental accounting may be able to provide important data on this and must, at a minimum, provide some basis for environmental disclosure and accountability. In addition, a sustainable society is also probably going to need to know quite a lot about the justice of its decisions, how wealth is distributed among its peoples, how its decisions affect this distribution as well as the way in which future generations are affected by present practices. This is a role that social accounting and social disclosure can play: this is the basis on which we offer our own policy choices for the development of CSR.

10.4 Developing CSR

Some of our preferred forms of social and environmental accounting will have been apparent to the reader throughout the book. We made some of our preferences more explicit in Chapters 2 and 3 when we committed ourselves to the accountability model, introduced the compliance-with-statute report and recognised the important role that education — especially in accounting — must play. We would now like to expand upon these themes.

Making suggestions for an 'ideal' form of 'accounting' runs the risk of being hopelessly utopian. That is, in a 'perfect world' (whose perfect world?) we might like to see a very significant restructuring of organisations and a complete revamping of both conventional and social accounting systems. It clearly falls somewhat outside the scope of this book to deliberate on what an ideal economic, social and political system might look like, what the consequential accounting system would look like[4] and how we might move from where we are to this idealised situation. On the other hand, to simply accept the world as it is would be to counsel doing nothing to improve that world. For reasons of pragmatism, therefore, what follows is a justifiable, practicable and potentially achievable mixture of current 'best practice' plus additional mechanisms to move current accounting towards a more accountability centred focus. The pragmatism has (at least) one crucial characteristic — any statement of a pragmatic ideal must change with time as what is considered desirable and achievable will develop as conditions alter (see, for example, Tinker et al., 1991).[5] With this in mind, what follows (reluctantly) accepts that financial statements are likely to remain the dominant form of organisational accountability for the foreseeable future and therefore any proposals for CSR need to be differentiated between recommendations that amend current conventional accounting practice and those which are for additional statements.

While it is a great deal easier said than done, the first steps in the development of systematic social and environmental accounting system are:

a identification of the **purpose and focus** of the report; and
b some specification of the way in which the organisation is **conceptualised** in an attempt to satisfy the information characteristic of **completeness**.

We have already dealt with the first of these: the purpose of the report is to discharge accountability and, as a result, its focus must be a societal one in which the organisation is perceived as a subsystem interacting with its social and physical environment (see

Chapters 2, 3 and 4). This then provides some guidance on point (b). 'Completeness', while a widely accepted characteristic of any good account (see, for example, ASSC, 1975) is almost certainly an impossibility (see, for example, Laughlin and Puxty, 1981). What *is*, however, possible is to convey a view of an organisation in such a way that a reader can relate to it and make their own assessment as to whether or not it is complete in its own terms and/or in the terms of the reader. In the environmental field this 'completeness' is addressed through the use of the **eco-balance** supported by life-cycle assessment (LCA). This analysis provides an overview of an organisation showing all its physical inputs, its pollutions, leakages and wastes plus a specification of all its outputs. LCA then tracks each of these inputs and outputs to their source.[6] It is thus a systems-perspective of the organisation which permits the reader to gain an overall conception of the organisation's interactions with its physical environment. It is increasingly employed by organisations (see, for example, Gray *et al.*, 1993; Gray *et al.*, 1995d).

Such a system could also be applied to the social, ethical and political interactions of the organisation (the economic interactions are presumed to be captured in the financial statements — of which more later). A **social balance** would similarly identify the human, community and social inputs and outputs of the organisational system. Such a social balance is not an easy thing to construct and has been far less widely experimented with than the eco-balance but *is* feasible (see, for example, Dey *et al.*, 1994, 1995) and involves the sorts of analysis we provided in Figures 3.1, 3.2 and 3.3 in Chapter 3.

These two (probably pictorial) representations of the organisation are then the starting point of the CSR. The second step involves the specification of stakeholders and their rights to information. These stakeholders will be represented, directly or indirectly, in the social- and eco-balances established above. Rights to information will, as we have discussed, derive from extant law, codes of practice and organisational policy statements. In addition there will be the much more difficult-to-derive empirically 'moral' rights. These will remain an area for political action to drive up the acceptance of these moral rights. The second element of an ideal CSR is, therefore, a policy statement from the organisation explicitly identifying the stakeholders that it recognises, the codes and laws to which it is subject and any other elements of policy which drive the organisation as a social and environmental institution.

This policy statement then provides the basis for the compliance-with-standard (CWS) report which we have illustrated in Chapter 3. This will form the backbone of the CSR and act as the principal form of the discharge of the *minimum* accountability that organisations owe to society, and will then need to be augmented by two additional elements. The first will be the additional accountability information which will not easily fit into the CWS statement. Statements of intention and descriptive outlines of actions undertaken will, undoubtedly, be necessary to 'flesh out' the bare bones of the CWS. Many examples spring to mind: how a stakeholder may obtain further information; how data has been collected; involvement of third parties; activities with local communities; regular discussions with local pressure groups; activities to involve employees in the decision making of the organisation and so on. To a large extent these statements will principally be of three sorts: explaining the organisation; discussing issues for which standards are not available, easily quantifiable or whose quantification diminishes the quality of the information; and information on additional channels of accountability over and above the *formal* channel offered in the CSR report itself. The second additional element will relate to **sustainability**.

A complete CSR which addresses sustainability issues will need to be extended to deal with eco-justice and eco-efficiency issues. Some, indeed many, of these issues may have been captured already in the foregoing. However, it seems likely that further detail will be necessary. Both aspects open a complex web of potential matters of concern. For the eco-justice issues there will need to be some means to analyse the role the organisation plays in wealth distribution between peoples (the issues of *intragenerational equity*). This is not a well-developed area at the time of writing. However, CSR experiments such as the value-added statement (which, ideally, show how the 'income' of the organisation is distributed between financial stakeholders), the segmental reporting attempts which could be developed to show the source of purchases and sales; segmental and geographic wage rates and the ASSC's recommendation of transactions between an organisation and governments and other nations (ASSC, 1975) may offer some guidelines. Even more difficult to predict are the organisation's impacts on wealth distribution between generations (the issues of *intergenerational equity*). Here, we also need to see further experimentation but some analysis of future employment prospects, the organisation's policy on activity in countries outside the 'home' country and detail on the organisation's provisions and reserves for future events (e.g. decommissioning, R&D, market changes) might be helpful. There is little question that these are areas which need a great deal of further experimentation and development before practicable solutions can be proposed.

We are on slightly firmer ground with the eco-efficiency issues. Several proposals have been made here to account for the environmental side of sustainability. The simplest are the **sustainable cost** calculations which would represent the amount of money an organisation would have *had* to spend in the preceding accounting period *if* it had acted sustainably. A sustainable organisation would replace, renew or substitute for every environmental item it took from the ecology and would not take from the ecology anything which was not replaceable, renewable or substitutable. The essence of the sustainable cost calculation is that the *notional* amount would comprise the costs of renewing, replacing or substituting environmental impacts plus a recorded amount of 'infinity' for all irreplaceable elements (e.g. impact on the ozone layer, species extinction, removal of nuclear wastes). This cost calculation would be shown at the foot of the existing profit and loss account and would, incidentally, show that no company, certainly in the West, is currently making a profit and, probably, would also show that they never had done so (see, for example, Bebbington and Gray, 1995a).

Which brings us, finally, to the current situation with organisational financial statements. Financial statements are, among other things, *a record of financial transactions* and a *construction of social reality* (see, for example, Hines, 1988; Morgan, 1988; Power, 1994). The record of financial transactions is represented in a particular way, employing the conventional categories of expenses, revenues, etc. These categories capture and reflect certain social costs as well as reflecting certain social, as well as economic, categories. Therefore, a traditional set of accounts will show certain categories of expenditure on employment, innovation and provisions for the future. Because these statements also reflect a sort of social reality they in effect paint a picture which emphasises certain aspects of the organisation's life. It is a relatively simple matter to re-code the bookkeeping systems of an organisation to identify revenues and costs separately from social, political and environmental perspectives. A simple re-working of the financial statements could reflect a more detailed analysis of employment costs, a reflection of energy, packaging and waste disposal costs, expenditure on replaceable and finite raw materials, forms of transport costs, environmental liabilities and expenditures, revenues from developing nations, legal fines and related costs, and so on. Quite how this might work is not entirely clear but it is highly likely that such a re-categorisation would: (a) encourage a more careful analysis of costs which, while perhaps not economically significant, will almost certainly be socially, politically and environmentally significant; and (b) change the way in which the organisation was viewed to increase the emphasis given to the socially orientated financial categories rather than the current conventional, predominantly economic categories. This re-statement, coupled with a sustainable cost calculation (plus, perhaps, an equivalent eco-justice calculation if such were possible and desirable) would have the effect of changing the ways in which we think of organisations, the analysis we do of those numbers and (through the information inductance effect; see, for example, Prakash and Rappaport, 1977) increase the importance which the management of organisations placed on these areas of transaction (see, for example, Gray *et al.*, 1993; Power, 1994).

The essence of these recommendations is summarised in Figure 10.1. We make no claim that these recommendations are either exhaustive or static; nor do we claim that such reporting would be easy or inexpensive. However, the recommendations would move organisations onto a more accountable and transparent path towards a less unsustainable future. Most of the elements have been tried at some stage by organisations and, indeed, we have reviewed many of them in the foregoing chapters. Furthermore, and of more immediate interest, data relating to many of these issues is already present somewhere in the 'best practice' reports of leading companies. A

Figure 10.1 *Summary of recommendations for developing a mandatory CSR*

- Disclosure of detailed eco-balance and social balance statements;
- Disclosure of a detailed policy statement itemising the laws, codes and additional issues which govern the organisation;
- Disclosure of a detailed Compliance-With-Standard report;
- Additional descriptive analysis of remaining accountability issues;
- Detailed eco-justice statement;
- Detailed sustainable cost calculation;
- Restatement of the financial statements to highlight social, political and environmental costs;

And, as a first step

- Bring together all *currently* disclosed social, environmental and employee information into a single social and environmental report *within* the existing conventional Annual Report.

major, but basically simple, first step would be to bring together the environmental, social, community, ethical and employee/employment information already contained in company reporting into a single **social and environmental report**. We have argued elsewhere that this would be a first, simple, cheap and eminently practicable first step towards the wider practice and acceptance of CSR (see, for example, Gray, 1995b). This suggestion is also added to the recommendation in Figure 10.1.

10.5 So what do we do now?

If you have managed to read this far then we must presume that you were either one of those 'converted' to CSR before you began reading or (we hope) have become somewhat more predisposed to the subject as a result of the foregoing; but is studying the subject — however novel the insights that it generates — sufficient? This book has been predicated on the assumption that identifying problems is not sufficient; one must also seek solutions and then look for ways in which to encourage their implementation. From a moral, educational and/or professional point of view this *must* be one of the principle purposes behind any form of scholarship.[7] More particularly, accounting academics have been roundly chastised for their continual failures to recognise the political and social implications of their work and then to act upon them (see, for example, Arrington, 1990; Sikka *et al.*, 1989, 1991; Tinker and Puxty, 1995; Tinker *et al.*, 1982; Willmott, 1990). The question must naturally emerge as to what we should do about the current state of accounting in general and CSR in particular?

First, as teachers we have a duty to stretch our students' intellectual abilities and to help them develop both such ethical and moral maturity as they are capable of. We must avoid indoctrination — and this means exposing the political, social and environmental implications of what we teach as well as not trying to fudge some of the less sensible practices that masquerade under the name of current accounting practices and GAAP. We also believe that social and environmental accounting offers an especially rich field in which to help students explore their world, their subject and themselves and, in doing so, to cast a more critical light on currently accepted principles of conventional accounting.

Secondly, as students, our education presents us with a wide range of techniques, issues, ideas and views with which to grapple. The easiest path is, without doubt, to accept these at face value and to ignore their basic idiocies (the 'rational economic man' is just such a mythical creature) and the moral vacuum in which they are presented. Our motivations for this will not just be the relative ease of following the line of least resistance. We will, in part, be motivated by the need for future employment and advancement. This is a fairly boring and self-centred approach to such an important part of our lives (and one wonders why accountants are thought to be boring!). Those of you who are the future of the profession owe it to yourselves — as well as to the society that has afforded you the privileges you currently enjoy — to explore your future profession as carefully as possible and to think what 'serving the public interest' will mean to you. Oddly enough this approach will also help you to enjoy the study of accountancy a great deal more — although it will not make professional examinations any easier.

Thirdly, as researchers, we all need to be conscious of the social construction of knowledge and the way in which our research influences and is influenced by the prevailing hegemony in academic life, in the profession and in the powerful elements of society. Can we justify what we do on a personal level? Can you encourage the maximisation of shareholder wealth when you believe in environmental desecration? Can you try to help markets be more 'efficient' if you are a socialist? Is the technical detail of new financial instruments really more important than the international debt crisis? Are make or buy decisions really nothing to do with employment issues or the remittance of international profits through TNCs nothing to do with third world poverty? There are many crucial human and environmental issues which cry out for our attention. Is it not our duty as privileged researchers to explore those *we* believe important, not what convention or the richest 5 per cent of the world believe is important to their interests?

Fourthly, as members of a profession (and we authors are all active members of at least one professional accountancy body), we have a duty to the public interest. This requires us to seek to educate and persuade our fellow professionals as to the implications of what we do and to the desirability of what we can do. CSR cannot become a recognised part of accounting orthodoxy until it is more widely recognised and accepted by the professions. Part of our duty is to proselytise the issues and their solutions. An important part of this is putting our weight behind calls for mandatory CSR and demonstrating that voluntary initiatives never work — despite our professions' preference to believe the contrary.

Finally, as global citizens we should surely recognise the enormous privilege we enjoy by living in the western 'democracies'. Most of us with professional careers — or the prospect of such — enjoy vast wealth when compared with the homeless and unemployed or the bulk of the population in developing countries. We enjoy a fairly substantial amount of freedom and freedom of speech (if rather subtly controlled) and have the right, to a fair degree at least, to exercise our democratic concerns through protest. This is a major function of the 'social audit' organisations we examined in Chapter 9 and their function in maintaining western democracy is incalculable. They need our help as professionals and as accountants. Accountability, transparency and sustainability is very much what such organisations are seeking to achieve.

Whatever one decides to do, it is surely better than a do-nothing, 'I'm all right thank you' sort of attitude. While many of us adopt such a view without really recognising we do so, we should never forget that we are part of the most privileged 5 per cent of humanity on this planet — of course it seems all right to us. Self-interest is only preached by those who are at the top of the pile. It is no good for the other 95 per cent. If we, the privileged, cannot do anything to try and change the system which keeps us so warm and cosy, there are not many alternatives — all of them very unpleasant indeed. 'It's nothing to do with me'? It is everything to do with all of us.

Notes

1. You may recall from Chapters 1 and 2 that this is not supposed to happen in capitalism as there is presumed to be a 'trickle-down effect' whereby the benefit of the best well-off 'trickles down' to enhance the poorer sections of society. This is not happening.
2. This chapter is less replete with references because the ideas herein draw much more explicitly from our work. For more detail see the authors' referenced work in the references and bibliography section at the back.
3. An important element of accountability as we have outlined it in this book is that accountability gives the human species the right to make itself extinct as long as it is informed that its actions are having this effect. We agree with the deep ecologists that if humanity cannot act in an ecologically sensitive way then it has no right to continued existence and deserves to become extinct.
4. For example, there is an argument that in a utopian world there would be no accountants as we currently understand the term (see, for example, Gray, 1992) as the need for formal accounting systems based on an economic model of the world is, in effect, an expression of an imperfect state of the world. However desirable one might (or might not) find this such a point of view has little to recommend it in terms of likely states of the world in the foreseeable future.
5. The historic analysis we presented in Chapter 4 illustrates this quite clearly. More specifically, by the early 1990s the very widespread environmental debates permitted discussion in political, business and academic circles of a range of matters which were considered trivial and irrelevant only a few years earlier (see, for example, Gray, 1990; Gray *et al.*, 1993; Owen, 1992).
6. It is impossible to track every input and every output through to every source as one very quickly hits an 'infinite regress'. For illustration, a purchased input involved transport, energy, manufacture of the input and raw materials. These in turn involved machinery which were themselves manufactured and thus based on previous manufacture, transport, energy and raw materials. These, in turn ... and so on. LCA therefore concentrates on the principal, first or second phase impacts. This is, first, for reasons of practicality and secondly, in recognition that if every organisation undertook such analysis then environmental impact could be traced back through other organisations' own LCA (for more detail see, for example, Business-in-the-Environment/SustainAbility, 1994; Gray *et al.*, 1993).
7. The usual rejoinder that it is the duty of the scholar to simply record and classify knowledge in as objective a way as possible not only smacks of ivory tower avoidance of the consequences of one's scholarship as well as a considerable misunderstanding about the nature of knowledge and knowledge creation but is a major abnegation of one's professional and personal duties to seek to change and improve practice.

References and bibliography

Abayo, A.G., Adams, C.A. and Roberts, C.B. (1993) 'Measuring the quality of corporate disclosure in less developed countries: the case of Tanzania', *Journal of International Accounting, Auditing and Taxation*, 2(2), pp. 145–58.

Abbot, W.F. and Monsen R. J. (1979) 'On the measurement of corporate social responsibility: self reported disclosures as a method of measuring corporate social involvement', *Academy of Management Journal*, 22(3), pp. 501–15.

Abercrombie, N., Hill, S. and Turner, B.S. (1984) *Dictionary of Sociology*, Harmondsworth, Middlesex: Penguin.

Abt, C.C. and Associates (ACCA) (1972 *et seq.*) *Annual Report and Social Audit*.

Accounting Education Change Commission (AECC) (1990) *Objectives of Education for Accountants* (Position Statement Number 1), Bainbridge Island: AECC.

Accounting Standards (formerly Steering) Committee (ASSC) (1975) *The Corporate Report*, London: ICAEW.

Ackoff, R.L (1960) 'Systems, organisations and interdisciplinary research', *General Systems Theory Yearbook*, 5, pp. 1–8.

Adams, C.A., Coutts, A. and Harte G. (1995a) 'Corporate equal opportunities (non-) disclosure', *British Accounting Review*, 27(2), pp. 87–108.

Adams, C.A., Hill, W.Y. and Roberts, C.B. (1995b) *Environmental, Employee and Ethical Reporting in Europe*, ACCA Research Report, No. 41, London: ACCA.

Adams, C.A. and Roberts, C.B. (1994) 'International accounting education in the UK', *Accounting Education*, 3(2) pp. 167–81.

Adams, C.A. and Roberts, C.B. (1995) 'Corporate ethics; an issue worthy of report?' *Accounting Forum*, 19(2/3) pp. 128–42.

Adams, R. (1990) 'The greening of consumerism', *Accountancy*, June, pp. 80–3.

Adams, R. (1992) 'Green reporting and the consumer movement' in *Green Reporting: Accountancy and the challenge of the nineties* Owen, D. (ed.), London: Chapman and Hall.

Adams, R., Carruthers, J. and Hamil, S. (1991) *Changing Corporate Values*, London: Kogan Page.

Adorno, T.W. and Horkheimer, M. (1947/1972) *Dialectic of Enlightenment* (trans. J.Cummings), New York: Herder and Herder.

Advisory Committee on Business and the Environment (1993) *Report of the Financial Sector Working Group*, London: Department of the Environment, Department for Enterprise.

Ahmed, Y.J., Serafy, S.L. and Lutz, E. (eds) (1989) *Environmental Accounting for Sustainable Development*, Washington, DC: The World Bank.

Alexander, J.J. and Bucholz, R.A. (1978) 'Corporate social responsibility and stock market performance', *Academy of Management Journal*, 21(3), pp. 479–86.

Allen, K. (1991) 'In pursuit of professional dominance: Australian accounting 1953–1985', *Accounting Auditing and Accountability Journal*, 3(1), pp. 51–67.

American Accounting Association (AAA) (1973a) 'Report of the committee on environmental effects of organisational behaviour', *The Accounting Review*, suppl. XLVIII.

American Accounting Association (AAA) (1973b) 'Report of the committee on human resource accounting', *Accounting Review Supplement*, pp. 169–85.

American Accounting Association (AAA) (1974) 'Report of the committee on the measurement of social costs', *Accounting Review Supplement*, pp. 98–113.

American Accounting Association (AAA) (1975a) 'Report of the committee on concepts and standards for external financial reports', *The Accounting Review*, 50(suppl), pp. 41–9.

American Accounting Association (AAA) (1975b) 'Report on the committee on social costs', *Accounting Review Supplement*, pp. 51–89.

American Accounting Association (AAA) (1977) *Statement on Accounting Theory and Theory Acceptance*, Sarasota Fl.: AAA.

American Institute of Certified Public Accountants (AICPA) (1977) *The Measurement of Corporate Social Performance*, New York: AICPA.

Anderson, J.C. and Frankle, A.W. (1980) 'Voluntary social reporting: an iso-beta portfolio analysis', *The Accounting Review*, 55(3), pp. 467–79.

Anderson, R.H. (1978) 'Responsibility accounting — how to get started', *Canadian Chartered Accountant Magazine*, September, pp. 46–50.

Anderson, V. (1991) *Alternative Economic Indicators*, London: Routledge.

Andrew, B.H., Gul, F.A., Guthrie, J.E. and Teoh, H.Y. (1989) 'Note on corporate social disclosure practices in developing countries: the case of Malaysia and Singapore', *British Accounting Review*, 21(4), pp. 371–6.

Anell, B. (1985) 'Exercises in arbitrariness and ambiguity — a study of twelve cost benefit analyses of industrial disinvestment decisions', *Accounting, Organizations and Society*, 10(4), pp. 479–92.

Armstrong, M.B. and Vincent, J.I. (1988) 'Public accounting: a profession at the crossroads', *Accounting Horizons*, March, pp. 94–8.

Armstrong, P. (1991) 'Contradiction and social dynamics in the capitalist agency relationship', *Accounting, Organizations and Society*, 16(1), pp. 1–26.

Arnold, P.J. (1990) 'The State and political theory in corporate social disclosure research: a response to Guthrie and Parker', *Advances in Public Interest Accounting*, 3, pp. 177–81.

Arrington, E. (1990) 'Intellectual tyranny and the public interest: the quest for the holy grail and the quality of life', *Advances in Public Interest Accounting*, 3, pp. 1–16.

Arrington, E. and Francis, J. (1989) 'Letting the chat out of the bag: deconstruction, privilege and accounting research', *Accounting, Organizations and Society*, 14(1/2), pp. 1–28.

Bailey, D., Harte G. and Sugden R. (1994a) *Making Transnationals Accountable: A significant step for Britain*, London: Routledge.

Bailey, D., Harte, G. and Sugden, R. (1994b) *Transnationals and Governments: Recent policies in Japan, France, Germany, the United States and Britain*, London: Routledge.

Bank-Jorgensen, H. (1993) 'The "Green Account" of the Danish Steel Works Ltd', *Social and Environmental Accounting*, 13(1), pp. 2–5.

Barach, P. and Baratz, M.S. (1962) 'Two faces of power', *The American Political Science Review*, 56, pp. 947–52.

Barnes, P. (1994) 'A new approach to protecting the environment: the European Union's environmental management and audit regulation', *Environmental Management and Health*, 5(3), pp. 8–12.

Barnsley Metropolitan Borough Council (1984) *Coal Mining and Barnsley*, Barnsley MBC.

Bartolomeo, M. (1994) 'A new tool for environmental accounting: an approach from Italy', *Social and Environmental Accounting*, 14(1), pp. 6–8.

Bauer, R.A. and Fenn, D.H. (1972) *The Corporate Social Audit*, New York: Russell Sage Foundation.

Beaver, W.H. (1981) *Financial Reporting: An accounting revolution*, Englewood Cliffs, NJ: Prentice Hall.

Bebbington, J. (1993) 'The European Community Fifth Action Plan: towards sustainability', *Social and Environmental Accounting*, 13(1), pp. 9–11.

Bebbington, K.J. and Gray, R.H. (1993) 'Accounting, environment and sustainability', *Business Strategy and the Environment*, Summer, pp. 1–11.

Bebbington, K.J. and Gray, R.H. (1995a) 'Incentives and disincentives for the adoption of sustainable development by transnational corporations', UNCTAD Report TD/B/ITNC/AC.1/3, UNCTAD: Geneva.

Bebbington, K.J. and Gray, R.H. (1995b) 'Accounting for profit and sustainability', *World Statesman*, 3(2) Spring, pp. 66–8.

Bebbington, K.J., Gray, R.H., Thomson, I. and Walters, D. (1994). 'Accountants attitudes and environmentally sensitive accounting', *Accounting and Business Research*, 94, Spring, pp. 51–75.

Beishon, J. and Peters, G. (1972) *Systems Behaviour*, London: Open University/Harper and Row.

Belkaoui, A. (1976) The impact of the disclosure of the environmental effects of organizational behaviour on the market, *Financial Management*, Winter, pp. 26–31.

Belkaoui, A. (1980) 'The impact of socio-economic accounting statements on the investment decision: an empirical study', *Accounting, Organizations and Society*, 5(3), pp. 263–83.

Belkaoui, A. (1984) *Socio-Economic Accounting*, Connecticut: Quorum Books.

Belkauoi, A. (1986) *Accounting Theory*, London: Harcourt Brace Jovanovich.

Belkaoui, A. and Karpik, P.G. (1989) Determinants of the corporate decision to disclose social information, *Accounting Auditing and Accountability Journal*, 2(1), pp. 36–51.

Benjamin, J.J. and Stanga, K.G. (1977) Differences in disclosure needs of major users of financial statements, *Accounting and Business Research*, 27, pp. 187–92.

Benn, H. (1992) Green negotiating: the MSF approach, in *Green Reporting: The challenge of the nineties* Owen, D. (ed.) London: Chapman and Hall.

Bennett, M. and James, P. (1994) *Financial dimensions of environmental performance: developments in environment-related management accounting*, paper presented to the British Association Annual Conference, Winchester College.

Benston, G.J. (1982a) 'Accounting and corporate accountability', *Accounting, Organizations and Society*, 7(2), pp. 87–105.

Benston, G.J. (1982b) 'An analysis of the role of accounting standards for enhancing corporate governance and social responsibility', *Journal of Accounting and Public Policy*,

1(1), pp. 5–18.

Benston, G.J. (1984) 'Rejoinder to "Accounting and corporate accountability: an extended comment" ' *Accounting, Organizations and Society*, 9(3/4), pp. 417–19.

von Bertalanffy, L. (1956) 'General Systems Theory', *General Systems Yearbook*, 1, pp. 1–10.

von Bertalanffy, L. (1971) *General Systems Theory: Foundations, development, applications*, Harmondsworth: Penguin.

von Bertalanffy, L. (1972) 'General Systems Theory — a critical review' in *Systems Behaviour* Beishon, J. and Peters, G. (eds) London: Open University/Harper & Row.

Bird, P. (1973) *Accountability*, London: Haymarket.

Bird, P. and Morgan-Jones, P. (1981) *Financial Reporting by Charities*, London: ICAEW.

Birkett, W.P. (1988) *Concepts of Accountability*, paper presented at British Accounting Association, Trent.

Birnberg, J.G. and Gandhi, N.M. (1976) 'Toward defining the accountants' role in the evaluation of social programmes', *Accounting, Organizations and Society*, 1(1), pp. 5–10.

Bloom, R. and Heymann, H. (1986) 'The concept of social accountability in accounting literature', *Journal of Accounting Literature*, 5, pp. 167–82.

Blum, R., Herxheimer, A., Stenzl, C. and Woodcock, J. (eds) (1983) *Pharmaceuticals and Health Policy*, London: Social Audit.

Bogiages, G.H. and Vorster, Q. (1994) *Green Reporting in the Republic of South Africa*, University of Pretoria, working paper.

Booth, P. and Cocks, N. (1990) 'Power and the study of the accounting profession' in *Critical Accounts* Cooper, D.J. and Hopper, T.M. (eds), Basingstoke: Macmillan, pp. 391–408.

Bougen, P. (1983) 'Value added' in *Financial Reporting 1983/84* Tonkin, D.J. and Skerratt, L.C.L. (eds) London: ICAEW.

Bougen, P. (1984) 'Review of *Linking Pay to Company Performance* by T. Vernon Harcourt', *British Accounting Review*, 16(1), p. 96.

Boulding, K.E. (1966) 'The economics of the coming Spaceship Earth' in *Environmental Quality in a Growing Economy*, Jaratt, H. (ed.), Baltimore: Johns Hopkins Press, pp. 3–14.

Bowen, H.R. (1953) *Social Responsibilities of the Businessman*, New York: Harper and Row.

Bowman, E.H. and Haire, M. (1975) 'A strategic posture toward corporate social responsibility', *California Management Review*, 18(2), pp. 49–58.

Bragdon, J.H. and Marlin, A.T. (1972) 'Is pollution profitable?' *Risk Management*, April, pp. 9–18.

Briloff, A.J. (1986) 'Accountancy and the public interest', *Advances in Public Interest Accounting*, 1, pp. 1–14.

Briston, R. J. (1984) 'Accounting standards and host country control of multinationals', *British Accounting Review*, 16(1), pp. 12–26.

Broadbent, J., Laughlin, R. and Read, S. (1991) 'Recent financial and administrative changes in the NHS: a Critical Theory analysis', *Critical Perspectives on Accounting*, 2(1), pp. 1–30.

Brockoff, K. (1979) 'A note on external social reporting by German companies: a survey of 1973 company reports', *Accounting, Organizations and Society*, 4(1/2), pp. 77–85.

Brooks, L.J. (1980) 'An attitude approach to the social audit: the Southam Press experience', *Accounting, Organizations and Society*, 5(3), pp. 341–55.

Brooks, L.J. (1986) *Canadian Corporate Social Performance*, Toronto: Society of Management Accountants of Canada.

Brown, D. (1990) 'Environmental investing: let the buyer beware', *Management Review*, June, pp. 18–21.

Brummett, R.L., Flamholtz, E.G. and Pyle, W.C. (1968) 'Human resource measurement — a challenge for accountants', *The Accounting Review*, 43(2), pp. 217–24.

Bruyn, S.T. (1987) *The Field of Social Investment*, Cambridge: Cambridge University Press.

Bryer, R.A. (1979) 'The status of the systems approach', *Omega*, 7(3), pp. 219–31.

Bryer, R.A., Brigall, T.J. and Maunders, A.R. (1984) 'The case for shadow planning', in *Fighting Closures*, Levie, H., Gregory, D. and Lorentzen, N. (eds), Nottingham: Spokesman.

Burchell, S. (1980) 'Casting around for a firm report base', *Accountants Weekly*, 1, August, pp. 24–5.

Burchell, S., Clubb, C. and Hopwood, A. (1985) 'Accounting in its social context: towards a history of value added in the United Kingdom', *Accounting, Organizations and Society*, 10(4), pp. 381–413.

Burchell, S., Clubb, C., Hopwood, A., Hughes, J. and Nahapiet, J. (1980) 'The roles of accounting in organisations and society', *Accounting, Organizations and Society*, 5 pp. 5–27.

Burck, G. (1973) 'The hazards of corporate responsibility', *Fortune*, June, pp. 114–17.

Burke, R. C. (1980) 'The disclosure of social accounting information', *Cost and Management*, pp. 221–4.

Burton, J.C. (1972) 'Commentary on "Let's get on with the social audit"', *Business and Society Review*, Winter, pp. 42–3.

Business-in-the-Environment/SustainAbility (1994) *The LCA Sourcebook*, London: BiE/SustainAbility/SPOLD.

Butler, D., Frost, C. and Macve, R. (1992) 'Environmental reporting' in *Financial Reporting 1991–1992: A survey of UK reporting practice*, Tonkin, D.J. and Skerratt, L.C.L. (eds), London: Institute of Chartered Accountants in England and Wales.

Cadman, D. (1986) 'Money as if people mattered,' in *The Living Economy: A new economics in the making*, Ekins, P. (ed.), London: Routledge and Kegan Paul.

Campanale, M., Willenbacher, A. and Wilks, A. (1993) *Survey of Ethical and Environmental Funds in Continental Europe*, London: Merlin Research Unit.

Campfield, W.L. (1973) 'The accountants' opportunity for participating in the solution of socio-economic problems' in *The Accountant in a Changing Business Environment*, Stone, W.E. (ed.) Florida: University of Florida Accounting Series, pp. 2–11.

Canadian Institute of Chartered Accountants (CICA) (1993a) *Environmental Stewardship: Management accountability and the role of Chartered Accountants*, Toronto: CICA.

Canadian Institute of Chartered Accountants (CICA) (1993b) *Reporting on Environmental Performance*, Toronto: CICA.

Carlin, F. M. (1995) 'The European Works Council Directive', *European Law Review*, 20(1), pp. 96–103.

Carson, R. (1962) *Silent Spring*, Boston: Houghton Mifflin.

Carter, R., Martin, J., Mayblin, B. and Munday, M. (1984) *Systems, Management and Change: A graphic guide*, London: Harper and Row.

Cartwright, D. (1990) 'What price ethics?' *Managerial Auditing Journal*, 5(2), pp. 28–31.

Centre for Alternative Industrial and Technological Systems (CAITS) (1984a) *Public costs of Unemployment*, London: CAITS.

Centre for Alternative Industrial and Technological Systems (CAITS) (1984b) *Economic Audit of the Costs of Closure of the Foundry at Dagenham by Ford*, London: CAITS.

Centre for Social Change/New Consumer (1993) *Good Business: Case studies in social responsibility*, Bristol: SAUS Publications.

Chan J.L. (1979) 'Corporate disclosure in occupational safety and health: some empirical evidence' *Accounting Organizations and Society*, 4(4), pp. 273–281.

Charkham, J.A. (1990) 'Are shares just commodities?' in National Association of Pension Funds (NAPF), *Creative Tension*, London: NAPF.

Chartered Institute of Management Accountants (CIMA) (1982) *The Evaluation of Energy Use: Readings*, London: CIMA.

Checkland, P.B. (1981) *Systems Thinking, Systems Practice*, Chichester: Wiley.

Chen, K. H. and Metcalf, R. W. (1980) 'The relationship between pollution control record and financial indicators revisited', *Accounting Review*, 60(1), pp. 168–77.

Cherns, A.B. (1978) 'Alienation and accountancy', *Accounting, Organizations and Society*, 3(2), pp. 105–14.

Choudhury, N. (1988) 'The seeking of accounting where it is not: towards a theory of non-accounting in organizational settings', *Accounting, Organizations and Society*, 13(6), pp. 549–57.

Chow, C.W. and Wong-Boren, A. (1987) 'Voluntary financial disclosure by Mexican corporations', *The Accounting Review*, LXII(3), pp. 533–41.

Christenson, C. (1983) 'The methodology of positive accounting', *The Accounting Review*, January, pp. 1–22.

Christophe, B. and Bebbington, K. J. (1992) 'The French Bilan Social: a pragmatic model for the development of accounting for the environment? A research note', *The British Accounting Review*, 24(3), pp. 281–90.

Church of Scotland (1988) *Report of the Special Commission on the Ethics of Investment and Banking*, Edinburgh: Church of Scotland.

Churchill, N.C. (1973) 'The accountants' role in social responsibility' in *The Accountant in a Changing Business Environment*, Stone, W.E. (ed.) Florida: University of Florida Accounting Series, pp. 14–27.

Churchill, N. C. and Toan, A. B. (1978) 'Reporting on corporate social responsibility: a progress report', *Journal of Contemporary Business*, Winter, pp. 5–17.

City of Edinburgh District Council and Lothian Regional Council (1985) *Rowntree Mackintosh plc Edinburgh, The Consequences of Closure: A Social Audit*, City of Edinburgh District Council.

Climo, T. (1976) *Disclosure of Information to Employees Representatives: a Wage Bargaining Decision Model*, unpublished, University of Kent.

Coalition for Environmentally Responsible Economies (CERES) (1993) *Directory of Members*, Boston, Mass: CERES.

Coker ,E.W. (1990) 'Adam Smith's concept of the social system', *Journal of Business Ethics* 9(2), pp. 139–42.

Cmnd 5391 (1973) *Company Law Reform*, London: HMSO.

Cmnd 6888 (1977) *The future of company reports — a consultative document*, London: HMSO.

Cmnd 7233 (1978) *Code of Conduct for Companies with Interests in South Africa*, London: HMSO.

Cmnd 7654 (1979) *Company Accounting and Disclosure*, London: HMSO.

Cmnd 9860 (1986) *Code of Conduct for Companies with Interests in South Africa*, London: HMSO.

Colwyn Jones, T. (1995) *Accounting and the Enterprise: A social analysis*, London: Routledge.

Confederation of British Industry (CBI) (1973) *The Responsibilities of the British Public Company*, London: CBI.

Confederation of British Industry (CBI) (1976) *Response to Aims and Scope of Company Reports*, London: CBI.

Confederation of British Industry (CBI) (1992) *Environment Means Business: a CBI action plan for the 1990s*, London: CBI.

Cooper, C. (1992) 'The non and nom of accounting for (M)other Nature', *Accounting Auditing and Accountability Journal*, 5(3), pp. 16–39.

Cooper, D.J. (1984) 'Accounting for Labour', in *Current Issues in Accounting*, 2nd edn, Carsberg, B.V. and Hope, A. (eds) Oxford: Philip Allen.

Cooper, D.J. (1988) 'A social analysis of corporate pollution disclosures: a comment', *Advances in Public Interest Accounting*, 2, pp. 179–86.

Cooper, D.J. and Essex, S. (1977) 'Accounting information and employee decision making', *Accounting, Organizations and Society*, 2(3), pp. 201–17.

Cooper, D.J. and Hopper, T.M. (eds) (1990) *Critical Accounts*, Basingstoke: Macmillan.

Cooper, D.J. and Sherer, M.J. (1984) 'The value of corporate accounting reports: arguments for a political economy of accounting', *Accounting, Organizations and Society*, 9(3/4), pp. 207–32.

Council on Economic Priorities (CEP) (1973) *Economic Priorities Report*, New York: CEP.

Council on Economic Priorities (CEP) (1977) *The Pollution Audit: A guide to 50 industrials for responsible investors*, New York: CEP.

Council of the European Communities, Commission of the European Communities (1992) *Agreement on the European Economic Area*, Luxembourg: Office for Official Publications of the European Communities.

Council of the European Union, European Commission (1992) *Towards Sustainability. A Community Programme of Policy and Action in Relation to the Environment and Sustainable Development*, Brussels: European Commission, March.

Council of the European Union, European Commission (1993) *Environmental Management and Audit Scheme*, Council Regulation EEC No. 1863/93, Brussels: European Commission, 29 June.

Council of the European Union, European Commission (1994) *Protocol Adjusting the Agreement on the European Economic Area*, Luxembourg: Office for Official Publications of the European Communities.

Counter Information Services (CIS) (1972 *et seq.*) *Anti Reports*, London: CIS.

County of Cleveland (1983) *The Economic and Social Importance of the British Steel Corporation to Cleveland*, County of Cleveland.

Cowen, S. S., Ferreri, L. B. and Parker, L. D. (1987) 'The impact of corporate characteristics on social responsibility disclosure: a typology and frequency-based analysis', *Accounting, Organizations and Society*, 12(2), pp. 111–22.

Craig-Smith, N. (1990) *Morality and the Market: Consumer pressure for corporate accountability*, London: Routledge.

Cressey, P. (1993) 'Employee participation' in *The Social Dimension: Employment policy in the European Community*, Gold, M. (ed.) Basingstoke: Macmillan.

Dahl, R.A. (1970) *Modern Political Analysis*, Englewood Cliffs, NJ: Prentice Hall.

Dahl, R.A. (1972) 'A prelude to corporate reform', *Business and Society Review*, Spring, pp. 17–23.

Daly, H.E. (ed.) (1980) *Economy, Ecology, Ethics: Essays Toward a Steady State Economy*, San Francisco: W.H. Freeman.

Daly, H.E. (1980) *For the Common Good: Redirecting the economy towards the community, the environment and a sustainable future*, London: Greenprint.

Daniel, W.W. (1976) *Wage Determination in Industry*, Political and Economic Planning (PEP) Report, No. 563, London: PEP.

Daniel W.W. (1981) 'Influences on the level of wage settlements in manufacturing industry', in *The Future of Pay Bargaining*, Blackaby, F. (ed.) London: Heinemann.

Dauncey, G. (1988) *After the Crash: The emergence of the rainbow economy*, Basingstoke: Greenprint.

Davis, S.W., Menon, K. and Morgan, G. (1982) 'The images that have shaped accounting theory', *Accounting, Organizations and Society*, 7(4), pp. 307–18.

Deloitte, Touche Tohmatsu International; International Institute for Sustainable Development and Sustainability (1993) *Coming Clean*, London: Deloitte Touche Tohmatsu International.

Den Uyl, D.J. (1984) 'The new crusaders: the corporate social responsibility debate', *Studies in Social Philosophy and Policy No.5*, Ohio: Social Philosophy and Policy Center.

Department of Trade (1976) *Aims and Scope of Company Reports*, London: HMSO.

Dey, C., Evans R. and Gray, R.H. (1994) *Emerging forms of accountability: the new social audits and social bookkeeping and accounting systems — the case of Traidcraft plc*, paper presented at Scottish Accounting Group, University of Paisley, September.

Dey, C., Evans, R. and Gray, R.H. (1995) 'Towards social information systems and bookkeeping: a note on developing the mechanisms for social accounting and audit', *Journal of Applied Accounting Research*, (2)3, pp. 36–69.

Dickson, D. (1974) *Alternative Technology and the Politics of Technical Change*, Glasgow: Fontana.

Dierkes, M. (1979) 'Corporate Social Reporting in Germany: conceptual developments and practical experience', *Accounting, Organizations and Society*, 4(1/2), pp. 87–107.

Dierkes, M. (1980) 'Corporate social reporting and performance in Germany' in *Research in Corporate Social Performance and Policy*, Preston, L. (ed.), Greenwich, CT: JAI Press, 2, pp. 251–89.

Dierkes, M. and Antal, A.B. (1985) 'The usefulness and use of social reporting information', *Accounting, Organizations and Society*, 10(1), pp. 29–34.

Dierkes, M. and Preston, L.E. (1977) 'Corporate social accounting and reporting for the physical environment: a critical review and implementation proposal', *Accounting, Organizations and Society*, 2(1), pp. 3–22.

Dobson, A. (1990) *Green Political Thought*, London: Unwin Hayman.

Domini, A. L. and Kinder, P.D. (1984) *Ethical Investing*, Reading, Mass: Addison Wesley.

Donaldson, J. (1988) *Key Issues in Business Ethics*, London: Academic Press.

Dowling, J. and Pfeffer, J. (1975) 'Organisational legitimacy: social values and organisational behaviour', *Pacific Sociological Review*, January, pp. 122–36.

Drucker, P. (1965) 'Is business letting young people down?' *Harvard Business Review*, Nov/Dec, p. 54.

Dyckman, T.R., Downes, D.H. and Magee, R.P. (1975) *Efficient Capital Markets and Accounting*, Englewood Cliffs, NJ: Prentice Hall.

Eckersley, R. (1992) *Environmentalism and Political Theory: Towards an egocentric approach*, London: UCL Press.

Ecumenical Committee for Corporate Responsibility (1989) *Churches, Companies and Share Ownership*, Fareham, Hants: ECCR.

Ecumenical Committee for Corporate Responsibility (1992) *The Greening of Industry?*, Fareham, Hants: ECCR.

Ekins, P. (1992a) *A New World Order: Grassroots movements for global change*, London: Routledge.

Ekins, P. (1992b) *Wealth Beyond Measure: An atlas of new economics*, London: Gaia.

Elkington, J. (1987) *The Green Capitalists*, London: Victor Gollancz.

Elkington, J. and Hailes, J. (1988) *The Green Consumer Guide: High street shopping for a better environment*, London: Victor Gollancz.

Emery, F.E. (ed.) (1969) *Systems Thinking*, Harmondsworth: Penguin.

Epstein, M.J., Epstein, J.B. and Weiss, E.J. (1977) *Introduction to Social Accounting*, California: Western Consulting Group Inc.

Ernst and Ernst (1976 *et seq.*) *Social Responsibility Disclosure*, Cleveland, Ohio: Ernst and Ernst.

Estes, R.W. (1976) *Corporate Social Accounting*, New York: Wiley.

Ethical Investment Research Service (EIRIS) (1989; 1992; 1993) *Choosing an Ethical Fund*, London: EIRIS.

European Economic Community (1957) *Treaty Establishing the European Economic Community*, Rome, 25 March, London: Her Majesty's Stationery Office.

Fédération des Experts Comptables Européens (FEE) (1993) *Environmental Accounting and Auditing: Survey of current activities and developments*, Brussels: FEE.

Firth, M. (1984) 'The extent of voluntary disclosure in corporate annual reports and its association with security risk measures', *Applied Economics*, 16, pp. 269–77.

Flamholtz, E.G. (1974) *Human Resource Accounting*, California: Dickenson.

Flamholtz, E.G. (1987) 'Valuation of human assets in a securities brokerage firm: an empirical study', *Accounting, Organizations and Society*, 12(4), pp. 309–18.

Foley, B.J. and Maunders, K.T. (1977) *Accounting Information Disclosure and Collective Bargaining*, London: Macmillan.

Folger, H.R. and Nutt, F. (1975) 'A note on social responsibility and stock valuation,' *Academy of Management Journal*, 18(1), pp. 155–60.

Francis, M.E. (1973) 'Accounting and the evaluation of social programs: a critical comment', *The Accounting Review*, April, pp. 245–357.

Frankel, B. (1987) *The Post Industrial Utopians*, Cambridge: Polity Press.

Frankel, M. (1978) *The Social Audit Pollution Handbook*, London: Macmillan.

Frankel, M. (1981) *A Word of Warning*, London: Social Audit.

Frankel, M. (1982) *Chemical Risk*, London: Pluto Press.

Freedman, M. and Jaggi, B. (1986) An analysis of the impact of corporate pollution disclosures included in annual financial statements on investment decisions, *Advances in Public Interest Accounting*, 1, pp. 193–212.

Freedman, M. and Jaggi, B. (1988) 'An analysis of the association between pollution disclosure and economic performance', *Accounting Auditing and Accountability Journal*, 1(2), pp. 43–58.

Freedman, M. and Stagliano, A.J. (1992) 'European unification, accounting harmonisation, and social disclosures', *International Journal of Accounting*, 27(2), pp. 112–22.

French, P.A., Jensen, R.E. and Robertson, K.R. (1992) 'Undergraduate student research programs: are they as viable for accounting as they are in science and humanities?' *Critical Perspectives on Accounting*, 3(4), pp. 337–57.

Friedman, M. (1962) *Capitalism and Freedom*, Chicago: University of Chicago.

Friedman, M. (1970) 'The social responsibility of business is to increase its profits', *The New York Times Magazine*, September 13, pp. 122–6.

Friends of the Earth (FoE) (1989) *The Environmental Charter for Local Government*, London: FoE.

Galbraith, J.K. (1973) *Economics and the Public Purpose*, Middlesex: England.

Galbraith, J.K. (1991) 'Revolt in our time: the triumph of simplistic ideology' in *Europe from below* Kaldor, M. (ed.), Harmondsworth: Penguin Books.

Gambling, T. (1977) 'Magic, accounting and morale', *Accounting, Organizations and Society*, 2(2), pp. 141–51.

Gambling, T. (1977) 'Accounting to society' in *Current Issues in Accounting*, Carsberg, B.V. and Hope, A.J.B. (eds) Oxford: Philip Allen.

Gambling, T. (1978) 'The evolution of accounting man', *Accountants' Weekly*, 10 November, pp. 30–1.

Garrod, N. (1987) 'Accounting regulation, efficient markets tests and information inductance', *The British Accounting Review*, 19(2), pp. 133–44.

Geddes, M. (1992) 'The social audit movement', in *Green Reporting: The challenge of the nineties* Owen, D. (ed.) London: Chapman and Hall.

General and Municipal Workers Union (GMWU) (1978) *Disclosure of Information Guide*, Esher: GMWU.

George, S. (1988) *A Fate Worse than Debt*, Harmondsworth; Penguin.

Gerboth, D.L. (1987) 'The conceptual framework: not definitions but professional values', *Accounting Horizons*, 1(3), pp. 1–8.

Gerboth, D.L. (1988) 'Commentary: on the profession', *Accounting Horizons*, 2(1), March, pp. 104–8.

Gibson, K. and O'Donovan, G. (1994) *Green Accounting in Australia: Myth or reality?*, paper for the 17th European Accounting Association Congress, Venice.

Giddens, A. (1976) *New Rules of Sociological Method*, London: Hutchinson.

Giles, W.J. and Robinson, D.F. (1972) *Human Asset Accounting*, London: Institute of Personnel Management.

Gjesdal, F. (1981) 'Accounting for stewardship', *Journal of Accounting Research*, Spring, pp. 208–31.

Gladwin, Thomas, N. (1993) 'Envisioning the sustainable corporation' in *Managing for Environmental Excellence*, Smith, Emily T. (ed.), Washington, DC: Island Press.

Glautier, M.W.E. (1976) 'Human resource accounting — a critique of research objectives for the development of human resource accounting models', *Journal of Business Finance and Accounting*, 3(2), pp. 3–21.

Glautier, M.W.E. and Underdown, B. (1976) *Accounting Theory and Practice*, London: Pitman, pp. 673–716.

Glyn, A. (1985) *The Economic Case Against Pit Closures*, Sheffield: National Union of Mineworkers.

Glyn, A. and Harrison, J. (1980) *The British Economic Disaster*, London: Pluto Press.

Goldsmith, E. *et al.* (1972) *Blueprint for Survival*, Harmondsworth: Penguin.

Gorz, A. (1989) *Critique of Economic Reason* (trans G. Handyside and C. Turner), London: Verso.

Gray, R.H. (1980) *An evaluation of the current UK practice in external social reporting with special reference to Social Audit and Counter Information Services*, MA (Econ) dissertation, University of Manchester.

Gray, R.H. (1990a) *The Greening of Accountancy: The profession after Pearce*, London: ACCA.

Gray, R.H. (1990b) 'Business ethics and organisational change: building a Trojan horse or rearranging deckchairs on the Titanic?' *Managerial Auditing Journal*, 5(2), pp. 12–21.

Gray, R.H. (1990c) 'Accounting and economics: the psychopathic siblings — a review essay', *British Accounting Review*, 22(4), pp. 373–88.

Gray, R.H. (1990d) 'The accountant's task as a friend to the Earth', *Accountancy*, June, pp. 65–9.

Gray, R.H. (1991a) 'Sustainability: do you REALLY want to know what it means?' *CBI Environment Newsletter*, 3, pp. 10–11.

Gray, R.H. (1991b) *Trends in Corporate Social and Environmental Accounting*, London: BIM.

Gray, R.H. (1992) 'Accounting and environmentalism: an exploration of the challenge of gently accounting for accountability, transparency and sustainability', *Accounting, Organizations and Society*, 17(5), pp. 399–426.

Gray, R.H. (1993) 'Current practice in environmental reporting', *Social and Environmental Accounting*, pp. 6–9.

Gray, R.H. (1994a) 'The accounting profession and the environmental crisis (or can accountancy save the world?)', *Meditari*, pp. 1–51.

Gray, R.H. (1994b) 'Corporate reporting for sustainable development: accounting for sustainability in 2000AD', *Environmental Values*, 3(1), pp. 17–45.

Gray, R.H. (1995a) 'The developing state of the art in environmental reporting in the UK and continental Europe' in *Green Reporting: Environmental protection and accounting* Yamagami, T. and Kikuya, K. (eds) pp. 323–42, Journal published annually by the University of Pretoria.

Gray, R.H. (1995b) 'The silent practice of social accounting and corporate social reporting in companies', University of Dundee Discussion Papers in Accountancy and Finance, ACC/9506..

Gray, R.H. and Bebbington, K.J. (1994) 'Sustainable development and accounting: incentives and disincentives for the adoption of sustainability by transnational corporations', Dundee Discussion Papers in Accountancy and Finance, ACC/9414, November.

Gray, R.H., Bebbington, K.J. and McPhail, K. (1994) 'Teaching ethics and the ethics of accounting teaching: educating for immorality and a case for social and environmental accounting education', *Accounting Education*, 3(1), pp. 51–75.

Gray, R.H., Bebbington, K.J. and Walters, D. (1993) *Accounting for the Environment: The greening of accountancy Part II*, London: Paul Chapman.

Gray, R.H., Bebbington, K.J., Walters, D. and Thomson, I. (1995a) 'The greening of enterprise: an exploration of the (non) role of environmental accounting and environmental accountants in organisational change', *Critical Perspectives on Accounting*, 6(3), pp. 211–39.

Gray, R.H. and Kouhy, R. (1993) 'Accounting for the environment and sustainability in lesser developed countries: an exploratory note', *Research in Third World Accounting*, 2, pp. 387–99.

Gray, R.H., Kouhy, R. and Lavers, S. (1995b) 'Corporate social and environmental reporting: a review of the literature and a longitudinal study of UK disclosure', *Accounting Auditing and Accountability Journal*, 8(2), pp. 47–77.

Gray, R.H., Kouhy, R. and Lavers, S. (1995c) 'Constructing a research database of social and environmental reporting by UK companies: a methodological note', *Accounting Auditing and Accountability Journal*, 8(2), pp. 78–101.

Gray, R.H. and Laughlin, R.C. (1991) 'The coming of the green and the challenge of environmentalism', *Accounting Auditing and Accountability Journal*, 4(3), pp. 5–8.

Gray, R.H. and Mallon, P. (1994) 'Bringing the environmental case to bear on investment appraisal', *Integrated Environmental Management*, 29, pp. 20–2.

Gray, R.H. and Morrison, S. (1991) 'Accounting for the environment after the Pearce Report', *Radical Quarterly*, 19, pp. 17–25.

Gray, R.H., Owen, D.L. and Adams, R. (1995d) 'Standards, stakeholders and sustainability', *Certified Accountant*, March, pp. 20–224.

Gray, R.H., Owen, D.L. and Maunders, K.T. (1986) 'Corporate social reporting: the way forward?' *Accountancy*, December, pp. 6–8.

Gray, R.H., Owen, D.L. and Maunders, K.T. (1987) *Corporate Social Reporting: Accounting and accountability*, Hemel Hempstead: Prentice Hall.

Gray, R.H., Owen, D.L. and Maunders, K.T. (1988) 'Corporate social reporting: emerging trends in accountability and the social contract', *Accounting Auditing and Accountability Journal*, 1(1), pp. 6–20.

Gray, R.H., Owen, D.L. and Maunders, K.T. (1991) 'Accountability, corporate social reporting and the external social audits', *Advances in Public Interest Accounting*, 4, pp. 1–21.

Gray, R.H. and Perks, R.W. (1982) 'How desirable is social accounting?' *Accountancy*, April, pp. 101–2.

Gray, R.H. and Symon, I.W. (1992) 'Environmental reporting: BSO/Origin', *Integrated Environmental Management*, 7, March, pp. 8–10.

Gray, S.J., Shaw, J.C. and McSweeney, L.B. (1981) 'Accounting standards and multinational corporations', *Journal of International Business Studies*, 11(1), pp. 121–36.

Gray, V. (1978) 'Accountability in policy process: an alternative perspective' in *Accountability in Urban Society*, Greer S., Hedlund, R.D. and Gibson, J.L. (eds) London: Sage.

Greenwood, E. (1957) 'Attributes of a profession', *Social Work*, July, pp. 44–55.

Greer, S., Hedlund, R.D. and Gibson, J.L. (eds) (1978) *Accountability in Urban Society*, Sage: London.

Gröjer, J.E. and Stark, A. (1977) 'Social accounting: a Swedish attempt', *Accounting, Organizations and Society*, 2(4), pp. 349–86.

Groves, R.E.V. (1981) 'Human resource accounting and reporting' in *Developments in Financial Reporting*, Lee, T.A. (ed.) Oxford: Philip Allen.

Gul, F.A.K., Andrew, B.H. and Teoh, H.J. (1984) 'A content analytical study of corporate social responsibility accounting disclosures in a sample of Australian companies (1983)', working paper.

Guthrie, J.E. and Mathews, M.R. (1985) 'Corporate social accounting in Australasia', *Research in Corporate Social Performance and Policy*, 7, pp. 251–77.

Guthrie, J. and Parker, L.D. (1989a) 'Corporate Social Reporting: a rebuttal of legitimacy theory', *Accounting and Business Research*, 9(76), pp. 343–52.

Guthrie, J.E. and Parker, L.D. (1989b) 'Continuity and discontinuity in corporate social reporting: a critical case study of BHP reporting 1885–1985', working paper.

Guthrie, J. and Parker, L.D. (1990) 'Corporate social disclosure practice: a comparative international analysis', *Advances in Public Interest Accounting*, 3, pp. 159–76.

Hackston, D. and Milne, M.J. (1995) 'Some determinants of social and environmental disclosures in New Zealand companies', working paper.

Hahn, F. (1984a) 'Reflections on the invisible hand' in *Equilibrium and Macroeconomics* Hahn, F. (ed.) Oxford: Basil Blackwell, pp. 109–33.

Hahn, F. (1984b) 'Economic theory and Keynes' insights, *Empirica*, 11(1), pp. 7–22.

Halford, R. (1989) 'Corporate social reporting, corporatism and feminism', paper presented at British Accounting Association, Bath University, March.

Harte, G. (1988) 'Human resource accounting: a review of some of the literature', in *Making Corporate Reports Valuable — The literature surveys*, Glasgow: ICAS, pp. 217–59.

Harte, G., Lewis, L. and Owen, D.L. (1991) 'Ethical investment and the corporate reporting function', *Critical Perspectives on Accounting*, 2(3), pp. 227–54.

Harte, G. and Owen, D. (1987) 'Fighting de-industrialisation: the role of local government social audits', *Accounting, Organizations and Society*, 12(2), pp. 123–41.

Harte, G. and Owen, D.L. (1991) 'Environmental disclosure in the annual reports of British Companies: a research note', *Accounting Auditing and Accountability Journal*, 4(3), pp. 51–61.

Haughton, G. (1988) 'Impact analysis — the social audit approach', *Project Appraisal*, 3(1), pp. 21–5.

Hayek, F.A. (1960) *The Constitution of Liberty*, London: Routledge.

Hayek, F.A. (1982) *Law, Legislation and Liberty*, vol.3, London: Routledge and Kegan Paul.

Hedlund, R.D. and Hamm, K.E. (1978) 'Accountability and political institutions' in *Accountability in Urban Society*, Greer, S., Hedlund, R.D. and Gibson, J.L. (eds) London: Sage.

Hekimian, J.S. and Jones, C.H. (1967) 'Put people on your balance sheet', *Harvard Business Review*, January/February, pp. 105–13.

Held, D. (1987) *Models of Democracy*, Oxford: Polity Press.

Herremans, I.M., Parporn, A. and McInnes, H. (1993) 'An investigation of corporate social responsibility reputation and economic performance', *Accounting, Organizations and Society*, 18(7/8), pp. 587–604.

Hetherington, J.A.C. (1973) 'Corporate social responsibility, stakeholders and the law', *Journal of Contemporary Business*, Winter, pp. 45–58.

Hicks, J.R. (1946) *Value and Capital*, 2nd edn, Oxford: Clarendon Press.

Hines, R.D. (1988) 'Financial accounting: in communicating reality, we construct reality', *Accounting, Organizations and Society*, 13(3), pp. 251–61.

Hines, R.D. (1989) 'The sociopolitical paradigm in financial accounting research', *Accounting Auditing and Accountability Journal*, 2(1), pp. 52–76.

Hines, R.D. (1991a) 'The FASB's conceptual framework, financial accounting and the maintenance of the social world', *Accounting, Organizations and Society*, 16(4), pp. 313–32.

Hines, R.D. (1991b) 'Accounting for nature', *Accounting Auditing and Accountability*

Journal, 4(3), pp. 27–9.

Hines, R.D. (1992) 'Accounting: filling the negative space', *Accounting, Organizations and Society*, 17(3/4), pp. 313–42.

Holden Meehan (1994) *An Independent Guide to Ethical and Green Investment Trusts*, 5th edn, Bristol: Holden Meehan.

Hood, N. and Young, S. (1979) *The Economics of Multinational Enterprise*, London: Longman.

Hopper, T. and Powell, A. (1985) 'Making sense of research into the organisational and social aspects of management accounting: a review of its underlying assumptions', *Journal of Management Studies*, 22(5), pp. 429–65.

Hopper, T., Storey, J. and Willmott, H. (1987) 'Accounting for accounting: towards the development of a dialectical view', *Accounting, Organizations and Society*, 12(5), pp. 437–56.

Hopwood, A.G. (1978) 'Towards an organisational perspective for the study of accounting and information systems', *Accounting, Organizations and Society*, 3(1), pp. 3–13.

Hopwood, A.G. (1983) 'On trying to study accounting in the contexts in which it operates', *Accounting, Organizations and Society*, 8(2/3), pp. 287–305.

Hopwood, A.G. (1984) 'Accounting and the pursuit of efficiency' in *Issues in Public Sector Accounting*, Hopwood, A.G. and Tomkins, C. (eds) Oxford: Philip Allen.

Hopwood, A.G. (1986) 'Economics and the regime of the calculative' in *Developing the Socially Useful Economy*, Bodington S., George, M. and Michaelson, J. (eds) London: Macmillan, pp. 69–71.

Hopwood, A.G. (1987) 'The archaeology of accounting systems', *Accounting, Organizations and Society*, 12(3), pp. 207–34.

Hopwood, A.G. (1990) 'Ambiguity, knowledge and territorial claims: some observations on the doctrine of substance over form: a review essay', *British Accounting Review*, 22(1), pp. 79–88.

Hopwood, A.G. and Miller, P. (eds) (1994) *Accounting as Social and Institutional Practice*, Cambridge: Cambridge University Press.

Hoskin, K.W. and Macve, R.H. (1988) 'The genesis of accountability: the Westpoint connections', *Accounting, Organizations and Society*, 13(1), pp. 37–73.

House of Lords (1982) *Report of the Select Committee on Unemployment*, London: House of Lords.

Huizing, A. and Dekker, H.C. (1992) 'Helping to pull our planet out of the red: an environmental report of BSO/Origin', *Accounting Organizations and Society*, 17(5), pp. 449–58.

Hundred Group of Finance Directors (1992) *Statement of Good Practice: Environmental Reporting in Annual Reports*, London: 100 Group.

Hussey, R. (1981) 'Developments in employee reporting', *Managerial Finance*, 7(2), pp. 12–16.

Ijiri, Y. (1983) 'On the accountability-based conceptual framework of accounting', *Journal of Accounting and Public Policy*, pp. 75–81.

Ingram, R.W. (1978) 'An investigation of the information content of (certain) social responsibility disclosure', *Journal of Accounting Research*, 16(2), pp. 270–85.

Ingram, R.W. and Frazier, K. (1980) 'Environmental performance and corporate disclosure', *Journal of Accounting Research*, 18(4), pp. 614–22.

Institute of Chartered Accountants in England and Wales (ICAEW) (1992) *Business, Accountancy and the Environment: A policy and research agenda* Macve, R. and Carey, A. (eds) London: ICAEW.

Institute for Workers Control (IWC) (1971) *UCS: A Social Audit*, London: IWC.

Institute for Workers Control (IWC) (1975) *Why Imperial Typewriters Must Not Close*, London: IWC.

International Accounting Standards Committee (1990) *Annual Review*, London: IASC.

Jackson, A. (1992) 'The trade union as environmental campaigner: the case of water privatisation', in *Green Reporting: The challenge of the nineties* Owen, D. (ed.) London: Chapman and Hall.

Jackson, P.M. (1982) *The Political Economy of Bureaucracy*, Oxford: Philip Allan.

Jackson-Cox, J., McQueeney, J. and Thirkell, J.E.M. (1984) 'The disclosure of company information to trade unions — the relevance of the ACAS Code of Practice on disclosure', *Accounting, Organizations and Society*, 9(3), pp.253–73.

Jacobs, M. (1991) *The Green Economy: Environment, sustainable development and the politics of the future*, London: Pluto Press.

Jacobson, R. (1991) 'Economic efficiency and the quality of life', *Journal of Business Ethics*, 10, pp. 201–9.

Jaggi, B. (1980) 'An analysis of corporate social reporting in Germany', *International Journal of Accounting*, 15(2), pp. 35–45.

Jasch, C. (1993) 'Environmental information systems in Austria', *Social and Environmental Accounting*, 13(2), pp. 7–9.

Jensen, M. and Meckling, W. (1976) 'Theory of the firm: managerial behaviour, agency costs and ownership structure', *Journal of Financial Economics*, October, pp. 305–60.

Jensen, R.E. (1976) *Phantasmagoric Accounting: Studies in Accounting Research No.14*, Sarasota, Fl: AAA.

Johnson, H.L. (1979) *Disclosure of Corporate Social Performance: Survey, evaluation and prospects*, New York: Praegar.

Jones, G.W. (1977) *Responsibility in Government*, London: London School of Economics.

Jones, M. (1993) 'Going green in the USA', *Certified Accountant*, November, pp. 33–4.

Jonson, L.C., Jonsson, B. and Svensson, G. (1978) 'The application of social accounting to absenteeism and personnel turnover', *Accounting, Organizations and Society*, 3(3/4), pp. 261–8.

Kaplan R.S. (1984) 'The evolution of management accounting', *Accounting Review*, 59(3), pp. 390–418.

Kaplan, R.S. and Norton, D.P. (1992) 'The balanced scorecard — measures that drive performance', *Harvard Business Review*, January–February, pp. 71–9.

Kapp, K.W. (1950/1978) *The Social Costs of Business Enterprise*, Nottingham: Spokesman.

Kast, F.E. and Rosenweig, J.E. (1974) *Organisation and Management: A systems approach*, McGraw Hill: Kograkusha.

Keenan, P. and Miller, K. (1988) 'Pension fund survey', *PIRC Bulletin*, 5, p. 3.

Keidanren (1991) *Global Environmental Charter*, Keidanren.

Keidanren (1992) *Towards Preservation of the Global Environment*, Keidanren.

Kempner, T.K., MacMillan, K. and Hawkins, K.H. (1976) *Business and Society*, Harmondsworth: Pelican.

Kern, W. (1975) 'The accounting concept in German labour oriented business management', *International Journal of Accounting*, 10(2), pp. 23–35.

Kestigan, M. (1991) 'The greening of accountancy', *Australian Accountant*, September, pp. 20–28.

Keuning, S. and Bosch, P. (1993) 'Dutch environment satellite accounts', *Social and Environmental Accounting*, 12(2), p. 12.

Kirkman, P. and Hope, C. (1992) *Environmental Disclosure in UK Company Annual Reports*, Cambridge University Press.

Kjellen, B. (1980) *Employee Consultants and Economic Information for Employees*, Research Report, Stockholm: University of Stockholm.

Knights, D. and Collinson, D. (1987) 'Disciplining the shopfloor: a comparison of the disciplinary effects of managerial psychology and financial accounting', *Accounting, Organizations and Society*, 12(5), pp. 457–77.

Kokubu, K. (1993) 'Corporate social activities and disclosures in Japan', working paper, Faculty of Business Osaka City University.

Kokubu, K. and Tomimasu, K. (1995) *Ethical Disclosure Embedded in the Japanese Socio-Political Context*, presented at the First Asian-Pacific, Interdisciplinary Research in Accounting Conference, Sydney.

Kokubu, K., Tomimasu, K. and Yamagami, T. (1994) *Green Reporting in Japan: Accountability and legitimacy*, paper for the Fourth Interdisciplinary Perspectives on Accounting Conference, Manchester.

KPMG (1993a) *UK Survey of Environmental Reporting*, London: KPMG.

KPMG (1993b) *International Survey of Environmental Reporting*, Canada: KPMG Peat Marwick Thorne.

KPMG (1994) *UK Environmental Reporting Survey*, London: KPMG.

Kreuze, J.G. and Newell, G.E. (1994) 'ABC and life cycle costing for environmental expenditures', *Management Accounting*, February, pp. 38–42.

Lamb, D. (1991) 'Morals and money', *Money Management*, September, pp. 34–46.

Laughlin, R.C. (1988) 'Accounting in the social context: an analysis of the accounting system of the Church of England', *Accounting Auditing and Accountability Journal*, 1(2), pp. 19–42.

Laughlin, R.C., Broadbent, J. and Shearn, D. (1992) 'Recent financial and accountability changes in general practice: an unhealthy intrusion into medical autonomy?' *Financial Accountability and Management*, 8(2), pp. 129–48.

Laughlin, R.C. and Gray, R.H. (1988) *Financial Accounting: Method and meaning*, London: Van Nostrand Reinhold.

Laughlin, R.C. and Puxty, A.G. (1981) 'The decision–usefulness criterion: wrong cart, wrong horse', *British Accounting Review*, 13(1), pp. 43–87.

Lee, T.A. (1978) 'The cash flow alternative for corporate financial reporting' in *Trends in Management and Financial Accounting*, Van Dam, C. (ed.) vol.1, Amsterdam: Martinus Nijhoff.

Lehman, C. (1992) *Accounting's Changing Roles in Social Conflict*, London: Paul Chapman.

Lehman, G. (in press) 'A legitimate concern for environmental accounting', *Critical Perspectives on Accounting*.

Lessem, R. (1977) 'Corporate social reporting in action: an evaluation of British, European and American practice', *Accounting, Organizations and Society*, 2(4), pp. 279–94.

Lev, B. and Schwartz, A. (1971) 'On the use of the economic concept of human capital in financial statements', *Accounting Review*, 46(1), pp. 103–11.

Lewis, L., Humphrey, C. and Owen, D. (1992) 'Accounting and the social: a pedagogic perspective', *British Accounting Review*, 24(3), pp. 219–33.

Lickiss, M. (1991) 'President's page: measuring up to the environmental challenge', *Accountancy*, January, p. 6.

Likert, R. (1967) *The Human Organisation*, New York: McGraw Hill.

Likierman, A. (1986) *Rights and Obligations in Public Information*, Cardiff: University College Cardiff Press.

Likierman, A. and Creasey, P. (1985) 'Objectives and entitlements to rights in government financial information', *Financial Accountability and Management*, 1(1), pp. 33–50.

Lindblom, C.E. (1984) 'The accountability of private enterprise: private — no. Enterprise — yes' in *Social Accounting for Corporations* Tinker A.M. (ed.) Manchester: MUP.

Lindblom, C.K. (1994) *The implications of organizational legitimacy for corporate social performance and disclosure*, paper presented at the Critical Perspectives on Accounting Conference, New York.

Linowes, D.F. (1972) 'An approach to socio-economic accounting', *Conference Board Record*, November, p. 60.

Loft, A. (1988) *Understanding Accounting in its Social and Historical Context: The case of cost accounting in Britain 1914–1925*, New York: Garland Publishing.

Lowe, A.E. (1972) 'The finance director's role in the formulation and implementation of strategy', *Journal of Business Finance*, 4(4), pp. 58–63.

Lowe, A.E. and McInnes, J.M. (1971) 'Control of socio-economic organisations', *Journal of Management Studies*, 8(2), pp. 213–27.

Lowe, H.D. (1990) 'Shortcomings of Japanese consolidated financial statements', *Accounting Horizons*, 4(3), pp. 1–9.

Lucas Aerospace Combine Shop Stewards Committee (1979) *Democracy versus the circumlocution office*, Pamphlet No. 65, Nottingham: Institute for Workers Control.

Lukes, S. (1974) *Power: A radical view*, London: Macmillan.

Luther, R.G., Matatko, J. and Corner, D. (1992) 'The investment performance of UK "ethical" unit trusts', *Accounting Auditing and Accountability Journal*, 5(4), pp. 59–72.

Luther, R.G. and Matatko, J.N. (1994) 'The performance of ethical unit trusts: choosing an appropriate benchmark', *British Accounting Review*, 26(1), pp. 77–89.

Lutz, E., Munasinghe, M. and Chander, R. (1990) *A Developing Country Perspective on Environmental Accounting*, Divisional Working Paper No 1990-12, August, Washington DC: World Bank Environment Dept.

Lyall, D. (1981) 'Financial reporting for employees', *Management Decision*, 19(3), pp. 33–8.

Lyall, D. (1982) 'Disclosure practices in employee reports', *Accountants Magazine*, July, pp. 246–8.

Lyndenberg, S.D., Marlin, A. T. and Strub, S.O. (1986) *Rating America's Corporate Conscience*, New York Council on Economic Priorities.

McBarnet D., Weston S. and Whelan C. J. (1993) 'Adversary accounting: Strategic uses of financial information by capital and labour', *Accounting, Organizations and Society*, 18(1), pp. 81–100.

McGuire, J.B., Sundgren, A. and Schneeweis, T., (1988) 'Corporate social responsibility and firm financial performance', *Academy of Management Journal*, 31(4), pp. 854–72.

McKee, A. (1986) 'The passage from theology to economics', *International Journal of Social Economics*, 13(3), pp. 5–19.

McMonnies, P. (ed.) (1988) *Making Corporate Reports Valuable*, Edinburgh: ICAS.

McSweeney, B. (1983) *The Influence of Legislation on the Disclosure and Use of Financial Information in UK Collective Bargaining*, London: Chartered Association of Certified Accountants.

MacGillivray, A. (1993) *A Green League of Nations: Relative environmental performance in OECD countries*, London: New Economics Foundation.

Macpherson, C.B. (1973) *Democratic Theory: Essays in retrieval*, Oxford: OUP.

Macpherson, C.B. (1977) *The Life and Times of Liberal Democracy*, Oxford: OUP.

Macpherson, C.B. (1978) *Property*, Toronto: University of Toronto Press.

Macpherson, C.B. (1985) *The Rise and Fall of Economic Justice and Other Papers*, Oxford: Oxford University Press.

Macve, R. (1981) *A Conceptual Framework for Financial Accounting and Reporting*, London: ICAEW.

Mahapatra, S (1984) 'Investor reaction to a corporate social accounting', *Journal of Business Finance and Accounting*, 11(1), pp. 29–40.

Mak, Y.T. (1991) 'Corporate characteristics and the voluntary disclosure of forecast information: a study of New Zealand prospectuses', *British Accounting Review*, 23(4), pp. 305–28.

Malachowski, A. (1990) 'Business ethics 1980–2000: an interim forecast', *Managerial Auditing Journal*, 5(2), pp. 22–7.

Marcuse, H. (1955/1986) *Reason and Revolution*, London: Routledge and Kegan Paul.

Marcuse, H. (1964) *One-Dimensional Man*, Boston: Beacon.

Marquès, E. (1976) 'Human resource accounting: some questions and reflections', *Accounting, Organizations and Society*, 1(2/3), pp. 175–8.

Marston, C. (1986) *Financial Reporting in India*, London: Croom Helm.

Mathews, M.R. (1984) 'A suggested classification for social accounting research', *Journal of Accounting and Public Policy*, 3, pp. 199–221.

Mathews, M.R. (1985) 'Social accounting: a future need', *Accountancy*, December, p. 139.

Mathews, M.R. (1987) 'Social responsibility accounting disclosure and information content for shareholders', *British Accounting Review*, 19(2), pp. 161–8.

Mathews, M.R. (1993) *Socially Responsible Accounting*, London: Chapman Hall.

Mathews, M.R. (1994) 'A comment on Lewis, Humphrey and Owen's "Accounting and the social"', *British Accounting Review*, 26(1), pp. 91–7.

Maunders, K.T. (1981) 'Social reporting and the employment report' in *Financial Reporting 1981–1982* Tonkin, D.J. and Skerratt, L.C.L. (eds) London: ICAEW, pp. 217–27.

Maunders, K.T. (1982a) 'Social reporting and the employment report' in *Financial Reporting 1982–1983* Tonkin, D.J. and Skerratt, L.C.L. (eds) London: ICAEW, pp. 178–87.

Maunders, K.T. (1982b) 'Simplified and employee reports' in *Financial Reporting 1982–1983* Tonkin, D.J. and Skerratt, L.C.L. (eds) London: ICAEW, pp. 173–7.

Maunders, K.T. (1984) *Employment Reporting—an investigation of user needs, measurement and reporting issues and practice*, London: ICAEW.

Maunders, K.T. and Burritt, R. (1991) 'Accounting and ecological crisis', *Accounting Auditing and Accountability Journal*, 4(3), pp. 9–26.

Maxwell, S. R. and Mason, A. K. (1976) 'Social Responsibility and Canada's Largest Corporations', Occasional Paper No. 9, Toronto: International Centre for Research in Accounting.

Mayo, E. (ed.) (1993) *Bank Watch*, London: New Economics Foundation.

Meadows, D.H., Meadows, D.L., Randers, J. and Behrens, W.H. (1972) *The Limits to Growth*, London: Pan.

Medawar, C. (1976) 'The social audit: a political view', *Accounting, Organizations and Society*, 1(4), pp. 389–94.

Medawar, C. (1978) *The Social Audit Consumer Handbook*, London: Macmillan.

Medawar, C. (1979) *The Consumers of Power*, London: Social Audit.

Medawar, C. (1984) *The Wrong Kind of Medicine*, London: Hodder and Stoughton.

Medawar, C. and Freese, B. (1982) *Drug Diplomacy*, London: Social Audit.

Meek, G.K. and Gray, S.J. '(1988)The value added statement: an innovation for US companies?' *Accounting Horizons*, June, pp. 73–81.

Merlin Research Unit (1993) *The Assessment Process for Green Investment*, London: Merlin Research Unit.

Mesarovic, M. and Pestel, E. (1975) *Mankind at the Turning Point*, Club of Rome, London: Hutchinson.

Mill, J.S. (1863/1962) *Utilitarianism* Warnock, M. (ed.) London: William Collins.

Miller, A. (1992) 'Green investment', in *Green Reporting: Accountancy and the challenge of the nineties* Owen D.L. (ed.) London: Chapman and Hall.

Millerson, G.L. (1964) *The Qualifying Association*, London: Routledge and Kegan Paul.

Milne, C. D. A. (1993) 'Environmental accountability: New Zealand's experience', *Social and Environmental Accounting*, 13(2), pp. 9–11.

Milne, M.J. (1991) 'Accounting, environmental resource values and non-market valuation techniques for environmental resources: a review', *Accounting Auditing and Accountability Journal*, 4(3), pp. 81–109.

Milne, M.J. (1995) 'Sustainability, the environment and management accounting', *Management Accounting Research*, in press.

Minns, R. (1980) *Pension Funds and British Capitalism*, London: Heinemann.

Mintz, S.M. (1990) *Cases in Accounting Ethics and Professionalism*, New York: McGraw Hill.

Mintzberg, H. (1983) 'The case for corporate social responsibility', *Journal of Business Strategy*, 4(2), pp. 3–15.

Mirvis, P.H. and Macey, B.A. (1976) 'Accounting for the costs and benefits of human resource development programs — an interdisciplinary approach', *Accounting, Organizations and Society*, 1(2/3), pp. 179–93.

Mitchell, F., Sams, K.T., Tweedie, D.P. and White, P.I. (1980) 'Disclosure of information — some evidence from case studies', *Industrial Relations Journal*, 11(5), pp. 53–62.

Moore, G. (1988) *Towards Ethical Investment*, Gateshead: Traidcraft Exchange.

Moore, R., Gold, M. and Levie, H. (1979) *The Shop Stewards Guide to the Use of Company Information*, Nottingham: Spokesman.

Moore, R. and Levie, H. (1981) *Constraints upon the Acquisition and Use of Company Information by Trade Unions*, Trade Union Research Unit, Ruskin College, Occasional Paper No 67.

Morgan, G. (1988) 'Accounting as reality construction: toward a new epistemology for accounting practice', *Accounting, Organizations and Society*, 13(5), pp. 477–85.

Moskowitz, M.R. (1972) 'Choosing socially responsible stock', *Business and Society Review*, pp. 71–5.

Most, K.S. (1977) 'Corporate social reporting: "model report" by Deutsche Shell', *The Accountant*, February.

Mueller, G.G. and Smith, C.H. (eds) (1976) *Accounting: a book of readings*, Illinois: Dryden, pp. 225–44.

Mulligan, T. (1986) 'A critique of Milton Friedman's essay "the social responsibility of business is to increase its profits" ', *Journal of Business Ethics*, 5, pp. 265–69.

Munkman, C.A. (1971) *Accountability and Accounting*, London: Hutchinson.

Murray, R. (1983) 'Pension Funds and local authority investments', *Capital and Class*, Summer, pp. 89–102.

Neale, C.W. (1989) 'Post-auditing practices by UK firms: aims, benefits and shortcomings', *British Accounting Review*, 21(4), pp. 209–328.

Neimark, M.K. (1992) *The Hidden Dimensions of Annual Reports*, New York: Markus Wiener.

Ness, K.E. and Mirza, A.M. (1991) 'Corporate social disclosure: a note on a test of agency theory', *British Accounting Review*, 23(3), pp. 211–18.

Newcastle City Council (1985) *Newcastle Upon Tyne Social Audit 1979–1984*, Newcastle City Council.

Newton, T.J. and Harte, G. (1994) *Green Business: Technicist Kitsch*, University of Edinburgh, Department of Business Studies, working paper 94/17.

Nielsen, R. and Szyszczak, E. (1993) *The Social Dimension of the European Community*, Denmark: Handelshojskolens Forlag.

Nikolai, L.A., Bazley, J.D. and Brummett, R.L. (1976) *The Management of Corporate Environmental Activity*, Washington: National Association of Accountants.

Nishiguchi, S. (1994) 'Social disclosure of Japanese companies' in *Social Disclosure: An international comparison*, Yamagami, T. and Iiada, S. (eds) Tokyo: Hakuto [in Japanese].

Noreen, E. (1988) 'The economics of ethics: a new perspective on agency theory', *Accounting, Organizations and Society*, 13(4), pp. 359–70.

Nozick, R. (1974) *Anarchy, State and Utopia*, Oxford: Basil Blackwell.

Ogden, S.G. (1986) *Trade Unions and the Disclosure of Information*, The University of Leeds, School of Economic Studies, working paper 86/4.

Ogden, S.G. (1993) 'The limitations of agency theory: the case of accounting based profit sharing schemes', *Critical Perspectives on Accounting*, 4(2), pp. 179–206.

Ogden, S.G. and Bougen, P.D. (1985) 'A radical perspective on disclosure of information to trade unions', *Accounting, Organizations and Society*, 10(2), pp. 211–24.

Owen, D.L. (1990) 'Towards a theory of social investment: a review essay', *Accounting, Organizations and Society*, 15(3), pp. 249–66.

Owen, D.L. (1992) *Green Reporting: The challenge of the nineties*, London: Chapman and Hall.

Owen, D. (1995, in press) 'In pursuit of eco-justice: A future role for green accounting?', in *The Accounting Framework: Essays in honour of Professor Shunji Hattori*, Fujita (ed.) 3 Kyushu University Press, in press [in Japanese].

Owen, D.L. and Gray, R.H. (1994) 'Environmental reporting awards: profession fails to rise to the challenge', *Certified Accountant*, April, pp. 44–8.

Owen, D.L., Gray, R.H. and Adams, R. (1992) 'A green and fair view', *Certified Accountant*, April, pp. 12–15.

Owen, D., Gray, R. and Maunders, K. (1987) 'Researching the information content of social responsibility disclosure: a comment', *British Accounting Review*, 19(2), pp. 169–76.

Owen, D., Humphrey, C. and Lewis, L. (1994) *Social and Environmental Accounting Education in British Universities*, ACCA Research Report No.39, London: ACCA.

Pallot, J. (1991) 'The legitimate concern with fairness: a comment', *Accounting, Organizations and Society*, 16(2), pp. 201–8.

Pang, Y. H. (1982) 'Disclosures of corporate social responsibility', *The Chartered Accountant in Australia*, 53(1), pp. 32–4.

Parker, L.D. (1976) 'Social accounting: don't wait for it', *The Accountants' Magazine*, February, pp. 50–2.

Parker, L. D. (1977) *The Reporting of Company Financial Results to Employees*, London: ICAEW.

Patten, D.M. (1990) 'The market reaction to social responsibility disclosures: the case of the Sullivan Principle signings', *Accounting, Organizations and Society*, 15(6), pp. 575–87.

Patten, D.M. (1992) 'Intra-industry environmental disclosures in response to the Alaskan oil spill: a note on legitimacy theory', *Accounting, Organizations and Society*, 17(5), pp. 471–5.

Patterson, N. (1976) *Nuclear Power*, Harmondsworth: Penguin.

Pearce, D., Markandya, A. and Barbier, E.B. (1989) *Blueprint for a Green Economy*, London: Earthscan.

Pensions and Investment Research Consultants Ltd (PIRC) (1991) *Pension Fund Investment and the Environment*, London: PIRC.

Pepper, D. (1984) *The Roots of Modern Environmentalism*, Beckenham: Croom Helm.

Pepper, D. (1989) 'Green consumerism — Thatcherite environmentalism', *New Ground*, Winter, pp. 18–20.

Perks, R.W. (1993) *Accounting and Society*, London: Chapman and Hall.

Perks, R.W. and Gray, R.H. (1978) 'Corporate social reporting: an analysis of objectives', *British Accounting Review*, 10(2), pp. 43–60.

Perks, R.W. and Gray, R.H. (1979) 'Beware of social accounting', *Management Accounting*, December, pp. 22–3.

Perks, R.W. and Gray, R.H. (1980) 'Social accounting: the role of the accountant', *The Accountants' Magazine*, May, p. 201.

Perks, R.W., Rawlinson, D. and Ingram, L. (1992) 'An exploration of ethical investment in the UK', *British Accounting Review*, 24(1), pp. 43–65.

Pezzey, J. (1989) *Definitions of Sustainability* (No.9), UK: CEED.

Pike, R.H. (1984) 'Sophisticated capital budgeting systems and their association with corporate performance', *Managerial and Decision Economics*, 5(2), pp. 91–7.

Pomeranz, F. (1978) 'Social measurement: a primer for implementation', *Journal of Accounting, Auditing and Finance*, Summer, pp. 385–90.

Pope, P.F. and Peel, D.A. (1981) 'Information disclosure to employees and rational expectations', *Journal of Business Finance and Accounting*, 8(1), pp. 139–46.

Porritt, J. (1984) *Seeing Green: The politics of ecology explained*, Oxford: Basil Blackwell.

Power, M. (1992) 'After calculation? Reflections on *Critique of Economic Reason* by Andre Gorz', *Accounting, Organizations and Society*, 17(5), July, pp. 477–500.

Power, M. (1994) *The Audit Society*, London: Demos.

Power, M. and Laughlin, R.C. (1992) 'Critical theory and accounting' in *Critical Management Studies* Alvesson, M. and Willmott, H. (eds) London: Sage, pp. 113–35.

Prakash, P. and Rappaport, A. (1977) 'Information inductance and its significance for accounting', *Accounting, Organizations and Society*, 2(1), pp. 29–38.

Preston, L.E. (1981) 'Research on corporate social reporting: directions for development', *Accounting, Organizations and Society*, 6(3), pp. 255–62.

Preston, L.E., Rey, F. and Dierkes, M. (1978) 'Comparing corporate social performance: Germany, France, Canada and the US', *California Management Review*, Summer, pp. 40–9.

Public Environmental Reporting Initiative (1994) *PERI Guidelines*, PERI.

Puxty, A.G. (1986) 'Social accounting as immanent legitimation: a critique of a technist ideology', *Advances in Public Interest Accounting*, 1, pp. 95–112.

Puxty, A.G. (1991) 'Social accountability and universal pragmatics', *Advances in Public Interest Accounting*, 4, pp. 35–46.

Puxty, A.G. and Laughlin, R.C. (1983) 'A rational reconstruction of the decision usefulness criterion', *Journal of Business Finance and Accounting*, 10(4), pp. 543–60.

Raines, J.P. and Jung, C.R. (1986) 'Knight on religion and ethics as agents of social change', *American Journal of Economics and Sociology*, 45(4), pp. 429–39.

Ramanathan, K.V. (1976) 'Toward a theory of corporate social accounting', *The Accounting Review*, 51, pp. 516–28.

Rawls, J. (1972) *A Theory of Justice*, Oxford: Oxford University Press.

Raynard, P. (1995) 'The New Economic Foundation's social audit: auditing the auditors?', *Social and Environmental Accounting*, 15(1), pp. 10–13.

Reeves, T.K. and McGovern, T. (1981) *How Shop Stewards Use Company Information — Ten Case Studies of Information Disclosure*, London: Anglian Regional Management Centre.

Reilly, B.J. and Kyj, M.J. (1990) 'Economics and ethics', *Journal of Business Ethics*, 9(9), pp. 691–8.

Rey, F. (1978) 'Corporate social responsibility and social reporting in France' in *The Status of Social Reporting in Selected Countries* Schoenfeld, H. (ed.) Urbana, Ill.: University of Illinois.

Ridgers, B. (1979) 'The use of statistics in counter information', in *Demystifying Social Statistics*, J. Irvine (ed.) London: Pluto Press.

Rivera, J. M. and Ruesschoff, N. (1992) 'Ethics disclosures in current annual reports' in *Ethical Considerations in Contemporary International Accounting Practice* Zimmerman, V. K. (ed.), University of Illinois: Center for International Education and Research in Accounting.

Roberts, C.B. (1990) *International Trends in Social and Employee Reporting*, Occasional Research Paper No.6, London: ACCA.

Roberts, C.B. (1991) 'Environmental disclosures: a note on reporting practices in Europe', *Accounting Auditing and Accountability Journal*, 4(3), pp. 62–71.

Roberts, J. and Scapens, R. (1985) 'Accounting systems and systems of accountability', *Accounting, Organizations and Society*, 10(4), pp. 443–56.

Roberts, R.W. (1992) 'Determinants of corporate social responsibility disclosure', *Accounting, Organizations and Society*, 17(6), pp. 595–612.

Robertson, D. (1986) *Dictionary of Politics*, London: Penguin.

Robertson, J. (1978a) 'Corporate social reporting by New Zealand companies', *Journal of*

Contemporary Business, 7, pp. 113–33.

Robertson, J. (1978b) *The Sane Alternative*, London: James Robertson.

Robertson, J. (1984) 'Introduction to the British Edition' in Capra, F. and Spretnak, C. *Green Politics: The Global Promise*, London: Hutchinson, pp. xxiii–xxx.

Robson, K. and Cooper, D.J. (1990) 'Understanding the development of the accountancy profession in the United Kingdom' in Cooper, D.J. and Hopper, T.M. (eds) *Critical Accounts*, Basingstoke: Macmillan, pp. 366–90).

Rockness, J. (1985) 'An assessment of the relationship between US corporate environmental performance and disclosure', *Journal of Business Finance and Accounting*, 12(3), pp. 339–54.

Rockness, J. and Williams, P.F. (1988) 'A descriptive study of social responsibility mutual funds', *Accounting, Organizations and Society*, 13(4), pp. 397–411.

Roslender, R. (1992) *Sociological Perspectives on Modern Accountancy*, London: Routledge.

Roslender, R. and Dyson, J.R. (1992) 'Accounting for the worth of employees: a new look at an old problem', *British Accounting Review*, 24(4), pp. 311–29.

Rowthorn, B. and Ward, J. (1979) 'How to run a company and run down an economy — the effects of closing down steelmaking in Corby', *Cambridge Journal of Economics*, 3, pp. 329–40.

Ryle, M. (1988) *Ecology and Socialism*, London: Radius.

Sackmann, S.A., Flamholtz, E.G. and Bullen, M.L. (1989) 'Human resource accounting: a state of the art review', *Journal of Accounting Literature*, 8, pp. 235–64.

Sattar, D. (1995) 'Funding the social economy', *Social Investment Forum*, 3, May.

Savage, A.A. (1994) 'Corporate social disclosure practices in South Africa: a research note', *Social and Environmental Accounting*, 14(1), pp. 2–4.

Scapens, R.W. and Sale, J.T. (1981) 'Performance measurement and formal capital expenditure controls in divisionalised companies', *Journal of Business Finance and Accounting*, Autumn, pp. 389–419.

Scarpello, V. and Theeke, H.A. (1989) 'Human resource accounting: a measured critique', *Journal of Accounting Literature*, 8, pp. 265–80.

Schoenfeld, H.M. (1978) '*The status of social reporting in selected countries*', *Contemporary Issues in International Accounting*, Occasional paper number 1, University of Ill.: Centre for International Education and Research in Accounting.

Schmidheiny, S. (1992) *Changing Course*, New York: MIT Press.

Schreuder, H. (1979) 'Corporate social reporting in the Federal Republic of Germany: an overview', *Accounting, Organizations and Society*, 4(1/2), pp. 109–22.

Schuller, T. (1986) *Age, Capital and Democracy: Member participation in pension scheme management*, Aldershot: Gower.

Schumacher, E.F. (1973) *Small is Beautiful*, London: Abacus.

Seabrook, J. (1990) *The Myth of the Market: Promises and illusions*, Bideford: Green Books.

Services to Community Action and Trade Unions (SCAT) (1985) *The Public Cost of Private Contractors*, Sheffield: SCAT.

Sethi, S.P. (1972) 'Getting a handle on the social audit', *Business and Society Review*, Winter.

Shane, P.B. and Spicer, B.H. (1983) 'Market response to environmental information produced outside the firm', *Accounting Review*, 58(3), pp. 521–38.

Shanks, M. (1978) 'What is social accounting?', *Social Accounting*, London: CIPFA.

Sheffield City Council (1985) *Sheffield Jobs Audit*, Sheffield City Council.

Sherer, M., Southworth, A and Turley, S. (1981) 'An empirical investigation of disclosure, usage and usefulness of corporate accounting information', *Managerial Finance*, 7(2), pp. 6–11.

Shocker, A.D. and Sethi, S.P. (1973) 'An approach to incorporating societal preferences in developing corporate action strategies', *California Management Review*, Summer, pp. 97–105.

Sikka, P. (1987) 'Professional education and auditing books: a review article', *British Accounting Review*, 19(3), pp. 291–304.

Sikka, P., Willmott, H.C. and Lowe, E.A. (1989) 'Guardians of knowledge and the public interest: evidence and issues of accountability in the UK accountancy profession', *Accounting Auditing and Accountability Journal*, 2(2), pp. 47–71.

Sikka, P., Willmott, H.C. and Lowe, E.A. (1991) ' "Guardians of knowledge and the public interest": a reply to our critics', *Accounting Auditing and Accountability Journal*, 4(4), pp. 14–22.

Simon, J.G., Powers, C.W. and Gunnemann, J.P. (1972) *The Ethical Investor: Universities and corporate responsibility*, New Haven: Yale University Press.

Singh, D.R. and Ahuja, J.M. (1983) 'Corporate social reporting in India', *International Journal of Accounting*, 18(2), pp. 151–69.

Singhvi, S. S. (1968) 'Characteristics and implications of inadequate disclosure: a case study of India', *International Journal of Accounting*, 3(2), pp. 29–34.

Skalak, S.L., Russell, W.G., Robinson, M., Miller, G. and Casey, G. (1993/94) 'Proactive environmental accounting and world-class annual reports', *Journal of Corporate Accounting and Finance*, Winter, pp. 177–96.

Social Audit (1973–1976) *Social Audit Quarterlies*, London: Social Audit.

Society of Management Accountants of Canada (1992) *Accounting for the Environment*, Hamilton, Ontario: The Society of Management Accountants of Canada.

Solomons, D. (1989) *Guidelines for Financial Reporting Standards*, London: ICAEW.

Speake, J. (1979) (ed.) *A Dictionary of Philosophy*, London: Pan.

Spicer, B.H. (1978) 'Accounting for corporate social performance: some problems and issues', *Journal of Contemporary Business*, Winter, pp. 151–70.

Stephenson, J. (1973) 'Prying open corporations — tighter than clams', *Business and Society Review*, Winter, pp. 66–73.

Stepien, M. (1994) 'Environmental protection in Polish accounting', *Social and Environmental Accounting*, 14(1), pp. 4–5.

Sterling, R. (1972) 'Decision oriented financial accounting', *Accounting and Business Research*, Summer, pp. 198–208.

Sterling, R.R. (1973) 'Accounting research, education and practice', *Journal of Accountancy*, September, pp. 44–52.

Stevens, W. (1984) 'Market reaction to environment performance', *Advances in Accounting*, 5, pp. 41–62.

Stewart, J.D. (1984) 'The role of information in public accountability' in *Issues in Public Sector Accounting* Hopwood, A. and Tomkins, C. (eds) Oxford: Philip Allen.

Stone, C.D. (1975) *Where the Law Ends*, New York: Harper & Row.

Stone, D. (1994) *No longer at the end of the pipe, but still a long way from sustainability! A look at management accounting for the environment and sustainable development in the United States*, Department of Accountancy and Business Finance, University of Dundee, Working Paper Series, ACC/9408.

Stone, D. (1995) 'Business social responsibility and accountability in the United States: a corporate initiative', *Social and Environmental Accounting*, 15(1), pp. 14–15.

Sturdivant, F.D. and Ginter, J.L. (1977) 'Corporate social responsiveness: management attitudes and economic performance', *California Management Review*, 19(3), pp. 30–9.

Tellus Institute (1992a) *Total Cost Assessment – Accelerating industrial pollution prevention through innovative project financial analysis*, Washington DC: US Environmental Protection Agency.

Tellus Institute (1992b) *Alternative Approaches to the Financial Evaluation of Industrial Pollution Prevention Investments*, Boston Mass: Tellus Institute.

Teoh, H.Y. and Thong, G. (1984) 'Another look at corporate social responsibility and reporting: an empirical study in a developing country', *Accounting, Organizations and Society*, 9(2), pp. 189–206.

Tinker, A.M. (1984a) 'Theories of the State and the state of accounting: economic reductionism and political voluntarism in accounting regulation theory', *Journal of Accounting and Public Policy*, 3, Fall, pp. 55–74.

Tinker, A.M. (1984b) (ed.) *Social Accounting for Corporations*, Manchester: MUP.

Tinker, A.M. (1984c) 'Accounting for unequal exchange: wealth accumulation versus wealth appropriation', in *Social Accounting for Corporations*, Tinker (ed.), Manchester: HUP.

Tinker, A.M. (1985) *Paper Prophets: A social critique of accounting*, Eastbourne: Holt Saunders.

Tinker, A.M., Lehman, C. and Neimark, M. (1991) 'Corporate social reporting: falling down the hole in the middle of the road', *Accounting Auditing and Accountability Journal*, 4(1), pp. 28–54.

Tinker, A.M., Merino, B.D. and Neimark, M.D. (1982) 'The normative origins of positive theories: ideology and accounting thought', *Accounting, Organizations and Society*, 7, pp. 167–200.

Tinker, A.M. and Okcabol, F. (1991) 'Fatal attractions in the agency relationship', *British Accounting Review*, 23(4), pp. 329–54.

Tinker, T. and Puxty, T. (1995) *Policing Accounting Knowledge*, London: Paul Chapman.

Tokutani, M. and Kawano, M. (1978) 'A note on Japanese social accounting literature', *Accounting, Organizations and Society*, 3(2), pp. 183–8.

Tonkin, D. J. (1991) 'Environmental protection statements' in *Financial Reporting 1990–1991: A survey of UK reporting practice*, Tonkin, D. J. and Skerratt, L.C.L. (eds) London: Institute of Chartered Accountants in England and Wales.

Touche Ross (1990) *Head in the clouds or head in the sands? UK managers' attitudes to environmental issues — a survey*, London: Touche Ross.

Trades Union Congress (TUC) (1991) *Greening the Workplace: A TUC guide to environmental policies and issues at work*, London: TUC.

Transport and General Workers Union (TGWU) (1971, 1977) *The Ford Wage Claim*, London: TGWU.

Transport and General Workers Union (TGWU) (1986) *Let's Take on the Takeovers*, London: TGWU.

Tricker, R.I. (1983) 'Corporate responsibility, institutional governance and the roles of accounting standards', in *Accounting Standards Setting — An International Perspective* Bromwich, M. and Hopwood, A.G. (eds) London: Pitman.

Trotman, K. (1979) 'Social responsibility disclosures by Australian companies', *The Chartered Accountant in Australia*, 49(8), pp. 24–8.

Trotman, K.T. and Bradley, G.W. (1981) 'Associations between social responsibility disclosure and characteristics of companies', *Accounting, Organizations and Society*, 6(4), pp. 355–62.

Ullmann, A.E. (1976) 'The corporate environmental accounting system: a management tool for fighting environmental degradation', *Accounting, Organizations and Society*, 1(1), pp. 71–9.

Ullmann, A.E. (1979) 'Corporate social reporting: political interests and conflicts in Germany', *Accounting, Organizations and Society*, 4(1/2), pp. 123–33.

Ullmann, A.E. (1985) 'Data in search of a theory: a critical examination of the relationships among social performance, social disclosure and economic performance of US firms', *Academy of Management Review*, 10(3), pp. 540–57.

UEC Working Party on Social Reporting (1983) *Socio-economic Information*, A report prepared for the ninth UEC congress, Strasbourg: UEC.

UNEP IE (1994) *Company Environmental Reporting: A measure of the progress of business and industry towards sustainable development*, Technical Report No.24, Paris: United Nations Environment Programme Industry and Environment.

United Nations (1991) *Accounting for Environmental Protection Measures*, Report by the Secretary General, March (E.C.10/AC.3/1991/5), New York: UN.

United Nations (1992) *Environmental Disclosures: International survey of corporate reporting practices*, Report of the Secretary General, 13 January (E/C.10/AC/1992/3), New York: UN.

United Nations (1994a) *Environmental Disclosures: International survey of corporate reporting practices*, Report of the UNCTAD Secretariat, 12 January (E/C.10/AC3/1994/4), New York: UN.

United Nations (1994b) *Review of National Environmental Accounting Laws and Regulations*, Report by the UNCTAD secretariat, 19 December (TD/B/ITNC/AC.1/2), Geneva: UN.

United Nations (1995) *Disclosure by Transnational Corporations of Environmental Matters at the National Level in Annual Reports*, Report by the UNCTAD secretariat, 6 January (TD/B/ITNC/AC.1/4), Geneva: UN.

United Nations Centre on Transnational Corporations (UNCTC) (1982) *Towards International Standardization of Corporate Accounting and Reporting*, New York: United Nations.

United Nations Centre on Transnational Corporations (UNCTC) (1984) *International Standards of Accounting and Reporting*, New York: United Nations.

United Nations Centre for Transnational Corporations (UNCTC) (1992) *International Accounting*, New York: UNCTC.

United Nations World Commission on Environment and Development (UNWCED) (1987) *Our Common Future* (The Brundtland Report,) Oxford: OUP.

Vance, S.C. (1975) 'Are socially responsible corporations good investment risks?' *Management Review*, 64(8), pp. 18–24.

Van den Bergh, R. (1976) 'The Corporate Report — The Deutsche Shell experience', *Accountancy*, December.

Vogel-Polsky, E. (1990) 'What future is there for a social Europe following the Strasbourg summit?', *Industrial Law Journal*, 19, pp. 65–80.

Wainwright, H. and Elliott, D. (1982) *The Lucas Plan — a new trade unionism in the making?* London: Allison and Busby.

Walker, M. (1989) 'Agency theory: a falsificationist perspective', *Accounting, Organizations and Society*, 14(5/6), pp. 433–54.

Wallace, R. S. O. (1988) 'Intranational and international consensus in the importance of disclosure items in financial reporting', *British Accounting Review*, 20(3), pp. 223–66.

Walton, C.W. (1983) 'Corporate social responsibility: the debate revisited', *Journal of Economics and Business*, 3(4), pp. 173–87.

Ward, S. (1991) *Socially Responsible Investment*, 2nd edn, London: Directory for Social Change.

Watts, R. and Zimmerman, J. (1979) 'The demand for and the supply of accounting theories: the market or excuses', *Accounting Review*, April, pp. 273–305.

Wells, D. (1985) 'Barclays is losing its fight with a shadow on points', *Accountancy Age*, 9, May, pp. 9–10.

West Lothian District Council (1985) *Report of the Public Inquiry into the Proposed Closure of Polkemmet Colliery, Whitburn*, West Lothian District Council.

Weston, J. (ed.) (1986) *Red and Green: The New Politics of the Environment*, London: Pluto Press.

Williams, K., Williams, J. and Thomas, D. (1983) *Why are the British Bad at Manufacturing?* Henley: Routledge and Kegan Paul.

Williams, P.F. (1987) 'The legitimate concern with fairness', *Accounting, Organizations and Society*, 12(2), pp. 169–89.

Willmott, H.C. (1986) 'Organising the profession: a theoretical and empirical examination of the development of the major accountancy bodies in the UK', *Accounting Organizations and Society*, 11, pp. 555–80.

Willmott, H. (1990) 'Serving the public interest? A critical analysis of a professional claim' in Cooper, D.J. and Hopper, T.M. (eds) *Critical Accounts*, Basingstoke: Macmillan, pp. 315–31.

Wiseman, J. (1982) 'An evaluation of environmental disclosures made in corporate annual reports', *Accounting, Organizations and Society*, 7(1), pp. 53–63.

Wokutch, R.E. and Fahey, L. (1986) 'A value explicit approach for evaluating corporate social performance', *Journal of Accounting and Public Policy*, 5(3), pp. 191–214.

World Industry Council for the Environment (1994) *Environmental Reporting: A manager's guide*, Paris: WICE.

Wright, R. (1970) 'Managing man as a capital asset', *Personnel Journal*, April, pp. 290–98.

Yamagami, T. and Kokubu, K. (1991) 'Note on corporate social disclosure in Japan', *Accounting Auditing and Accountability Journal*, 4(4), pp. 32–9.

Zadek, S. and Evans, R. (1993) *Auditing the Market: A practical approach to social accounting*, London: New Economics Foundation.

Zeff, S.A. (1987) 'Does the CPA belong to a profession?', *Accounting Horizons*, June.

Zeff, S.A. (1989) 'Recent trends in accounting education and research in the USA: some implications for UK academics', *The British Accounting Review*, 21(2), pp. 159–76.

Zeghal, D. and Ahmed, S.A. (1990) 'Comparison of social responsibility information disclosure media used by Canadian firms', *Accounting Auditing and Accountability Journal*, 3(1), pp. 38–53.

Index

Copyright acknowledgements

Acknowledgement is made to the following companies and organisations for permission to reproduce their material. pp 130–1, Figure 5.1, p 132, Figure 5.2 and p 133, Figure 5.3: SustainAbility Limited, London. p 136, Figure 5.5: reproduced with permission from *Environmental Reporting* (WICE, 1994), permission given by the World Business Council for Sustainable Development. p 137, Figure 5.6: ICC Business Charter for Sustainable Development, ICC Publication No. 210/356A, published by the International Chamber of Commerce, Paris, copyright © 1991 International Chamber of Commerce (ICC), available from: ICC Publishing SA, 38 Cours Albert 1er, 75008 Paris, France, and from: ICC United Kingdom, 14/15 Belgrave Square, London SW1X 8PS. p 143, Table 5.1: United Nations Conference on Trade and Development. p 154, Table 5.3: MCB University Press, Bradford. p 162, Figure 5.14: reprinted from *Accounting, Organizations and Society*, 9(2), H.Y. Teoh and G. Thong: 'Another look at corporate social responsibility and reporting: an empirical study in a developing country', © 1984, pp 189–206, with kind permission from Elsevier Science Ltd, The Boulevard, Langford Lane, Kidlington OX5 1GB, UK. pp 172 (Table 6.1), 191 (Table 6.3) and 205 (Table 6.4): extracts from 'Environmental, employee and ethical reporting in Europe' (1994), Certified Research Report 41. This research report was funded and published by the Chartered Association of Certified Accountants (ACCA) and is available from ACCA, PO Box 66, Glasgow G41 1BS; extracts are reproduced with ACCA's kind permission. p 174, Figure 6.2: MCB University Press, Bradford. p 184, Figure 6.8: reproduced with permission of the Eni Enrico Mattei Foundation (FEEM). p 197, Figure 6.15, p 206, Figure 6.18: MCB University Press, Bradford. p 225, Figure 8.1: The Cooperative Bank, Manchester. p 256, Figure 8.2: Sbn Bank/Spaarkassen Nordjylland. pp 282 and 232, Figure 9.3: *New Consumer*. p 288, Figure 9.4: Traidcraft Exchange.